SAMUEL JOHNSON
AND THE SCALE OF GREATNESS

SAMUEL JOHNSON
AND THE SCALE
OF GREATNESS

ISOBEL GRUNDY

THE UNIVERSITY OF GEORGIA PRESS

ATHENS

Published in Great Britain in 1986 by Leicester University Press
Published in the United States of America in 1986 by
the University of Georgia Press, Athens, Georgia 30602

Designed by Douglas Martin
Set in Linotron Janson by Alan Sutton Publishing Limited
Printed and bound in Great Britain

CONTENTS

2306922

FOR
MY PARENTS

of whom I will not violate their modesty by boasting,
but I do not believe that any body else has parents like them.

ABBREVIATIONS

Adv.	Johnson's essays in *The Adventurer* (Y, II)
Boswell	James Boswell, *The Life of Samuel Johnson, LL. D.*, ed. G.B. Hill and L.F. Powell, 6 vols (1934)
GM	*The Gentleman's Magazine*
Journey	Johnson, *A Journey to the Western Islands of Scotland* (Y, IX)
Letters	(cited by number): Johnson, *Letters*, ed. R.W. Chapman, 3 vols (1956)
Lives	Johnson, *The Lives of the English Poets*, ed. G.B. Hill, 3 vols (1905)
Ram.	Johnson, *The Rambler* (Y, III, IV, V)
Rass.	Johnson, *The History of Rasselas, Prince of Abissinia*
Works	Johnson, *Works*, 9 vols (1825)
Y	*The Yale Edition of the Works of Samuel Johnson* (1958–)
I	*Diaries, Prayers, and Annals*, ed. E.L. McAdam, Jr, and Donald and Mary Hyde (1958)
II	*The Idler and The Adventurer*, ed. W.J. Bate, John M. Bullitt and L.F. Powell (1963)
III–V	*The Rambler*, ed. W.J. Bate and Albrecht B. Strauss (1969)
VI	*Poems*, ed. E.L. McAdam, Jr, and George Milne (1964)
VII, VIII	*Johnson on Shakespeare*, ed. Arthur Sherbo, introduction by Bertrand H. Bronson (1968)
IX	*A Journey to the Western Islands of Scotland*, ed. Mary Lascelles (1971)
X	*Political Writings*, ed. Donald J. Greene (1977)
XIV	*Sermons*, ed. Jean Hagstrum and James Gray (1978)
XV	*A Voyage to Abyssinia* (translated from the French), ed. Joel J. Gold (1985)

In my notes I have used standard abbreviations for scholarly journals, and short forms for all book titles: for full reference see List of Works Cited. The abbreviations above appear thus in the text as well as in the notes, in order to keep the number of those 'necessary evils' down as far as possible.

PREFACE

HE – OR SHE – 'that makes a book from books may be useful, but cannot be great'. Johnson would surely value himself more on his continuing incomparable usefulness to readers than on his greatness, about which so much has been written and spoken. It is his usefulness which gives those who write about him some confidence in their own.

I began to think out the opinions which this book now contains in Toronto in 1975–6, and they have given me much enjoyment since then. I have spent more time on the pursuit in the houses of friends and relatives than in my own, which means that I have the pleasure of gratitude for much hospitality.

When I first began to pursue these ideas I marvelled that among the many views offered of Johnson nobody seemed to have taken my own, although it pressed itself upon me as central – a position from which the landscape of his works may be triangulated, new prospects opened and confusions removed. Since then I have found others whose concerns do overlap with mine, increasingly I believe though still to a remarkably small extent. For their work and for all the 'successive labours of innumerable minds' carried out by readers and scholars of Johnson and his contemporaries, I am grateful. The steps by which I became a Johnsonian were variously furthered by Miss Kirstie Morrison, Professor Robert Halsband, the late Professor James L. Clifford, Miss Mary Lascelles, Mr Lewis Raddon, Dr David Fleeman, and students at London (Queen Mary College), Toronto and Princeton. Having become a Johnsonian, I have enjoyed the hospitality of Lady Eccles (then Mrs Mary Hyde), of the Johnson Society of London, and of Pembroke College, Oxford.

I am vividly conscious of having relied on the help and support – often direct and indispensable, sometimes indirect or even remote from the eventual goal and yet equally indispensable – of people far too numerous to list and thank. They include teachers, librarians, colleagues, students, friends, family, and others. My parents will, I hope, understand the kind and degree of gratitude implied by my dedication. Pat Clements has been my acutest critic ever since she caused me first to revise and then to scrap the earliest page on Johnson which I ever wrote with a hope of publication. My warmest thanks go to those and others who read the MS either whole or in parts (Skip Brack, Warren Chernaik, Cornelia Cook, Mel Cooper, Sandy Cunningham, Paul Korshin, Rob Merrett, Isabel Rivers, Pat Thomson) and to those who typed it either whole or in parts (my sister Janet Orr, Doreen Barnes, Kate Entwhistle, Linda Pasmore).

INTRODUCTION

SAMUEL JOHNSON is known as a Christian moralist. Among the makers of our literature, none is more deeply Christian and none more deeply committed to the view of the writer as moralist, first and last. Yet he differs from the established tradition of Christian morality in one important area, never sufficiently remarked. This is his whole complex of attitudes to greatness – in Christian moralist terms, to 'worldly greatness'.

Literature has had, since Homer's heroes and Aristotle's magnanimous man, a long and in the main an honourable connection with an ideal of greatness. Epic, that 'with no middle flight intends to soar', has been the most respected genre; tragedy has always lived close to 'Pride, pomp, and circumstance'.[1] The fall from greatness, the decline of fortune's wheel, has been no less poetically compelling than its ascent. 'Queenes have died yong and faire'; sceptre and crown must 'in the dust be equal made/With the poor crooked scythe and spade.' Christianity, too, especially in churches by law established, has built up its own relationship to worldly greatness, and evolved a temporal and literary pomp of its own. Johnson, merely respectful of the greatness of birth, was acutely sensitive to issues involving the greatness of ability and the greatness of attainment. He thought the advice which a Homeric hero is given by his father – 'ever to be bravest and pre-eminent among all' – was 'the noblest exhortation that could be instanced in any heathen writer'.[2]

The exhortations of Christian moralists, however, have generally been for renunciation of this lure – of 'all the kingdoms of the world' as rejected by Christ, or of that 'fame, that darling fame' which Dryden feared his God might demand in sacrifice – in accordance with the paradox which Christ opposed to his disciples' rivalry for greatness: 'he that is least among you all, the same shall be great'.[3] The Christian poets (even those not primarily moralists, and those who do not go personally so far as to aim at being the littlest and least) betray a feeling that moralizing and greatness belong in different worlds, or at least different works. To the preacher, including the literary preacher, goodness and greatness compose a well-worn and serviceable antithesis. Lord Lyttelton instructs female readers in proper humility: 'Seek to be Good, but aim not to be Great'. Thomas Gray closes his 'Progress of Poesy' by claiming humility himself as he espouses a rank 'Beneath the Good how far, but far above the Great.' Henry Fielding takes the distinction for granted as he satirically embroiders it: 'no two things can possibly be more distinct from each other, for greatness consists in bringing all manner of mischief on mankind, and goodness in removing it from them'.[4]

We should expect Johnson to follow suit, but not so. 'Greatness' (identified rather more closely than we might expect with superiority to one's fellows) is one of the most frequent topics in his writings; deprecation of it is, quite unexpectedly, rare. Direct urging of humility is not a high priority of his moral writing, and he seldom depicts the practice of humility, either fictional or biographical. He even goes so far sometimes as to make goodness or virtue sound like a means towards greatness rather than an end in itself. 'Nothing can be great which is not right' (*Ram.* 185: Y, V, 209); the 'first step to greatness is to be honest' (*Works*, VI, 311); 'virtue is the highest proof of a superior understanding, and the only solid basis of greatness'.[5] Even in a sermon Johnson (admittedly endorsing heathen philosophers) deduces greatness from virtue rather than the other way round (no. 3: Y, XIV, 30–1). These examples subordinate what is right, honest or virtuous to the aim of becoming great, and they not only admit but accept that aim as the driving force of human action.

Johnson's literary criticism does nothing unusual when it subordinates lesser literary qualities to those of greatness or genius. In this particular area we are accustomed to the use of this scale of judgment, to regarding moral congruence as a necessary first step rather than a final aim. Indeed, Johnson has aroused more modern cavil by emphasizing morality than by emphasizing genius. Our notions of literary quality, though often including some specifically moral demands, are essentially comparative and competitive. Johnson's age in particular paid close attention to the quality of greatness in art, under the rubric of 'the sublime'.[6] But in the realm of moral criticism of life we expect to hear rightness recommended for itself, not because it leads to greatness. It is not, of course, that Johnson omits to inculcate virtue, or that he is insensitive to the potential conflict between virtue and ambition. But in the area of this conflict his emphasis falls markedly to one side of most moralists' accustomed target. Unusually alert to the moral dangers of pursuing greatness, he is nevertheless prepared to entertain the possibility of investing the pursuit itself with positive moral value; at the least he declines to follow the moralist tradition of decrying it without careful examination. Since he is also by temperament and principle outside the tradition, which had run strongly from Sir Philip Sidney to Dryden, of writers as celebrants of individual greatness, he stands in an ambivalent position, receptive to greatness in theory though sceptical of it in practice.

Johnson's occasional subordination of goodness to greatness is only the most surprising effect of a persistent concern which seems to me the single most distinguishing characteristic of his thought. This concern preserves at the heart of all his writing about human nature and the human condition a vital question which is not essentially one of moral good or evil, the question 'How *important* is this?' (To this question Lyttelton and Gray sound confident that they know the answer, and Fielding sounds confident that he knows the world's usual answer is wrong.) To present this question in many contexts as one admitting debate, and to provide the means of answering it, is a dominant aim of all Johnson's literary works.

This concern of Johnson's has received useful critical attention recently, mostly under the term *achievement*. In the preface to his seminal study, Walter Jackson Bate wrote that what interested Johnson most was 'the possibility of human achievement'; he closed his preface by quoting from A.N. Whitehead: 'moral education is impossible apart from the habitual vision of greatness'.[7] Others have emphasized that Johnson 'regards the fulfillment of man's potentialities as one of the ultimate ends of morality'; that in the *Rambler* 'the dream of literary greatness came almost inevitably to dominate'; that he is 'concerned with the nature and, more importantly, the limits of human achievement'; that he distinguishes 'a central paradox regarding man's nature: the infinite importance and infinite irrelevance of human achievement'; that his prayers and meditations show 'implicit realization of the importance of petty events and the littleness of even the greatest'; and that *Rasselas* employs 'a double perspective, seeing human wisdom and morality as at once important and vain'.[8] Howard Erskine-Hill, in an article particularly germane to the topics discussed here, on 'Johnson and the petty particular', finds that 'much that is most humanly impressive in Johnson's art . . . arises from a kind of dialogue between the general and the particular, or between the petty and the great'.[9] The aim of this book is a detailed investigation of the second aspect of that dialogue, which, astonishingly, has never been attempted.

The topic of greatness, its attractions and its dangers, is never absent from Johnson's works for long. He approaches it more regularly from the direction of the limitations of greatness than from the contrast with moral goodness, but he reveals ambiguous responses to it, revulsion as well as attraction. *The Lives of the Poets*, which catalogues a myriad unsuccessful and just a few triumphant aspirants to greatness, is only the final sounding of a dominant theme. Johnson began his metropolitan writing career in the Swiftian school of attack on Robert Walpole as great man. In *London* he lamented the slow rise of personal worth and the decline of national stature; in the life of Savage he anatomized an individual convinced of superiority, who nevertheless achieved little. In other early biographies (for instance, of Boerhaave and Drake) he portrayed a readily recognizable historical greatness; in the 'Debates in the Senate of Magna Lilliputia' he depicted in action the more dubious greatness of the contemporary political scene.

This sketch of Johnson's literary beginnings reminds us that he was not, any more than Swift or Fielding, naïvely respectful of greatness, which was an idea ripe for the satirist's hand, both through its relation to moral issues and through its associations with the purely physical, with bulk or height.

To Swift and Fielding these associations had been invaluable – making, for example, Walpole's title of 'the great man' richly ambiguous. Such satire depends on confidence that the physical and the figurative meanings of *great* are quite distinct from each other and that to confuse them is therefore a joke, a joke from which goodness is exempt. For Johnson, whose practice in the *Dictionary* was to tie the 'primitive' or root meaning of a word to physical qualities, and to branch out in secondary senses to the intellectual or the moral, the distinction was less firm, and the potential double meaning a device less simple in its effect. (Swift is often cited as making the moral or the spiritual concrete, but he does so for the sake of an intentionally jarring effect, where Johnson does so routinely. *Swelling*, for instance, is a word which Johnson likes to use simply as a more colourful equivalent of *proud*: they appear together as his tenth definition of *great*.)

Johnson seems to have taken special care with his *Dictionary* entries on *great* and *good*, revising each for the fourth edition. His first definitions of *great* ('Large in bulk or number') and of *good* ('Having such physical qualities as are expected or desired') relate equally to *material* qualities. The illustrations of *good*, however, lose no time in moving beyond the material. The first is from the opening book of *Genesis*: 'God saw every thing that he had made, and behold it was very *good*', which enriches the word's physical sense with moral and spiritual suggestion, making it both potentially absolute and potentially all-embracing. It becomes more emphatically all-embracing in the succeeding illustrations, which gather together good effects, good verses, good digestion, good nature, and good sense. It becomes more emphatically absolute in the expanded definition of 1773, which reads: 'Having, either generally or for any particular end, such physical qualities as are expected or desired. Not bad. Not ill.' Goodness can stoop to describe efficient digestive processes, or it can expand to take in those moral qualities expected and desired in humanity by God.

Under *great*, on the other hand, it is not until his fourth definition that Johnson moves away from the physical, or suggests the idea of human greatness. He then supplies complex suggestions of subjectivity and exclusiveness, and paints the dazzling prize with an allure that satiric moralists hardly dare allow it. '4. Important; weighty. 5. Chief; principal. 6. Of high rank; of large power. 7. Illustrious; eminent. 8. Grand of aspect; of elevated mien. 9. Noble; magnanimous.' (The fourth edition, altering and expanding, added a newly discriminated sense: 'Venerable; adorable; awful.') Johnson does not sink the moralist in the lexicographer, however: his illustrative quotations under these senses of *great* go some way towards counteracting his powerfully attractive or tempting definitions. Under 'Of high rank; of large power' he quotes Shakespeare, Pope and Rowe unanimously voicing criticism, in varying degrees, of 'the great', and to these in 1773 he adds Parnell, and Milton explicitly contrasting the great with the good. A definition thus illustrated very naturally branches out into the tenth meaning: 'Swelling; proud.' Nevertheless the *Dictionary* clearly reveals Johnson's sensitivity to the allure of greatness,[10] which he recognizes more candidly than either Swift or Fielding. To him this concept, encumbered as it was with notions of bulk or height (bulk perhaps swollen, height perhaps tottering or remote), was yet a concept both celebrated and aspired to by the poets, a concept of eminence, grandeur, magnanimity, significance, which worked more powerfully on his imagination even than the idea of goodness.

Unlike goodness, however, it is a concept essentially relative, as those fifth and seventh definitions made clear. Having defined *big*, almost identically with *great*, as 'Great in bulk; large', Johnson inserted a new primary meaning in the revised fourth edition: 'Having comparative bulk, greater or less'.[11] To say that good is *not ill* conveys an objective meaning; but to say that big, or great, is *not little* would remain a meaningless statement unless some scale of measurement had been established. Johnson is further stressing absoluteness for one word, relativity for the other. The great is chief among others, eminent among others, while the good is not bad, not ill. Other writers seek to explode greatness by deriding it as merely physical or by contrasting it with goodness. Johnson nearly always contents himself with seeking a scale of measurement. To be great is to be larger or more elevated than others, yet to surpass the human scale altogether, if that were possible, would be to become merely a giant or a monster.

Johnson's age gave much attention to the marking out of scales of measurement, both physical and moral: an attention which Paul Fussell calls 'the evaluative obsession', a 'vertical' cast of mind 'impelled to order everything in rank'.[12] Development of the microscope and telescope had increased the known range of objects much bigger than and much smaller than mankind, increasing also awareness of relativity. It had always been possible for writers to contrast the littleness and lowness of man with the greatness and height of God, the short sight of man with the all-seeing eye of God, as the writer of *Isaiah* had done with particular force and brilliance: 'Behold, the nations are as a drop of a bucket, and are counted as the small dust of the balance: behold, he taketh up the isles as a very little thing. . . . For as the heavens are higher than the earth, so are my ways higher than your ways, and my thoughts than your thoughts' (xl, 15; lv, 9). Now more scientifically informed writers seized on a clearer knowledge that what is large when measured by one scale is small according to a different scale.[13]

To these scientific developments there has been traced a group of literary works which choose to see the human scale physically magnified or diminished: pre-eminently *Gulliver's Travels*, but also *The Rape of the Lock*, Fielding's *Tom Thumb the Great*, and the Latin 'Battle of the Pygmies and Cranes', written by the young Addison and translated into English by the young Johnson.[14] Other contemporary works besides these relate the moral to the physical scale. Pope shrinks his antagonists (who in life were to a man, and even to a woman, larger than he) to insects or to puny degenerates in comparison with their ancestors. His exemplary figures seem to perform the work of giants ('roll obedient Rivers thro' the Land'); conversely, Timon's grotesquely gigantic setting necessarily shrinks him in comparison:

> His pond an Ocean, his parterre a Down:
> Who but must laugh, the Master when he sees,
> A puny insect, shiv'ring at a breeze![15]

Philip Stevick, writing of 'Miniaturization in eighteenth-century English literature', finds a deliberate irony in apparently inappropriate scales 'that forces us to ask, as we read, how such a subject can possibly be contained in so small a structure'.[16]

Throughout his writings Johnson makes play with scales of magnitude. He seems never to ask himself the question, so frequently asked by less solidly empirical thinkers, whether what he could see was really there.[17] He relies on the evidence of his eyes – yet not in all respects securely. In matters of scale he expects the eye to mislead. The question he repeatedly asks is whether what he sees is really the size he sees it.

Johnson makes a practice of carefully defining the standard of judgment he is using, and he regularly employs for his standards the metaphors of seeing and of size. William R. Keast writes that morals and criticism 'both involve referring actions to their agents and measuring the powers or accomplishments of those agents against a general standard. The great problem is to fix the general standard.'[18] This, however, ignores the problem of relativity. Johnson likes to compare one scale of measurement with another, keeping both in play. In *A Journey to the Western Islands* he frequently contrasts metropolitan and Hebridean standards of expectation; in *Rambler* 192 he contrasts urban and rural standards of riches: different standards are valid in different circumstances.

In his moral essays and again in *The Lives of the Poets* (which together embody his most detailed study of the themes of comparative judgment and of true and false greatness) Johnson alternates two different scales of measurement: his little people, wits and money-grubbers and busy strivers for parochial renown, are presented comically and with inexhaustible tolerance, often in their own epistolary words; contenders for more extensive renown, like the major poets or the collective audience whom Johnson addresses in the discursive essays, are warned again and again that their standards must be submitted in the end to a still larger scale. Johnson operated comparable double standards in literature and in life. Sir John Hawkins noted on the one hand the 'asperity' with which he pointed out Shakespeare's faults, and on the other his care 'ever to forbear exercising his critical talents on the effusions of men inferior in learning and abilities to himself'; on the one hand his ferocious maintenance of 'superiority over all with whom he conversed', on the other his forbearance (which Hawkins calls 'pusillanimity' or 'imbecility') towards his dependants ('people of the lowest and vulgarest minds').[19]

Johnson frequently points out errors traceable to standards which are wrong in varying ways. He judges that Swift's high opinion of Stella's mind was formed according to an unreasonably low opinion of women in general: 'she was great because her associates were little' (*Lives*, III, 42–3). Wide-ranging errors can result from too petty standards of measurement, but equally misleading is the opposite error, that of enlarging the standard and diminishing the thing compared. Lack of interest in ordinary lives 'arises from false measures of excellence and dignity' (*Ram.* 60: Y, III, 320), and these false measures may lead us to diminish ourselves as easily as other people.

> Man is seldom willing to let fall the opinion of his own dignity, or to believe that he does little only because every individual is a very little being. . . .
> From this mistaken notion of human greatness it proceeds, that many who pretend to have made great advances in wisdom so loudly declare that they despise themselves. . . . a little more than nothing is as much as can be expected from a being who with respect to the multitudes about him is himself little more than nothing. (*Idler* 88: Y, II, 274–5)

In these cases Johnson defends the importance of the ordinarily small. He sees clearly how the greatness, not in bulk but in number, of the mass of humanity tends to diminish any individual in comparison, but how, for the puny individual, even slight achievement is significant.

This idea lies behind his many references to his own works as 'little', in which it is not necessary to suspect false modesty or self-contempt. He characterizes *Rasselas* as 'a little story book' (it was still the 'little Book' when honoured with an American edition and five translations); his last major literary project consists of 'little Lives, and little Prefaces, to a little edition of the English Poets', or of 'Little lives and little criticisms', or of 'little books'; the *Journey to the Western Islands* comprises 'the thoughts of one who has seen but little', just as his letters covering the same ground are 'the story of me and my little ramble'.[20] In fact (though *Rasselas* is undeniably brief, and the volumes in which the *Lives* appeared were smaller – and cheaper – than most editions of poets[21]) Johnson intends primarily a recognition that his works are to be measured by the human scale according to which only a little more than nothing can be expected. 'Surely every hour convinces a thinking man how little he does, how little he has done, how little he can do for himself' (*Letters*, no. 1003.1). In this he stands at the opposite pole from Gulliver, who after all his opportunities for learning about comparative scales, still succumbs to the expectation of single-handedly transforming the world.[22]

Johnson resembles Swift and Pope in his acute perception of the moral and physical pettiness of the human scale, but unlike them he does not urge his readers to despise or condemn, but merely to measure. Few of his remarks are better remembered than 'There is nothing, Sir, too little for so little a creature as man.' Boswell recorded (as well as his warning against 'big words for little matters') his pleasure in 'little things' and small jokes, Hester Thrale his concern with 'daily life' and 'common manners'.[23] To accept the pettiness of the human scale is itself a liberation.

But for Johnson, as for Swift, the human scale, even when accurately adjusted, is not the only one. Although 'we see a little, very little', still 'we can repose with comfort' on 'the care of Providence, whose eye takes in the whole of things' (*Adv.* 107: Y, II, 445). In comparison with immortal life, 'how little are all other things!' (Boswell, II, 358). The Christian believes that in the end humanity has to be judged by standards not its own, just as a writer of genius ought to lift his eyes 'beyond his own performances' and elevate 'his views to that ideal perfection which every genius born to excel is condemned always to pursue, and never overtake' (*Lives*, II, 253). Therefore, although a certain falsely inflated measure may unnecessarily diminish our view of ourselves, almost any true measure (whether that of human beings in the mass, or of individuals alone, or of all-seeing God), will tend to qualify or deflate that human greatness which other false measures conspire to glorify. To pursue excellence is to fail at perfection.

Johnson consistently gives his best attention, in the moral as in the literary field, to the man born to excel. Aspiration is the keynote of his psychological interpretations, greatness the goal of his fictional and actual subjects as well as of his own writings. He depicts the goal as ever desirable, yet the aspiration as morally neutral or dangerous, as well as unpredictable in outcome. He regards all human activity as competitive, as a struggle to become, in images from the material world, greater or higher or brighter than one's neighbour; at the same time he regards competition as productive of envy and malignancy. Hobbes had pointed out that virtue, by which he meant something like *faculty* or *ability*, 'is somewhat that is valued for eminence; and consisteth in comparison. For if all things were equally in all men, nothing would be prized'.[24] Johnson fully shares this opinion, and he has an acuter sense than Hobbes of the wide-ranging personal and social damage (as opposed to large-scale political disturbance) resulting from the battle for eminence. His sermons return again and again to this struggle for distinction, and the ravages it inflicts. (The topic seems even more like an obsession here, appearing as an important theme in Sermons 4, 5, 6, 8, 11,

12, 14, 17, 23 and 24, than it does in the moral essays, where it is perhaps more expected.)

Nor is desire of superiority a guarantee of greatness or even of dignity: pride 'is seldom delicate, it will please itself with very mean advantages' (*Rass*. IX). The *Rambler* teems with characters who expend limitless effort and ingenuity in struggles for superiority which are often of a strikingly petty kind. A girl in the country aspires after 'the highest honours of the female world'; her account of a rival's triumphs dwells naturally upon numbers ('a thousand civilities . . . a hundred lovers . . . twenty visits in an afternoon . . . six balls in an evening'), since she is noting the score which she will have to surpass (no. 62: III, 330, 333).

The ambition to excel involves, almost inescapably, ill-will towards rivals and towards those already excellent. Such ill-will plays a major part in *The Lives of the Poets*. Johnson has constructed this work to revolve round two poles: one is the greatness achieved by some of his subjects and vainly aspired to by others; the other is the inescapably paltry humanity of even the greatest, which shows itself often, ironically, in being pleased with mean advantages. The poets are measured by a grander scale than the *Rambler* characters, since they are judged against the ancients and are to be judged again by posterity. Yet the recurrent appearance of death in the scenes of this work serves to invoke a scale still grander. The last sentence of the life of Hughes calls Pope to witness that Hughes had 'no claim to poetical reputation but from his tragedy' – which succeeded after work upon work by Hughes had somehow failed to catch or hold the public attention, and in the teeth of overruling by the actors of the author's intentions. But Hughes outlived his sense of its importance: he 'paid no regard to the intelligence' of its success, 'being then wholly employed in the meditations of a departing Christian' (*Lives*, II, 163–5). His doggedly disputed claim to poetic stature suddenly becomes nothing to him. Here, as in *Rambler* 17, where thoughts of death are urged to lessen any 'great object which we have placed before us', or in no. 54, where a dying man is represented as no longer affected by 'visions of greatness' or 'accounts of the growth of his reputation' (Y, III, 93, 291), death alters the scale: the human standard of judgment is set aside for the divine standard. Johnson seems to have been deliberately correcting what he regarded as misjudgment of scale: *Biographia Britannica* had called Hughes's play 'worthy of the latest cares of so eminent a poet and so good a man'.

Johnson's sermons and other writings employ a whole series of periphrases for death (recalling the famous 'Being . . . whom I fear to name', in *Rasselas*, XLVIII), which suggest that he habitually associated death with the negation of distinctions of superiority more closely even than with the blotting out of vitality or consciousness. It is 'a state, where wealth or honour shall have no residence', 'a place where vanity and competition are forgotten for ever', 'a state, in which all distinctions will be for ever obliterated, but those of virtue'.[25]

Johnson has one ideal to oppose significantly against competitiveness: that of community, 'the secret concatenation of society, that links together the great and the mean, the illustrious and the obscure' (*Adv.* 67: Y, II, 386), a mutual exchange of help and benefits which includes in some cases a voluntary renunciation of superiority. Carey McIntosh finds in Johnson's fiction 'no sense of community' but only the pursuit of goals 'relative, and therefore comparative, and therefore competitive';[26] but this is because Johnson's fiction is mainly satirical. His sermons, essays and biographies regularly urge a willed co-operation. They regularly remind us, too, of our involuntary equality. We are all atoms in the great mass, the 'one vast republick' of mankind (*Idler* 19: Y, II, 59) which imposes common experience with or without our assent. Even for those who consistently reject the ideal of mutuality, death in the end imposes a community not to be evaded.

The interweaving of these ideas constitutes a habitual structure in Johnson's thought, indeed the figure in his carpet, to which everything else relates. The ideal of greatness, an ideal inescapably attractive, cannot be dealt with by simple moral obloquy. The appropriate response is to remember the relativity of greatness: to measure, which can be done only by comparison. Comparison, the making of judgments, is the central energy of Johnson's writing, as it is in his view the central activity of the human intellect, and it is associated with the drive to be judged highly. 'There is in every mind, implanted by nature, a desire of superiority' (Sermon 11: Y, XIV, 120); 'no two people can be half an hour together, but one shall acquire an evident superiority over the other' (Boswell, II, 13). The desire for excellence, if natural, cannot be simply prohibited, yet it leads to competition, to malevolence towards others, to mean triumph in petty advantages. To be superior is not necessarily to be great. To rank high in too diminutive a scale is valueless; a rational being must be able to measure one scale against another. Moreover, every scale perceptible by the human eye shrinks to nothing before that of eternity. Awareness of this ultimate relativity may provoke a choice of goodness rather than greatness as an ideal, but this is a solution which Johnson turns to less readily and less firmly than do many other moralists. He even seems sometimes to associate the pursuit of goodness with passive or negative ideas (obedience to commands and prohibitions), and he links the virtues he most admires – courage, generosity, struggle with adversity or with the dead weight of one's own psyche – with the pursuit of greatness, although that pursuit is also ineradicably linked with moral evils.

This complex of ideas held in tension against one another, threatening contradictoriness, is responsible for much vitality in Johnson's writings, much dialectical move and countermove, much irony both comic ('the highest honours of the female world') and shocking (Hughes lived to hear that his play 'was well received; but paid no regard to the intelligence'). It receives its fullest working out in *The Vanity of Human Wishes*, Johnson's finest single achievement. This poem represents at one view the allurements of greatness and the pathetic inadequacy of those who achieve it, the savagery of the struggle for superiority and, at the end, its inconsequentiality. It measures human beings by at least three different scales: the 'extensive view' which takes in whole nations of pygmy-sized people striving and sinking; the detailed view which displays Wolsey, Charles XII, and other champions in gigantic poses; and the one-to-one approach of the conclusion, which so strangely brackets the personal (*thou* and *thy*) with the impersonal ('the supplicating voice', 'the mind').

Elsewhere in Johnson's writings the same complex of ideas governs his choice of topics: ambition, rivalry, false greatness exploded, heroic greatness defeated, quotidian littleness vindicated. It governs also some favourite structures: that of 'mount . . . shine, evaporate, and fall',[27] that of the narrative which covers simultaneously a climb to eminence and a narrowing down of potentiality, that of the carefully measured judgment overruled on appeal to a different scale. It adds a depth and resonance of implication to several much used groups of words: the vocabularies of size, of comparison, of malice, for instance. It provides a number of favourite images which link the spiritual with the material,[28] size or height with often questionable intellectual or moral elevation: precipices (where a man standing may think he has left the earth beneath him, but is still subject to the law of gravity), vultures (which rejoice at destruction and prey on the fallen), heroes (often a type of what seems great by a false standard), and (bearing some relation to each of the previous three images) that of the observer from above and beyond the struggle, a less easily classified example of superiority, and to Johnson a disturbing image, frequently set before his readers and as frequently rejected.

To trace the varying play of these ideas will be to elucidate a particular and vital pattern in Johnson's works. The pattern fits together tightly, and it is hard to separate each topic for discussion from the others which help to define it. My argument is organized to move from one theme to another, not one work to another, and some important works or passages will be considered more than once in different contexts. It begins with Johnson's use of comparison and of different scales or standards in the processes of measuring and judging, his use of Swift's Lilliputian techniques in the 'Debates in the Senate of Magna Lilliputia', and his varying treatments of human pettiness, which he sometimes vindicates and sometimes mocks or reproves. It then moves on to a series of topics connected with the struggle to excel: the related issues of competitiveness and malignity, placed on either side of the ideal of community which Johnson opposed to them. It looks in some detail at the various figures of the watcher from on high, at the hero or achiever of more than is generally possible for humanity, and finally at that superiority or greatness whose common humanity is nevertheless insisted on. In the course of the argument I hope to make clear why Johnson, in his fascination with greatness, sees goodness as a necessary preliminary step towards it, in a way that no kind of greatness is to goodness. Whether or not greatness emerges from Johnson's surveys as a desirable quality or a justifiable object of pursuit, it is true to say that he finds its full realization beyond the grasp of humanity. Greatness is the most syren-like of all our 'treach'rous phantoms in the mist',[29] and until we recognize how strongly he is tugged by and how doggedly he resists its steadily exerted pull, we shall never accurately gauge the current of Johnson's thought.

1

COMPARISON

Undoubtedly Philosophers are in the Right when they tell us,
that nothing is great or little otherwise than by Comparison.

(*Gulliver's Travels*, II, i)

JOHNSON PRONOUNCES through Imlac that 'all judgment' and in *Rambler*
127 that 'all human excellence' is comparative (*Rasselas* XXX; Y, IV, 315).
In his own person he says the same both of happiness and of many of our
miseries (*Adv.* 111: Y, II, 451). To compare, according to the *Dictionary*'s
careful and analytical definition, is 'To make one thing the measure of
another; to estimate the relative goodness or badness, or other qualities, of
any one thing, by observing how it differs from something else.' This
mental operation is the basis of most of Johnson's moral, critical and
creative thinking, and the necessary preliminary to any assessment of
greatness. (That one may estimate relative goodness does not really
contradict the view that its nature is absolute. Goodness exists in relative
amounts; greatness can exist *only* relatively.) The definition reminds us,
however, that to compare is to make a value judgment: 'in whatever respect
a man differs from others, he must be considered by them as either worse or
better' (*Adv.* 131: Y, II, 485).

Even in the *Dictionary*, Johnson's uses of comparison reflect a never-
sleeping concern for worse or better. He often defines by comparison,
in particular by contraries (as his first meaning for *fat* is 'the contrary to lean'),
especially in explanation of those words which are 'too much known, to
be happily illustrated'. Being more aware than his predecessors that
'nothing can be defined but by the use of words too plain to admit a
definition', he makes more use of contraries than they do, but in an
interestingly selective manner.[1] He defines many pairs of words (*light* and
heavy, *thick* and *thin*, *lean* and *fat*, *long* and *short*) each in terms of its opposite.
Long is 'not short' and *short*, contrariwise, 'not long'. He uses these

contraries even more profusely when defining conditions which indicate a lack of something: *little*, *low*, *small* and *dark* are defined more in terms of contraries than *light/heavy*, and so on, while on the other hand *great*, *high*, *quick* and *light* (opposite of dark) are not defined by this method. Of Johnson's five definitions of *little*, three employ 'not'. His first definition of *small* includes 'not great' and his last 'not strong'; five out of six quotations under its first sense make an explicit comparison with something larger. For the adjective *low*, nine of the sixteen definitions begin with 'not'; but only one among nineteen senses for *high* uses a negative comparison, and that is the special sense of 'high treason'.[2] The illustrative quotations under *petty* not only make implicit or explicit comparisons with grander things, but five out of nine of them apply the word to things which clearly ought to possess dignity – princes (twice), gods, commonwealths, the river Rhine – so that pettiness is either a surprise or a reproach. 'Not' or its equivalent appears in each of Johnson's seven definitions of the adjective *dark*, but only once in the first edition for its opposite, *light* (noun and adjective).

Little, *low*, *small*, *petty* and *dark*, it seems, which invite definition by negatives, differ from their opposites – and also from both *light* and *heavy*, *thick* and *thin*, which correspond to Locke's primary qualities of solidity, extension, figure, mobility[3] – in carrying a sense of privation. Johnson defines *privativeness* as 'Notation of absence of something *that should be present*' (my italics).[4] So greatness, height, brightness (like human achievement) are things which somehow *ought* to be, whose absence is not simply the presence of a contrary quality but is a lack, a deprivation.

These comparative qualities, measurable by gradual scales of greatness, height, or brightness, are the terms of physical measurement which also, in figurative senses, play an important role in Johnson's psychological and critical vocabulary.[5] This unequivocally material basis does not exclude implications of value judgment, the same implications which Johnson attaches to other, less directly physical, critical terms. The *Dictionary* explains the several senses of *pretty* in terms of deprivation, in a manner increasingly derogatory: '1. Neat; elegant; pleasing without surprise or elevation. 2. Beautiful without grandeur or dignity. 3. It is used in a kind of diminutive contempt in poetry, and in conversation. . . .' Even in making definitions, to compare is to prefer or to reject, 'to estimate the relative goodness or badness', to suggest of greatness and its related qualities that we cannot do without them as we can do without weight or thickness. From Johnson's comparative method of defining we learn to expect that when he comes to discuss human greatness – which means, comparatively, the excelling of others – he will see it as a desideratum or requisite.

The other part of the *Dictionary*'s definition of *to compare*, 'To make one thing the measure of another', raises the question of what to compare with, what to make the measure or scale. This question had exercised other thinkers of the generations before Johnson, to whom the possibility had first opened of considering mankind in relation to almost the whole range of natural objects. Locke wrote

> There are . . . words of time, that ordinarily are thought to stand for positive ideas, which yet will, when considered, be found to be relative [as *young* and *old*, when used of human beings, are reckoned by comparing with seventy years]. . . . But the sun and stars, though they have outlasted several generations of men, we call not old, because we do not know what period God hath set to that sort of beings.[6]

Newton himself, knowing more than most people about the sun and stars, provided the groundwork for scientific belief that 'there is no great or little, but with regard to ourselves'.[7] Johnson endorsed to some extent the choice of a measure based on ourselves, our own perceptions and experience.

> One general method of judging, and determining upon the value, or excellence of things, is by comparing one with another. Thus it is, that we form a notion of wealth, greatness, or power. It is by comparing ourselves with others, that we often make an estimate of our own happiness, and even sometimes of our virtue. (Sermon 16: Y, XIV, 177)

Rambler 108 tells us that we cannot cope directly with either extreme, with extensive surfaces or with atoms: 'our faculties are fitted to images of a certain extent, to which we adjust great things by division, and little things by accumulation' (Y, IV, 211).

So far this is simply orthodox empiricism, our ultimate reliance on our own sense-impressions and experience. But for Johnson the mental operation of comparing and judging is a far from simple one. In the case of physical measurement, the self can never be a standard objectively seen, for as Locke wrote and as Johnson quoted him under *size*: 'Objects near our view are thought greater than those of a larger *size*, that are more remote'.[8] That we have, literally speaking, our own point of view makes objectivity, if attainable at all, a matter of compensation, of readjusting the natural bias against which Sermon 16 goes on to warn us.

Johnson makes a parliamentary orator observe: 'It is well known, Sir, tho' it is not always remembered, that political as well as natural Greatness is merely comparative, and that he only is a powerful Prince, who is more powerful than those with whom he can have any Cause of Contention' (*GM*, XII, 1742, p. 285). Actual comparing, by experience, will supersede a subjective view (whereby a prince near at hand looks more powerful than one remote), and may be endlessly modified through contention and competition. In matters of mere size our brain learns to reinterpret the evidence of our eyes; in the case of more subtle measurables, like political power or artistic beauty, the range of comparison extends and elaborates itself.

In *Rambler* 92 Johnson says of literary beauty also that it is 'merely relative and comparative': 'we transfer the epithet as our knowledge encreases, and appropriate it to higher excellence, when higher excellence comes within our view' (Y, IV, 121–2). This remark introduces an attempt to establish critical principles on which distinctions may be based. Critical principles follow from comparison, yet their establishment does nothing, in Johnson's view, to supersede the operation of comparative criticism, which can never reach a final assessment of what it seeks to value.

The only irreversible conclusions which comparative criticism can reach are negative ones. 'He that reads many books must compare one opinion or one style with another; and when he compares, must necessarily distinguish, reject, and prefer' (*Lives*, III, 94). In this complex series of actions, to distinguish involves preferring but also rejecting. To keep our eyes open for higher excellence is to be ready to relinquish the lower.

All Johnson's critical writings demonstrate his concern with mensuration as an essential, but also exacting, even dangerous, tool. The candid critic, whose use of himself as standard does not bring himself into distorting competition with the thing measured, has the satisfaction of preferring as well as rejecting, of recognizing greatness as well as littleness. If we mostly perceive Johnson's judgments as generous and not carping, this is because of the flexibility with which they deploy appropriate standards; those who dislike his criticism may agree with Sir John Hawkins in finding it 'mechanical. . . . a kind of arithmetical process, subtracting from [a writer's] excellencies his failings'. Hawkins says this about the preface to Shakespeare, where he works out the sum very oddly, concluding that Johnson 'endeavoured . . . to persuade us, against reason and our own feelings, that the former [excellencies] are annihilated by the latter [failings]'.[9]

Most of Johnson's readers would probably reach a different total here. The preface, in fact, contains his most magnificent statement of the value of comparison to the critic, and it is by no means simply a mathematical value:

> To works, however, of which the excellence is not absolute and definite, but gradual and comparative; to works not raised upon principles demonstrative and scientifick, but appealing wholly to observation and experience, no other test can be applied than length of duration and continuance of esteem. What mankind have long possessed they have often examined and compared, and if they persist to value the possession, it is because frequent comparisons have confirmed opinion in its favour. As among the works of nature

no man can properly call a river deep or a mountain high, without the knowledge of many mountains and many rivers; so in the productions of genius, nothing can be stiled excellent till it has been compared with other works of the same kind. . . . Of the first building that was raised, it might be with certainty determined that it was round or square, but whether it was spacious or lofty must have been referred to time. (Y, VII, 59–60)

This passage is instructively characteristic. Johnson here advises logical comparison while extending his own measure to include non-logical, imaginative comparison of plays with rivers, mountains, and buildings. Advising comparison of like with like, he practises comparison of like with unlike as well. He enjoyed mathematical calculation as a pastime and distraction, and valued it as a means to knowledge,[10] but its very uniformity made it less valuable as a scale of human achievement than the relative standards of the natural world.[11] The critic's estimation of the spaciousness or loftiness of artistic works adds evaluative comparison to simple measurement. To compare one work with another is a preliminary exercise in estimating them rightly; to compare a work of the brain with rivers or mountains – objects quite unlike itself – works in a manner both flattering and cautionary, as well as imaginatively descriptive. Such are the natural images – field or lawn, flight, and fire – by which Johnson compares Pope with Dryden, which David Daiches calls 'diagnostic and clarifying', although he agrees with Hawkins in finding Johnson's comparative method usually mechanical and arithmetical.[12] What the purely quantitative method is like, and what Johnson adds to it, may be seen by making our own comparison of his passage on Shakespeare with Hume's advocacy of comparing 'the several performances, admired in different ages and nations', in order to 'rate the merits of a work . . . and assign its proper rank among the productions of genius'.[13] Johnson's scale of reference, unlike Hume's, implicitly ranks the productions of genius in their turn in relation to other things.

To compare the material of books with the facts of actual life fruitfully supplements the mathematical comparison of like with like, as Johnson suggests in another characteristic passage. He has been saying that poverty bears two different meanings, in books and in reality:

Poets have their imaginations filled with ideas of magnificence; and being accustomed to contemplate the downfal of empires, or to contrive forms of lamentation for monarchs in distress, rank all the classes of mankind in a state of poverty, who make no approaches to the dignity of crowns. To be poor in the epick language, is only not to command the wealth of nations, not to have fleets and armies in pay.

So poetic poverty is compared with actual poverty, like with unlike; at the same time, within the scale of actual poverty, comparison of like with like is doggedly enforced. In cold prose nobody 'can, with any propriety, be termed poor, who does not see the greater part of mankind richer than himself' (*Ram.* 202: Y, V, 288–9). As comparison with the measurable works of nature helps Johnson to assess the less amenable works of human genius, so comparison with life helps him to assess books: in each case a simple comparison opens into a wider and more suggestive one.

From the outset of his career Johnson voiced the necessity of knowing what comparative terms like riches and poverty meant over as large a range as possible of the human scale. In the *Gentleman's Magazine* in 1738 he wrote that the satisfaction of reading travel books 'arises from a comparison which every reader naturally makes' between the familiar and the new (Y, X, 15). The same idea recurs later: travel-writers need the ability both to make comparisons and to lead their readers to make their own (Boswell, III, 301–2; *Idler* 97: Y, II, 298). In a letter to Hester Thrale he wrote, 'If the world be worth wining let us enjoy it, if it is to be despised let us despise it by conviction. But the world is not to be despised but as it is compared with something better' (no. 409). The tendency of all Johnson's writings about human life is to lead his readers to extend their range of such comparisons, as a vital step in the hard endeavour 'to see things as they are'.[14] Since all 'indifferent qualities and practices are bad if they are compared with those which are good, and good if they are opposed to those that are bad' (*Idler* 56: Y, II, 177), it is always desirable to draw on more than one scale of comparison.

Johnson believed that figurative language works by means of comparison, but he expected more from it than a simple parallel of like with like. 'A poetical simile is the discovery of likeness between two actions in their general nature dissimilar.' A successful one will ennoble as well as illustrating. Johnson uses the word 'comparison' for Pope's simile of the 'Alps on Alps', which he calls 'perhaps the best that English poetry can shew'. He distinguishes simile, which compares two things 'generally unlike, as unlike as intellect and body', from mere exemplification – the comparison, for instance, of one river with another (the kind of comparison on which judgment of relative size can be formed). Comparison, therefore, the vigorous composite activity which embraces distinguishing, rejecting, and conferring value, lies at the heart of poetic statement. It involves two separate spheres, and 'the force of metaphors is lost when the mind by the mention of particulars is turned more upon the original than the secondary sense, more upon that from which the illustration is drawn than that to which it is applied'.[15] (Johnson's remarks about metaphor and simile are interchangeable, for although his own images more frequently take the form of metaphor, he had no separate theory of its nature and function – he did not think, for instance, that it constituted perception of any actual identity – but saw it as simile couched in a different form or, as the *Dictionary* rather confusingly has it, 'a simile comprized in a word'.)

As well as relying on comparison for definition, for moral judgment, for illumination and ennobling, Johnson relied on it for humour, for a salutary jolt to mechanical perceptions. He makes Mr Rambler complain from time to time about readers comparing his essays with those of his predecessors, and the complaints vary in tone from dignified self-justification to transparent mock-modesty (Y, III, 128–9; IV, 204–5). He prefaces his Eskimo romance of Anningait and Ajut with a solemn warning that in order to avoid dissatisfaction we ought to compare our own state only with that of others less fortunate than ourselves and never with the more fortunate – a warning which the developing context warns us not to take too seriously (*Ram*. 186: Y, V, 211–12). *Idler* 34 opens, 'To illustrate one thing by its resemblance to another has been always the most popular and efficacious art of instruction' – but develops not as a dissertation on poetic imagery or on knowledge of the world, but as a light-hearted conceit paralleling the ideal blend of ingredients for stimulating conversation with that for making punch (Y, II, 106–8). This is not only to compare great things with small, but also deliberately and comically to compare things unlike. The fifth *Idler* plays the same trick, ironically weighing the respective merits of soldiers and pets as companions for fine ladies, making especially good fun of the apparent abandonment of the comparison: 'but a parrot, after all, is a poor little creature, and has neither sword nor shoulder-knot, can neither dance nor play at cards' (Y, II, 17–18). Such playful uses of comparison spring from Johnson's delight in contrasts and incongruities of all kinds, from comic interpolation (about the holder of a new record for long-distance riding, the Idler is 'far from wishing either to the Amazon *or her horse* any diminution of happiness, or fame'[16]) to the 'delightful contrariety of images' in the Hebrides: of 'the beating billows and the howling storm' outdoors with 'the song and the dance' indoors, of 'the ruggedness of moors' with 'seats of plenty, gaiety, and magnificence', of the expected 'gross herdsman, or amphibious fisherman', with the actual 'gentleman and two ladies' offering 'all the kindness of hospitality, and refinement of courtesy' (Y, IX, 66, 77, 142–3). Johnson demands from his readers an alertness to observe *how* 'one thing . . . differs from something else', and rewards such alertness with innumerable discoveries of contrast, surprise and re-evaluation.

2

SCALE

Greatness and littleness are terms merely comparative; and
we err in our estimation of things because we measure them by
some wrong standard.

(*Adventurer* 128)

AMONG OTHER delightful contrarieties, Johnson had an eye for and an
enjoyment of incongruities in physical size. He makes incisive comment on
the disproportion between his own bulk and a twelve-hand Island pony
carrying him, or between Hester Thrale's 'Lilliputian' littleness and a
fashion more appropriate to somebody taller.[1] His juvenile translation of
Addison's Latin 'Battle of the Pygmies and Cranes' juxtaposes the warfare
of 'enormous gyants' with 'little ghosts' of pygmies appearing by moonlight
to shepherds (lines 136–70: Y, VI, 26–7). He chose a giant and a dwarf, too,
when he needed a quick summary of the incongruous subject-matter of the
romances (Y, VII, 64). As his chief example of the 'little pursuits' and
'narrow views' of Frederick William of Prussia, he used that monarch's
devotion to his carefully collected 'tall regiment' (*Works*, VI, 436, 441).

Johnson thought it unlikely to be true, as reported, that the negroes of
Africa thought the first Portuguese ships they saw were fish, birds or
phantoms. A native, he said, would recognize the ship as related to the tiny
boats he would know already, and, 'perhaps, suppose it to be a hollow
trunk of a tree, from some country where trees grow to a much greater
height and thickness than in his own'.[2] That is, he expected primitive
people to distinguish one *kind* of object clearly from another, but to have in
their minds the concept that the same object might exist on quite a different
scale – as if the experience of Gulliver had entered as deeply into their
imaginations as into his own.

These remarks refer to strictly physical bulk, but in Johnson's mind the
'primitive' physical meaning and the figurative meaning of words never lie

far apart. The *Dictionary* follows its first definition of *size* as 'Bulk; quantity of superficies; comparative magnitude' with '3. Figurative bulk; condition'. Johnson's treatment of greatness never loses touch with the root connotations of dimension, and his critical and moral judgments constantly express themselves through the notion of physical size. In the first volume of *Praeterita*, Ruskin expressed his gratitude to Johnson for having 'taught me carefully to *measure* life', 'to think and judge as Johnson thought and *measured*'.[3]

Ruskin's word is appropriate. To measure the little against the great is one of the most characteristic activities of Johnson's mind. Of course he was not alone in this. Virgil's 'to compare great things with small'[4] was perhaps the most overworked tag of the period, for classicists and non-classicists alike. Gray's 'How low, how little are the Proud,/How indigent the Great!' provoked from Johnson not one but two slightly sour comments: 'the thoughts have nothing new. . . . The morality is natural, but too stale'.[5] It is odd that Johnson (who himself wrote in a letter of those 'whom we condescend to call Great'[6]) failed to appreciate the way in which Gray took the deliberately trite reflection of his Muse-accompanied poet and embedded it in a series of delicately balanced comparisons of one scale of measurement with another, for this technique lies at the heart of Johnson's own thinking, and his methods of constructing literary works.

He himself wrote of *standards* or *measures* rather than *scales*. He defines *standard*, the word he employs to emphasize the relativity of greatness and littleness – after '1. An ensign in war, particularly the ensign of the horse' – as '2. That which is of undoubted authority; that which is the test of other things of the same kind'. The fixity which this definition suggests is modified by the examples, which include mention of false standards and of things inappropriately proposed as standards, as well as an appeal to the cosmos, from Holder: 'The heavenly motions are more stated than the terrestrial models, and are both originals and *standards*.' Johnson's first definition of the noun *measure*, 'That by which any thing is measured', is illustrated by, among others, another quotation from Holder about relativity: 'All magnitudes are capable of being measured; but it is the application of one to another which makes actual *measures*.'

The relevant definition of the noun *scale* is one of a series: '5. Ladder; means of ascent. 6. The act of storming by ladders. 7. Regular gradation; a regular series rising like a ladder. 8. A figure subdivided by lines like the steps of a ladder, which is used to measure proportions between pictures and the thing represented.' Senses five and seven are further linked by their first illustrative quotations, both from *Paradise Lost*. Johnson takes the word to indicate a means of climbing in 'Love . . . is the *scale*/By which to heav'nly love thou may'st ascend',[7] but as the series of the Chain of Being in all seven quotations[8] under the seventh definition, including:

> . . . the *scale* of nature set,
> From centre to circumference; whereon
> In contemplation of created things,
> By steps we may ascend to God.[9]

Other writers usually allude to the scale of being in order to assert the perfect adaptation of humanity to its place there; Johnson, by his choice of this quotation, almost makes it sound as if he holds progression to be possible from one position in the scale to a higher.

Johnson tells us that he had often considered the doctrine of the Scale of Being, 'but always left the inquiry in doubt and uncertainty' (*Works*, VI, 51). He included in the *Dictionary* some quotations (such as the second under *magnificent*, from Locke) which support the doctrine, but himself held that 'those, who repose their reason upon the scale of being' have little cause 'to triumph over them who recur to any other expedient of solution'.[10] The doctrine itself is efficiently propounded by Soame Jenyns and quoted by Johnson in the review which is elsewhere so scathing:

> The universe is a system, whose very essence consists in subordination; a scale of beings descending, by insensible degrees, from infinite perfection to absolute nothing; in which . . . the beauty and happiness of the whole depend altogether on . . . the comparative imperfections of the several beings of which it is composed. . . . It is, moreover, highly probable, that there is such a connexion between all ranks and orders, by subordinate degrees, that they mutually support each other's existence, and every one, in its place, is absolutely necessary towards sustaining the whole vast and magnificent fabrick.[11]

Were it not for its early origins, this doctrine might have been invented expressly to assuage the unease caused by the scientists' expansion of the scale of the visible universe, an unease variously recorded, accepted, and protested against, by writers of the seventeenth century.[12] Pascal, famous for voicing the fear of a different kind of man – an unbeliever – before the eternal spaces, had himself been fascinated by them:

> Que l'homme contemple donc la nature entière dans sa haute et pleine majesté. . . . que la terre lui paraisse comme un point au prix du vaste tour que cet astre décrit, et qu'il s'étonne de ce que ce vaste tour lui–même n'est qu'une pointe très délicate à l'égard de celui que les astres qui roulent dans le firmament embrassent.[13]

Locke also felt it salutary for humanity to recognize its own littleness in comparison with the immensity of the universe. He would not have forgotten in writing the following passage, any more than Johnson did in quoting from it in the *Dictionary*, that the root meaning of *immensity* indicates not bigness but impossibility of measuring.

> He that will not set himself proudly at the top of all things, but will consider the immensity of this fabric [the universe], and the great variety that is to be found in this little and inconsiderable part of it which he has to do with, may be apt to think that in other mansions of it there may be other and different intelligent beings, of whose faculties he has as little knowledge or apprehension as a worm shut up in one drawer of a cabinet hath of the senses or understanding of a man.[14]

Shaftesbury, who differed from Locke about so much, nevertheless put forward the same idea:

> Yet is this mansion-globe, this man-container, of a much narrower compass even than its other fellow-wanderers of our system. How narrow then must it appear compared with the capacious system of its own sun? And how narrow, or as nothing, in respect of those innumerable systems of other suns? Yet how immense a body it seems compared with ours of human form.[15]

Literature did ample justice to this concept. Milton, as Marjorie Nicolson has pointed out,

> makes much of the difference between this earth as it seems to those who dwell upon it and to those who survey it from afar, to whom it shows its relative unimportance in the cosmic scheme. To Adam and Eve . . . earth seems fixed and secure, the center of the universe. . . . But to those who view it from far off – whether God or Satan – and see it in its relation to the vast expanse of space . . . [it is] a tiny body, merely one of many stars.[16]

Milton, dramatizing the different viewpoints belonging to different measures of size, appropriates the cosmic view to beings other than human. Our sight is fitted only to the earth. Pascal found the human measure insufficient to grapple with the greater one. 'Nous avons beau enfler nos conceptions au delà des espaces imaginables, nous n'enfantons que des atomes, au prix de la réalité des choses.'[17] Shaftesbury describes almost the same experience of time that Pascal describes of space. 'In vain, too, we pursue that phantom time, too small, and yet too mighty for our grasp, when, shrinking to a narrow point, it escapes our hold, or mocks our scanty thought by swelling to eternity.'[18] The language describing each experience (humanity attempting to enlarge its ideas; time enlarging out of its grasp) is eloquent of a sense of relativity, therefore immeasurability; mankind seems to shrink as its environment expands.

The obvious conclusion for the moralist from these premises, and the one encouraged by the doctrine of the scale of being, was that humanity must employ its sense of proportion to re-evaluate its own littleness in relation to the new vastness of the universe. Pascal told his readers what humility ought to follow from contemplation of the cosmos:

> Que l'homme . . . se regarde comme égaré dans ce canton détourné de la nature; et que, de ce petit cachot où il se trouve logé, j'entends l'univers, il apprenne à estimer la terre, les royaumes, les villes et soi-même son juste prix.[19]

Locke, however, refused to be intimidated by the disparity between the immense universe and the simple ideas which are our only tools of knowing:

> All those sublime thoughts which tower above the clouds, and reach as high as heaven itself, take their rise and footing here; in all that great extent wherein the mind wanders, in those remote speculations it may seem to be elevated with, it stirs not one jot beyond those *ideas* which *sense* or *reflection* have offered for its contemplation.[20]

Simple ideas, he maintained, can hold their own as material for investigation even with remote speculations:

> Nor let anyone think these too narrow bounds for the capacious mind of man to expatiate in, which takes its flight farther than the stars, and cannot be confined by the limits of the world; that extends its thoughts often even beyond the utmost expansion of matter, and makes excursions into that incomprehensible inane.[21]

Here the discrepancy in proportion between the immediate and the distant remains, but the human mind is now seen as mediating between vast and minute, and even as sharing, through its imaginative extension, the nature of the vast.

During Johnson's own lifetime the contemplation of immensity was used by writers for a whole range of purposes: to inculcate humility, acceptance, reverence or ecstasy. Henry Baker published in 1727 *The Universe, A Poem. Intended to restrain the Pride of Man*. Pope uses the cosmic scale for two contrary effects: to assert and to undermine the dignity of the human. Between 1711 and 1714 he imagined himself standing

> betwixt Earth, Seas, and Skies;
> The whole Creation open to my Eyes;
> In Air self-ballanc'd hung the Globe below.

In 1733 he sardonically instructed the human being, that 'wond'rous creature', to:

> Go, soar with Plato to th'empyreal sphere. . .
> Then drop into thyself, and be a fool![22]

Johnson's own uses of this imagery differ interestingly from any yet mentioned here. He comes nearest to using it as an argument for humility in his review of Soame Jenyns, whom he advises on the topic of the universe

> a little to distrust his own faculties, however large and comprehensive. . . . the petty distinctions of locality, which are of good use upon our own globe . . . have no meaning with regard to infinite space, in which nothing is *high* or *low*. (*Works*, VI, 59)

Compared with Henry Baker or Pope, however, this is a gentle reproof, and even this is unusual for Johnson.

In *Rambler* 118 he traces the idea of cosmic comparison far back beyond the Copernican revolution to the time of Cicero. He opens the essay as if he were going to follow the pattern of employing the vastness of heaven to inculcate humility in human beings, closely paraphrasing 'Somnium Scipionis', a passage of Cicero's *De Republica* in which the dead hero Scipio Africanus 'point[s] at the earth from the celestial regions' and proclaims the narrow limits of human fame.[23] The globe is so small, the inhabited portion still smaller: how few, he says, can become known *even* as far as the bounds of human knowledge, which are *only* the Ganges and the Caucasus! Ganges to Caucasus may well seem a narrow span to an observer in the 'celestial regions' – but we may remember how in *The Vanity of Human Wishes* Observation herself finds the survey from China to Peru (an updated version of what Dryden's Juvenal calls 'the Habitable World') an extensive one. Cicero, through his elevated exemplar Scipio, sees fit to humble humanity with a sense of littleness; he uses his earlier cosmography, as Pascal, Locke and Baker were to use theirs, to 'restrain the pride of man'. Johnson's essay, however, contradicts Cicero, choosing to present him as the advocate of a biased case. Cicero professes to diminish fame, but Johnson finds his profession not only disingenuous but illogical:

> he confines not its extent but by the boundaries of nature, nor contracts its duration but by representing it small in the estimation of superior beings. He still admits it the highest and noblest of terrestrial objects, and alleges little more against it, than that it is neither without end, nor without limits.

So much for the attempt to measure human endeavours by a standard formed in the celestial regions.

Johnson devotes the rest of his essay to a careful consideration of the limitations of individual fame *within* the range to which Cicero reduces it: 'a narrower compass; a single nation, and a few years, [which] have generally sufficient amplitude to fill our imaginations'. Within this compass he reminds us how few people have any attention to spare for those who bid for fame. Most are busy with their own livelihood and pastimes. Either they have 'their heads filled with a fox or a horse-race, a feather or a ball', or they live 'below the flight of fame . . . in the vallies of life', or they 'are with-held from attending his triumph by different persuits'.[24] These images work to aggrandize the candidate for fame and belittle the potential audience: interest in sport or fashion is ludicrously concretized as having a fox or feather in one's head; to be famous is to soar above valley-dwellers or to hold a garlanded and trophied triumph. From these images alone we might suppose that Johnson's 'humble version' works, just as much as the 'Ciceronian eloquence' whose tendentiousness he had stigmatized, to exalt the 'fever of renown'.[25] Yet the pursuer of fame is not exempt from diminishing definition, any more than the pursuer of foxes, but becomes one 'who places happiness in the frequent repetition of his name'. Science is made ridiculous by the same concretizing technique that was applied to fashion and sport: someone 'that is growing great and happy by electrifying a bottle, wonders how the world can be engaged by trifling prattle about war or peace'. Both these remarks are examples of what W.J. Bate calls Johnson's 'reductionism',[26] or what *Adventurer* 128 calls 'a detail of minute circumstances to make every thing little' (see below, p.28). The essay which begins by finding fault with Cicero ends by endorsing the message of his Scipio Africanus that we must 'raise our eyes to higher prospects' than merely human praise and reward.

The differences between Cicero and Johnson resolve themselves into differences of measurement. Cicero seeks to reduce his readers' idea of fame by first showing, from a superhuman perspective, the small size of the globe and the smaller part that human renown can reach. Fame may fill the known world, he says, but that world is smaller than we think. Johnson reduces the range of fame from Cicero's known world to the 'nearer bounds' of few only among our fellow-creatures; the candidate for fame is to 'subduct' the small total of his 'encomiasts' from those who for various reasons ignore him. The mathematical word ironically indicates the uncertain nature of this calculation. Having enforced choice of the human scale in preference to Cicero's cosmic one, Johnson further complicates the processes of judgment. Within his 'nearer bounds' or 'narrower compass' his mind moves back and forth, now recognizing and now denying stature in the pursuers of fame and in those indifferent to it; he demonstrates the human standard to be not only more just but also more flexible, incorporating the different values (some endorsed, some satirized) of different individuals, capable of dealing with the infinite variety of life which the Ciceronian passage ignores.

Johnson used the cosmic scale again in another essay which tests one standard of judgment against another. *Adventurer* 128 (Y, II, 476–81) takes as its subject the contempt and scorn with which each group regards the activities of others, and proceeds as advised in *The Vanity of Human Wishes*: 'How just that scorn ere yet thy voice declare,/Search every state'.[27] This essay's third paragraph rejects a celestial overview of its

> question, which a distant prospect of the world will not enable us to answer. We find all ranks and ages mingled together in a tumultous confusion, with haste in their motions and eagerness in their looks; but what they have to persue or avoid, a more minute observation must inform us.

Such observation resembles the 'minute discriminations' which on his way to Scotland Johnson was inclined to think beyond any traveller's capability;[28] but in this essay he comprehends various sorts of 'minute observation'. First comes a survey of all those motions and eagerness, which runs through different occupations from collecting fossils to card parties and betting on horses; from this follows the irresistible conclusion 'that some of these lives are passed in trifles . . . by which no man could be long engaged, who . . . had knowledge enough to compare what he is with what he might be made'. Johnson diminishes the human race to something very like an ant-hill under a microscope; then, however, he descends from his vantage-point to deprecate 'that universal contempt and haughty negligence, which is sometimes associated with powerful faculties' and which masquerades as greatness of mind.

It then emerges that all this was only prelude. We perceive that fossils, flowers, mistresses and cards are too predictably a quarry for the satirist to engage us other than in warning against that 'contempt and arrogance' which 'is the easiest philosophy'. The heart of the essay lies in opposition between the wonderment of the philosopher La Bruyère that reasonable beings should spend their days 'in rubbing two smooth stones together, or in other terms in polishing marble' and the stone-cutter's wonderment at the laborious and purposeless employment of the writer, whom he would be glad to see 'seized by an order of the government, and obliged to labour at some useful occupation'. The reader is led successively through sympathy for the despised workman's initial innocence and good will ('The sight of a man who works so much harder than myself, excited my curiosity'), through amusement at the description, both detailed and economical, of the pains of authorship ('disquieted with doubts, about the propriety of a word which every body understood'), to some sense of shock at the workman's hostile and politically reactionary conclusion, and therefore relief when Johnson himself intervenes: 'Thus, by a partial and imperfect representation, may every thing be made equally ridiculous.'

Word-polisher and stone-polisher are equally myopic, though it is usually the man of words who can enforce his biased scale of measurement with distorting language. So ploughing becomes either, on the one hand, 'driving a piece of sharp iron into the clay' ('a detail of minute circumstances to make every thing little', a very Swiftian technique), or, on the other, 'changing the face of nature, diffusing plenty and happiness over kingdoms, and compelling the earth to give food to her inhabitants' ('an aggregation of effects to make every thing great'). Observation must be close, but it must not omit to allow for the effects of perspective: 'the mind, as well as the eye, is deceived by distance' (*Adv.* 111: Y, II, 452).

Into this context drops the characteristic aphorism which stands at the head of this chapter. Illiberal standards expose littleness in their user, whether satirist or philospher. 'He that despises for its littleness any thing really useful, has no pretensions to applaud the grandeur of his conceptions.' For instance, to neglect the care of a family out of a desire to do something greater, to diffuse blessings 'over all the globe', is mistaken because

> even this globe is little, compared with the system of matter within our view; and that system barely something more than non-entity, compared with the boundless regions of space, to which neither eye nor imagination can extend.

Here again Johnson, like Pascal, Locke and Shaftesbury, compares diminutive earth with boundless space, but makes the comparison serve different ends. He takes the value and significance of the world as agreed: its cosmic insignificance rebukes the grandiose ambition to shine 'over all the globe', but also sets its human inhabitants free to accept and to feel comfortable with their domestic insignificance. Because we do not despise our planet, though it is in reality little, we have neither right nor duty to despise even littler things. Johnson, seeking a scale of measurement, proposes a two-fold one, in relation to ourselves and in relation to God. On the one hand, 'the present moment', 'the smallest point of time', is 'inconceivably short'; on the other, 'its effects are unlimited', since they extend 'either to our hurt or our advantage, through all eternity' (*Ram.* 41: Y, III, 225). On the one hand, whoever 'steadily perseveres in the exertion of all his faculties, does what is great with respect to himself'. On the other, we 'have powers very scanty in their utmost extent' according to God's ultimate scale (*Adv.* 128: Y, II, 480–1). Only with both these measures in mind may we consider the different proportions of faculties or powers in different people.

One of the processes that take place in *Rasselas* is the enlargement of the material available for comparison, the gradual expansion of the characters' sphere of activity, from the Happy Valley, to Cairo, and out beyond the city as far as 'the extremity of Egypt' whither Pekuah is abducted (XXXVII), as well as backwards in time by means of the catacombs and the pyramids. When Rasselas first feels the valley to be small he longs for the great world outside; the world gradually becomes small and circumscribed too (see below, pp.158, 163–4). The decision to return to Abyssinia, which comes to many readers as a shock, sounds like an exchange of the wider for the narrower. Such an exchange need not, however, be constricting: of the two characters in the book who allow their imaginations to range the heavens, the would-be aeronaut is nearly stifled when he comes down to earth, but the astronomer, who suffers severely for his desire to diffuse blessings 'over all the globe', is liberated by the narrow bounds of a social group. One could say that while the astronomer has adjusted a scale of vision which made the world look too small, Rasselas and his companions have adjusted one which once made the world took too great.

Mindful of the parallel between physical and mental perception, of the well-known fact of the mind's and eye's deception by distance, Johnson frequently borrows images from telescopes, microscopes, and other optical phenomena, for their power to indicate both relativity and the possibility of substituting one scale for another.[29] (He quoted Newton's *Opticks*, the only Newton work he used, 461 times in the *Dictionary*.[30]) When Dryden forms an inaccurate telescope image, Johnson is quick to point it out (*Lives*, I, 463). He uses this image himself in at least two ways: sometimes as if the instruments of seeing distort a true scale, based on our own size and perceived correctly by our senses, and sometimes as if they provide a healthily corrective standard.

Both Pope and Thomson had drawn on the magnifying and distorting properties of mist and fog: for the confused visions of Dulness, for objects rendered indistinct 'beyond the life', and for the shepherd who 'stalks gigantic'.[31] Instead of the enlarged vagueness which these poets differently delight in, Johnson uses the image for a measurable and therefore correctable distortion. Frederick the Great was saved by an upbringing unworthy of his station from the myopia of most kings, which sees 'the world in a mist, which magnifies every thing near them, and bounds their view to a narrow compass' (*Works*, VI, 440). In the first paragraph of *The Lives of the Poets* Johnson reverts to this image for a different kind of distorted perception: Sprat, he says, included so little detail in his life of Cowley that 'scarcely any thing is distinctly known, but all is shewn confused and enlarged through the mist of panegyrick'. In the same way, as Johnson claimed later in the same work, Cowley and his school produced by hyperbole and amplification 'combinations of confused magnificence', and Dryden writing on the death of Charles II distorted his images 'by endeavouring to enlarge them' (*Lives*, I, 1, 21, 438). Johnson's statement about Sprat also states what he himself intended to avoid in the *Lives*.[32] He

Scale 29

had shown in *Adventurer* 128 how either aggregation or too-minute detail can distort the scale of judgment: the mist image suggests a cause (both for lack of detail and for aggrandizement) which, unlike distance, can be easily remedied: from it Johnson's life of Cowley moves straight to the eminently clear and unfogged 'His father was a grocer, whose condition Dr. Sprat conceals under the general appellation of a citizen'.[33]

Johnson uses the example of Julius Libri, who refused to look through Galileo's telescope and 'see the experiments by which [his errors] were confuted', to contrast wilful blindness with enlightenment (*Ram.* 31: Y, III, 169 and n. 3). Telescope truth, this suggests, is a corrective to personally limited vision. When Johnson chooses to depict the writer or moralist as surveyor of mankind (see below, pp. 154ff.) he sometimes evokes a hint of the telescope image; but in those passages, such as *Rambler* 54, he generally rejects remote observation for a closer view, and the corrective properties of the instrument are therefore inappropriate. Telescope truth is distant truth, potentially objective but sometimes wilfully evaded or distorted.

In *Idler* nos 78 and 83 Johnson presents the conversational style of the company at Tunbridge Wells. The restricted circle of this resort, he says, acts like a microscope to provide

> opportunities for more exact observation. The glass that magnifies its object contracts the sight to a point, and the mind must be fixed upon a single character to remark its minute peculiarities. The quality or habit which passes unobserved in the tumult of successive multitudes, becomes conspicuous when it is offered to the notice day after day. (Y, II, 243)

The minute peculiarities noted in 'this envied party' consist of tics or obsessive habits (of, for instance, the 'vehement asserter of uncontroverted truth', the man of sensibility, the quotation-monger). The reader recognizes these compulsions from experience of real life, where, though not concentrated each in a single individual, they flourish in many. Such traits are isolated and magnified by writers of fiction or satire in a manner which Johnson here acknowledges to be intentional distortion, like the laboratory study of mites.[34] To limit one's attention to such minutiae is a choice which itself can be blamed or satirized, but Johnson often defends it. The microscope image suggests to him a scale, different from that of everyday vision, which has its own uses. Microscope truth lies very near at hand, but needs some exaggeration to make it visible.

Both telescopic and microscopic vision can be misused, in ways connected with the general tendencies of human vision to focusing wrongly: 'As a glass which magnifies objects by the approach of one end to the eye, lessens them by the application of the other, so [our own] vices are extenuated by the inversion of that fallacy, by which virtues are augmented' (*Ram*. 28: Y, III, 153). 'An object, however small in itself, if placed near to the eye, will engross all the rays of light; and a transaction, however trivial, swells into importance, when it presses immediately on our attention' (*Ram*. 106: Y, IV, 202). In *Rambler* 112, on disproportionate peevishness over trivia (evidently written with the *exemplum* of Swift constantly in mind though never mentioned), Johnson frames his two biographical examples between the reminders that 'exposed to a microscope, the smoothest polish of the most solid bodies discovers cavities and prominences' and a fine complexion 'repels the eye with excrescences and discolorations', and that 'such is the limitation of the human powers, that by attention to trifles we must let things of importance pass unobserved: when we examine a mite with a glass, we see nothing but a mite' – meaning not that the creature we see is *nothing but* a mite, but that our whole field of vision is for the moment filled with *nothing but* it (Y, IV, 232, 236).

It is a sign of Johnson's appetite for greatness that he rebukes the misuse of the microscope more frequently than that of the telescope. As he explains at the end of his preface to Shakespeare (which introduces so much minute and detailed comment), great works demand, through their very greatness, the use of a kind of intellectual telescope before a nearer scrutiny.

> Parts are not to be examined till the whole has been surveyed; there is a kind of intellectual remoteness necessary for the comprehension of any great work in its full design and its true proportions; a close approach shows the smaller niceties, but the beauty of the whole is discerned no longer. (Y, VII, 111)

Johnson's most extended use of his optical image takes in misuse of both types of artificially augmented vision. It comes as climax to *Rambler* 176, which tells us that the purpose of codified criticism is to supply the defects of the 'eye of the intellect', and that 'rules are the instruments of mental vision'. Such instruments are necessary to help us comprehend 'an object so great that we can never take it into our view' (*Ram*. 125: Y, IV, 300), but they can have a corrective function only if properly used.

> Some seem always to read with the microscope of criticism, and employ their whole attention upon minute elegance, or faults scarcely visible to common observation. The dissonance of a syllable . . . the smallest deviation . . . the slightest defect . . . swell before their eyes into enormities. As they discern with great exactness, they comprehend but a narrow compass, and know nothing of the justness of the design . . . the harmony of the parts; they never conceive how small a proportion that which they are busy in

contemplating bears to the whole, or how the petty inaccuracies with which they are offended, are absorbed and lost in general excellence.

Others are furnished by criticism with a telescope. They see with great clearness whatever is too remote to be discovered by the rest of mankind, but are totally blind to all that lies immediately before them. They discover in every passage some secret meaning . . . which no other reader ever suspected; but they have no perception of . . . the various colours of diction, or the flowery embellishments of fancy; of all that engages the attention of others, they are totally insensible, while they pry into worlds of conjecture, and amuse themselves with phantoms in the clouds. (Y, V, 166, 167)

'In the first of these two paragraphs Johnson probably had in mind *The Dunciad*, IV, 233–8, where Bentley advocates the microscopic criticism which examines 'hairs and pores', but never how 'parts relate to parts':[35] he had announced the satirical direction of this essay by introducing authors' experience of criticism as among 'the principal of comick calamities' (Y, V, 164). Abuse of critics for short-sightedness had become traditional. *The Lives of the Poets* were themselves condemned in 1782 for 'microscopical sagacity', and, ironically, later commentators have found Johnson's blame too particularized and his praise too generalized: have charged him, that is, with both microscopy and telescopy.[36] It is not my concern here to investigate these charges, but to point out that in *Rambler* 176, as in his life of Cowley, Johnson is describing two contraries of his own aim. To judge according to an accurate scale, neither inflated nor contracted, was for him the most central necessity of criticism.

'The true strong and sound mind' can adjust its scale or focus, 'can embrace equally great things and small' (Boswell, III, 334). Johnson praises Thomson for this two-fold focus. Like Blake's Orc, who contracts his 'eyes, the lights of his large soul' in order to see the hidden things of earth, minerals and growing buds, and expands them to see 'the terrors of the Sun & Moon' and other planets,[37] Johnson's Thomson 'at once comprehends the vast, and attends to the minute' (*Lives*, III, 299). Similarly, Goldsmith is praised for being both general and minute successfully (*Lives*, II, 49), and Imlac attempts to balance the 'awfully vast' and the 'elegantly little' (see below, pp. 170–1).

It is at key points in his writings (the opening of *The Lives of the Poets*, Imlac's dissertation, the close of the preface to Shakespeare) that Johnson uses the image of double vision. He too embraces both vast and minute: the *Lives* and the preface, famous for their judicious general pronouncements, also triumphantly justify the examination of parts, as do his Shakespearean notes. But he keeps us in mind, while we apply one scale of criticism, of the existence of the other. Nor does he forget to relate criticism to something beyond itself. Leopold Damrosch points out the value of his constantly relating it to 'the wide purview of humanist thought. . . . the larger concerns subsumed under the name of "truth"'.[38] The measure of criticism is tested in its turn by Johnson's bringing it into comparison with a wider scale.

3

SWIFT AND THE
DEBATES IN THE SENATE
OF MAGNA LILLIPUTIA

thoughts or incidents in themselves ridiculous, grow still
more grotesque by the solemnity of great* characters . . .
what is despicable and absurd, will not, by any association
with splendid titles, become rational or great.

(*Rambler* 125)

MICROSCOPE and telescope experience had, before Johnson, been most
memorably dealt with by Swift, who was also the leading exponent of
moral and intellectual judgments couched in physical terms. I have written
elsewhere on Johnson's general indebtedness to Swift, which has been until
recently consistently ignored or underestimated.[1] This chapter emphasizes
the key role which Swift played in the development of Johnson's concept of
scales of greatness. As well as his major work, Swift's minor writings bear
witness to his preoccupation with scale. *An Essay on Modern Education* says of
an uneducated nobleman that he is just the same 'if you should look at him
in his Boyhood through the magnifying End of a Perspective, and in his
Manhood through the other'.[2] 'Thoughts on Various Subjects' include
'Elephants are always drawn smaller than the Life, but a Flea always
larger.'[3] Harrison's *Tatler* no. 2, of which Swift said he had given 'hints',
describes in very Johnsonian terms the writer's visit to the parish where he
grew up, where 'to my utter Disappointment I found [things] wonderfully
shrunk, and lessened almost out of my Knowledge'.[4] Many of Swift's
poems, notably those on Vanbrugh's house and on Castleknock, turn on
comic misapplication of a scale.

Great things and small are equally embraced, of course, in the first two
parts of *Gulliver's Travels*: the hero painfully discovers the fact of relativity
when he finds himself in the land of the giants 'as inconsiderable in this
Nation, as one single *Lilliputian* would be among us'.[5] Gulliver's mind
proves not strong or sound enough to preserve its sense of proportion in

* The reading of the original text.

relation to great things and small, to distinguish between twelve miles' circumference and the extremities of the globe, or between a narrow prejudice and the magnanimity of the King of Brobdingnag. Johnson in *Rambler* 112 uses images which recall Gulliver in Brobdingnag, to enforce his advice against measuring by false scales. Whatever he might have thought about the strength or soundness of Swift's own mind, he was profoundly receptive to the depiction of a man grappling with the experience of relativity and unstable scales of measurement. He absorbed Swift's influence, and that consciously.

To maintain this may seem to be flying in the face of the evidence. Johnson in his life of Gay calls *Gulliver* 'an unnatural fiction' (*Lives*, II, 284). What he says of it in his life of Swift is remarkable chiefly for its ambivalence and negativity of approach. The book was 'new and strange', says the life; readers responded with 'avidity' and 'a mingled emotion of merriment and amazement'.

> Criticism was for a while lost in wonder: no rules of judgement were applied to a book written in open defiance of truth and regularity. But when distinctions came to be made the part which gave least pleasure was that which describes the Flying Island, and that which gave most disgust must be the history of the Houyhnhnms. (*Lives*, III, 38)

This leaves parts I and II with some claim to please without (or without *much*?) disgusting, as well as with their claim to the accolade of originality with which Johnson closes this life (III, 66); yet he has not *explicitly* given them credit for any of these things, but has, as it were, allowed his left hand to do it without his right hand knowing.

This life (for which see further below, pp.227–9) seems to shuffle out of criticizing or judging rather as Johnson says the public did on the appearance of *Gulliver*. All the considerable *Lives of the Poets* (except 'Savage') follow either the pattern laid down in 'Cowley' and 'Denham', in which the biographical section leads directly to an evaluation of the works, or that of 'Milton', where an account of character, sometimes with physical description and other details, intervenes between biography and criticism. The life of Swift looks as if it will conform to the first pattern as it follows the account of his death with a paragraph beginning 'When Swift is considered as an author it is just to estimate his powers by their effects'. Instead of actually considering Swift as an author, however, Johnson follows this paragraph on effects with four on prose style, and then turns away, as if with relief, to his 'political education', his churchmanship, appearance, habits, and to his character as drawn by Delany. The critical section, when finally reached, turns out to consist of three very short paragraphs on the poems: it opens with the statement that they (like

Gulliver) offer 'not much upon which the critick can exercise his powers' (III, 50–66). The reader is left with an overwhelming sense of Johnson's reluctance to discuss any of Swift's literary work (though he is willing enough to discuss prose in the life of a poet when that poet is Addison).

This is not the place to speculate as to the reasons for Johnson's reticence, or to run over at any length the old but evergreen discussion of his attitudes to Swift. I have argued elsewhere that Swift's *literary* influence on Johnson was strong, that he was early one of Johnson's favourite authors and that Johnson retained throughout his career, despite conversational gibes, an appreciation of Swift's humour and a serious regard for him (amply evidenced in the *Dictionary*) as a historical, political, and religious writer.[6] The argument here is that Swift had preceded Johnson in entertaining very many of the cluster of ideas and preoccupations which this book discusses; and particularly that Johnson derived his technique of shifting the measurement of moral or intellectual scale, which lies at the heart of this investigation, at least partly from what Swift does with the physical scale in *Gulliver's Travels*.

Johnson must have been as well acquainted with *Gulliver* as his conversational and *Dictionary* quotations show he was with Swift's poems and political writings. His famous disparagement, 'When once you have thought of big men and little men, it is very easy to do all the rest' (Boswell, II, 319), plays down originality and indicates that, unlike most of the book's first readers, he found the germ of its story commonplace rather than new and strange: he speaks as if he had thought of big men and little men himself. The *Dictionary* (in which the choice of illustrative quotations reflects Johnson's estimate of writers quoted[7]) makes heavy use of the opening of Part I and the close of Part II (Gulliver's arrival in Lilliput and in its capital, and his eagle-assisted escape from Brobdingnag), some slight use of the rest of Part I, and apparently none at all of Parts III or IV. When compiling the *Dictionary* Johnson did not turn to *Gulliver*, as he did to the rest of Swift's writings, for the serious, specialized or technical words which abound in it.[8] He drew on it, however, for many common concrete nouns like *ladder* and *pulley*, for onomatopoeic or strongly physical words like *shove*, *jolt*, *bang*, *squash*, *squall*, *jump* and *soporiferous*, and for less classifiable but highly characteristic words like *maligner*, *maliciously* and *familiar*. Johnson's *Dictionary* use of Swift would suggest that he saw *Gulliver* as a romance or adventure story rather than as an ironical anatomy of human nature and society. It suggests also – unlike his life of Swift – that Parts I and II were what he both enjoyed and remembered best (though he undoubtedly read the rest, and alluded to Part III in essays[9]). We may further suspect that what he most enjoyed, since he had them at his fingertips, were Gulliver's experiences with the shrunken humanity of Lilliput and his nerve-wracking flight with the eagle, both of which exemplify to the full Swift's delight in the *mechanics* of his converted scales of measurement.

The play they both make with the concept of scale is certainly the most striking parallel between Swift and Johnson, and it is a far-reaching parallel, extending itself from the centre of this habitual structure of thought to every one of those related aspects to be discussed in later chapters. David Oakleaf, examining the importance of observation and distortion to *Gulliver's Travels*, concludes that the book replaces a fixed with a shifting viewpoint: 'there is no escape from differences of point of view and the appearances that trick the eye'.[10] Both Swift and Johnson insist on relativity, and especially relative size. Each was attentive to little things. Essays like *Rambler* 12 and *Idlers* 13 and 46 show Johnson equalling Swift's eye for the 'minute occurrences' of domestic detail, though he put it to such different use from those *Directions to Servants* which he used as a lexicographer and disapproved as a biographer.[11] Johnson's vindication of the humanly little and commonplace in the delightful teasing of his letters to Hester Thrale (below, pp.70ff.) has a precedent in Swift's *Journal* and poems to Stella. Not only did Johnson quote key passages from these poems in the *Dictionary*, once at least from memory, but Mrs Thrale chose to compare herself to Stella – and therefore, implicitly, Johnson to Swift – to get him to write her birthday verses.[12]

Swift's general views on ambition and competitiveness seem to have resembled Johnson's (see below, pp.102ff.). Under *appetite* Johnson quoted from *A Project for the Advancement of Religion*, 'Power being the natural *appetite* of princes, a limited monarch cannot gratify it'.[13] Swift's *Essay on the Fates of Clergymen* (originally *Intelligencer* 5 and 7), much quoted in the *Dictionary*,[14] sounds somewhat Johnsonian in its dry accounts of the plodder and of the talented man doomed to unsuccess, and very Johnsonian in the dying fall with which talent becomes 'utterly undistinguished and forgotten; only some of the Neighbours have accidentally heard, *that he had been a* notable Man *in his Youth*'. Johnson would have handled the specific examples differently, but he would have agreed wholly with Swift's general proposition (from the full text of which the *Dictionary* quotes twice) that an exceptional man can rise only by accident, and is more frequently '*disgraced*, or *banished*, or *suffered Death*, merely in Envy to . . . Virtues and superior *Genius*', that he meets 'universal Opposition, when he is mounting the Ladder, and every Hand ready to turn him off, when he is at the Top'. Johnson was aware that his views on and imagery for success and envy resembled Swift's, since he was fond of the 'Verses on the Death of Dr. Swift' and often quoted it, even as he approached his deathbed.[15] He used a poem of similar purport in the *Dictionary* to illustrate *altitude*: 'Your *altitude* offends the eyes/Of those who want the power to rise'.[16]

Swift, like Johnson (see below, pp.120ff.), opposed the ideal of community to a world riddled with rivalry and competition. His sermon 'On Mutual Subjection'[17] proposes a Johnsonian antidote for these things:

'you cannot envy your Neighbour's Strength, if he maketh use of it to defend your Life, or carry your Burden'. This sermon includes a resounding statement of the roots of human interdependence which strongly suggests Johnson's sermon 11 on brotherly love, and also *Rambler* 104 (see below, p.129).

> God Almighty hath been pleased to put us into an imperfect State, where we have perpetual Occasion of each other's Assistance. There is none so low, as not to be in a Capacity of assisting the Highest; nor so high, as not to want the Assistance of the Lowest.

'On Mutual Subjection' suggests the idealism of Johnson's Rasselas when it maintains that power, 'no Blessing in itself', may become so 'when it is employed to protect the Innocent', a sentiment from which Johnson quoted, under *power*, and again in considerably altered form – that is, from memory – under *oppressor*.

But in Swift's world, as in Johnson's, assisting the lowest and protecting the innocent tend to be subordinated to a goal of self-advancement. The rhapsody with which Gulliver responds to the idea of outliving most of mankind catches exactly the tone of Johnson's many fictional characters who hope to become similarly superior and exceptional (e.g. below, p.169ff.). He plans first to achieve wealth as a necessary preliminary (to independence: benevolence is to be a by-product), then to achieve a counterpart of Nekayah's dream 'first to learn all sciences, and then . . . preside, that, by conversing with the old, and educating the young, she might . . . raise up for the next age models of prudence, and patterns of piety'.[18] The immortal Gulliver, having arrived 'in time to excel all others in Learning', would be free to satisfy simultaneously his instincts both for benevolence and for his fellows' recognition of his superiority: he would 'become the Oracle of the Nation' and 'would entertain myself in forming and directing the Minds of hopeful young Men' and 'probably prevent [the] continual Degeneracy of human Nature'. Yet 'Length of Time would harden me to lose [you Mortals] with little or no Reluctance . . . just as a Man diverts himself with the annual Succession of Pinks and Tulips in his Garden. . . . Add to all this, the Pleasure of seeing the various Revolutions of States and Empires. . . .' There is no clearer case, in all Johnson's many treatments of this theme, of the divisive, anti-communal and hardening effect of the desire for even the most benevolent eminence above one's fellows.

Swift, like Johnson (see below, pp.135ff.), classes the extreme of malignity as that which works without hope of reward. Ireland, he says, suffers such unmotivated 'Hatred and Contempt . . . without the least Grounds of Provocation' from the English, 'who rejoyce at our Sufferings, although sometimes to their own Disadvantage'.[19] Johnson's careful and attentive definition of *animosity* ('Vehemence of hatred; passionate malignity. It implies rather the disposition to break out into outrages, than the outrage itself') is illustrated from Swift among others. Swift, of course, often wrote about the outrage of man to man, both public and private. Two passages in his *Discourse of the Contests and Dissentions . . . in Athens and Rome* (one of them expansively quoted by Johnson under *acquisition*) employ Johnson's favourite battle image of vultures hovering over the dead and dying (cf. below pp.173–4ff.).[20] The Yale editors find 'obvious' parallels between the vulture fable which was Johnson's original *Idler* 22 and *Gulliver's Travels* Part IV, and attribute his exclusion of the essay from the collected edition to his resistance against his own affinity with Swift (Y, II, 317n.).

Swift also shares Johnson's less sharply defined image of evil, the Lucretian unconcerned spectator, especially of battlefields (see below, pp.164ff.). The steadily increasing frequency of the 'word *observe* and its derivatives' in *Gulliver's Travels*[21] can be taken as indicating Gulliver's disconnection, as a non-participating observer, from the societies which he visits, a less extreme version of the isolation of longevity. Johnson was alert to the complex and sinister implications of the spectator in another of Swift's works: under *amusement* he chose to quote from a passage in the Drapier's fifth letter where Swift depicted his persona as receiving bitterly ironic advice about non-participating watchers from Swift's non-participating, concealed self:

> The *Dean* further observed, That I was in a Manner left alone to
> stand the *Battle*; while others, who had Ten thousand Times better
> Talents than a *Drapier* . . . perhaps thought it no unpleasant
> Amusement to look on with Safety, while another was giving them
> *Diversion* at the Hazard of his Liberty and Fortune.

Swift here has caught Johnson's attention by touching on Johnson's nightmare of the observer who enjoys another's pain or danger; he touched on it again in the Drapier's next letter ('a quiet Stander-by, and an indolent Looker-on'), in the remote inhabitants of the flying island of Lagado,[22] and in *A Short View of the State of Ireland*. In this essay (quoted at least seven times in the *Dictionary*, vol. I) the visiting Englishman finds the miseries of Ireland both 'comfortable' and profitable. We are left in some doubt whether to find his profit or his comfort more revolting,[23] as we are again over the comparable war profiteers in Johnson's 1770s pamphlets. Swift never directly connects his culpably unmoved spectators with the opening of Lucretius' *De rerum natura* book II, as Johnson does; but he applies the passage in fun to watching the bloodless warfare of cards, as Johnson applies it to garret-dwelling.[24]

Swift's and Johnson's common stock of war-images extends further than this. They share an attitude to the spoils of battle, like Swift's 'few Rags' hung up as trophies, 'which cost an hundred Millions, whereof [posterity will be] paying the Arrears, and boasting, as Beggars do, that their Grand-fathers were rich and great', which Johnson quoted under *arrears* and remembered in 'And mortgag'd states their grandsires wreaths regret,/From age to age in everlasting debt'.[25] Swift in *Examiner* 16 with bitter humour compares Marlborough's enormous war profits with the cost, meticulously tabulated, of rewarding a general of ancient Rome: triumphal arch £500, laurel crown 2d.[26] Johnson adapts this technique of computation for *Idler* 6, which similarly compares the rewards of fame in an ancient idealistic age and a modern venal one. Swift, speaking behind a mask, contributed a note of bitter disillusion to the re-evaluation of heroic greatness which paved the way for Johnson's writing on this theme. *A Tale of a Tub* describes heroes as vermin preying on humanity (see below, p.181); the 'Additions' to that work sarcastically propound that 'greater Souls in proportion to their superior merit claim a greater right to take every thing from meaner folks. This is the true foundation of Grandeur & Heroism'.[27] Johnson's complicated and more subtle approach to greatness is not in Swift's style of complication and subtlety; but Swift was an important influence in shaping it.

That Johnson in his mature thought continued to remember Swift becomes less surprising when we consider his earliest published writings, especially the parliamentary reports published in the *Gentleman's Magazine* as those of 'Magna Lilliputia', a name which is the radical or primitive joke of this Swiftian scheme.

We are now realizing that the strain of mockery which launched the scheme was more characteristic of Johnson than used to be recognized.[28] I hope to show here that this was carried over as a minor yet important element into the debates themselves; and that, though primarily intended to evade the ruling (13 April 1738) against reporting the proceedings of Parliament, the scheme was also exploited for purposes of very Johnsonian balancing of greatness and pettiness. My argument here may have some appearance of circularity. Since I find a Johnsonian irony in the passages which established this machinery I maintain that Johnson wrote them; since I believe he wrote them I take them as instances both of his early, Swiftian or Scriblerian manner, and of the consonance of this manner with those aspects of his later writing discussed below. I am not alone in believing that the Lilliputian device owed its establishment and method to Johnson's key position in the *Gentleman's Magazine* team. I shall briefly note the basis of this opinion before exploring its implications for my main argument.

We know that Johnson was altering or revising the 'Lilliputian' debates by September 1738, three months after their inception; we know he was solely responsible for writing them between July 1741 (when he reported a debate of 13 February 1741) and, probably, the 1744 Supplement.[29] About the part he played in starting up the Lilliputian machinery, that imaginative 'device of indirection', in June 1738, we have speculation and probability but no evidence.[30] The scheme was introduced by somebody steeped in the work of Swift (which Johnson was), who shares some hallmarks of Johnson's style and later attitudes. Edward A. Bloom's assumption that 'Cave probably had more enthusiasm for the Lilliputian scheme . . . than did Johnson' rests on an expectation that Johnson would neither admire nor copy anything of Swift's,[31] which we now know to be unfounded.

Johnson's earliest works as a London writer – *London* itself, *Marmor Norfolciense*, *A Compleat Vindication of the Licensers of the Stage*, his annual prefaces for the *Gentleman's Magazine* – resemble *A Tale of a Tub* in treating matters of national importance with irreverent, self-conscious, virtuoso wit. Scriblerian devices abound: the concretizing of the abstract, the catalogue incorporating incongruities which signal disproportion: 'a Lawyer, a Pickpocket, a Colonel, a Fool, a Lord'; 'masquerades, operas, birth-nights, treaties, conventions'. The fictional narrators of Johnson's pamphlets show, like many of Swift's satiric personae, an eager, credulous, submissive reverence for all authority. The licenser is 'this great man' charged with 'this great office', a 'great work', 'this great affair'.[32]

Johnson's reliance on Swift at this period does not in itself prove that he only could have hit on the Lilliputian device for reporting debates. Other admirers and imitators of Swift were not hard to find in these years, and some were to be found on the staff of the *Gentleman's Magazine*. Yet it seems to me overwhelmingly likely that Johnson was instrumental in giving the parliamentary debates their Swiftian direction, in view of his opinions, style and editorial position on the magazine,[33] and the very different flavour of other *Gentleman's* uses of Swift. The Lilliputian device produced a blend of serious and comic unmatched in Johnson's later writings until perhaps the opening *Idlers* (see below, pp.93ff.), but not at all foreign to his early ones. Circumventing the ban on parliamentary reporting was a serious matter, since the reports had become the most successful feature of both monthly magazines.[34] Yet the first response from the *Gentleman's* appeared in the guise of a *jeu d'esprit*. Under the picture of St John's Gate on the June 1738 cover are listed:

I.   APPENDIX to Capt. *Lemuel Gulliver*'s Account of the famous Empire of LILLIPUT.
II. The Constitution, Interests, and Politics of that powerful Nation further discover'd.
III. DEBATES of the Senate held at *Belfoborac* [*sic*: later Belfaborac], introduc'd, on the Measures that were to be taken for repairing or avenging the Losses of their Merchants.
IV. SPEECH of the Prime Minister, in the House of CLINABS, to

prepare them against a Bill proposed by the great Patriot *Wim-gul Pulnub*, for encouraging and securing the trade to *Columbia*.

Irony directed at national institutions is present from the beginning: 'the famous Empire', 'that powerful Nation'. The more detailed table of contents on the verso elaborates these four items to seventeen, the second of which reads 'The Veracity and extensive Genius of Capt. *Gulliver*, the Discoverer of *Lilliput*'. The unnamed prime minister and the great patriot Wim-gul Pulnub do not gain in stature from their association with the veracious Captain Gulliver. From this any reader would expect satire rather than straight reporting.

The promised 'Appendix to Capt. Lemuel Gulliver's Account' actually appears under the heading 'DEBATES *in the Senate of* MAGNA LILLIPUTIA', and is not in fact divided by heading or subheading from the speech which eventually follows. It has recently been reprinted as Johnson's under the title (from its running head) 'The State of Affairs in Lilliput'. I shall adopt this title with some regret: taking a form popular for serious political analysis, it emphasizes seriousness and minimizes Swiftian diminishment.[35] The essay's ostensible object is to vindicate Gulliver's reputation by proving the basic truth of his account, excusing and correcting its flaws, and buttressing it with additional material gleaned on a voyage by Gulliver's grandson. The British ban on parliamentary reporting is casually mentioned on the first page as having made space available for this project. Despite the initial mention of 'Debates', the unsignposted shift from travel-book material into the (Lilliputian) Prime Minister's speech comes as a jolt. The oblique approach to the main topic matches that of many *Ramblers*.

The parallel drawn between Britain and Lilliput obviously subjects British politicians to a demeaning scale of measurement. The satirical implications would have been disturbing for readers familiar with the pettiness, unreason and cruelty of Lilliputian politics in Swift; but the disturbance is offset by its pleasing ingenuity, and by flourishes of light-hearted irony beyond the strictly necessary. Gulliver's grandson, as befits the family temperament, sails 'in the Ship named the *Confidence*'. He gathers information from '*Flibo Quibus*, the Royal *Historiographer*', a man whose name debars him from our respect as surely as do those of Swift's Flimnap and Skyresh Bolgolam.[36] Similarly deflating names stud the debates: Rub. (or Retrob) Walelop, the Boship of Odfrox (a reference to clerical and academic gowns), Ptit (an inescapable suggestion of *petit*, well befitting a Lilliputian), and the Rednetrep or Pretender (an evocatively named bugbear who first appears outside the table of contents in the words, 'Sir, I have indeed one Fear, and but one Fear . . . Sir, I fear the *Rednetrep*': *GM*, VIII, 518).

Satire through names of the anagram type is of course a chancy and limited business.[37] The magazine's Slewyn, or at other times Slenwy, cannot be said to be more risible than sober Selwyn; Waknits (or sometimes Waknitz) Wimgul Ooynn, though grotesque, is hardly more so than Watkins William Wynne, or Whynd-Kotnot than Hynde Cotton. In time *Gentleman's Magazine* readers must have ceased to notice individual names, the eye seeing Santhepo or Swandich but the brain reading Stanhope or Sandwich and approving or disapproving according to its already formed prejudice. But there is no doubt that these 'quaint and barbaric pseudonyms' are as far as possible made comic in themselves as well as suggestive of *Gulliver's Travels*. They also represent the widest possible contrast with those of the *London Magazine*. That journal argued that anonymity would make the substance of the debates appear 'trifling'; it named its speakers after Cicero, Cato, Scipio Africanus and others, in accordance with their 'no small importance'.[38] Johnson's magazine did not fear to make its rulers sound trifling: at least on occasion there is glaring discrepancy between the risibility of its names and the serious tone of the debates themselves, moments when particular words or situations co-operate with the names to give the reader of great affairs momentarily a full-size perspective on Lilliputian antics (or, which is the same thing, a Brobdingnagian perspective on human ones).

'The State of Affairs in Lilliput' cannot have been written without satirical intent: its readers cannot have failed to recognize that intent, or to expect at the outset some diminishing of the rulers of Britain in the reports to follow. The magazine offered such diminution again the next month, outside the Lilliputian debates, in a letter from 'Eubulus' on China and England (VIII, 365–6: Y, X, 14–18). The writer of the letter, Johnson's persona, supposes that an account of Chinese political virtue, of honest ministers and emperors who voluntarily submit to 'reason, law, and morality', will have the value of absolute and astounding novelty to English readers. Comparisons, whether with China, Lilliput, or the past, regularly implied comment, usually hostile, on present-day politicians. The preface to Johnson's life of Blake (1740) disclaims '*any Parallel between his Atchievements and those of our present Admirals*' – equivocally, since comparison was clearly intended. The record of the contemporary British navy was being regularly decried in debates by the opposition, and had recently been fulsomely celebrated by a government supporter in the Clinabs or Commons (*GM*, X, 301, 257–8, 270). Later the same year *Gulliver's Travels* was used for another ironical attack on the government in 'A Proposal humbly offered to the Senate of Great Lilliput' by T.B.[39] *Gentleman's Magazine* readers were certainly given little opportunity during these early years of the debates to close their eyes to their satire on the great. Hoover points out the literary importance of the title 'Debates in the

Senate of Lilliput'.[40] He might have gone further, and emphasized the oxymoron 'Magna Lilliputia' or later 'Great Lilliput', which, though seldom appearing in the running head to the debates, figured elsewhere in the magazine with fair and increasing regularity through 1739, 1740, and the years of Johnson's parliamentary reporting. Such elaborate apparatus would have been entirely inappropriate as a frame for straight reporting of political affairs estimated at their conventional magnitude.

English parliamentary procedures were from the beginning sharply belittled through readers' recollections of Swift's

> GOLBASTO MOMAREN EVLAME GURDILO SHEFIN MULLY ULLY GUE, most Mighty Emperor of *Lilliput*, Delight and Terror of the Universe, whose Dominions extend five Thousand Blustrugs, (about twelve Miles in Circumference) to the Extremities of the Globe: Monarch of all Monarchs: Taller than the Sons of Men,

by almost the breadth of Gulliver's nail.[41] Swift's Lilliputians were petty in size, and their attitude to affairs of state was as trivializing as it was pompous. Subscribers to the *Gentleman's Magazine* would have been accustomed to thinking of *Gulliver*, a publication twelve years old, as a scandalous topical satire instead of, in our terms, as a hallowed literary classic. Its circulation had been, and still was, wide. Readers would not have forgotten the creeping, the rope-dancing, the solemn announcement of mercy before the infliction of a cruel punishment.[42] 'The State of Affairs in Lilliput' builds on this foundation. It requires us to believe that the pure and vigorous British parliament has succeeded in its much-resented move to prevent the magazines from reporting its proceedings: it is the 'miserably degenerate' as well as dwarfish Lilliputian one whose debates we shall soon be reading.

The subject of the first debate to be reported, England's quarrel with Spain, gives opportunity for the 'State' to prolong itself into a background sketch of international affairs. This uses the Lilliputian-Iberian disguise to diminish both Spanish ambition and Britain's heroic past. Memories are awakened of the miniature jingoism of Swift's Lilliput, and the ships drawn as if on pack-thread by Gulliver. The transparent disguise does not conceal national identity, but forces the reader to see it by a different scale. The 'State' presents the facts of the case as partly to England–Lilliput's credit and partly the reverse. It has a balance and moderation which is hardly to be expected in the parliamentary oratory to follow; yet through all this the fictional framework causes moderation to verge on detachment, and detachment to suggest the traveller's comfortable sense of superiority to the pygmy beings he observes.

The question remains as to how far the incisive diminishing produced by the 'State' was later forgotten. During the early months the Lilliputian effects are being, as it were, worked out: they are very largely concentrated in the editorial matter (notes, etc.) which accompanies the actual speeches. While some notes are entirely staid and matter-of-fact (e.g. VIII, 394), others address the greatness theme with sparkling wit. The 'Advertisement' which concludes the 1738 Supplement combines self-congratulation (of the type found in Johnson's *Gentleman's Magazine* prefaces) for popularity and for Gulliverian '*Honesty, Impartiality and Exactness*', with a reference to '*great Men and Women of Distinction*' of Lilliput, and the claim that they make a more instructive comparison with actuality than do the animals of Gay's *Fables* (which, of course, are also satirical). The first speech to be reported (in June 1738, given by the Prime Minister) is introduced by an inscrutable note informing us that the principles of the low-heeled or opposition party are now '*not exactly the same as when his Grandfather, Capt. Lemuel was in that Country*' (p.[288]). Since Swift gave this party no principles whatever except height of heel,[43] we are none the wiser. Another note on the same page glosses 'Gentlemen' at its first appearance, 'So Mr. *Gulliver* translates URGOLIN, a Diminutive of URGOL, *Esquire*'. 'Gentleman', recognized as next rank below Esquire, is not strictly a diminutive. Johnson – or somebody – has deliberately chosen a term which would once again emphasize small stature.

Editorial comments in the *Gentleman's Magazine* on the disputes of party are almost without exception ironical. In June 1739 we are told, 'The Party, which in the Days of Capt. *Gulliver* was known by the Title of LOW-HEELS, espoused the moderate peaceable Measures of the Ministry, which was advantageously enough set forth in his Majesty's Speech' (IX, 300). The questionable irony of language ('moderate', 'peaceable', 'advantageously enough') works independently of the Lilliputian reference, but is in its turn subjected to a faint additional hint of contempt. In November 1738 it is noted that readers 'are divided in their Opinions, whether the *Slamecsans* or *Tramecsans* have had the most disinterested Patriots or the greatest Orators on their Side; but Mr *Gulliver*'s Accuracy and Impartiality are equally acknowledg'd by all Parties' (VIII, 558). It was of course important for Cave to preserve both sides of his readership by an appearance of impartiality;[44] but to claim impartiality in Lilliputian terms converts it into a suggestion that the issues are essentially trivial or ridiculous. It is hard to believe with Edward A. Bloom that Johnson 'compromised with his principles' in the debates by 'lending his pen to the cause of opposition'. On the whole the debates firmly deny either side 'the best of it', keeping the reader in oscillation.[45] They question the political process more fundamentally than by simply asking which side is right.

One fairly obvious technique to which the Lilliputian device lends itself is ironical panegyric. In 1738 '*Mr* Gulliver's *Preliminary Discourse on the Power, high Privileges, hereditary and other Honours of this antient Body of*

Lilliputian *Nobility*' is promised but deferred (VIII, 399). Again in February 1740 information is promised on great men because without it their excellencies *'cannot but with Difficulty be conceived by the most penetrating and comprehensive Understanding'* (X, 50). The process reaches its climax in panegyrics on members of the Royal Family, the House of Lords (March 1740: X, 100–3), and the Commons (May: X, 227ff.). Much of this praise is either heightened or barbed truth, like mention that Heryef (John, Lord Hervey, Walpole's right-hand man in the Lords and in pamphlet warfare) possesses 'a vast Copiousness of Diction' and 'great Obligations to the Court' (X, 103). Much is ironically inappropriate, like praise of the King for 'preferring Men to Posts, both Civil and Military, especially the latter, according to their Merit and Services' (X, 100).

All in all, these long-promised 'Sketches' (X, 50) of *great* Lilliputians hold greatness up to Democritean laughter in the same manner as Johnson's *Compleat Vindication*. Scholars differ about the limits of Johnson's part in the character sketches (especially since he was out of London from August 1739 until, probably, late March or early April 1740).[46] This is not, however, to deny the connection. Whatever the systems followed at the *Gentleman's Magazine*, it was clearly the first of Johnson's many collaborative enterprises, the first of many works in which he supplied either the basic conception or the final touches to the inventions of others.

Broadly, there are two possible ways of looking at the elaborate preparations and later Lilliputian trappings to the debates. Either they are simply a disguise designed to be seen through, a perhaps regrettable encumbrance necessitated by the accidental circumstance of governmental edict, and soon forgotten; or they are a means of introducing, as an accompaniment to serious parliamentary debate, a faint but continuous undertone of satire, a distortion of scale giving the reader *something* of the detachment and wonder of a Gulliver looking on at the petty doings of Lilliput. The early part of the first *Gentleman's Magazine* item, the 'State of Lilliput', inclines a reader to the second view; the later part, the speech by Walpole – not yet Sir Rub., or Retrob, Walelop – in a debate on navigation and commerce (really, therefore, on the approaching war), full of apposite material and forceful argument, on the whole inclines one to the first view. The first view sees these ironical comments as more or less irrelevant intrusions on the debates; the second sees serious and ironical elements as held together in an uneasy relationship both at the beginning and later, since the satire is not such as to make us discount the serious content of the speeches.

The first view was held in a pure form by editors who early collected the debates, from Richard Chandler in 1742 to John Stockdale printing them as Johnson's in 1787, who called the Lilliputian apparatus 'barbarous jargon' and excised it. Those other editors who transferred speeches written by

Johnson into the printed works of their supposed authors, and those readers who admired them there, bear witness that independent of Lilliputian context Johnson wrote with splendid rhetoric, majesty of style and efficacy of argument. Hoover leans towards the first view when he considers that 'the *Gentleman's Magazine* must occasionally have been found irksome by reason of the heavy sprinkling of grotesque Lilliputian terms within its speeches', or when he emphatically repeats that the debates' 'original purpose . . . was not to entertain readers . . . but to inform them of the issues'.[47] He also holds that the effect faded fairly quickly:

> For several months the magazines were highly conscious of the new clothing of their debates and seemed to put more emphasis on the device than on the real business at hand, to communicate parliamentary intelligence to their readers. . . . In time the disguises came to be worn more comfortably.

Yet now and again he inclines slightly towards the second view.

> However the eighteenth-century reader may have received them, the terms seem appropriate to the air of unreality in the Lilliputian *Debates*, especially as those speeches, in the 'forties, took on the full strength of Johnson's classical eloquence.[48]

Conversely, W.K. Wimsatt finds that the debates 'tend toward a rhetorical emptiness which may reflect what was actually said'. Carlson writes, 'There is something almost ludicrous in the seriousness with which the whole matter is handled in the *London Magazine* and one turns to the *Gentleman's* with a sense of relief'.[49] To this one must add that the relief arises from the fact that in the *Gentleman's* the 'something almost ludicrous in the seriousness' is deliberately brought out. There have been other periods since Johnson's death when journalists' mockery of politicans has become hard to distinguish from what the politicians do for themselves.

Let us admit that the 'real business' of Johnson and his associates *was* 'to communicate parliamentary intelligence' rather than to hold up the proceedings of Parliament to ridicule; it was not therefore necessary to effect a total separation between informing and satirically criticizing. Johnson, as editor and writer, wished to do justice to the politicians by giving them such speech as would become their office; but his idea of their office was a somewhat disenchanted one, unimpressed by 'false measures of excellence and dignity' (*Ram.* 60: Y, III, 320). In *Rambler* 125 he writes that great titles accentuate, rather than veil, absurdity;[50] the titles he means are those of the monarchs and generals of tragedy, but the same point is apt for Members of Parliament.

It is not that Johnson's debates set out to satirize the conventions of a genre, in the manner of Swift in *A Meditation upon a Broomstick* or Gay in *The*

What D'ye Call It (each of which was taken seriously by listeners who failed to notice the parody).[51] Yet that very classical eloquence which is in itself most impressive becomes most ridiculous in the mouths of Urgs and Hurgoes, orators six inches high. It is characteristic of the later Johnson to see how a shift in scale can render the gravest human activities disastrously petty. He was to subject to gentle mockery even devotion to poetry, to learning, to science;[52] devotion to a party or even to national interest could not be immune. Johnson must have foreseen and worked for the effect of ridicule, within certain limits. In most contexts the Lilliputian element would not obtrude, but sometimes it would be hard or impossible to avoid. It works impartially to undermine both government supporters – the Urg; Hewo (John Howe) on 'the *Lilliputian* Youth, the Sons of noble Families, and the Hopes of the Nation' and Hynrec Feaux, Urg; (Henry Fox) on the idea of balancing 'our Lives, our Liberties, our Patrimonies, and our Posterity, against thirty thousand Sprugs' (XII, 690; XIII, 15) – and violent partisans of opposition, like Lettyltno (George Lyttelton) in a peroration hoping 'to see *Lilliput* again courted and feared, her Monarch considered as the Arbiter of the World, the Protector of the true Religion, and the Defender of the Liberties of Mankind' (XIII, 300). Whenever anything is admitted to be petty and undignified, or conversely whenever speakers appeal to institutional dignity and grandeur, the fiction of miniscule size would tend to be recalled, and Swift's original text would provide a tacit comment.

Such comment is often achieved by explicit denial of pettiness, as in a protest 'that the Representatives of a mighty Nation beset with Enemies . . . seem to forget their Importance and their Dignity, by wrangling from Day to Day upon a Pint of Small-beer' (XII, 178). It is suggested equally by mention of 'the mighty People of *Lilliput*. . . . whose Bravery is celebrated to the most distant Corners of the Earth' and of Blefuscu as 'this gigantick State', about to be 'disabled from being any longer the Disturbers of the Peace of the Universe' (XIII, 340, 400, 507), and of 'the Reverence due to the . . . great Council of the Nation' as 'a Place sacred to Justice and to Honour, into which Passion, Partiality and Faction have been very rarely known to intrude' (XIII, 459, 525). (The last high claim is as manifestly inaccurate of Britain as of Lilliput.) Again and again in the debates, claims to greatness are countered by implications of pettiness, just as flowers of rhetoric are countered by appeals against rhetoric's specious power.

Johnson writes almost consistently in a grand and dignified style, and as long as his subject-matter matches it the effect is grand and dignified; irony creeps in with discrepancy between style and content, and the reader who is not alert to the implications of content will not notice the irony. The Lilliputian device was of course mechanical. Johnson could not turn it on and off at will; but, by a kind of mechanical serendipity, it works to produce irony at precisely those moments when irony is appropriate, whenever a speaker strikes an exaggeratedly noble attitude by grand-iloquent reference to his House, his party or his country.

In December 1738 (Johnson revising) the magazine reported a Bill brought in according to a petition in April 1738 'by the Manufacturers of Raw Silk and Mohair, and of Needle-work Buttons, and of the Traders and Dealers therein . . . in several Towns and Counties in *Great Lilliput*'. The petition, quoted in *Gentleman's Magazine* VIII, 627–8, is a serious and competent piece of prose explaining economic matters: the government wished to encourage the trade with Turkey of 'Woollen and other Manufactures' in return for raw silk and mohair; since the latter were used for buttons and button-holes, making these articles of any other stuff was forbidden; but now horsehair ones were being illegally manufactured, to the 'Prejudice of the Woollen Manufacturies of the Empire'. It seems to have been editorial policy to draw attention to the triviality of this subject as well as to its wider repercussions:

> It is generally agreed that little Incidents, or casual and unpremeditated Remarks, give a clearer Insight into the Characters of Great Men, than their studied Discourses, or more conspicuous Actions. . . . This Observation may be extended to the Character of Nations in general, which discovers itself sometimes most evidently in the Transaction of Affairs not of the greatest Consequence.
>
> It was undoubtedly with this View, that the Accurate Mr *Gulliver* thought it proper to subjoin to the great and elaborate Debates concerning *War*, *Depredations*, *Conquests*, and *Dominion*, the following Controversy upon *Buttons* and *Button-holes*. A Question, of which the *Lilliputian* Senate did not think the Discussion below their Dignity, tho' it could not engage Attention by pompous Sounds, or mag-nificent Images. Does it not plainly appear from this Part of their Behaviour, that, in their Opinion, Industry is the Strength of a Nation, and that nothing is inconsiderable which affects the Public.

This passage, despite its foreshadowing of *Tristram Shandy*, bears some hallmarks of Johnson's mature style and thinking.[53] The sentence first quoted suggests *Rambler* 60 (see below, pp.62–3); the development of the thought leaves us, as does *Adventurer* 128 (see above, pp.27–8), if not actually uncertain where the writer stands, at least convinced that the two viewpoints which make things great or little are interchangeable. Like many of Johnson's periodical essays, the report on the petition begins at a point far removed from its central concern, and works round (further than has been quoted here) to a serious reminder of the importance of trade. Without the Lilliputian element it might be regarded as simply a justification of using trivial detail for serious purposes, a defensive argument against those readers who might think the component parts of button-holes below their notice, like 'Further Thoughts on Agriculture' (see below, pp.76–7). But that element ('the Accurate Mr *Gulliver*', 'the great and elaborate Debates concerning *War*', etc., the Lilliputian senate's attention to their dignity) considerably complicates its effect. It takes a pompous and self-conscious compromise with pettiness and renders that in turn petty and ridiculous. This whole account may have reminded eclectic readers, by contrast, of the *London Magazine*'s statement of intention, three months earlier, to ignore all trivial debates and concentrate on those 'upon Questions of great Importance'.[54] The *Gentleman's* places its great and elaborate debates concerning war at the opposite end of a scale which also embraces the button-hole question.

Hoover observes that we cannot distinguish Johnson's House of Lords from his Commons style, because 'there is so much dignity running through all the debates'.[55] It is, however, precisely this which most clearly invites an ironical response. The very first Lilliputian speech, that of Walpole delivered on 8 May and reported in June 1738, recalls *Gulliver* by such phrases as 'the Honour of the Nation, and the Dignity of the Imperial Crown of *Lilliput*' (VIII, [288]), and such phrases continue popular among Johnson's parliamentarians. Toblat (William, 2nd Baron Talbot, Opposition patriot and eccentric) begins a speech by outbidding any of the others in grandeur, though with ironical intentions: 'So high is my Veneration for this great Assembly, that it is never without the utmost Efforts of Resolution that I can prevail upon myself to give my Sentiments upon any Question' (XII, 519). Archbishop Secker's accounts of debates, taken from his shorthand notes, never give Talbot a formula like this; nor does the *London Magazine*'s account of this debate. Nor do Secker or the *London Magazine* provide parallels to other claims to dignity which have been or will be quoted here: such phrases as 'the Happiness, the Glory, and the Security of our Constitution'[56] do occur, but far less frequently than in the *Gentleman's*. This is no proof that they were not uttered (Secker and perhaps the *London Magazine* journalists had no time or space for such frills); but Johnson's insertion of them has a reason. To portray the Lords and Commons as so attentive to their own greatness is to portray them as disappointingly, pettily concerned with those things 'which it is a mark of greatness to despise; as fortunes, offices,' etc.[57] If we make any classification of topics frequently belittled in Johnson's debates, the parade of the parliamentary process or the little brief authority of its representatives ranks high on the list (closely followed by military swashbuckling and personal status). These politicians, unlike the old man in *Rasselas*, are not too wise to enjoy what Nekayah mistakenly expects to be a pleasure of old age, 'the consciousness of [their] own dignity' (XLV).

Any analytical reading of the debates must constantly question and re-evaluate that dignity. The Hurgo Sholmlug (George, third Earl

Cholmondeley, Walpole's son-in-law) begins a speech on 13 February 1741, the day of the debate on removing Sir Robert from office, with a strong assertion of dignity, not for himself but for his setting.

> I rise thus abruptly to preserve that Order and Decency which is essential to public Councils, and particularly suitable to the Dignity of this Assembly . . . that Respect which it has hitherto preserved, not only by the Justice of its Determinations, but by the solemn Grandeur of its Procedure.[58]

It is nearly always the opening remarks of speeches which concern themselves with issues of dignity, and one might argue that, coming closest after the Lilliputian titles, these remarks are the most vulnerable to ironical reading. Unarguably, Johnson here causes his speaker to assume two acutely vulnerable positions: that grandeur is as worthy of respect as justice, and that 'this Assembly' is more dignified than others. Cholmondeley would presumably have invited comparison with the Commons; behind this is shadowed a comparison with the grandeur and the justice of Lilliput as Gulliver experienced them when *he* was removed from office. If we read naîvely we might suppose in the absence of contrary evidence (this part of the debate is unrecorded by the *London Magazine*; Secker's notes record only the briefest allusions to the dignity of the House[59]) that these high flourishes were put together, with no sense of their absurdity, by Cholmondeley himself, or else that Johnson simply conceived them as suitable to the character of this speaker and his place in the debate. But since Johnson, as author of *A Compleat Vindication* and *Marmor Norfolciense*, had amply demonstrated both his own lack of respect for solemnly grand procedure and his awareness that not all parliamentary determinations are just, it is worth looking more closely at the context.

We need a firm grasp on the factual background of this speech for probing Johnson's purpose in it, a moralist's rather than a politician's grasp, won by investigating the basis of dignity in parliamentary assemblies rather than the relative value of competing party programmes. Cholmondeley was speaking in a subsidiary debate which followed on the defeat of the motion urging Walpole's removal.[60] The subsidiary motion was '*That any Attempt to inflict any kind of Punishment on any Person without allowing him an opportunity to make his Defence . . . is contrary to natural Justice*' (XI, 106). Two points advanced about this motion by the opposing sides in the House of Hurgoes seem to me indisputable: that it is in principle 'a known Truth [such] as never was denied'; but also that to put it forward for debate just then was disingenuously 'designed to imply . . . Censure of the Proceedings of this Day' (XI, 416–17). These two points, neither of them in itself controvertible, were of course the grounds on which battle was to be joined.[61] Both positions are true, as high and low heels both exist; yet every member of the House would be bound by political allegiance to defend one and attack the other – not with the weapons of reason, since reason must recognize both positions, but with rhetoric.

When Sholmlug speaks in Johnson's debate, Toblat (a leading advocate of the anti-Walpole motion just defeated) has just threatened to make personal aspersions not only on his adversaries' conduct but on 'the visible Motives to which it may be ascribed, their Places, their Dependence' (XI, 418). Such language is one kind of threat to order, decency and solemn grandeur; but it takes a mind only moderately critical of parliamentary procedure to see the whole debate on punishment without defence, presented as an impersonal abstract issue, as a charade which demands some kind of undercutting. In making inflated claims for the dignity of the charade, Cholmondeley becomes Sholmlug: a tiny pompous figure unaware of the programmed element in his own activity: truly a Lilliputian.

In July 1742 Johnson reported the Commons' choice of Speaker on 1 December 1741;[62] between election and report, at the end of January 1742, came Walpole's historic decision to resign. Re-election of Olswon (Arthur Onslow, the existing Speaker, originally a Walpole man) was proposed by Plemahm (Henry Pelham, at the time of speaking Walpole's deputy; by the time of publication on the point of succeeding him as leader of the Commons). Plemahm enumerates the 'Qualifications required in the Person who shall fill the Chair'. A satisfactory Speaker, he says, must possess an unshakable 'perpetual Serenity', an absolute 'Firmness of Mind'; and finally, to

> procure Veneration to his Decisions, he must from his general
> Character and personal Qualities, derive such Dignity and
> Authority, as may naturally dispose the Minds of others to
> Obedience, as may suppress the Murmurs of Envy, and prevent the
> Struggles of Competition.

Aside from the fact that the historical Onslow was accused of the opposite behaviour, currying favour with both sides, this list of requirements cannot possibly be filled by ordinary humanity. In particular the goal of extirpating envy and competition is one which, as we shall see below, Johnson can never have regarded as attainable in any situation, let alone that in which the idol Walpole was just tottering to his fall. The requirements suggest Lucretius' ideal of the wise man unmoved by tumult, an ideal which the later Johnson abhorred (see below, pp. 165ff.); more specifically, they suggest the equally taxing qualifications demanded by Imlac for a poet (see below, pp. 170–1), by Johnson's Walelop for a political journalist (who must be a politician *and* a writer, 'at once a Man of Business, and a Man of Leisure'), and by Johnson in his own person for an emending critic.[63] In each of these three later cases Johnson was, like Imlac, aggrandizing a profession of his own, ironically suggesting just those demands which cannot be met.

Olswon's series of acceptance speeches heightens the impression that this House, whose bitter intestine struggle is just coming to a head, is being revealed as in love with the idea of its own august authority. The respectful compliments turned by Mr Onslow in the *Journals of the House of Commons* are elaborated into 'too high an Idea of the Wisdom of this Assembly', 'so important a Trust', and 'exalted to this important Office, for which it is not n[e]cessary to mention how little I am qualified' (XII, 345–6), which recall the terms in which Johnson wrote of the licensers of the stage. In view of Johnson's spoofing of veneration in that pamphlet and *Marmor*, and of his later attitude towards it (see below, pp.183ff.), I assume that he is here mocking the reverential tone of Olswon and more particularly of Plemahm, painting an exercise in group hubris. In view of the unbounded veneration in which the Speaker's office has been held and continues to be held today this assumption may be open to argument. What is not arguable is the way he makes Plemahm's seconder, Cluckerbutt (Thomas Clutterbuck, a Walpole supporter until his fall, and friend of Onslow), tip head over heels into the risible. He can add nothing to Plemahm's encomium, says Cluckerbutt, but is 'confident that in the Opinion of this Assembly his Name alone includes all Panegyric, and that he who recommends the Urg; *Olswon*, will never be required to give the Reason of his Choice'. On this magnificently Swiftian dismissal of reason (not paralleled in Clutterbuck's modest and sensible speech in the *Journals*) 'the whole Assembly cried out, with a general Acclamation, Olswon, Olswon' (XI, 345). As Hoover says, the 'whole would not be inappropriate to *Gulliver's Travels*'.[64] To this judgment two important points must be added: that the 'touch of grotesqueness' which Johnson achieves through his 'Lilliputian trappings' is one which to this day forces itself upon the lay eye and ear in such traditional rituals of pure procedure (as radio and television coverage of them has now made plain), and that Johnson achieves the effect with such a slight heightening of actual parliamentary language that without the fictional framework it would be natural to take his speakers straight.

Johnson's orators regularly exult in their own dignity and that of the parliamentary institutions to which they belong, in the past perspective of national greatness and the world-wide range of national influence, and in the weightiness of the questions at issue, whether international, economic, social, or having to do with the integrity of Robert Walpole. The dignity of these things is by no means always as easy to undermine as Cholmondeley's respect for solemn grandeur. Of those consistent notes of Johnson's voice which make themselves heard behind his speakers' many and different voices,[65] one is a note of excitement and urgency over these burning issues, that note we hear again in 'Law in his voice, and fortune in his hand', in 'For such the steady Romans shook the world', and 'nations on his eye suspended wait'.[66] But another is that note which was to dismiss Wolsey and Charles XII to petty ends and the Romans to childishly flashy rewards, and to maintain that nothing is too little for so little a creature as man.

The debate speakers are much given to comparisons of scale: the heroic past with the sordid present, the ideal statesman with the corrupt placeman, 'the great Employments of the Empire' with 'every petty Post' (XIII, 71), the dignity of their office with the meanness of some of the details (like button-holes) which they have to attend to, or, politely, their own inferior abilities with those of their colleagues. Such comparisons are too closely involved with the stuff of life ever to be entirely avoided, but the *London Magazine* speakers seem to devote much less attention to them. There, for instance, lengthy debates early in 1742 on army diet, on small beer and a groat a day, pass, as they do not in the *Gentleman's*, without reference to scale, to the debaters' dignity, or to the magazine's initial resolution to stick to questions of great importance. In pursuing such comparisons, Johnson's speakers repeatedly recognize littleness, either their own or that of others, either reluctantly, or judiciously, or exultingly. In the course of one debate Levol (Walpole's neighbour and supporter Thomas Coke, Lord Lovel, from 1744 Viscount Coke of Holkham and Earl of Leicester) claims that 'from our Resolutions whole Nations are waiting for their Sentence' (much the same language as the *London Magazine* gives a different speaker in this debate, and as Johnson was to use of nations waiting on the eye of Charles XII);[67] at once the anti-Walpole Whigs Castroflet (Johnson's future patron Lord Chesterfield), Toblat (Talbot) and Quadrert (John, Viscount Carteret, later Earl Granville) follow suit with appeals to various kinds of greatness (XII, 347, 350, 402, 408). Yet none of these speakers is shown as wholly believing in this grand scale. Levol goes on to picture the expectant nations 'disappointed when they shall hear, that instead of declaring War . . . or raising Armies to regulate the State of the Continent, we met here in a full Assembly, and disagreed upon the Form of an Address' (XII, 347). No *London Magazine* speaker says anything like this; Secker's notes read simply '*Lovel*. Seconded'.[68] Castroflet, Toblat and Quadrert concur in using appeals to greatness to usher in accusations of wilful declension into pettiness: the grand scale is for them largely rhetorical.[69]

The complaint that greatness is not maintained constitutes a chief and recurrent theme of Johnson's Opposition. Whether we should assume that he himself endorsed the complaint is questionable and ultimately irrelevant: *London* and the lives of Blake and Drake suggest that he would have; *Marmor Norfolciense* makes fun of the notion of a heroic past. Commentators have on the whole paid more attention to the dignifying than to the belittling process, though Hoover observes that the Whig Opposition leader Samuel

Sandys as reported by Fox is 'reasonable, persuasive, straightforward', while Snadsy as reported by Johnson is 'acidly and rather violently ironic'.[70] When he put reductionist language into his orators' mouths, Johnson was not diverging from actual parliamentary practice. Where he makes his Opposition leader the Nardac Agryl (John Campbell, 2nd Duke of Argyll) jeer elaborately at the army as 'this stupendous Collection' of striplings performing the pettiest imaginable actions (XI, 618–19), Secker gives similar terms to Argyll and to Talbot.[71] But Johnson's mockery is much the stronger, through its use of terms inherited from *Gulliver*, as when he has Pulnub mock the army's 'utmost Exertion of heroic Fury' in breaking eggs in the market-place (XII, 678), and the sorrowful parting of newly made boy officers from 'the Maid that has fed them with Sweet-Meats, and defended them from Insects' (XII, 684).

For Johnson the Lilliputian device is not an alternative scale to offer in place of the normal human one, but rather an important resource (though not his only one in the debates) for guarding us against measuring by a wrong standard and arriving at a wrong estimation of things (*Adv.* 128). For his speakers, both Walelop and Pulnub, government and opposition, it is a versatile weapon to be opportunistically used: each has at different times something to gain by it.

In February 1743 the *Gentleman's Magazine* at last turned back to give its attention to the Commons debate of 13 February 1741 on the removal of Walpole (having reported the Lords' debate eighteen months before). Johnson gives Snadsy a single attacking speech which rings the changes in techniques of scale manipulation, echoing both Swift and Pope in words which must be of his own devising, not that of Samuel Sandys (XIII, 59–74). (The *London Magazine*'s equivalent, as by L. Junius Brutus, though it has him mentioning vast preparations and pusillanimous actions, makes no use of scale manipulation as such; nor do the speeches which follow there. Nor do other versions of the debate.[72]) Snadsy at an extreme stage in his argument, implying that Walelop was not only incompetent or dishonest but even treacherously desirous of Blefuscan victory, aggrandizes Blefuscu, which now cherishes a 'Scheme of universal Empire' (XIII, 60), and diminishes Lilliput, whose once mighty people now find themselves 'insulted like a petty State' (XIII, 64, 66, 67). If his words here had been 'France' and 'England' an element of uncertainty or instability about size, and an important reference to the sickening betrayals of *Gulliver* (I, vii and viii), would have been lost; but whether we associate or contrast Walelop with Swift's tiny creatures at this point is very much up to us. Though on one hand memory of Swift makes us more willing to believe in Walelop's guilt, on the other hand it makes his behaviour more trivial, more despicable, perhaps less serious. When Snadsy draws on Pope, and paints Walelop as 'an Idol [with] all that surround him cringing to his superior

Power, and making humble Offerings of their Consciences, their Votes, their Liberties, and their Posterity' (XIII, 71), the effect is more straightforward. The echo of the recent (1738) *Epilogue to the Satires, Dialogue I*, about the same man's idol-mistress – 'See thronging Millions to the Pagod run,/And offer Country, Parent, Wife, or Son!' (lines 157–8) – makes Walpole unquestionably gigantic, his countrymen dwarfish, and the speaker a merely verbal warrior who sees his cause as hopeless.

Walpole's reply also turns on issues of scale. Views of him as either dwarfed by Blefuscu or dwarfing his followers are replaced in his own speech of defence by disclaimers of greatness and also by an almost weary admission of human littleness. Denying the charge of assuming 'exorbitant Power', he calls the title of Prime Minister 'a Kind of mock Dignity' and claims he has never acted 'otherwise than as one among many' (XIII, 179–80). Denying the charge of amassing great wealth from office, he describes his gains as nothing but 'a little House' and the 'little Ornament upon my Shoulder', the Garter (XIII, 181). His defence of the 'little Ornament' – that the Lords may resent his having it but the Commons should surely feel honoured by its bestowal on one of their number – implies that his enemies' anxiety over details of status is hardly magnanimous. (Some of his speech, however, is more rhetorically effective at a distance of centuries than it can have been in close-up: the epithet in 'little House' accurately contrasts a suburban retreat from work with his mansion at Houghton, where the estate was inherited, but ignores the vast sums of money spent at both and certainly not inherited.) Some of these phrases have counterparts in other contemporary accounts of Walpole's self-defence (as Hoover points out). But the estimate of human beings as very little creatures, which underlies every point of Walpole's succinct, dignified defence, plays no such part in any other version[73] – as, of course, no other version has him reckon his gains in Lilliputian sprugs.

The House of Lords debate on spirituous liquors (that is, on regulations governing the sale and taxing of gin for the sake of military expenditure), which took place on 22–25 February 1743 and which Johnson reported between November 1743 and February 1744,[74] provided particular opportunities for exploring the relationship between great things and small: opportunities less focused but more varied than those of the Walpole struggle. Every speaker in it recognizes the exceptional importance of the issues raised by what Johnson editorially calls '*this memorable Debate*' (XIV, 64). The Bill's supporters, however (who were in life Cholmondeley, Carteret, Archibald Campbell Lord Islay, who between the debate and the report had succeeded his dead brother as Duke of Argyll, and others) locate its importance in the international military projects hanging on it, while its opponents (most notably Hervey, owning a changed allegiance since Walpole's fall, and Chesterfield) dwell on the effect it will have on the health and virtue of the nation. Questions of scale are equally important in both cases, for each side means to claim stature as well as virtue for itself. Sholmlug (Cholmondeley) equates the war with preventing 'the Ruin of a great Part of Mankind' (XIV, 17); his opponents suggest that the war is negligible and that such ruin is what the Bill will cause, not prevent. Johnson gives these latter far the stronger arguments, though he does not, like Secker, give them a monopoly on moral fervour. He shares between both sides an acute sense of scale discrepancies: either between the dignity of governing and the indignity of gin-swigging, the heights of authority and the depths of demoralization, the grandeur of the projected war and the unimportance of *how* essential money is raised for it; or else between paltry sprugs and 'the general Happiness', 'the Strength and Virtue' of the nation (XIV, 16, 60). It is an issue to raise this kind of awareness: both Secker and to a lesser degree the *London Magazine* represent some speakers as defiantly maintaining the greater importance of ordinary people than of the proceedings of government. Secker's Viscount Lonsdale, for instance, is dismayed to find that when he urges 'the lives and morals of the people, and the condition of the next generation . . . I am answered, The Committee of Supplies may be closed, the Commons must sit a fortnight longer, the manufacture will go to decay'.[75] But neither of these reports approaches Johnson's in presenting the contradictory scales of human life, the interaction of great generalities (as well as great pretensions) with minute particulars.

Johnson's Heryef, opening the debate, shows himself well aware of the disproportion between on the one hand 'stated and invariable Principles', 'that Zeal for the Promotion of Virtue, and that Regard to publick Happiness, which has on all Occasions distinguished this illustrious Assembly', and on the other hand the petty details of gin-shop transactions, and the tiny successive steps of degradation for those whom he later calls 'the Dregs of the Populace' (XIII, 564, 569–71; XIV, 20). The Johnsonian question, 'How important is this?' and the question specific to the Debates of how ironically we should take aggrandizement of 'this illustrious Assembly', remain crucial, and Heryef in his opening speech provides an answer which is very Johnsonian in its deduction of the great from the little. He claims that the significance of his squalid stories will be clear to all those who have 'ever looked upon the various scenes of Life with that Attention which their Importance demand[s]' (XIII, 571); his terms foreshadow those which state the brief of Observation in *The Vanity of Human Wishes*. His argument of 'the general Concatenation of Society', that 'to the Plow, and the Anvil, the Loom and the Quarry, Pride is indebted for its Magnificence, Luxury for its Dainties and Delicacy for its Ease' (XIII, 565) is a favourite theme of Johnson's, discussed further below. On such humdrum foundations, says Heryef, rests not only the stability of society but also ambition, the power to 'give Law to Mankind' and 'fight for the Liberty of distant Nations' (XIII, 566). Heryef casts doubt on the great scale of intervention in the affairs of distant nations by pointing out its dependence on littleness.

Heryef claims for government a dignity which is founded in little matters, though he indignantly rejects any inflation of personal littleness, any thoughts of immortalizing one's name by inventing 'a new Method of raising Money' (XIII, 574). He logically grounds in sordid detail his reminder that government exists not 'only to raise Money' but 'only to promote Virtue'. Although he continues less Johnsonianly to maintain that of virtue 'Happiness is the Consequence' (XIII, 573–4), this claim for the essential dignity of government is made to seem much less shaky than the claim with which his speech had begun, about the House of Hurgoes' invariable attention to the public good. Heryef's speech fulfils Johnson's ideal (see above, p.32) of combining general and particular; it relies on the insistent organizing principle of opposed relatedness of little and great. It is remarkable how much of the same ground is covered by the *London Magazine*'s Hervey (C. Helvius) without reference to this principle.[76]

When the Bill moves to committee, Heryef, in an equally impassioned speech which he ironically recognizes to be 'inconsistent with that Delicacy, with which the Debates of this august Assembly have generally been carried on', calls it 'a Bill by which the Sense of Morality and Religion will be extinguished, and the Restraints of Law made ineffectual' (XIII, 680). Though he once glances at tactics (how to 'preserve the Nation without irritating the other House': XIII, 681), Heryef concentrates on matters of principle. Johnson presents the first response to his speech as a violent shift from morality to tactics, a sudden narrowing of the frame of reference, which the other reports of this debate avoid by sharing the various elements more evenly between various speakers. Heryef's urgency produces first '*a short Silence*', then replies which shun questions of principle for those of strategy and procedure, for what is or is not proper for a committee, for the relative status and character of the two Houses and the relations between them (XIII, 681ff.).

As readers, however, we are not allowed to rest on the security of contrasting large principle with petty tactics. As rhetoric counters rhetoric, as 'one produces against a Proposal the very Argument which another offers in its Favour' (Castroflet, XIV, 8), the reader begins to feel, not only that each side claims that it is against gin and the other side is for it, but also a dizzy uncertainty as to what is the true relationship between principle and situation, humble individuals and national pride. Quadrert's reply to Heryef is staggeringly illogical and inconsistent: to reject the Bill would cause cruel hardship among distillers (by sudden decrease in consumption); to pass it would not only bring good (public revenue) out of undefeatable evil, but also produce gradual and painless decrease in consumption, until at last 'the Vice of drinking Spirits will be forgotten among us' (XIII, 684–5).

Johnson can hardly have intended these arguments to convince. They open the way for Castroflet brilliantly to debunk them in a deliberately fallacious argument, what a modern writer on irony calls a 'patently false enthymeme' of blame-by-praise.[77] Castroflet speaks of 'this excellent and wonder-working Bill, this Bill which is to lessen the Consumption of Spirits, without lessening the quantity which is distilled . . . and correct Vice by indulging it'. To this Swiftian 'Irony and Burlesque', as Yali (Islay) calls it with grave disapproval of Castroflet's flightiness (XIV, 6, 14), he adds indignant questioning of the generally accepted social scale, by scornful satire on those who think themselves great. He is, he says, 'always desirous of gratifying those great Men to whom the Administration of Affairs is entrusted', who 'conceived, that they had reformed the common People without infringing the Pleasures of others' (XIV, 6, 8). He pictures how those higher ranks who will still be able to afford drunkenness will 'over a full flowing Bumper look down with Contempt' on 'the inferior Classes of Drunkards' who will now be forced to pass 'many tedious Hours in a languishing Possession of their Senses and their Limbs' (XIV, 8). His sketch of topnotch drunkards is matched by one of grovelling lawgivers: it would be less undignified to

> establish a certain Number of licensed Wheel-barrows, on which the laudable Trade of Thimble and Button might be carried on for the Support of the War, and Shoe-Boys might contribute to the Defence of the House of *Aurista*, by raffling for Apples. (XIV, 11)

Heryef grounds his serious arguments in a recognition of the importance of little things; Castroflet's sarcasm alternately mock-aggrandizes and belittles. His playing with standards of measurement gives a natural opportunity for Yali to protest against infringement of 'the Dignity of this Assembly' and against 'turning the great Affairs of the Nation to Ridicule', to accuse Castroflet of 'divert[ing] himself with the Sight of Misery', and to assert that 'our Deliberations can receive very little Assistance from Merriment and Ridicule' (XIV, 13, 14). This particular bone of contention, over which each side is angered by the other's alleged lack of dignity or greatness, has no place in the other accounts of the debate. Nor has a more persuasive speech by Quadrert, in which he reasserts his belief that the Bill will prove beneficial, but in much more tentative, less inflated terms. Instead of promising universal reform, he now hopes for slight improvement. His defence is now grounded, like Walelop's earlier, in admission of littleness. 'To charge any Scheme with Imperfection is only to allege, that it is the Production of Men, of Beings, finite in their Capacity and liable to Error'

(XIV, 62). Lowering his sights has considerably strengthened his argument.

This report, Johnson's penultimate one for the *Gentleman's Magazine*, performs most of its shifting of scale without reference to the Lilliputian device. Such reference as it does make is not very important, and the degree of its ironical tendency not very clear. On this topic Johnson hardly needed Swift. Among the activities of government the raising of revenue from alcohol most notably straddles principle and grossness, the high-flown, the immensely serious, and the risible. This debate by Johnson combines grotesque physicality and tragic mortality, the cheapness of outcast lives and the grandeur of military ambition, the savagery of moral accusation and the predictability of party loyalty, the impossibility of distinguishing pleasure from self-destruction, or disentangling 'stated and invariable Principles' from committee procedure or an adverse effect on the income of barley-growers. Secker's and the *London Magazine*'s reports are by no means unaware of these issues, but Johnson shows a finer and more acute sense of their shifting proportions.

Elsewhere in the debates as well as in this one the task of measuring and estimating issues is often shown as not only hard but almost impossible. Hickrad (Lord Chancellor Hardwicke) observes resoundingly that 'Names will not change the Nature of the Things to which they are applied' (XII, 568); but this, like so many Johnsonian aphorisms, conceals under its monolithic appearance a need for difficult and complicated application. When Walelop has to reply to a charge that abuses have occurred in pressing men for the navy, he admits that they may, 'for it is not in the Power of any Administration to make all those honest or wise whom they are obliged to employ; and when great Affairs are depending, minute Circumstances cannot always be attended to' (XI, 457). He makes, in fact, exactly the same defence that Imlac makes of Rasselas's father the emperor, when his rule is found to be imperfect (VIII). Ought we as readers to accept Walelop's brushing off of the fate of individuals as 'minute Circumstances' contrasted with national 'great Affairs', or ought we to listen to the contention of the previous speaker, Branard (opposition Tory Sir John Barnard), that 'every Question by which the Liberty of a *Lilliputian* may be affected, is of Importance'? This last-quoted phrase is obviously not susceptible to the same kind of dismissive contempt that it would be in Swift, and in its context of great and elaborate debate the fictional name is less striking than in a short excerpt.

While the Lilliputian device is clearly not designed to drain such issues as this of significance, it does work to the detriment of politicians: in this naval example both to that of Walpole, who claims the sanction of 'great Affairs', and of Barnard, who claims the importance of a Lilliputian's liberty. Johnson seems not to have intended in the debates to show, as Secker does, one party as consistently preferable to the other. What is unquestionable is that in these debates the scale, to a sensitive reader, shifts and reshifts disturbingly. The speakers' recurrent assertions of their own importance, their reductive ironical attacks on each other, together with the overall effect of the Swiftian machinery, produce moments of withdrawal to an Olympian perspective which, as will be argued below, are characteristic of Johnson's later writings, though lingering on such heights is not (see below, pp.174–5).

The debates, which still deserve more attention than they have received, have by now begun to collect complimentary superlatives. The preface to the first *Gentleman's Magazine* index (probably by Johnson himself) called them 'such a Series of Argumentation as has comprised all Political Science'.[78] Yet they also question and qualify the dignity of politics, and demonstrate the range and readiness, in the young Johnson, of those mental habits which, for want of a better word, we have to call satirical. They fulfil the design of 'The State of Affairs in Lilliput' – 'to display the Policy of the most refined, and celebrate the Atchievements of the most warlike Nation' (VIII, 283) – but the display and the celebration are just as ambivalent as Johnson's other treatments of policy and warlike achievement, from *Marmor Norfolciense* to *Falkland's Islands*. Lords and Commons, burdened with great affairs, aspiring to the language of Demosthenes and Cicero and to the political principles of great statesmen, display from time to time disconcerting touches of Dogberry or of squeaking and unprincipled miniatures. Appeals are confidently made to absolute standards which a moment's thought reveals to be only relative, like the grandeur 'particularly suitable to the Dignity of this Assembly'. It is never possible for the reader to relax and take the credentials of any one speaker (whether these rest in power and dignity on one side or professed commitment to abstract principle on the other) as necessarily acceptable. Johnson's parliamentary speakers exert great energies of intelligence and rhetoric to escape the littleness of humanity, but they are always shown to fail.

4

VINDICATION OF
LITTLENESS

Exploding many things under the name of trifles, is a
very false proof either of wisdom or *magnanimity*.

(Swift, quoted in the *Dictionary*)

JOHNSON'S WRITINGS constantly challenge his readers' scales of measurement. We are not permitted to admire our leaders as great without being
shown them as Lilliputians; equally, we are not permitted to dismiss them
as Lilliputians without being shown their claims to moral dignity. Both
Johnson's awareness of relativity and his antithetical spirit press him to
contradict his readers' expectations, repeatedly telling us that what we look
up to is little and what we overlook is important. The littleness which he
vindicates to us is of two kinds, the human and the non-human, personal
detail and the detail of the world in which we live; and the more insisted on
of the two is the littleness of the frail and single individual, the daily lives of
unimportant people. Johnson often employs a scale which shows us people
as petty, but acceptably petty: often his reductionism is entirely non-
satirical.

Johnson's best-known biographical writings resemble his parliamentary
ones in taking for the majority of their subjects those who are
conventionally considered as great, and whose position reminds us of the
different stature conventionally accorded to different individuals. Nevertheless, like the debates, they often remind us of the standards by which all
human powers are scanty, and of our need to come to terms with a scale
which makes us little. His famous *Rambler* on biography tells us, in case we
think nobody worth reading about but those 'whose sphere of action was
. . . extended', that such a notion 'arises from false measures of excellence
and dignity, and must be eradicated'. The biographer ought

> often to pass slightly over those performances and incidents, which
> produce vulgar greatness, to lead the thoughts into domestick pri-

vacies, and display the minute details of daily life, where exterior appendages are cast aside, and men excel each other only by prudence and by virtue.[1]

The reader, in other words, is too anxious for an answer to the question 'Was this man great?' which it is not the biographer's primary purpose to supply. To discover and portray the truth about an individual life, a writer needs to question and ultimately to adjust what is likely to be too grand a scale of judgment.

Six years later, in his life of Sir Thomas Browne, which reassesses, endorses, and puts into practice many of the views of *Rambler* 60, Johnson again argues the vital need to preserve 'silent excellencies . . . soon forgotten . . . those minute peculiarities which discriminate every man from all others, [and which] if they are not recorded by those whom personal knowledge enables to observe them, are irrecoverably lost', in preference to those qualities which are publicly recognized (*Works*, VI, 493–4). The biographer's viewpoint is one particularly apt to distort, to celebrate 'vulgar greatness' and pass over the minutiae of personal behaviour whose consequences may be momentous. To his determination to substitute a true measure for a false one, we may attribute Johnson's varying biographical tributes to people whose lives were either strikingly unsuccessful, or successful on a scale less than imposing. These individuals, discriminated from all others, *do* deserve our notice: Richard Savage, poet and outcast; Edmund Cave, whom Johnson praises for tenacity in struggles not only with the Stamp Office and the *London Magazine* but before that with his schoolmaster and early employers (excise collector, timber merchant, printer) and their wives; Anna Williams's father Zachariah, movingly pictured as an aged unrewarded toiler; Isaac Watts and Elizabeth Rowe, the pious Dissenters now 'applauded by angels and numbered with the just'; and finally Dr Robert Levet.[2]

The same cause contributes in Johnson's lives of conspicuous achievers to something which has often been interpreted as a sour note,[3] but which is actually an appeal to the scale which makes even such achievement inconsiderable. Milton's rancorous politics, Dryden's pamphlet warfare, Pope's stealthiness, Swift's narrowness about money and other things, are insisted on not to detract from literary stature but to balance it by an assertion of humanity: 'our reverence for a genius [must not] dispose us to forget' to call his failings by their true names (*Lives*, I, 10).

In his life of Browne, Johnson tackled a subject who delighted, more freely and unquestioningly than his biographer, in minute peculiarities. Johnson responded by applying his measures of excellence and dignity in an especially ambiguous or paradoxical manner. On the one occasion when he finds Browne, on his travels, withholding details of information as perhaps not wôrthwhile, he blames him but also finds excuses for him: 'to minds naturally great, few things appear of so much importance as to deserve the notice of the publick'. Browne here shares a handicap of great minds: their poor adaptation to the scale of the common person (*Works*, VI, 477). Later, when Browne has overcome his greatness of mind sufficiently to claim public notice for all kinds of bits and pieces, Johnson responds ambivalently. He finds in *Religio Medici* 'many passages, which, relating merely to his own person, can be of no great importance to the publick'; he is inclined to be harsh about the classification of his own life-story as 'a miracle'; and he cannot resist merriment at the obsession that writes as if 'nature and art had no other purpose than to exemplify and imitate a quincunx' (*Works*, VI, 477, 479–80, 486). He describes the subject-matter of Browne's omnivorous interests and voluminous notes – plants and fish of the Bible, abstruse verse forms, burial mounds and barrows, tombs in Norwich Cathedral – with touches to hint, with varying degrees of irony, that they do not incorporate 'matter proportionate to the skill of the antiquary' (*Works*, VI, 487, 488, 491). He balances positive approval of these researches (the 'fanciful sports of great minds are never without some advantage to knowledge') with modified disapproval:

> Some of them are of little value, more than as they gratify the mind with the picture of a great scholar, turning his learning into amusement; or show upon how great a variety of inquiries, the same mind has been successfully employed. (*Works*, VI, 486, 490–1)

On the whole he still sounds better pleased with these trivialities than with Browne's neglect of triviality on his journey abroad.

Browne provides the occasion for a general survey of the pleasure given

> by learning and genius, exercised upon subjects of little importance. It seems to have been, in all ages, the pride of wit, to show how it could exalt the low, and amplify the little. To speak not inadequately of things really and naturally great, is a task not only difficult but disagreeable; because the writer is degraded in his own eyes, by standing in comparison with his subject . . . but it is a perpetual triumph of fancy to expand a scanty theme, to raise glittering ideas from obscure properties, and to produce to the world an object of wonder, to which nature had contributed little. To this ambition, perhaps, we owe the frogs of Homer, the gnat and the bees of Virgil, the butterfly of Spenser, the shadow of Wowerus, and the quincunx of Browne. (*Works*, VI, 485–6)

Writers on petty subjects may be neglecting or evading sterner tasks, yet may produce objects of wonder. The list of names is impressive. Johnson might have added *The Rape of the Lock*, *The Dunciad*, Swift's *Journal to Stella* (in whose 'diurnal trifles' he found 'some odd attraction': *Lives*, III, 23), and other important Scriblerian works, as well as many of his own moral essays, not only the yet-to-be-written *Idlers*.

Throughout this biography we sense the stirrings of its author's natural impulse, rigorously repressed, to condemn his subject for pettiness. Johnson frequently applies the adjective *great* to Browne, taking his stature as assumed, though he only once, when writing about literary style, elaborates or explains (*Works*, VI, 499–500). He dwells repeatedly on Browne's attention to the by-ways of scholarship, assuming their pettiness as he assumes Browne's greatness; he does not attack him for this, but by defending him reveals that he supposes defence to be called for. The life concludes with a resounding celebration of Browne, at first printed in capitals for greater emphasis, for having lived 'a zealous adherent to the faith of Christ . . . and died in confidence of his mercy' (*Works*, VI, 503): here at last Johnson is using a measure which cannot be questioned, and which sinks human greatness and littleness to a single proportion. In its apparent inconsistencies of scale, and in the manner in which it resolves them, this is a pattern for *The Lives of the Poets*.

Johnson maintains the importance of the minute details in daily life perhaps most movingly in his later writings (letters, *A Journey*, and the *Lives*), but he has already begun to do so in his essays. He opens *Adventurer* 128 (already discussed) with the statement that all classes commonly charge others with unworthily wasting time on trifles 'below the dignity of our nature', and then investigates and rejects this 'contempt' (Y, II, 476, 478). Johnson does not despair of reconciling human dignity with the detail of quotidian living.

Rambler 12, the first consisting wholly of a letter from an imaginary correspondent, describes the petty humiliations meted out to the well-born but destitute Zosima in her efforts to find a job in service; it has been praised for its command of vivid colloquial phrasing, of which the flavour can be given by quoting the parting shot of each interview:

Pray, Mrs. gentlewoman, troop down stairs. . . . What, you never heard of the foundling house? . . . I suppose, Mrs. Flirt, if I was to see your work, it would be fine stuff! – You may walk. . . . I suppose, Mrs. Minx, these fine hands cannot bear wetting – A servant indeed! Pray move off – I am resolved to be the head person in this house – . . . Such trollops! Get you down. What, whimpering? Pray walk. . . . What will this world come to, if a gentleman may not jest with a servant? Well, such servants! pray be gone, and see when you will have the honour to be so insulted again. Servants insulted – a fine time. – Insulted! Get down stairs, you slut, or the footman shall insult you. (Y, III, 64–7)

The prospective employers comprehend the usual satirist's cross-section of only moderately good society; the pain they inflict is trivial but ingeniously various and cumulative (having been abused for wearing too fine a gown, her best, to one interview, Zosima chooses a plain one for the next and is abused as a slattern). It is almost nothing to the inflictors, almost unbearable to the victim – who, besides, really needs a job to survive. Zosima's name, as Edward A. Bloom has noted, comes from one of the epitaphs in *The Greek Anthology* which Johnson chose to translate into Latin as well as English, and which his 'Essay on Epitaphs' (1740) calls an inspiration to us 'to support the dignity of human nature under the most pressing afflictions'. 'Zosima, who in her life could only have her body enslaved, now finds her body likewise set at liberty.'⁴ This Greek name gives the English girl's status the full horror of slavery, and her person the inalienable dignity of death. She introduces her story as recounting 'one species of cruelty, with which the life of a man of letters perhaps does not often make him acquainted; and which . . . may become less common when it has been once exposed in . . . its full magnitude' (Y, III, 62). The essay is a lens for the adjustment of scale.

Several of Johnson's invented *Rambler* correspondents introduce themselves with some apology for the apparent triviality of their topic. Eubulus, the writer of nos 26 and 27, admits that his 'narrative will not exhibit any great variety of events, or extraordinary revolutions' (Y, III, 141): his situation of dependence and inferiority, with the unimportance in his affluent friends' eyes of their slights and omissions towards him, makes it akin to Zosima's. The writer of no. 147 begins, 'Sir, As little things grow great by continual accumulation, I hope you will not think the dignity of your character impaired' by his account (Y, V, 18). (Others conversely, introduce trivial matter with a statement of self-importance; these will be considered after we have established Johnson's capacity for taking small things seriously.)

Some *Rambler* correspondents, far from apologizing, criticize their author quite sharply for not taking small things seriously enough. In no. 57 Sophron writes in terms which prefigure *Adventurer* 128, already quoted:

Sir,
    I am always pleased when I see literature made useful, and scholars descending from that elevation, which, as it raises them above common life, must likewise hinder them from beholding the ways of men otherwise than in a cloud of bustle and confusion. Having lived a life of business, and remarked how seldom any occurrences emerge for which great qualities are required, I have learned the necessity of regarding little things. . . .
    Your late paper on frugality was very elegant and pleasing, but,

in my opinion, not sufficiently adapted to common readers, who pay little regard to the musick of periods, the artifice of connection, or the arrangement of the flowers of rhetoric. (Y, III, 305)

It is true that the paper on frugality, no. 53 (Y, III, 284–8), includes elaborately musical periods – the two long ones which make up paragraph five, for instance – and that Johnson had compared different causes of poverty to precipices, to 'gulphs', to 'a slow poison, hourly repeated', and to 'Syrens that entice . . . to shipwreck, and Cyclops that are gaping to devour'; but it seems just as well adapted to common readers as most *Ramblers*, so that Johnson voices, in no. 57, a quite fundamental doubt about his own approach.

Philomides in no. 72, writing on good humour, and Eutropius in no. 98, writing on politeness, are if anything even more trenchantly critical, on grounds of matter rather than style. Each admits that the *Rambler* has sometimes acknowledged, with 'more truth than novelty', the importance of the 'petty transactions' in which our lives glide away, but neither thinks it has gone far enough. Johnson is severely taken to task by his own creatures as one of those 'who exalt themselves into the chair of instruction', who 'would not have injured your reputation, if you had sometimes descended to the minuter duties of social beings . . . difficult as they may prove to be detailed with dignity' (Y, IV, 12–13, 160–1).

The accusations made in these letters are less just than those of Sophron. As the Yale editors point out, Johnson had recently devoted *Rambler* 68 (as well as an eloquent passage in no. 66) to the importance of 'small incidents, and petty occurrences' (Y, III, 351, 359). He can therefore hardly have believed that he was gravely at fault. But to measure by too grand a scale is a constant temptation for the writer, especially one who (like Johnson's debaters and his poets, like Johnson himself in his writings) *does* aim at dignity. He uses these correspondents to dramatize the conflicting demands of the great and the trivial, the occupational hazard of becoming remote by an effort at greatness. Johnson later concurred with the sentiments of his own invented characters when he praised Milton and Isaac Watts for their 'voluntary descent from the dignity of science' to the teaching of subaltern endowments; everyone 'acquainted with the common principles of human action will look with veneration' on such descent (*Lives*, I, 132, 147; III, 308; cf. *Ram*. 137: Y, IV, 364).

It is not always possible to separate Johnson's satire on individuals for disproportionate pettiness (to be discussed in the next chapter) from his vindication of the small scale, for often one process leads into the other. The unnamed correspondent of *Rambler* 161 (Y, V, 90–4) makes a descent from the dignity of science which at first appears involuntary, even unconscious, and therefore ludicrous, but the end of the essay seems to show him capable of learning to let his own dignity slip from sight and to accept and justly value a minute scale. He opens with a pompous harangue (backed with the names of Cicero and Archimedes) in praise of historical curiosity, even when addressed to such humdrum material as the past vicissitudes not of a nation but of one's own country estate. He is here urging the worthiness of comparatively petty material ('The same disposition, as different opportunities call it forth, discovers itself in great or little things'); but he does so by an attempt to aggrandize little things rather than by use of a true measure. After his grand preamble he rehearses the history not even of an estate but of a garret (a rather littler scene than he has led readers to anticipate), and confesses himself 'somewhat mortified' that his *dramatis personae* are not 'politicians, philosophers, and poets' but a bankrupt tailor, a prostitute, a counterfeiter and a struggling author. Readers begin by smiling at the correspondent who writes to the *Rambler* in default of any 'employment equal to his ambition or genius'; we go on to find within this 'narrow space' a marvellous accumulation of comic detail (the way of life of the successive tenants, with the interpretations of the landlady, and perhaps best of all the paragraph of inane comments uttered by those who look at the room but do not take it); finally, with a sense of shock and even of outrage, we are brought face to face with death. The most recent tenants, two sisters, came to the garret when one was in the last stages of illness. The other

> followed her to the grave, paid the few debts which they had contracted, wiped away the tears of useless sorrow, and returning to the business of common life, resigned to me the vacant habitation.

It is a common experience among Johnson's readers to forget that the story of the two sisters belongs in this predominantly funny essay, and to file it elsewhere in the memory. The pathos of this paragraph is achieved, like the hilarity of the rest, through accumulation of detail. Death is prepared for and responded to in a series of minute yet significant actions: it causes less turmoil than the forger's suspense when waiting to receive his change or the author's composition of tragedy. Death is made to appear no great matter; it gives place immediately to 'the business of common life', which is in no way magnified and yet which is surely made to appear more precious by this glimpse of its end. We may conclude that the correspondent has experienced, through bending his attention on the minutiae of life, a shifting of his scale of reference. He begins as a man who needs the authentication of Cicero and Archimedes, of 'elegance in disguise, and learning in distress', to enable him to see any value in human traces snatched from the past; he becomes first a vividly ironic, then a deeply moving recorder of the actions of those 'of whom nothing [is] remembered' but a few sparse facts. This phrase is applied to the tailor; the very similar 'name which mankind have conspired to forget' was applied in the first paragraph to Archimedes. At the beginning of the essay a forgotten name suggests a famous one whose monument lies hidden under bushes and brambles; by the end it suggests the more truly forgotten – all the unnamed and departed tenants of the garret, especially the two sisters, the dead and the survivor – those who, in the words with which George Eliot ended *Middlemarch*, 'rest in unvisited tombs'. Despite its mocking start, this essay ends as a vindication of littleness. There no longer remains the slightest possibility of sneering at the correspondent's decision to describe little things as we smiled earlier at his ambition for greatness.

In his letter-essays Johnson links the ideas of too much height, too much attention to one's own glory, seeing indistinctly (through 'a cloud'), and judging by too large a scale (cf. above, p.29). From these dangers a writer will be preserved by contact with little things; but Johnson does not discuss little things without reference to any larger scale. He regularly weighs little matters against great qualities, great abilities, 'the more awful virtues', and finds them important despite recognizing their littleness (*Ram.* 72, *Adv.* 131: Y, IV, 12; II, 483). Even his journal of his health, a chronicle of humiliating minutiae, has an obvious reference to the great goal of preserving life.

The essay form itself, in which much of Johnson's best work was done, was, like the imitation, a genre whose name and conventions suggested a modest limitation of aims. A 'sharp, dismissive, almost pettish edge', like something intended as a joke, has been detected in the definition which Johnson the essayist composed for *essay* in its literary sense: 'A loose sally of the mind; an irregular indigested piece; not a regular and orderly composition.'[5] But the definition which sharply limits the modest genre is balanced by illustrative quotations (from Bacon and from a poem in praise of Roscommon) which agree in finding in essays a greater value than the term implies. Taken together, definition and quotations evaluate this little form both precisely and appreciatively.

It is worth notice in passing that although Johnson's essays devote less space than the *Tatler* and *Spectator* to social minutiae, he is also far less apt than his predecessors to exalt himself 'into the chair of instruction'. Johnson often presents in the epistolary first person matter which Steele or Addison would recount in the third; this makes the fictional character's experience loom larger, and helps to preserve it from being condescended to. Although the last *Rambler* admits that readers may have been put off by its unrelieved 'severity of dictatorial instruction' (Y,V, 319), the weightier essays had never made the *Spectator*'s judicial claim to *banish* vice and ignorance or to *scourge* vice and folly, nor had the lighter ones made use of any equivalent to such playful bullying as Addison indulged in: 'In order therefore to put a stop to this absurd practice, I shall publish the following edict, by virtue of that spectatorial authority with which I stand invested.'[6]

Rambler 152 says that in order to master the art of letter-writing, 'it is necessary to learn how to become little without becoming mean' (Y, V, 44). Littleness is the almost unavoidable characteristic of the letter-writer's subject-matter; avoiding meanness depends on the way the subject-matter is handled. Even in his familiar letters, Johnson continues to link minutiae with weighty themes, as he explains to Baretti in 1762 to account for the tone in which he has described his reactions to a visit to Lichfield:

> Moral sentences appear ostentatious and tumid, when they have no greater occasions than the journey of a wit to his own town: yet such pleasures and such pains make up the general mass of life; and as nothing is little to him that feels it with great sensibility, a mind able to see common incidents in their real state, is disposed by very common incidents to very serious contemplations. (*Letters*, no. 142)

Others of his letters, especially those of the 1770s to Hester Thrale, delight in trivia for their own sake:

> My Love to all
> Both great and small.
> These verses I made myself, though perhaps they have been made by others before me. (*Letters*, no. 289)

(Editors of Johnson's poetry have so far drawn the line at this distich, though the necessity of printing hardly more weighty *jeux d'esprit* with pompous notes has proved a problem for them, which Johnson would have enjoyed.)

Writing to Hester Thrale, he played endlessly with the words *great* and *little*, for the purposes of self-mockery, mockery of the pretensions of others, and celebration of the domestic, the diminutive, the merely human, 'a little talk . . . a little frolick' (*Letters*, no. 686). Tags from the epic poets jostle others from nursery rhymes like 'Boys and girls come out to play' (*Letters*, no. 592).[7] He frequently combines a gusto for petty detail with a measuring comparison or allusion. His wish for a 'little frolick' follows in the next paragraph after one touching on work (lives of poets), mortality, and past 'hopes of excellence' now relinquished; perhaps what he missed in the 'diurnal trifles' of the *Journal to Stella* was any explicit recognition of the scale employed.

Many of his best examples of measured minuteness were called forth by the tedium of visits to Ashbourne and Lichfield: 'To strawberries and cream which still continue, we now add custard and bilberry pye. Our two last fawns are well; but one of our swans is sick. Life, says Foresight, is chequer-work' (*Letters*, no. 262). Foresight, in Congreve's *Love for Love* (II, i), elaborately deduces this commonplace from a mixture of good and bad omens (getting out of bed backwards and putting on a stocking inside out as against stumbling on the stairs and meeting a weasel) but, unlike Johnson, he regards these portents as anything but trivial.

Another time (in no. 408) Johnson pursues his theme with more flourishes:

> Lady Smith has got a new postchaise, which is not nothing to talk on at Lichfield. Little things here serve for conversation. Mrs Aston's Parrot pecked my leg, and I heard of it some time after at Mrs Cobb's.
>
>   – We deal in nicer things
>   Than routing armies, and dethroning kings.
>
> A week ago Mrs Cobb gave me sweetmeats to breakfast, and I heard of it last night at Stowhill.
>
> If you are for small talk
>   – Come on, and do the best you can.
>   I fear not you, nor yet a better man.
>
> I could tell you about Lucy's two cats, and Brill her brother's old dog, who is gone deaf, but the day would fail me. Suadentque cadentia sidera somnum. So said Aeneas but I have not yet had my diner. I have begun early for what would become of the nation if a Letter of this importance should miss the post?

The first quotation has not been traced, but we cannot doubt that its author's 'nicer' subject-matter was less nice than Johnson's. Aeneas spoke the Latin sentence ('And setting stars to kindly rest invite', in Dryden's rendering) when pressed by Dido for the whole story of the Trojan war and his subsequent wanderings.[8]

The joke takes more complicated form in no. 293, also to Mrs Thrale:

> The inequalities of human life have always employed the meditation of deep thinkers, and I cannot forbear to reflect on the difference between your condition and my own. You live upon mock turtle, and stewed rumps of beef; I dined yesterday upon crumpets.[9] You sit with parish officers, caressing and caressed, the idol of the table, and the wonder of the day. I pine in the solitude of sickness. . . . You sleep away the night, and laugh or scold away the day. I cough and grumble, and grumble and cough. . . . and am disordered by very little things. Is it accident or age?

The beginning of this letter exhibits the amusement or irritation which Johnson frequently voices in face of truisms: those facts which everyone knows but which cannot be escaped, which confront the writer at every level of deep speculation or light-hearted banter.[10] (It also, as it were, smuggles in the identification of himself as deep thinker.) The worldly disproportion between him and his correspondent, which begins as a comic grievance, becomes progressively less certain. Her elevation diminishes through mention of parish officers (a parish being always an emblem of narrowness), and of being the wonder of the *day*. There are sharp points lurking under the unremarkable surface of this letter. Sleeping, laughing and scolding seem only moderately alluring as alternatives to coughing and grumbling; but Johnson's nights differ from his days only as coughing predominates over grumbling instead of vice versa (sleep is out of the question), while Hester Thrale enjoys the humdrum yet precious alternation of sleep and waking. Some doubt hangs over the 'little things' that disorder Johnson: if the cause is accident, that indeed is trivial; if it is age, then the 'little things' are symptoms of something graver. The whole passage explores the ironic implications of a trite comparison: Hester Thrale's condition may be less grand, Johnson's complaints less trivial, when carefully measured, than they at first appear; and of life's inequalities the most universal and least glamorous are the most pressing.

These letters run the whole gamut of possible relationships between the great and the little. They draw parallels which are ludicrous yet valid, like 'Many families that paid the parish rates are now extinct, like the race of Hercules' in a letter (no. 233) which compares, implicitly, a local rate-book to heroic legend, and (in Horace's words) the human race to dust and a shadow. Some letters mock the little with grand expression: Johnson says of a gout which has passed from his ankle to his toe, 'I have hunted it, and starved it, and it makes no figure'; he sends 'the history of one of my toes' (nos 632, 631). Of a rediscovered childhood acquaintance who 'has had as he phrased it *a matter of four wives*, for which neither you nor I like him much the better,' he comments satirically,

> Such, Madam, are the strange things of which we that travel come to the knowledge. We see *mores hominum multorum* [a quotation from Horace, on the observations made by Ulysses in his wanderings].[11] You that waste your lives over a book at home, must take life upon trust. (*Letters*, no. 256)

Such comparisons inflate petty detail in a way that makes us recognize its pettiness as we seldom do – but does not make us scorn or reject it. A sentence which sounds like a straightforward expression of preference for the grand ('I am of my friend's opinion, that when one has seen the Ocean, cascades are but little things') turns out to have been written to mock Bishop Percy's use of this comparison (*Letters*, no. 288 and n. 3).

To the child Queeney Thrale, Johnson writes in November 1772, with more pathos and less irony than usual:

> I am glad to hear of the improvement and prosperity of my hen. Miss Porter has buried her fine black cat. So things come and go.

Generations, as Homer says, are but like leaves; and you now see the faded leaves falling about you. (*Letters*, no. 282.1)

To her mother he writes with a gravity appropriate to a topic of absolute, not relative, significance: 'When the mind is drawn toward a dying bed, how small a thing is an election?' But this letter (no. 197) reverts immediately to the less important, and almost immediately to the deliberately trivial. When birth not death is the great event, he describes a circular transition from trivia to significance back to trivia:

Miss Porter is very kind to me. Her dogs and cats are all well.

In all this there is nothing very memorable, but *sands form the mountain*. I hope to hear from Streatham of a greater event, that a new being is born that shall in time write such letters as this, and that another being is safe that she may continue to write such.

(The quotation, adapted from Edward Young's *Love of Fame*, had headed *Rambler* 126.) Johnson may have felt that he had diminished his correspondent too sharply, since he went on, 'She can indeed do many other things; she can add to the pleasure of many lives' (*Letters*, no. 252). To limit the destiny of Hester Thrale and her new baby to the writing of 'such letters as this' is to make them inconsiderable indeed, in view of the way Johnson later joked about the correspondence as embodying 'the great epistolick art' of writing a letter with nothing in it: 'a power of which I will not violate my modesty by boasting, but I do not believe that every body has it'.[12] In this correspondence Johnson consistently and touchingly does what he tells us in *Idler* 88 that man is seldom willing to do: 'to let fall the opinion of his own dignity, or to believe that he does little only because every individual is a very little being' (Y, II, 274).

In the *Journey to the Western Islands*, as in letters from outside London, Johnson regularly invokes comparison with metropolitan standards, but works to prevent the comparison from diminishing too crushingly. He finds it necessary to translate from one scale of measurement to another: 'a house of lime and slate and glass' is an 'image of magnificence'; a village consists of 'many huts, perhaps twenty', since it follows hard upon a village 'of three huts, one of which is distinguished by a chimney' (Y, IX, 48, 42, 35). The letters have familiarized the technique which he applies to the headman of Iona 'whom Fame, but Fame delights in amplifying, represents as worth no less than fifty pounds' (Y, IX, 148). Only occasionally does he resort to satiric magnification of the little, as of a four-acre uninhabited island 'named Sandiland, I suppose, in contempt':

Having wandered over those extensive plains, we committed ourselves again to the winds and waters; and after a voyage of about ten minutes, in which we met with nothing very observable, were again safe upon dry ground. (Y, IX, 144)

Sandiland had nothing human to ward off contempt, and Johnson takes no steps to protect either his subject or himself from it here. He takes a more characteristic tone in his account of the aged widow living in a vault under the site of a demolished conventual building in St Andrews.

> She thinks however that . . . as her husband's name was Bruce, she is allied to royalty, and told Mr. Boswell that when there were persons of quality in the place, she was distinguished by some notice; that indeed she is now neglected, but she spins a thread, has the company of her cat, and is troublesome to nobody. (Y, IX, 8–9)

This sentence seems to me to approach again the spirit of epitaphs from the *Greek Anthology* (see above, p.66). Some of these celebrate past greatness (inscriptions for Priam, for Alexander, and for Archedicè who was daughter, sister, wife and mother of rulers); some record the deaths of the lowly (Crethis the sweet work-mate, Zosima the slave, and Epictetus, slave, cripple and favourite of heaven); but each group expresses with stark dignity a sense of how little of human life survives (Y, VI, 315–21, 340). Johnson's lines on old Mrs Bruce have a lapidary terseness; 'she thinks' contrasts with 'indeed', royalty with her cat, and 'was distinguished by some notice' with 'is troublesome to nobody', to make vivid the gulf that separates her imagined from her actual status; of the two last-quoted phrases, the former has the rotund emptiness that characterizes paragraphs of newspaper compliment,[13] and the other the pathetic dignity of low expectations and independence painfully preserved. Johnson's polished account of this meeting is much shorter but far more striking than his early version (*Letters*, no. 321). The phrase 'spins a thread,' so much more evocative than knitting or even weaving would be, succeeds in connecting the old woman simultaneously with the ancient female Fates (she is immediately rehumanized by mention of the cat), and with her husband's famous ancestor in the incident when, in company with his thread-spinning spider, he learned the lesson of perseverance which his later representative practises so well. She touches us both by her bare survival and by her tenuous hold on romance and royalty. (The fact that her interlocutor, Boswell, also plumed himself on descent from the Bruce, adds an extra, private irony.) This passage, in its intricacy and simplicity, celebrates the value of mere unaccommodated humanity as Johnson's poem on Levet does (see below, pp.236–9).

The chord struck here reverberates through the *Journey*. The Highlanders are poor, neglected, solitary, yet self-reliant; they cherish an unrealistic imaginative pride in what they take to be the splendour of their history; the huge harsh mountains and the sea intensify our sense of their actual littleness, as do the ruins where Mrs Bruce lives. Johnson meticulously gives credit for innumerable tiny achievements: from the woman at Auknasheals who was advised to ask more than a shilling for her milk, 'but she said a shilling was enough', to the deaf and dumb girl who demonstrated her mathematical ability on the sum Johnson set her, though 'probably disdaining so easy an operation'.[14]

Johnson justifies his attention to such petty details in the famous passage which follows his account of the lack of devices for keeping windows open.

> These diminutive observations seem to take away something from the dignity of writing, and therefore are never communicated but with hesitation, and a little fear of abasement and contempt. But it must be remembered, that life consists not of a series of illustrious actions, or elegant enjoyments; the greater part of our time passes in compliance with necessities, in the performance of daily duties, in the removal of small inconveniences, in the procurement of petty pleasures. . . . The true state of every nation is the state of common life. . . . The great mass of nations is neither rich nor gay: they whose aggregate constitutes the people, are found in the streets, and the villages, in the shops and farms. (Y, IX, 22)

These views echo those expressed in *Ramblers* 57, 98 and 202: to give a true account, to resist the temptation to see life as illustrious or elegant, may ask some sacrifice of dignity. In the essays Johnson had already presented the writer's predicament as a personal one. Here, publishing under his own name, he goes further in revealing his own vulnerability. To descend to petty detail involves hesitation, actual fear of abasement and contempt.[15] The dignity which the writer must renounce is no abstraction, but a shield against possible humiliation. But the fear of abasement and contempt is a *little* fear; of itself it reveals the writer's true kinship with the aggregate of little people. By thus including himself in his own picture, Johnson should have forestalled any objection that his concept of, and his sympathy with, the 'great mass of nations' is too general – even if his detailing of individuals (old woman, milk woman, deaf girl) did not forestall it.

Johnson had passed much of his own writing career in recording 'diminutive observations'. The 'voluntary descent' from a dignified to a utilitarian genre, which he admired in Milton and Isaac Watts, was no unusual experience to himself. His journalistic writings cover a wide range of everyday concerns – tea, bridge-building, fireworks, giving to charity – which cannot be called illustrious or elegant. Several of these writings recommend to public notice some particular topic which great minds might have considered unworthy of it, and do so with an admonishment about wrong scales of judgment. His labour on the Harleian Library produced 'An Essay on the Origin and Importance of Small Tracts and Fugitive Pieces' (1744: *Works*, V, 190–7), a fine defence of the value of minutiae in learning. The student of history 'that only reads the larger writers . . . will see none of the changes of fortune which every opinion has passed through . . . but will be to him, who traces the dispute through into particular gradations, as he that hears of a victory, to him that sees the battle' (V, 193).

His preface to *The Preceptor* (1748: *Works*, V, 231–46) recommends that educational work as 'applicable to the purposes of common life', purposes which are humble yet of incalculable importance (V, 232). Teaching to read and write is 'an attempt of little magnificence, but in which no man needs to blush for having employed his time, if honour be estimated by use' (V, 236). Johnson recommends each particular subject of study in terms of everyday practicality. Letter-writing, including letters on contracts and debts, is more useful and necessary than 'writing panegyricks or epithalamiums' (*Works*, V, 237). Logic must be 'frequently and familiarly applied', lest it 'fail to produce its effects upon common occasions' (*Works*, V, 242). Ethics or morality is inculcated as 'the study of himself, the knowledge of his own station in the ranks of being, and his various relations to the innumerable multitudes which surround him, and with which his Maker has ordained him to be united for the reception and communication of happiness' (*Works*, V, 243).

For five weeks early in 1751 Johnson devoted alternate numbers of the *Rambler* (beginning with no. 86) to a study of Milton's versification, a topic which he felt he must repeatedly warn his readers not to despise. Addison, he writes, never 'thought the art of numbers unworthy of his notice'. He quotes (hoping, presumably, that the authority will outweigh the sentiment) from Virgil's introduction to his mock-heroic account of beekeeping: '*In tenui labor.* What toil in slender things!'[16] He also justifies such toil directly:

> however minute the employment may appear, of analysing lines into syllables, and whatever ridicule may be incurred by a solemn delib-eration upon accents and pauses, it is certain that without this petty knowledge no man can be a poet; and that from the proper disposition of single sounds results that harmony . . . that shackles attention, and governs passion. (Y, IV, 99)

It is characteristic of Johnson that he should choose a series of general essays, not even predominantly literary, as the place in which to write his justification of minute critical studies.

'Further Thoughts on Agriculture' (1756: *Works*, V, 315–20) follows up the argument of *Rambler* 145 that 'vocations and employments of least dignity are of the most apparent use' (Y, V, 8). Agriculture, a subject 'not considered with attention proportionate to its importance', is 'the great art' which governments ought to protect and individuals improve. As in the *Preceptor* preface, Johnson characteristically avoids bald utilitarianism: he argues not simply that practical skills are useful, but that, being useful, they are or ought to be honourable. Common opinion is guilty of wrong measurement in

> the little regard which the disposers of honorary rewards have paid to agriculture, which is treated as a subject so remote from common life, by all those who do not immediately hold the plough, or give fodder to the ox, that I think there is room to question, whether a great part of mankind has yet been informed that life is sustained by the fruits of the earth. (*Works*, V, 315)

As he wrote this, Johnson may have recalled his own *Adventurer* 128 (see above, pp.27–8); certainly he here employs the same technique on the same subject, for the phrases about the plough and the ox make agriculture little by 'a detail of minute circumstances', while that about the sustenance of life makes it great by 'an aggregation of effects'.

Johnson's care always to deduce effects from causes leads him perpetually to delve down to those details or circumstances, generally dismissed as trivial, which underlie impressive aggregations. Though he is acutely aware of the minuteness of some of Sir Thomas Browne's or his own chosen scholarly concerns, he does not devalue them, but rather relates them on the one hand to their larger effects and on the other to that inescapable immersion in minutiae which we try at our peril to evade. He was deeply suspicious of any estimate of human dignity that might lead to dismissing this or that occupation as below it. *Dark, low, little* may suggest privation (see above, p.14), but they also suggest humanity. His own strong sense of the dignity of mankind was grounded on his belief in our accountability to God for all our actions, a belief which ensures that, though the greatest human event is petty *in itself*, the smallest is immense in its eternal consequences. His biographies emphasize domestic detail both purposely and purposefully. In Savage's melodramatic life story of heroes and villains, the kindness of the Bristol gaoler shines with the unemphatic splendour of genuine goodness. It is 'little, nameless, unremembered acts/Of kindness and of love',[17] which reveal an individual as the proper disposition of single sounds reveals a writer. Neither can be judged, as neither can be enacted, without attention to detail.

Johnson's vindication of pettiness is not in any way out of step with Christian tradition. No Anglican churchgoer could fail to be familiar with the rejoicing of the humble handmaid who became the mother of her Lord that 'He hath put down the mighty from their seat: and hath exalted the humble and meek'. It was a commonplace to whole generations as to George Herbert that a pious intention 'makes drudgerie divine'.[18] Johnson was always willing to lend his weight to restating the truism that the earthly human scale dissolves in face of the divine one. But it is also important to him to readjust the human scale without reference to anything more than human, to inculcate measurement by a scale more humane than those customarily used by literature or morality.

Johnson presents both the moral choices of ordinary people (how to treat a job applicant, how much money to ask for milk) and the moral infirmities of great men (see below, pp.215ff.) in all their minute particularity. The greatest works of literature depend on this mean material and these frail producers, as biography and history depend on minute facts, the pomp of royalty on the existence of spectators,[19] the educated intellect on practical instruction, epic poems on scansion, and the dignity of human nature on ploughs and oxen, custard and bilberry pie, and devices to prop open windows.

5

CRITICISM OF PETTINESS

his subjects are often unworthy of his care.

(life of Waller)

JOHNSON'S INSISTENCE that we should recognize and accommodate ourselves to the inbuilt, inescapable pettiness of the human scale does not debar him from joining in the far more familiar cry of moralists and satirists against the adoption of scales which are disproportionately, wilfully petty.[1] Having made fairly frequent use in the *Rambler* of the word *trivial* to signify 'Light; trifling; unimportant; inconsiderable' he then gave it as his view in the *Dictionary* that this sense, though 'more frequent', was 'less just' than the more etymologically accurate 'Vile; worthless; vulgar; such as may be picked up in the highway', and changed it in almost every case for a more 'exact' word like '*petty, trifling, minute, degenerate, slender, vain, slight,* or *silly*'.[2] In reclaiming the significance of the trivial or inconsiderable, he was washing his hands of the vain, slight or silly: these were fair game. Pure contempt is rare in Johnson's writings, but a revealing hint of contempt tamed and mastered by rigorous judgment is less so.

His validation of little things rests on allegiance to accuracy in scale; to undervalue them is not the only possible mistake for human judgment to make. The very letters to Hester Thrale which so delight in little things – which seem to have limitless space for dogs and cats and fowls – circle and recircle with measuring eye the topic of Dr Taylor's 'great Bull'. *We*, says Johnson, 'yet hate the man that had seen a bigger Bull': Taylor's petty obsession with size is made more and more disproportionate.[3] Hester Thrale recorded (*à propos* the cases, 'in a world that is bursting with sin and sorrow', of someone troubled with severe guilt at having committed thefts of string from his employer and someone else disapproving strongly of bird-catchers pursuing their trade on a Sunday) that 'Mr. Johnson had indeed a real abhorrence of a person that had ever before him treated a little thing like a great one'.⁴ Even in biography, or rather in journal-keeping, which is a subordinate branch of it, he qualified his claims for the significance of detail with 'an intemperate attention to slight circumstances . . . is to be avoided' (*Letters*, no. 542).

As the significance of daily life is to be appreciated by accepting the littleness of the human scale, so details are to be limited to no more than proper significance by keeping them to their proper place in that scale. Johnson's objections to overstatement of minutiae in literature and life are probably better known than his defence of vital minutiae. They are also equally central to his work: so much so that almost all of his whole-hearted satire is aimed at this kind of scale distortion. Donald T. Siebert, Jr, has analysed the techniques by which the edition of Shakespeare presents 'the ordinary editorial critic' as 'a puny disputant, pert, vain, and often pompous', utterly unable 'to see his undertakings for what they are, as modest, possibly useful inquiries but not the indispensable concern of human life'. He compares Johnson to 'the king of Brobdingnag or Gulliver's master Houyhnhnm – looking with pity, wonder, and horror at the spectacle of man's vicious smallness'.⁵ These scholars invite contempt not because their activities are trivial but because, judging by a wrong scale, they fail to acknowledge the fact as Johnson the scholar does. They remain glued to their microscopes, incapable of the double vision with which Johnson concludes his preface (see above, pp.31ff.).

Johnson could flap such insect writers away with ease, here or in conversation or in certain *Lives of the Poets*. He was also alert for mistaken pettiness in even very much more considerable writers. His famous pronouncement about Edgar's description of Dover Cliff in *King Lear* clearly stems from the same principle of opposition between detail and aggregate that he had adumbrated in *Adventurer* 128.

> He that looks from a precipice finds himself assailed by one great
> and dreadful image of irresistible destruction. But this over-
> whelming idea is dissipated and enfeebled from the instant that the
> mind can restore itself to the observation of particulars . . . distinct
> objects . . . enumeration.

Discussing the same passage later, he referred to Shakespeare's enu-merating of things seen, as if to measuring the downward drop by subdivisions: 'you pass on by computation, from one stage of the tre-mendous space to another'.⁶ The same principle informs his complaint about another example of seventeenth-century exuberance of detail, the imagery of Cowley and the Metaphysicals. What 'might in general expres-sions be great and forcible he weakens and makes ridiculous by branching it into small parts'. The fault is 'that of pursuing his thoughts to their last ramifications, by which he loses the grandeur of generality, for of the greatest things the parts are little; what is little can be but pretty, and by claiming dignity becomes ridiculous' (*Lives*, I, 53, 45). As with the editors and others, it is the *claim* to dignity which reveals a judgment out of scale, and invites rebuke.

According to this reasoning, Shakespeare's Edgar was caught in a dilemma: the higher the cliff, the smaller the objects at its foot would appear; but the smaller the objects, the more they would detract from the greatness of the image of destruction. The dilemma has a parallel in Johnson's system of psychology: the greater the man, the greater the temptation to the 'arrogance and contempt' which cannot co-exist with true magnanimity. Johnson's criticism of the Dover Cliff passage in effect suggests that the precipice (one of his own favourite images) ought to be illustrated not by visual means at all, but perhaps by spatial ones. He wants to be offered the sensation of readiness to fall, not the visual distortion of vertical height (an idea which interested him deeply, but for different reasons: see below, pp.169ff.). One is tempted to reply to his objections by invoking intention: if Shakespeare had meant Edgar to aim *chiefly* at frightening his father, and the audience, then he might have found better means of doing so, and Johnson's criticism would therefore be just; if he meant chiefly to insist on the different or distorted aspects of things from different viewpoints, and if he was preparing already for the debunking of Gloucester's terror by his survival of imaginary danger, then Johnson has overestimated the passage's need to be great and dreadful.

To put Johnson's comments on *King Lear* together with those on the ramifications of Metaphysical imagery is to feel that he was exercising some restraint in not calling the crows and choughs 'pretty', like Cowley's inadequate imitation of Pindar's 'deep mouth' (*Lives*, I, 43). The *Dictionary* definition of *pretty*, we recall (see above, p.14), makes it exclude just those qualities – elevation, dignity – which Johnson demands from literature.

> The noblest beauties of art are those of which the effect is
> co-extended with rational nature, or at least with the whole circle of
> polished life; what is less than this can be only pretty, the plaything
> of fashion and the amusement of a day. (*Lives*, III, 333)

The life of Waller maintains that the reader of poetry has a *right* to expect 'enlargement of his comprehension and elevation of his fancy'. When Johnson describes Waller as 'growing illustrious in his own opinion', he echoes phrases from his essays: on the giver of advice 'growing great in his own eyes at our expence' and the man 'growing great and happy by electrifying a bottle' who dismisses world affairs as 'trifling prattle' (*Lives*, I, 292, 283–4; *Rams*. 87,118: Y, IV, 95; see above, p.26). The bottle brought a touch of satire to a serious comparative estimate of human attempts at fame, offering, as the essays often do, a character's deluded opinion without direct authorial judgment. In the life of Waller, Johnson opposes his own opinion to the poet's, which is therefore firmly marked as contemptible. He has exchanged a technique of satire for one of measured statement.

> It is not easy to think without some contempt on an author who is growing illustrious in his own opinion by verses, at one time,
> *To a Lady, who can do any thing, but sleep, when she pleases.* At another,
> *To a Lady, who can sleep, when she pleases. . . . On a tree cut in paper*; or, *To a Lady, from whom he received the copy of verses on the paper-tree, which for many years had been missing. . . .*
> Of these petty compositions, neither the beauties nor the faults deserve much attention. . . . Little things are made too important.
> (*Lives*, I, 283–4, 287)

It is not only because an author hopes to become illustrious by his work that it is beneath him to devote himself exclusively to trifles. Johnson believes that the attention necessary for writing should be focused not on mites but only on such matters as deserve attention from both author and reader. 'Such books therefore', he continues, 'may be considered as shewing the world under a false appearance.' Poets who concentrate our vision on ladies cutting paper distort its scope as unjustifiably as moralists who look down from celestial regions.

Johnson touches on another way in which a writer can distort a great subject into pettiness when in the life of Cowley he writes that 'words being arbitrary must owe their power to association' – that is, like other scales of measurement they are relative – and that 'the most heroick sentiments will lose their efficacy . . . if they are conveyed by words used commonly upon low and trivial occasions' (*Lives*, I, 58–9). He had made the same point in *Rambler* 168, on the low words in *Macbeth*. Whether or not we share his estimate of these particular words, we can assent to the principle of relativity of diction, which he seeks to establish by comparing it with the scale of wealth and poverty discussed in *Rambler* 202 (see above, pp.17–18).

> The cottager thinks those apartments splendid and spacious, which an inhabitant of palaces will despise for their inelegance; and to him who has passed most of his hours with the delicate and polite, many expressions will seem sordid, which another, equally acute, may hear without offence; but a mean term never fails to displease him to whom it appears mean, as poverty is certainly and invariably despised, though he who is poor in the eyes of some, may by others be envied for his wealth.

The disproportion of the words to which Johnson objects (*dun, knife, peep* and *blanket*) will be 'wholly imperceptible to a foreigner' and 'will strike a solitary academick less forcibly than a modish lady' (Y, V, 126, 128). It is necessary to know the scale against which measurements are made.

Low and little as the human scale may be, it is still possible to fall below it. Johnson obsessively repeated the word *little* throughout his diary entries made at 11 p.m. on Good Friday and on Easter Eve 1779, with an entirely different tone from that in which he applied it to his writings (see above, p.7). There can be no doubt of the reproachfulness of the word here, where Johnson is describing *not* himself as little in relation to Almighty God, but his achievement as little in relation to his capabilities:

I am now to review the last year, and find *little* but dismal vacuity . . . much intended and *little* done. . . . my nights afford me *little* rest . . . I have made *little* acquisition. . . . a *little* Charity. . . . *Little* done. . . . I have read *little*, almost nothing. . . . Of resolutions I have made so many with so *little* effect. (Y, I 294–5: italics added)

Here the consoling consciousness of human beings as little creatures from whom little can be expected (which touches even Johnson's view of Shakespeare's editors) is in abeyance. He is measuring himself against a scale to which he cannot, yet ought to, conform.

Such unusually unqualified reproach of littleness is also prominent in other writings which date from the same decade as the scathing self-review, but are in almost every other respect a contrast to it. They are his political pamphlets of the 1770s, where reductionist techniques, which in the parliamentary debates had been scattered among the orators on either side, are concentrated relentlessly in the tone taken by Johnson the pamphleteer. A final paragraph of *Taxation No Tyranny* was to have begun with a sneer at the colonies' current size – 'Their numbers are at present not quite sufficient for the greatness which, in some form of government or other, is to rival the ancient monarchies' – and to have continued by mocking their predicted future increase by reducing it to mere mathematics: 'rule of progression. . . . thus multiplied. . . . to double and to double' (Y, X, 455 n.). This, which Johnson admitted to be 'indeed rather contemptuous' (*Letters*, no. 381), was deleted, but the pamphlet as published twice employs parochial comparisons (cf. above, pp.71–2). The first is made more insulting by the plea that it should not be taken as insulting: 'The legislature of a colony, let not the comparison be too much disdained, is only the vestry of a larger parish' (Y, X, 432). Johnson drives this home by comparing it with 'superior authority'; on the next page Maryland is 'one little settlement' as against 'the general interest of the empire'. He compares greater with less in the same way in *Thoughts on Falkland's Islands*, setting 'the whole fabrick of our empire' against

a bleak and gloomy solitude . . . an island which not the southern savages have dignified with habitation . . . and which, if fortune smile upon our labours, may become a nest of smugglers in peace, and in war the refuge of future buccaniers.[7]

The contempt which animates the 1770s pamphlets is something startling, a tone which had rarely been heard in Johnson's work before, and never before allowed to predominate. Here he allies himself with Democritus instead of with those who search and canvas before they will pronounce on the justice of Democritus' scorn. The reason is clear. For almost the first time outside a frame of reference borrowed from Swift's Gulliver, he was measuring public affairs according to a scale which accepts greatness as a norm. Contrary to his usual practice, he does not remark that pettiness is merely human; instead he laments the absence of dignity and grandeur from the political scene as a privation of what should be present. The colonies resemble 'every parish' in claiming the right to tax themselves; the likeness in this respect between a parish and a mighty kingdom (whose difference is one of scale but not of kind) is less present to Johnson's mind than his earlier writings would lead the reader to expect. He now assumes that 'the whole fabrick' or 'the general interest' of *our* empire outweighs questions about small islands, where earlier he had implied that interest in 'all the globe' is likely to lead to mistaken neglect of a smaller unit, and that too breathless a conviction of the importance of politics denotes a petty mind.

The full, unquestioning endorsement of the overriding importance of large units like kingdom or empire is, unlike reductionist techniques, new in Johnson's political writings. His early Swiftian pamphlet satires had conveyed, through their energy and elaboration, a sense of the vital significance of national affairs, but they did so by an extremely roundabout route which satirized their supposed writers' sense of significance. Johnson's political personae in those pamphlets voiced an extreme degree of 'proper deference' for authoritative names and weighty subjects; that of *Marmor Norfolciense* conveyed his vicarious importance in conjuring up

> a full and distinct view of all the negotiations, treaties, confederacies, of all the triple and quadruple alliances, and all the leagues offensive and defensive, in which we were to be engaged, either as principals, accessaries, or guarrantes.

Like the writer of the prophetic verse within the pamphlet, he

> knew that our negotiators would interest us in the affairs of the whole earth, and that no state could either rise or decline in power, either extend or lose its dominions, without affecting our politics and influencing our councels. (Y, X, 26, 37–8)

Readers, faced with the separate inanities of both prophecy and interpretation, and forced to work out their own scale of judgment, must supply their own scepticism about these eager claims to importance, and also any faith they may entertain that more intelligent politics (and greater causes than setting up a Society of Commentators) do exist. This persona's views of his own moment of history, 'this urgent occasion' when his country's fate hangs in the balance (Y, X, 51), are as exaggerated as those which Johnson attributes to the crisis mongers of *The False Alarm*. But the earlier pamphlet lacks the serious, accusing, diminishing figure of Johnson himself.

Similarly the interlocking ironies of the parliamentary debates keep us suspended between accepting the politicians' own pleasing sense of their global significance, and dismissing their affairs as Lilliputian, as a reader of *Gulliver* would do, and as they themselves do about their opponents (see above, pp.48ff.). Johnson's political writings of the 1750s, like 'Observations on the Present State of Affairs. 1756', which likens imperial annexation to robbery (Y, X, 188), take a no-nonsense attitude which is very far from magnifying the struggles of the international arena, though at the same time they convey a sense of urgency and also of moral dilemma. The *Idler* papers (see below, pp.93ff.) and the life of Frederick the Great (especially its conclusion: see below, pp.197ff.) move towards regarding the combats they describe as petty, but at least the combatants on both sides are measured by the same scale. The famous tirades of the 1770s, more clearly than anything written earlier, imply a superior, unimplicated judgment of the scene they depict: the dignity of constitution or empire attacked by trivial antagonists on trivial grounds. As Boswell said (II, 112), the 'contemptuous' *False Alarm* 'endeavoured to infuse a narcotick indifference, as to publick concerns, into the minds of the people'. *Marmor Norfolciense*, though it made fun of hysteria, could hardly have been said to advocate indifference; it showed more ironical or questioning measurement of the scale of public affairs than does the later work.

The False Alarm (1770) embodies much close reasoning on constitutional issues – what its author admired as 'subtlety of disquisition' (Boswell, II, 147). The difficulty for a reader is to reconcile this subtlety ('Every diffuse and complicated question may be examined by different methods, upon different principles': Y, X, 324) with the hilarious, Hogarthian account of the progress of a petition. The solution may be that they are intended to be irreconcilable. In this essay Johnson reports the complexities of principle as incompatible in scale with the muddle of electioneering, and dismisses the latter as unacceptably petty. As in *Taxation No Tyranny*, the lasting institution is great, the individual trouble-makers despicable. (These were the years of the very different letters about little things, which poke fun but not contempt at Hester Thrale's electioneering, and accept the petty scale of Lichfield life with equanimity: see above, pp.70–3). When *The False Alarm* compares the present political furore with the superstitious terror of savages at eclipses or meteors, Johnson is thinking of the only temporary shadow on the great light of government, the only temporarily distracting brilliance of Wilkes (Y, X, 317–18). The '*alarming crisis*' has no real existence and calls for no response (Y, X, 330, 345). There can be no connection or interaction between 'subtlety of disquisition' and 'these puny controvertists', the rabble, divided between those 'who are sober enough' to sign their names and those who are not (Y, X, 331, 337).

Falkland's Islands (1771) has been admired for its horrific account of the sufferings of war and the wickedness of those who profit by it. Its focus, though, is on the unworthiness of the *object* of war, as its first sentence makes clear: 'To proportion the eagerness of contest to its importance seems too hard a task for human wisdom.' Its second sentence calls its own substance 'the discussion of useless questions'; a later paragraph comments on the frequent inadequacy of causes to effects. To the islands under dispute 'nothing has happened . . . but that they have been sometimes seen by wandering navigators, who passed by them in search of better habitations' (Y, X, 349, 366, 350). They are little more than nothing; to fight for them would gain nothing. 'Let us not think our laurels blasted by condescending to inquire, whether we might not possibly grow rather less than greater by attacking Spain' (Y, X, 372). Johnson does not now see the condition of being little more than nothing as simply the human norm. Instead, he makes his opponents the rabble – and, in an even more striking image from *Taxation no Tyranny*, makes *both* sides of the contention – into something less than human: 'no man hates a worm as he hates a viper; they . . . may therefore quietly slink into holes, and change their slough unmolested and forgotten'; 'When the cranes thus begin to flutter, it is time for pygmies to keep their eyes about them' (Y, X, 376–7, 386, 448). He here comes close to regarding, contrary to his own earlier prescription, some concerns of his fellow-beings as 'below the dignity of our nature, and unworthy of the attention of a rational being' (*Adv.* 128: Y, II, 476).

Johnson had not foreshadowed this contempt in the *Rambler* and hardly in the *Idler*. He had, however, as well as vindicating involvement in 'little things' and 'common occasions', ranged through elegiac regret for this littleness as far as lively satire on privative pettiness and on the misjudgment which calls petty things great. He tells us in *Rambler* 20 that his correspondents love to conceal themselves under names redolent of grandeur, like Penthesilea, Ajax Telamonius, Sesostris, Dioclesian; of the names he issues them, on the other hand, a striking number are diminutives, mostly (unlike the later Drugget, Minim and Shifter) classically based. Some are merely perfunctory, like Flirtilla (no. 10), Misellus (no. 16), Zephyretta (no. 18); many of the more remarkable ones end in *–ulus* or *–ula*, a diminutive suffix well known to literature from the emperor Hadrian's address to his soul, 'Animula vagula, blandula . . . Pallidula, rigida, nudula', from which Johnson quoted in a letter of 1780

(*Letters*, no. 655). They are a pointer to Johnson's readiness to diagnose human stuntedness or underdevelopment.

Gulosulus, in *Rambler* 206, practitioner of the trivial art of dining at the expense of others, is a particularly acute example of the narrowing of human potential. He has no sense of dignity in himself, 'no opinion' that might antagonize any host; he 'has learned to consider rudeness and indignities as familiarities that entitle him to greater freedom'. As well as diminishing himself he magnifies eating: his knowledge of food is described in high terms as 'chief policy' and 'dictatorial authority'; he believes in 'the dignity of feasting' and 'is fully satisfied with his own conduct'. Unlike some other exemplars of pettiness, Gulosulus does not offend out of ignorance. He knows 'that those who value themselves upon sense, learning, or piety, speak of him with contempt'; his own opinion of himself remains unaffected (Y, V, 307–9).

Gulosulus has voluntarily chosen, as Leviculus the fortune-hunter of no. 182 has vainly sought, the life of a client depending on patrons. Johnson is much concerned in the *Rambler* with the corrupting effects he finds in relationships between superior and inferior, to which topic diminutive names are often – as in nos. 26, 27, 149, 162 and 189 – a pointer.[8]

Of Nugaculus in *Rambler* 103 (from *nugax*, frivolous), whose early promise has led him 'by an accidental declension to minuteness' to become nothing more than an unauthorized connoisseur of people's private secrets, Edward A. Bloom writes: 'The diminutive is characteristic of Johnson's application . . . when he wishes to express contemptuous disregard'.[9] This I believe is not accurate of Nugaculus, though *contemptuous disregard* does nicely describe the views in the pamphlets of the 1770s, and Johnson's attitude to minor *Rambler* characters: towards Gulosulus, Leviculus and peripheral figures in nos 113 and 119 who by treating little things as great ones arouse Johnson's real abhorrence.

He entertains more complex attitudes than contempt, however, towards characters treated in more detail (most of them correspondents), including those whose names end in *–ulus*. (Gulosulus is an exception in being treated in some detail yet also despised.) Nugaculus of no. 103 (the virtuoso of scandal), Florentulus of no. 109 (*little* as well as *flowery*), and Dicaculus of no. 174 (from *dicacitas*, 'raillery', which Cicero calls a trivial name for a trivial thing)[10] are all treated with psychological penetration and imaginative sympathy. Each has begun the world with ability and ambition, and without malevolence. Each has chosen some kind of dependence on other people. Florentulus, brought up by a dominating mother and submissive father, has devoted his life to the arts of pleasing ladies; Dicaculus has devoted his to making people laugh – and, he hopes, love him – by entertaining them with satiric and destructive wit. Too late they recognize the force of the world beyond their chosen sphere of influence. The one finds himself despised by the 'new flight of beauties', and 'hunted from all masculine conversation by those who were themselves barely admitted'; the other finds that since every joke requires a victim he has 'united mankind against' him.

Most interesting of all is Nugaculus, presented as exemplifying the:

> necessity of doing something, and the fear of undertaking much, [which] sinks the historian to a genealogist, the philosopher to a journalist of the weather, and the mathematician to a constructor of dials.

He has chosen, with 'an intention, innocent at first, if not laudable', the field of human psychology for his study. His friends initially cannot see any value in it, 'yet they could not deny [it] . . . worthy of a wise man'. The trouble is that the chosen subject is pre-eminently composed of petty particulars of the mind, observed through petty particulars of behaviour. Nugaculus pursues particulars with energy, but is not equal to the larger undertaking of synthesizing them into anything coherent or valuable, and so he declines into a gossip, becoming gradually not only foolish but vicious. Johnson judges him, like other characters with diminutive names, as guilty of pettiness, but he has been 'betrayed' into it by the very nature of humanity. Nugaculus begins as a hopeful young man and ends as a contemptible old one. Johnson's own interest in psychology (amply demonstrated in this particular essay, if we had no other evidence) and in the other fields he mentions here, those of history, science (the modern meaning of 'philosophy'), and mathematics, seems to indicate a degree of self-identification with this fictitious character, who might have made an excellent literary biographer. Similarly, Florentulus is preserved from our entire contempt by being allotted a passage of the most delicious mockery of his indolent, solitary, inelegant creator, and Dicaculus by the chastened mood in which he writes to Mr Rambler, out of obedience to the 'laws of social benevolence', to 'assist others by his experience'. By these means their creator voluntarily descends to association with the pettiness of his characters.

Nugaculus and Dicaculus have been betrayed into moral evil almost without having noticed that they are moral agents. Their one serious error is that of judgment, of accepting too trifling a scale. Having once aimed at recognition for 'intellectual excellence', Dicaculus dwindles to delight 'only in petty mischief' and 'obstreperous applause'. Nugaculus is ridiculous, with his inside knowledge of mortgages and the pilferings of butlers; he is culpable for 'a thousand acts of treachery' in acquiring information; he is pathetic, 'since he cannot enjoy this knowledge' without breaking confidences which every day increase his enemies; yet he is even tragic, too, having missed his chance of a more expanded, honourable and useful life.

These characters are not entirely contemptible and very far from disregarded.

Apparently the opposite of the socially active Florentulus and Dicaculus, Verecundulus in no. 157 has pursued and won 'academical laurels', and has now discovered that he lacks that social presence of mind which an earlier *Rambler* correspondent 'has presumed to mention with some contempt'. His name comes from Latin *verecund* (modest, bashful).[11] One might expect a verdict that Verecundulus had aimed too *high* in neglecting 'petty accomplishments' for virtue and learning, but instead he now finds that he must remedy his neglect in order to *rise* 'to a level with my fellow beings' (Y, V, 70–5). He has miscalculated the scale of human values and narrowed his own being as surely as Gulosulus or Nugaculus. Seeking no mean dependence, he still needs the countenance of his fellows as much as they; and he has omitted to secure it. He is, however, still willing to recognize his mistake and able to learn from it. This essay makes a point which is important in context. Most of Johnson's diminutive names are given to people seen in domestic settings, their activities the traditionally feminine ones of house and family management and social intercourse: Venustulus and Flosculus show their pettiness in frailties which are generally considered feminine, Ferocula hers by aping in miniature a peculiarly masculine code of challenge and defiance. But Johnson, though he is willing to diagnose and exemplify faults connected with gender, does not assume the traditional scale which ranks as important the masculine and extensive, and as unimportant the feminine and domestic. Verecundulus, having rejected the merely social for the academic, is diminished by his choice as clearly as Florentulus or Dicaculus by their opposite choices, and must *rise* to the quotidian level of others.

In case Johnson's readers have not understood the necessity of rising, rather than sinking, by acquisition of petty accomplishments, he presses the point in a discursive sequel, no. 159:

> No cause more frequently produces bashfulness than too high an
> opinion of our own importance. . . . the truth is, that no man is
> much regarded by the rest of the world. He that considers how
> little he dwells upon the condition of others, will learn how little the
> attention of others is attracted by himself. (Y, V, 84)

Here the workings of the scale are paradoxical: self-importance produces the cramping of bashfulness, while attention to our own littleness can enlarge us. The narrowness which Johnson exposes has not generally been sought by his characters, but has closed around them while they neglected comparison with any broader scale (such comparison as Johnson constantly makes in his letters).

They see a little, and believe that there is nothing beyond their sphere of vision, as the Patuecos of Spain, who inhabited a small valley, conceived the surrounding mountains to be the boundaries of the world, (*Rambler* 169: Y, V, 131)

Without constant and careful attention, Johnson suggests, the scope of the mind and soul diminish with time. He is more inclined to worry that humanity will limit its own scope to that of a worm in a cabinet drawer, than that the Creator's scheme may have pre-enforced such limitation (see above, p.23).

The regret implied in *Ramblers* 103 and 157 over a narrowing and constricting choice of life is more explicit in nos 83 and 177, in which the constriction is less chosen and to which Johnson provides his own authorial comment. The name of Vivaculus (no. 177: Y, V, 168–72) draws both on the *Dictionary*'s second and on its first sense of *vivacious* from Latin *vivax*: 'Long-lived' as well as 'Sprightly; gay; active; lively'. Both senses are qualified in the name by the diminutive form, which reminds us that neither sprightliness nor longevity is an absolute quality, but that the degree of each available to humanity is small. Vivaculus, with more extensive ambition than most diminutively-named characters, early resolves 'without any confinement of my excursions or termination of my views, to wander over the boundless regions of general knowledge'. Finding that studious life proves less broadening in practice than in expectation, he then hopes to restore his lost mental agility and conversational quickness in London coffee-house society. Its members, however, turn out to be even less lively than his new less lively self, and more severely limited by narrow specialization: 'totally ignorant of all that passes, or has lately passed, in the world', collecting not even ancient books but only lost fragments of books, halfpence, newspapers.

Having first pursued 'for some years' a plan of study broad enough to occupy more than the very longest life, Vivaculus finds himself cut off from 'the living generation'; but the effort he makes (like Verecundulus) to reunite himself with it seems doomed to fail. His solitude makes him a kind of intellectual Rip Van Winkle; but the tavern scholars he encounters are even more like that than he is. This essay differs from others in showing the effects of narrowing and diminution working not only on a single misguided correspondent but on a whole society. Vivaculus fails in his attempt at scope and extension; others do not even try. Johnson's concluding comment only partly mitigates the gloom of these findings: the tavern intellectuals, with their 'minute emulation and laborious trifles', were perhaps never capable of anything better, and 'he who does his best, however little, is always to be distinguished from him who does nothing'. Johnson is resigned to their narrowness; but that of Vivaculus causes him pain and regret in proportion as Vivaculus himself looks, rightly, 'with uneasiness on the waste of life', and seeks to become more like his name's root meanings and less like its diminutive suffix.

This essay develops the theme of an earlier one, a letter from Quisquilius,[12] who also presents himself as a broad and extensive genius. Quisquilius despises the options of either utilitarian or specialized studies: 'I took the whole region [of knowledge] into my view, and wished it of yet greater extent.' He boasts ingenuously of his scientific collection: 'the honour which my labours have procured to my country'. Like the collections of his fellows in no. 177, however, his consists of minute tokens of great originals: in it the tombs of Persepolis are represented by 'three letters broken off by a learned traveller', and the Great Wall of China by a snail (or more properly, one assumes, the shell of a snail) which once crawled there.[13] The reader mentally refuses to honour and prefers to despise this collection; but Johnson intervenes in the next paper (Y, IV, 70–6) to compel our minds to more complicated exercises than simple contempt. He tells us that Quisquilius has achieved more than many people, and that some of his kind have achieved all that their faculties would reach to. He even finds extenuation for wilful confinement of more promising faculties. As for those collected objects at which the reader has so willingly sneered:

> If what appears little be universally despised, nothing greater can be attained, for all that is great was at first little, and rose to its present bulk by gradual accessions, and accumulated labours. . . .
>
> To collect the productions of art, and examples of mechanical science or manual ability, is unquestionably useful, even when the things themselves are of small importance, because it is always advantageous to know how far the human powers have proceeded.

Even on the subject of personal mementoes,

> I am afraid to declare against the general voice of mankind, and am inclined to believe, that this regard, which we involuntarily pay to the meanest relique of a man great and illustrious, is intended as an incitement to labour.

Perhaps even a snail-shell from China may serve as an inspiration. Poor Quisquilius, like Vivaculus, finds his vindication in the inescapable littleness of humanity, painfully collecting the shards of greatness. In these essays satire is only briefly given its head before being swallowed up in regretful acceptance.

The virtuosos, practitioners of an obviously petty hobby which it was the done thing – as in *Dunciad* book III – to despise, compel the *Rambler*'s sympathy. Other petty practices, equally easy targets, demand his serious attention because other moralists had seriously recommended them. In no. 51 (Y, III, 273–9) a correspondent named Cornelia reports on Lady Bustle, whose life passes in the sublime mysteries of housekeeping, who initiates her daughters into the arts 'to turn rose-leaves in the shade, to pick out the seeds of currants with a quill'. The effect of this essay depends both on its own minute details and on the language that reflects and mocks Lady Bustle's large estimation of narrow concerns: 'treasure of hereditary knowledge . . . opportunity of consulting the oracle'. The word 'projection' confounds cooking with alchemy;[14] the stopping of the oven's mouth on its secret suggests state security, the silencing by assassination of unhappy human tools.

Lady Bustle is clearly a figure of fun: yet her servants and family credit her with greatness, dignity, excellence; and Cornelia, the correspondent who describes her, wonders 'whether I am to look on these ladies as the great patterns of our sex'. Her eagerness for Mr Rambler's judgment need not be taken as sarcastic. Lady Bustle's activities, housekeeping, harvesting, preserving, nourishing, had been and still are frequently proposed as a model for women to follow. This differentiates her from Eriphile of *Rambler* 112 (Y, IV, 234–5), the house-proud spinster who 'lives for no other purpose but . . . the great employment of keeping gravel from grass, and wainscot from dust'. Eriphile, though the Yale editors compare her to Lady Bustle in a footnote, though she too finds satisfaction or disturbance only in trivia and might be cured by considering 'the dignity of human nature', is a conventional satirist's butt, produced by Johnson as an example of what 'generally' becomes of women 'imbittered by age or solitude'. Lady Bustle is a much more original conception. Eriphile's pettiness expresses itself in malign negativity, while Lady Bustle's has at least a kind of vitality. Through her Johnson questions what may well be his reader's own scale of judgment. Eriphile is obviously a hopeless distortion of the female pattern of neatness; of Lady Bustle as pattern the question to be asked is parallel to the one Johnson raises in connection with Quisquilius and the tavern antiquaries: are women capable of anything greater? must they be measured by this scale? Johnson offers no answer in his own person, but he allows Cornelia to hint that she reciprocates Lady Bustle's contempt; and Cornelia's name, that of the mother of the Gracchi, may remind an alert reader that different standards have sometimes been entertained of great patterns of the female sex.

Innumerable invented characters in the *Rambler* (like Quisquilius, like the *Gentleman's Magazine* parliamentarians) lay claim to greatness, and whether satirically or not their claims are always denied. Florentulus of no. 109, 'universally skilful in all the changes of expensive finery', is yet more especially knowing about Brussels lace, in conformity with the cliché about 'genius' that 'every one, they say, has something to which he is particularly born' (Y, IV, 218). The city-bred mother of Misocapelus 'frequently displayed her father's greatness . . . the heaps of gold which he used on Saturday night to toss about with a shovel' (*Ram.* 116: Y, IV, 254). Such ludicrous ideas of greatness (shovelling gold, being particularly born to understand Brussels lace or acknowledged as an authority on custard) are precisely designed to expose the pettiness of those who entertain them.

Not surprisingly, Johnson carried on his investigation of different scales of magnitude, of petty matters and our inflation of them, from the *Rambler* and *Adventurer* into the *Idler*. Indeed the plan of the later series, expressed in its name, is to embody and satirically to praise all those narrowing forces which Johnson despised in others and feared in himself – sloth, petty-mindedness, purposelessness, and denigration of the achievement of others – to make us re-evaluate little things as little. The opening number of the *Rambler* had taken its name for granted and seriously, even solemnly, compared the range of strategies and techniques available to a writer for making his first overtures to the public, assuming that his motives are the lofty ones of improvement for his readers and fame for himself. The opening *Idler* on the other hand begins with the question of naming the paper, clearly a lesser one than the question of the purpose of writing.

This title must have surprised attentive readers who remembered the *Rambler*'s resounding condemnations of idleness (nos 85, 134: Y, IV, 86–7, 347–8). But it is as an idler that Johnson in his new first number promises only two things ('diminutive history' and the pulling down of rising names) and welcomes contributions only if they are not long (Y, II, 5, 6). Many commentators have been unwilling to recognize his intention in the *Idler*, signalized by its title. Hawkins, who believed that 'Johnson's mind was never occupied on trifles; his speculations were grand and noble', considered the name chosen 'not improperly' because Johnson was writing only to avoid getting to work on Shakespeare, but that it was 'a designation that imports little; or rather, its most obvious meaning is a bad one. Johnson . . . chose an irony, and meant that his readers should understand by it just the reverse of what it signified'. He thought it a compliment to say that 'in the execution, it must be owned, it merited a better name'.[15] The Yale editors say that the *Idler*'s style is 'pithy' only 'when the subject is not trivial (as it occasionally is in the earlier papers)' (II, xx). Critics have dwelt on the resemblance in subject-matter between these and the *Rambler* and *Adventurer* essays, rather than on the contrast in style and form which transforms the total effect.[16] In fact Johnson chooses his trivial subjects deliberately and purposefully throughout his series, and is never at a loss for means of conveying his actual endorsement of the qualities the Idler despises, and vice versa. The *Idler* amounts to a sustained ironic reversal of the *Rambler*'s position. The early numbers, whatever their particular subject-matter, expand their underlyng theme of idleness until it embraces a denial of almost every principle of life and action. It comes to embody, in the personal and psychological sphere, the qualities that Pope gave, in the mythological and public spheres, to the goddess Dulness, who included among her powers that of shrinking men to the size of swarming insects.

Idler no. 2 belittles the literary community and the contributions which the Idler-editor solicits from it; no. 3 belittles the writer's search for subjects; nos 5, 6, 7, 8 and 12 belittle newspaper material and newspaper announcements. No. 3 justifies its concern with microscope truth, with 'minute industry, and distinctions too subtle for common eyes', on the grounds that previous periodical writers have used up the more considerable subjects (Y, II, 10). The detail that fills these papers (the new, plebeian breed of writers, trivial 'essays and epigrams', events of the day, sales and auctions, cards and shellwork, lapdogs and operas) was part of the stock-in-trade of the eighteenth-century satirist, but also part of what Johnson's readers every day passed unquestioningly among. When in *Adventurer* 128 Johnson had determined to avoid that 'easiest philosophy' which consists in nothing more than 'contempt and arrogance', and had undertaken to consider whether or not ordinary day-to-day human activities are worthy of the dignity of a rational being, he had based his consideration not on these modish occupations but on the useful ones of masonry and agriculture (see above, p.28). In deciding that the *Idler* should be more topical than the *Rambler* or his *Adventurer* essays, he was choosing areas of interest that he regarded as essentially trivial; he was also choosing that confinement to a smaller circle which *Idler* 78 mentions as affording 'opportunities for more exact observation' of 'minute peculiarities' (see above, p.30). He was putting under the microscope what he generally passed over. The question is whether he is to be blamed by his own standards for devoting *too* much attention to trivial objects, or praised for descending to petty transactions.[17] Critics of the *Idler* have sometimes accused it of breaking butterflies on a wheel, concentrating a too powerful instrument on mites.

The first topical numbers are the fifth, which ridicules the departure of 50,000 soldiers for 'the pathless desarts of the Isle of Wight', and the sixth, which ridicules the 'great performance' of a Miss Pond, who, for a wager, rode the same horse a thousand miles in a thousand hours (Y, II, 16–22). In each of these astonishingly complex pieces of ironic discourse, Johnson's major target is the disproportion of public opinion, which insists on making mountains of these two molehills. Each essay begins with a grand announcement ('Our military operations are at last begun; our troops are marching in all the pomp of war'); each ends in an extreme of bathos ('let it be added, that at this time . . . the love of praise was extinct; the fear of infamy was become ridiculous; and the only wish of an Englishman was, "to win his wager"'). In each Johnson professes to share in the general enthusiasm, and his minor points of dissent from majority opinion – about the hardships of the women the army leaves behind, about the adequacy of the acclamations offered Miss Pond – simply take him even further overboard than the majority. The dignified tone fitted to a *Rambler* essay of morality is now used to disguise national fantasy as reasonable: at the departure of troops 'to that side of the kingdom which faces France'

> the heart of every Englishman now swells with confidence, though somewhat softened by generous compassion for the [non-existent] consternation and distresses of our enemies. . . . [Tender maidens mourn, but] men, of a more political understanding, are persuaded that we shall now see, in a few days, the ambassadors of France supplicating for pity.

A nation which gives its best attention to lapdogs and swordknots takes a trivial manoeuvre as heroic exploit. In the next essay it celebrates a Guinness Book of Records 'heroine' with ecstasy which, however, borders on the hypocritical, since it offers no hard cash, the only thing it *really* values. Johnson is reducing to their actual littleness matters which others have conspired to inflate, but is doing it through further inflation by his persona. Three months later, during the same campaign, he was calling, in 'serious' political essays as well as in the *Idler*, for use of a more accurate scale in estimating military acquisitions, relative both to their actual value and to the enemy's estimate.[18]

He does something similarly reductive in *Idler* 12 (Y, II, 39–42), where, however, the claim to greatness is made by 'vulgar characters', and is recognizable at once by the 'supercilious and severe' as hopeless. Johnson indeed seems to be exercising some severity and superciliousness of his own. He represents his reader (akin to the public depicted in nos 5 and 6) scanning the newspapers 'with eager curiosity in quest of statesmen and heroes' and fobbed off instead with the wedding announcement of 'an eminent salesman' and 'the only daughter of an eminent [gin] distiller'. These nearest available approximations to greatness are then reduced to the stark factual accuracy of 'the sons and daughters of lanes and alleys'. (The scale is shifted by the same technique in no. 16, where Ned Drugget's 'reputation soon extended', not without a recollection of the dominions of Lilliput, 'from one end of the street to the other': see above, p.44; Y, II, 51.) These announcements designed for getting a *name* stand in the same columns as the names of a stallion at service and a lost pet. But Johnson has still not completed his evaluation of these attempts at eminence. The close of the essay accords ambiguous status to 'Mr. Settle, a man whose "eminence" was once allowed by the "eminent". . . . the rival of Dryden', who was eventually reduced from royal performance of his play to the level of hawking round every death or marriage his 'standing elegy and

epithalamium, of which only the first and last leaves were varied occasionally'. An *Idler* essay cannot end on this note; Johnson follows it with a
paragraph which re-establishes light-heartedness. But for a moment we
have heard a voice more characteristic of *The Lives of the Poets*, one which
gravely records the scope of human achievement *sub specie aeternitatis*.
Settle's eminence, however far above that of salesmen and distillers, was
still conferred by people with claims as suspect as his own, according to a
scale which cannot endure.

Johnson does not consistently adhere to his persona of Idler (no. 4 is a
direct, unfictive plea for charitable enterprises; no. 24 condemns with some
violence the mental torpor which it describes), but he adheres pretty
consistently to the theme of idleness, and this embraces not only denial but
also denigration of greatness and of either competitive or communal
endeavour. No wonder, therefore, that a wry or biting tone is commoner
than that which invokes the scale of eternity. A memorable *Idler* victim is
the girl in no. 13 (Y, II, 42–5) who 'knows not, at sixteen, the difference
between a Protestant and a Papist, because she has been employed three
years in filling the side of a closet with a hanging that is to represent
Cranmer in the flames', on account of her mother's views about the
undesirability of idle hands. Not all who laugh at this essay remember that
by its end this woman has her daughters employed full-time in a win-
dowless attic, spinning rough linen for the servants (£5 worth in a year
between the three of them); or that her husband 'remonstrated, that with
larger wheels they might dispatch in an hour, what must now cost them a
day; but she told me, with irresistible authority, that any business is better
than idleness'. The delightful detail about Cranmer is in fact a sweetener to
make tolerable a picture far more crushing than that of *Rambler* 177 of 'the
waste of life' (see above, p.90–1). There some men of intellectual ability
voluntarily choose to restrict the range of their minds, and suffer for it; here
female children are subjected to physical restraint and mental extinction.
Idler 13 fiercely exposes the girls' mother as a perverted anti-idler; but the
father, who cares for his own ease – 'the quiet of my house' – more than for
his daughters, is a classic idler, and is if anything the more repellent of the
two.[19]

Not all the *Idlers* have even a touch of sourness. No. 40, on newspaper
advertising, recalls no. 12 on announcements; but here Johnson stays
consistently within his persona, irrepressibly treating little things as great
ones. He is anxious that future fame be equitably 'distributed among the
tailors and boddice-makers of the present age'. Anyone composing an
advertisement 'should remember that his name is to stand in the same paper
with those of the King of Prussia, and the Emperor of Germany, and
endeavour to make himself worthy of such association'. Advertisements
must be carefully positioned, since the 'noblest objects may be so associated

as to be made ridiculous. The camel and dromedary themselves might have lost much of their dignity between "The True Flower of Mustard" and "The Original Daffy's Elixir"'. Camel and dromedary (which one advertisement had puffed as 'Creatures of surprising Magnitude'), tailor, king and advertiser, jostle each other promiscuously as candidates for eminence; the Idler is impartially ready to dignify them all (Y, II, 124–8). Johnson here, with Burke in mind, gently mocks the 'sublime in the little world which parallels that in the great', and through it the 'great' world's anxious, unworthy attention to worldly greatness in king and emperor; he also mocks the sententious giver of advice.[20]

The death of Johnson's mother (which gave rise to the famous *Idler* 41, on bereavement) seems to have turned him away from trivial studies for a few numbers. *Idler* 46, however, a complaint from a servant about her mistress's 'mean indulgence of petty malevolence' (Y, II, 145), opens a series which plays every possible variation on the single theme of pettiness. No. 47 describes a city wit who has renounced what he now calls 'the minutiae of a shop' (II, 148), hoping to increase his stature by idling about the theatre and attempting to write plays, no. 48 the idleness of busy triviality and making a fuss about nothing. No. 49 allows full rein to Will Marvel's hyperbolical narration of his journey and no. 50 comically reduces the hyperbole to an accurate scale. No. 51 (see below, pp.214–15) puts, with a seriousness unusual in the *Idler*, a question as to the utility of greatness in common life. No. 52 comes up with a surprise answer to this question in the exemplum of the Roman general who, being content to eat turnips, was therefore immune to temptation by the rewards of greatness.

Johnson's hankering for a larger scale than that of 'slight occasions', 'cursory business' (*Idler* 57: Y, II, 177) is nowhere more certain, though nowhere more covert, than in the *Idler* series. Many *Idlers* recoil from human pettiness, yet other responses are also voiced: some mock our puniness with perfect good humour, even enjoyment; some preach acceptance of it. The final essay, bringing to an end the 'series of trifles', once again sets them in the scale against great things, reminding us 'that an end must in time be put to every thing great as to every thing little' and of the overwhelming importance of the last hour of life.

In this frame of mind Johnson hopes his readers 'are already disposed to view every incident with seriousness, and improve it by meditation' (Y, II, 316). A modern reader may be in danger of finding this conclusion foreign to the spirit of the whole collection, inappropriate to the comedy which informs, for instance, the journey of Will Marvel (no. 49: Y, II, 152–5). In that essay Johnson restores the true scale with his closing sentence, which translates Will's 'dreadful story' into 'proper terms'; but no 'proper terms' can spoil our delight in the gusto for 'minute relation' of Will, who when he buttons up his cape and keeps going through a shower, feels that his 'soul

disdained to turn back. He did what the king of Prussia might have done.'
Yet it is true that the *Idler* views every incident with seriousness: its most
purely risible essays tend to be followed, as predictably as those in the
Rambler, by a careful exposure of the message which the joke might obscure;
the sequel to the Will Marvel essay reminds us of the damage done through
the commonplace temptation to make 'the picture . . . bigger than the life'
instead of seeing 'every thing as it is' (Y, II, 157–8). The degree to which the
series concentrates on trifles and our exaggeration of them is the key to
every important difference between it and Johnson's other periodical
essays, which will 'solve all the phaenomena' of the *Idler* (Y, VIII, 974). It
sticks to its theme with the same persistence that Johnson was to recommend to Boswell for speaking to Members of Parliament: 'you must
consider, that they do not listen much'. You 'must say the same thing over
and over again, in different words' (III, 224; IV, 74).

There is not necessarily any contradiction or paradox involved in
Johnson's at one time vindicating the importance of the minutiae of
existence, and at another time insisting on the danger of magnifying them,
any more than in his at one time satirizing and at another time sympathizing
with the narrowing effects of experience. His apparent inconsistency stems
from something other than mere whim or disputatiousness: an awareness of
the variability of standards of measurement and of the urgency of making a
proper choice. It was in the same conversation that he told Boswell, both
that 'There is nothing so minute or inconsiderable, that I would not rather
know it than not', and that a journal (which, however, should be kept 'fully
and minutely') ought 'not to mention such trifles as, that meat was too much
or too little done, or that the weather was fair or rainy' (II, 357–8). Little
things have their place, and should be kept there. On the one hand, Johnson
measures by what we may aspire to; on the other hand he is still generally
willing to settle for what is possible for little beings like ourselves. The
Idler, like Johnson's thinking in general, moves towards rather than away
from acceptance of human littleness; but its characteristic tone is not one of
acceptance.

Johnson excoriates pettiness most strongly when it verges on nothingness. He has a particular horror of *doing nothing*, of 'the vacuities of our
being', of 'chasms . . . of wide and continued vacuity, and . . . interstitial
spaces unfilled'. He concurs with the 'old peripatetick principle, that
"Nature abhors a Vacuum"'.[21] Many of his ironic and epigrammatic phrases
descriptive of some trivial action are demonstrably designed to show how
closely that action verges on nullity. His Euphelia, killing time in the
country ('I go out and return. . . . I walk in the great hall, and watch the
minute-hand upon the dial') is a direct descendant of Pope's rusticated
Teresa Blount who will 'Count the slow clock, and dine exact at noon'.[22]
But for Johnson such existential blanks are not confined to the country; they

recur in one after another of his fictional characters' summaries of their existence, as well as on a grander or public scale. His political writings from the 1740s to the 1770s employ almost identical phrases to express his dissatisfaction with English armies and navies which, like Euphelia, 'went out, did nothing, and came home'.[23] In other than military contexts a wider variety of language expresses a wider range of attitudes to little-more-than-nothingness, and a more sympathetic understanding of the forces which produce it. The French, he maintains, colonized Canada out of 'that impatience of doing nothing, to which mankind perhaps owe much of what is imagined to be effected by more splendid motives' (Y, X, 136). People who fail to make their mark in conversation are reduced to animal imitations (*Ram.* 188: Y, V, 224), or horseplay (*Ram.* 141: Y, IV, 388); boys resolved on painting the town red are reduced to marching 'up to a row of chairs, and demolish[ing] them for standing on the pavement' (*Ram.* 195: Y, V, 255); romantics are reduced to taking 'a wife like the wives of others' (*Ram.* 196: Y, V, 260) – all in order to have done *something*. Writers especially face the dilemma of 'the necessity of doing something, and the difficulty of finding something to do' (*Lives*, I, 216). The yawning threat is ever present of having nothing to do, nothing to think, as well as nothing to say; it is this which gives a note of desperation to the comically rhetorical outburst in *Idler* 24:

> To every act a subject is required. He that thinks, must think upon something. But tell me, ye that pierce deepest into nature, ye that take the widest surveys of life, inform me, kind shades of Malbranche and of Locke, what that something can be, which excites and continues thought in maiden aunts with small fortunes . . . in soldiers absent from their regiments, or in widows that have no children?

In this essay, one from which the Idler persona is absent, we feel the stirring of both 'impatience and exasperation' against those 'mortals whose life is certainly not active, for they do neither good nor evil . . . but rise in the morning, look round them till night in careless stupidity, go to bed and sleep, and rise again in the morning' (Y, II, 75, 76).

The suggestion of nihilism harks back to the sensibility of the late seventeenth century. Johnson's detailings of meaningless, repetitive action – 'go out and return', 'go to bed and sleep, and rise again' – recall Swift's Peter, Martin and Jack as men about town who 'Whor'd, and Slept, and Swore, and took Snuff', and also such poems as 'I Rise at Eleven', printed in Rochester's *Poems on Several Occasions* (1680), which describes a daily round both squalid and inane.[24] Johnson made some penetrating remarks on Rochester's paradoxical 'poem upon *Nothing*', calling it the 'strongest effort of his Muse'. It was fitting, for a poet whose biographer could find no other closing comment than one about what he *might* have been, to have 'chosen this barren topick for the boast of his fertility'. Johnson concluded his life of Rochester by quoting, in full, a Latin poem by Jean Passerat on the same subject, which seems to have been important to him, since Hawkins says he gave the text entirely from memory.[25] It is a most striking association between the brilliant young life thrown away, and the two productions of intellect exercised upon nullity.

Johnson expresses two opposed emotional responses to the 'interstitial spaces unfilled': on the one hand comic desperation, as in *Idler* 24's appeal to the shades of Malebranche and Locke; on the other, elegiac recognition, in which he commonly associates himself with those he writes about. Even without Hester Thrale's testimony that he portrayed himself in 'my old friend Sober', we should perceive the degree of sympathy with which he parallels 'poor' Sober's experiments in distillation, 'which he knows to be of no use', with the substance of his life: he 'sits and counts the drops as they come from his retort, and forgets that, while a drop is falling, a moment flies away'.[26] The pettiness of life and its brevity are topics logically allied though emotionally opposed. *Doing nothing*, which Euphelia writes about so plaintively and amusingly, was accorded its full weight of horror in *Rambler* 41, the essay preceding hers.

> Life, in which nothing has been done or suffered to distinguish one day from another, is to him that has passed it, as if it had never been, except that he is conscious how ill he has husbanded the great deposit of his Creator. (Y, III, 225)

This passage, like others in which Johnson contemplates the vacuities of life, gives the impression that he was more strongly repelled by the idea of passing our time in nothingness than in wickedness. In the following sentence he tells us that: 'Life, made memorable by crimes, and diversified thro' its several periods by wickedness, is indeed easily reviewed, but reviewed only with horror and remorse.' The second sentence is less strongly phrased than the first, which echoes *Ecclesiasticus* ('as if it had never been')[27] and in its last clause ('how ill . . . Creator') enacts the horror and remorse that the second sentence only mentions. Here Johnson's plangent sense of life's emptiness is modified by Christian belief in it as 'great deposit'. Towards the end of the *Rambler* he expresses, just as hauntingly, a view much closer to that of the ancients:

> We know . . . that we must soon lie down in the grave with the forgotten multitudes of former ages, and yield our place to others, who, like us, shall be driven awhile, by hope or fear, about the surface of the earth, and then like us be lost in the shades of death. (No. 203: Y, V, 294)

For this kind of littleness, neither reformation nor palliation can be attempted. Johnson here at least approaches the celestial viewpoint of Scipio Africanus, a view which comprehends past generations and the whole surface of the earth (see above, pp. 25–6); but he avoids the detachment of Cicero's mouthpiece by his repeated *we, we, like us, like us*. Whether Johnson vindicates, reprehends, or merely points out the littleness of humanity, he seldom omits to include himself. Hence the personal tone of even the most formal essays; hence the complex dramatization of others, in which a character who comments is also commented upon; and hence at last the self-mockery of the letters to Hester Thrale which accept the charge of amounting not only to little but to nothing.

6

COMPETITION

The hostility perpetually exercised between one man and
another, is caused by the desire of many for that which
only few can possess. Every man would be rich, powerful,
and famous; yet fame, power and riches, are only the
names of relative conditions, which imply the obscurity,
dependance, and poverty of greater numbers.

(*Rambler* 183)

THE PETTINESS which Johnson mocks most vehemently is that which
struggles, like Quisquilius and Will Marvel and electioneering politicians,
to surpass others. The theme of competitive struggle to excel holds such an
important place in his writings that it is amazing to find it still awaiting
adequate critical attention.

Johnson's own penchant for competition, for defying littleness and
grasping at achievement, impressed most of those who knew him and is still
a vivid part of his legend. Walter Jackson Bate finds 'a side of Johnson's own
temperament' in the 'scene of headlong competition' which opens *The
Vanity of Human Wishes*.[1] Boswell loved to pit Johnson against a promising
conversational opponent. Hester Thrale places a group of anecdotes
together: how his cousin Cornelius Ford, coming on an inscription
recording a famous leap, immediately emulated it; how Johnson took pride
in his uncle Andrew 'who kept the ring in Smithfield (where they wrestled
and boxed) for a whole year, and never was thrown or conquered'; and how
he himself, like Cornelius Ford, performed a leap in response to an assumed
challenge.[2] Sir John Hawkins wrote of Johnson's university days, 'He had
at this time a great emulation, to call it by no worse a name, to excel his
competitors in literature'; of his early time in London, 'Johnson was an
adventurer in the wide world, and had his fortunes to make'; of his
maturity, 'he looked on every dignitary under a bishop . . . as occupying a

station to which himself had a better title, and, if his inferior in learning or mental endowments, treated him as little better than an usurper'; and of his criticism, that he noted Shakespeare's faults 'with such a degree of asperity as critics discover' towards a rival.[3] A modern writer sees the life of Milton as exhuming a dead titan in order to engage in a perverse battle for mastery.[4]

Johnson, who praised as noble the advice to be 'ever . . . pre-eminent above all' (see above, p.1), relished any effort in actual life to follow it. This is shown by his eagerness that the newly 'discovered' Fanny Burney (far too modest and retiring for a conversational combatant) should 'fly at the eagle' (the reigning bluestocking Elizabeth Montagu) and 'Down with her, Burney! – down with her! – spare her not! – attack her, fight her, and down with her at once!' He did not hide his self-identification with his pupil: 'You are a rising wit, and she is at the top; and when I was beginning the world, and was nothing and nobody, the joy of my life was to fire at all the established wits! and then everybody loved to halloo me on.' A few years later he staged a repeat performance with Fanny in the Montagu role and Susy Thrale in Fanny's; he had already used similar language to Charlotte Lennox about her supposed assault on Shakespeare.[5] (As well as savouring such combats, he perhaps thought of them as instruments for establishing truth: in *Idler* 25 he classes 'mistaken notions of superiority' among failings which will necessarily 'be brushed away by the wing of time': Y, II, 79–80.) All this serves as contrasting background to the deep fear and distaste for competition which he regularly evinces.

The *Dictionary* includes neither *competitive* (apparently a later coinage) nor *compete*, which dates from 1620 (*OED*). *Competition* for Johnson still carried a strong sense of its origins in Latin *con* and *petitio*: a legal cause pleaded against an opponent. He defines *competition* as the 'act of endeavouring to gain what another endeavours to gain at the same time; rivalry; contest'. The definition can do little to show just how fundamentally Johnson believed that what one person endeavours to gain, another *will* be endeavouring to gain at the same time; but his *Dictionary* entries for this word, and for *emulate*, *excel*, *superiour* and their derivatives, do reflect the complex of ideas which he associates with competition.

Under *superiority* ('Pre-eminence; the quality of being greater or higher than another in any respect') Johnson quotes Stillingfleet quoting Bellarmine about adoration of a superior and concluding, 'mere excellency without *superiority* doth not require any subjection but only estimation'. This distinction, though etymologically suspect, would, if it were present to the minds of those who compete for superiority, eliminate the impulse to cry 'down with' a rival; but, as we shall see, Johnson usually writes as if he disagreed with Stillingfleet, as if both superiority and excellence entail the subjection of inferiors. Such subjection is assumed in his second quotation under *superiority*, from *The Spectator*: 'The person who advises, does in that particular exercise a *superiority* over us, thinking us defective in our conduct or understanding.' The fact that to accept advice is a tacit admission of inferiority helps to explain humanity's universal unwillingness to do so, a point which Johnson himself made more than once in his moral essays.[6]

Johnson defines *emulate* first as 'To rival; to propose as one to be equalled or excelled'; under *emulation* he quotes Sprat: 'Aristotle allows that some *emulation* may be good, and may be found in some good men; yet envy he utterly condemns, as wicked in itself, and only to be found in wicked minds.' This distinction was echoed by Pope,

> Enry, to which th'ignoble mind's a slave,
> Is emulation in the learn'd or brave,[7]

and by Swift

> Her End when Emulation misses,
> She turns to Envy, Stings and Hisses.[8]

Johnson himself, however, does not always observe it: 'Where there is emulation there will be vanity, and where there is vanity there will be folly' (*Lives*, III, 351–2). Johnson particularly hated envy, and his sermons often dwell on it. Bate found 'either the word itself or the idea' in 57 *Ramblers* (more than 25 per cent), and commented that the theme 'crawls like a tortoise through the moral essays'. According to Hawkins, Johnson 'was candid enough to confess he was subject to' envy and 'laboured through his life to eradicate' it.[9] He therefore had reason to uphold Aristotle's and Sprat's distinction, yet he frequently links competition and envy, as in *Ramblers* 165 and 183 (Y, V, 112, 197).

Johnson defines *to excel* in terms which collect together his various physical images for intellectual or spiritual superiority, and also hint at subjection of what is excelled. As a transitive verb it means to 'outgo in good qualities; to surpass', as intransitive to 'have good qualities in a great degree; to be eminent', and in 1773 'to be great' replacing the tautologous 'to be excellent'. The *Dictionary*'s first three definitions for *eminence* are physical ('1. Loftiness; height. 2. Summit; highest part. 3. A part rising above the rest'), so that to *excel* means to go further, faster, or higher than another, or to be great. Johnson's view of greatness as the goal of human striving will be discussed later; here I want to discuss his views of the strife itself, and of the strivers' feelings towards each other. Johnson often regards success, like his speaker in *Rambler* 165, in terms of defeated competitors:

> They who once persued me, were now satisfied to escape from me; and they who had before thought me presumptuous in hoping to overtake them, had now their utmost wish, if they were permitted at no great distance quietly to follow me. (Y, V, 113)

The idea of human beings as basically competitive animals had become a familiar one since it achieved notoriety in the writings of Hobbes, who believed that the desire for power can never rest satisfied, since power includes the means of retaining and increasing power, and that one person's power can only be increased by lessening that of another.[10] In this Johnson's opinions coincide with those of Hobbes:

> The same disposition which inclines any man to raise himself to a superiority over others, will naturally excite the same desires of greater elevation while he sees any superiour to himself. There is therefore no hope that, by pursuing greatness, any man can be happy, or, at least, this happiness must be confined to one, because only one can be without a superiour. (Sermon 14: Y, XIV, 152)

The Restoration writers, in the wake of Hobbes's stirring doctrines, applied imagery of hawking and hunting, such as Johnson used in his exhortation to Fanny Burney, to every field of human rivalry. Although Hobbes's view of all individuals as each other's natural enemies did as much as anything to make his reputation suspect to his own and to succeeding generations, although the various theories of benevolence reflected a widely felt need to confute his views, still the belief that humans are basically competitive continued to hold its own even among earnest Christians.

In mid-eighteenth century Richardson left it to Anna Howe (whose whole-hearted enlistment in the sex war gives her a faintly Restoration aura) to remark, on the topic of men, women and power, that 'All the animals in the creation are more or less in a state of hostility with each other'. Yet even his exemplary Clarissa, unwittingly following Aristotle, recognizes that 'Noble minds, emulative of perfection . . . may be allowed a little generous envy', as well as that little minds, from some 'malignant principle . . . wish to bring down the more worthy characters to their own low level'.[11] Johnson remembered how Hogarth saw rivalry as the basis of all professional relationships.[12]

Isaac Watts, admired by Johnson as a real-life exemplary figure, presented the very struggle for salvation in terms of competition and 'holy ambition'. Even in heaven, Watts stated categorically and repeatedly, achievement will be recognized: 'St Paul, the greatest of the apostles' will reach a heavenly rank 'superior to that of the crucified thief' and King David one superior to his own infant child; Deborah the prophetess will sit higher than Dorcas the seamstress, and Dorcas in turn higher than Rahab the penitent harlot. It is therefore worth contending in 'the christian race . . . for some of the brighter prizes, some of the richer crowns of glory': 'methinks I would not have you contented with the lowest seat there'.[13] The issue of competition for the highest place unexpectedly sets the pious Watts in tune with the worldly Lord Chesterfield, who deduces the ambition to excel from the need to escape from mere animality:

> Every rational being (I take it for granted) proposes to himself some object more important than mere respiration and obscure animal existence. He desires to distinguish himself among his fellow-creatures.[14]

Johnson sounds most Hobbesian in *London* and in certain *Ramblers*. *London* presents a vivid picture of unrestrained competitiveness: on the rocks of Scotland some survive hunger but some do not (lines 9–12); in the city one must prey parasitically on a patron or be preyed on oneself. The fell attorney and fiery fop, even the sober trader and silken courtiers, are all in their different ways out for victory (lines 16, 226, 162–5). The poet puts forward no hope of community outside the struggle for eminence, but only enduring 'rage' against one's more successful fellows (lines 256–63).

Rambler 33, said to be Johnson's favourite among his allegorical fictions (Y, III, 179, n.1), gives a (fabulous) explanation of the origin of competition. Primitive ages were ruled by the gentle deity Rest, until

> pride and envy broke into the world, and brought with them a new standard of wealth; for men . . . now rated their demands, not by the calls of nature, but by the plenty of others. . . . Now only one could be happy, because only one could have most, and that one was always in danger, lest the same arts by which he had supplanted others should be practised upon himself. (Y, III, 179–80)

The situation allegorized is that which Hobbes saw as natural to humanity, and which Locke described in *The Second Treatise of Government* (1690: V, 36–7).

Johnson assumes the universality of Hobbesian competition for wealth or material benefits. The *Dictionary* sees *poor*, *weak*, *obscure* and their derivatives as signifying privation, and employs negative comparison to define them as it does not for *rich*, *powerful*, *famous*, or similar words. His writings, while they do not ignore the competition for riches, are more interested in competition for fame, fame of every sort, from the pettiest to the longest-lasting, most widely disseminated, and most deeply revered. Everyone, says *Rambler* 193, 'resolves' to be praised, and 'pants for the highest eminence within his view', whether that view extends to the praise of 'all ages and nations', or of a county, or of a club, or only of himself (Y, V, 244). This essay presents the difference between petty and vast ambitions as one of degree only, not of kind.

The only thing more desired, in Johnson's view, than fame itself is that of which fame is only the outward sign or by-product – the state called superiority, excellence, distinction, being the best or the greatest – a state which scarcely anybody, no matter how virtuous or prudent, will decline (*Ram.* 49, 114: Y, III, 265; IV, 241). Each *Dictionary* definition of this state (unlike those of the simple *fame*) embodies a comparative or superlative, recognizing that it is to be attained only by competition, by the outgoing of somebody, or everybody, else. Every description of it in Johnson's writings employs imagery of brightness, magnitude, height, strength, or swiftness – qualities whose absence is deprivation. To excel is to be light where others are dark, large where others are small, high where others are low. The goals which Johnson assumes his readers to be interested in (and which his biographers tell us he sought, and which he makes his fictional characters seek) are those which to attain is to prevent their attainment by somebody else. As Sermon 12 trenchantly puts it, '*the happiness of a few* must arise from *the misery of many*' (Y, XIV, 132). This is the very nature of all competitive achievement.

Our own century confesses its uneasiness about such achievement in the way in which it uses the word *elitist*; Johnson's character Seged faces the same problem when he observes with sorrow the anxiety and jealousy caused by his offer of prizes for those who should entertain him best. Seged loses his nerve and

> thinking . . . it would be cruel to oppress any heart with sorrow, he declared that all had pleased him alike, and dismissed all with presents of equal value.
> Seged soon saw that his caution had not been able to avoid offence. They who had believed themselves secure of the highest prizes, were not pleased to be levelled with the crowd; and . . . they departed unsatisfied, because they were honoured with no distinction, and wanted an opportunity to triumph in the mortification of their opponents. (*Ram.* 205: Y, V, 303)

Seged, recoiling from the expected 'malignity' of the losers, draws upon himself the malignity of the winners. He exemplifies the impossibility of opting out of the struggle for superiority, as does the unbearably insipid lady in *Idler* 100, *née* Miss Gentle, who considers it ill-natured to 'distinguish excellence from defect' (Y, II, 308).

Johnson's emotional response to competitiveness was a double one, like so many of his attitudes, because it was dramatic. While Boswell rejoiced in Johnson's triumphs, but Hawkins was inclined to sympathize with the defeated rivals, Johnson himself entered imaginatively into two different sets of feelings, those of the winner and the loser, though the latter required an act of both imagination and will. In Sermon 14, endeavouring to show the rewards of competition as hollow, Johnson suggested that even the one who proves superior to *all* the rest 'must surely feel his enjoyments very frequently disturbed, when he remembers by how many the station which he possesses is envied and coveted' (Y, XIV, 152). Elsewhere, however, he generally confesses the even more unpalatable likelihood that the superior person will *enjoy* the envy of others. Unlike Chesterfield, who began urging his son to excel his fellows as early as his seventh year (e.g. 30 September 1738), Johnson felt that to praise a child for excelling was not only to excite 'emulation and comparisons of superiority' but even to 'make brothers and sisters hate each other' (Boswell, I, 46). The hatred generated is reciprocal. In writing as well as in conversation Johnson uses the first person plural, to convince his readers that we are none of us immune either from 'that scorn with which the universal love of praise incites us all to drive feeble competitors out of our way' (*Ram*. 189: Y, V, 226), or from disappointed resentment when we are overtaken (*Ram*. 172: Y, V, 146–7). In the latter case he uses the first person plural (introduced midway in the fourth paragraph) to shock those readers who may have begun to identify with the front runner. The temptation to malignity awaits both winners and losers.

At the same time, competing is natural and human. Not to fight is to remain nothing and nobody, one of those who 'never ventured to excel, lest they should unfortunately fail' (*Ram*. 129: Y, IV, 323), or the despicable creature whose mask Johnson assumed in starting *The Idler*:

> Scarcely any name can be imagined from which less envy or competition is to be dreaded. The Idler has no rivals or enemies. . . . though such as tread the same track of life, fall commonly into jealousy and discord, Idlers are always found to associate in peace, and he who is most famed for doing nothing, is glad to meet another as idle as himself. (Y, II, 4)

Even here, as in illustrating *emulation*, and as in *Rambler* 165 and Sermon 14, Johnson has linked competition with envy and malevolence. If he makes the apathy of the Idler repellent, this is because he wishes to provide a contrast as shocking as the shocking vision, reiterated throughout his works, of the energy of competition.

This constant, universal struggle forms part of the background to Johnson's view of the human condition, something to be taken for granted, referred to as a given, even a truism, rather than a debatable question. Everyone, 'however unactive or insignificant, discovers [the inclination] of representing his life as distinguished by extraordinary events' (*Ram*. 198: Y, V, 266). Therefore those unable to rise pull others down (*Ram*. 76: Y, IV, 35), and those unable to aim at distinction aim, like Will Marvel, at a false representation of their actions as distinguished. Attempts at superiority engross persons both low and high, in situations both comic and serious. In the anonymity of a stage-coach journey 'the general ambition of superiority' is freely indulged by a nobleman's butler, a broker's clerk, a cookshop keeper: 'When the first ceremony was dispatched, we sat silent for a long time, all employed in collecting importance into our faces, and endeavouring to strike reverence and submission into our companions'; then each attempts to impose upon the others with a 'fictitious excellence' and a transparently aggrandized account of his or her station in life. Johnson writes this essay (*Adv.* 84: Y, II, 407–11) in the guise of a correspondent, which permits the use of the first person: 'Thus we travelled on four days with malevolence perpetually increasing, and without any endeavour but to outvie each other in superciliousness and neglect.' The only one to preserve her dignity is a woman who makes no 'struggle for distinction or superiority' and so has 'assumed no character', who is made by the recurrent use of *we* to figure as the exception, not the norm.

Since no discussion as to its existence or importance is necessary, Johnson scatters his remarks about competitiveness as asides in discussions of other topics. The ostensible subject of *Adventurer* 84 is deceit or disguise; underlying this as its root cause is the general ambition of superiority. In a discursive, more generalized essay, Johnson identifies 'the general dream in which we all slumber out our time' of one day leaving 'all those competitors behind, who are now rejoicing like [ourselves] in the expectation of victory', before he gets to grips with his subject, which is the folly of trusting to schemes for the future (*Adv.* 69: Y, II, 390). *Rambler* 164, whose topic is the way in which the illustrious serve as examples or patterns, opens by remarking that competitive ambition excludes nobody, 'however hopeless his pretensions may appear to all but himself' (Y, V, 106). In an allegory of life as a voyage 'many sunk unexpectedly while they were . . . insulting those whom they had left behind' (*Ram.* 102: Y, IV, 180).

The mutual contest has almost infinite fields in which to exercise itself. Different professions and occupations despise each other (*Adv.* 128). Different geographical areas vie with each other (*Journey*: Y, IX, 45). Individuals rival each other in every particular occupation: scholarship, sport, dress, moneymaking, writing and conversation, even in folly (*Ram.* 57: Y, III, 309). The

ambitious man has at all times been eager of wealth and power; but these hopes have been gratified in some countries by supplicating the people, and in others by flattering the prince: honour in some states has been only the reward of military atchievements, in others it has been gained by noisy turbulence and popular clamours. (*Adv.* 95: Y, II, 428)

Even unselfish 'care for the interests of friends, or attention to the establishment of a family, generates contest and competition, enmity and malevolence' (Sermon 3: Y, XIV, 32).

Almost every distortion or perversity of behaviour and deterioration in character can stem from a single cause: pleasure in the defeat of rivals. Lady Bustle the champion housekeeper (see above, p.92) draws her satisfaction from making others look mean, in exactly the same way as the Indian shepherd Raschid, who wished to have the Ganges diverted through his land while his neighbour Hamet wished only for 'a little brook', and who 'pleased himself with the mean appearance that Hamet would make in the presence of the proprietor of the Ganges' (*Ram*. 38: Y, III, 210). The conversationalist 'gratifies the pride of airy petulance' with victory which Johnson describes in terms of a fencing match or duel (*Adv*. 85: Y, II, 415). The collector of fossils 'when he has stocked his own repository, grieves that the stones which he has left behind him should be picked up by another. The florist . . . repines that his rival's beds enjoy the same showers and sun shine with his own' (*Adv*. 128: Y, II, 477).

The most violently competitive arenas, and also most damaging to the disposition, are those in which success involves becoming some kind of star: the arenas of public power in Johnson's early biographies and *The Vanity of Human Wishes*, but in the essays more usually those frequented by wits, authors and social darlings of both sexes. Johnson's moral essays frequently draw a parallel between the psychology of beauties and that of what we now call academics. Each has a self-centredness, a narcissism, which the male world regards as peculiarly feminine and the non-intellectual world as peculiarly highbrow.

> The friendship of students and of beauties is for the most part equally sincere, and equally durable: as both depend for happiness on the regard of others, on that of which the value arises merely from comparison, they are both exposed to perpetual jealousies, and both incessantly employed in schemes to intercept the praises of each other. (*Adv*. 45: Y, II, 360–1)

Instances accumulate. In his early poetry Johnson describes beauties as extending their reign despite malice and envy, or seeing 'conquer'd crowds confess [their] sway', in a phrase that anticipates *The Vanity of Human Wishes* (line 244). He describes the young author, in a poem also later reincarnated in *The Vanity of Human Wishes*, as scorning the 'dull croud' while he feels 'Secure of praise from nations yet unborn' (Y, VI, 83, 36, 72–3). Victoria (aptly named, though her conquests are later cut short by smallpox) passes through a childhood in which 'Mr. Ariet used to reproach his other scholars with my performances on the harpsichord', to her first sally into society, where her triumph is 'made more pleasing by the apparent envy of those whom my presence exposed to neglect' (*Ram*. 130: Y, IV, 328–9). Any public library will remind us of the analogous pleasures of authors: 'how often wit has exulted in the eternal infamy of his antagonists' (*Ram*. 106: Y, IV, 200). The acrimonious rivalries of editors and commentators make a blot on the fame of Shakespeare (Y, VII, 93–100). Having occasion to note the endeavours of Sir Thomas Browne and his polite critic Sir Kenelm Digby 'to grow bright by the obscuration of each other', Johnson introduces this incident with a general picture of an author entering the lists to fight for fame (*Works*, VI, 478–9). A combat held in 'the lists' as public, formalized, ostentatious; Johnson often places the contests of both wits and beauties in this chivalric and unreal setting.

But Johnson's attacks on competitiveness, like his attacks on pettiness, do not exclude a sympathetic understanding of causes. The author is necessarily competitive,

> considered as a kind of general challenger, whom every one has a right to attack; since he quits the common rank of life, steps forward beyond the lists, and offers his merit to the publick judgment. (*Ram*. 93: Y, IV, 133–4)

Writers have depicted writers as especially attentive to ranking order, because they know their own profession better than others, and because its rivalries are publicly visible; but such rivalry, 'diffused thro' all human nature, [mingling] itself with every species of ambition and desire of praise', embraces also the partisanship of readers, who are therefore no better than those they read (Y, III, 216–7). Johnson subjectively, self-revealingly, participates in the feelings of those who, aspiring to notice, see all around them as rivals and enemies.

In *Rambler* 15 (Y, III, 80–4) a girl complains that the ambition which she brought to London, 'to extend my victories over those who might give more honour to the conqueror', is frustrated by the current passion for occupying all social gatherings with cards. Having hoped to excel in wit, she disingenuously complains 'of want of opportunity for thinking . . . a condemnation . . . to perpetual ignorance', and sees it as 'a contrivance to level all distinctions of nature . . . to sink life into a tedious uniformity'. The card-players, she says, enviously refuse to join her in the contest of charm and fashion, at which she would excel. Johnson endorses her complaint, and agrees with her that the craze for cards 'threatens . . . to destroy all distinctions . . . to crush all emulation'. In his own persona Johnson here presents attitudes essentially identical to Cleora's, though with an extra twist. Mr Rambler would like to change the fashion in periodical journalism as Cleora would like to change the fashion in social gatherings. Each blames other people for combining competitiveness (in those others' field of excellence) with mean refusal to play in the critic's own field. Mr Rambler, however, tells Cleora that complaint is useless: in each case the people they criticize will return on them the accusation of envying the elevation they cannot reach and seeking to bring others down to their own level. By such elaborately devious means does Johnson both associate himself with and distinguish himself from the would-be competitive beauty, both admit to entertaining envy and complain that it is entertained against him.

For Johnson it is writers, if anybody, who may sometimes compete acceptably with their peers, with emulation rather than envy. He is prepared to praise colleges and academic societies for inciting competition and stimulating honest rivalry. In the life of Pope he writes approvingly that excellence is achieved by following a path begun by 'some accident which excited ardour and emulation' (*Lives*, III, 174). In *Rambler* life-stories such accidents often lead not to excellence but rather to ardour misdirected and ultimately dimmed. But writing more generally, as in *Adventurer* 45 and *Rambler* 154, Johnson recognizes some beneficial effects of competition. Individuals will be urged on by 'impatience of inferiority . . . and the scorn of obscurity while the rest are illustrious'. Although students may be, like beauties, insincere or treacherous in friendship, their 'emulous diligence' cannot fairly be disapproved by anyone hoping for the 'great attainments' to which it may lead. Indeed, in the essentially individualistic realm of literature, the force of rivalry may even serve to forward co-operative achievement (Y, II, 360–1; V, 57).

Johnson delights in pointing out to his readers that they are involved with him in his own struggle for excellence. The third *Rambler* reminds them that if they allow him to advise them, they 'must allow that he from whom they are to learn is more knowing than themselves' (Y, III, 15). The second had already put forward the proposition that 'Censure is willingly indulged, because it always implies some superiority'. The reader is likely to take this at first sight as ascribing the willing indulgence to the censured, and to register immediate, almost instinctive, disagreement: he or she does *not* willingly indulge assumptions of superiority by others! Then as the eye pursues the sentence further, it becomes clear (as a reader familiar with Johnson will expect) that it is the censurers and not the censured who are willing, who 'please themselves with imagining that they have made a deeper search, or wider survey, than others' (Y, III, 9). It is hard to believe that Johnson perpetrated this ambiguity unconsciously, and failed to notice it in two careful revisions of *The Rambler* for collected publication (1752 and 1756: Y, III, xxxivff.). Rather we must suppose that he designed this trap, to dramatize for us the difference in interest between writer and reader. He calls out our own unwillingness to be censured, in order to compel us to notice the author's willingness to censure, his motivating wish (beyond or apart from more creditable motives) for 'opportunities of triumphant exultation' (Y, III, 10). The moralist may 'please himself, and his auditors, with learned lectures on the vanity of life'; but he pleases his auditors in a different way from the way he pleases himself. This is not because he differs from them in kind – indeed he is 'acting upon principles which he has in common with the illiterate and unenlightened, angry and pleased like the lowest of the vulgar' – but because he differs from them in relation to his writings, which keep him 'swelling with the applause which he has gained by proving that applause is of no value' (*Ram.* 54: Y, III, 289–90). Johnson's ambiguous 'willingly' in *Rambler* 2 reminds us of two things: that writers are separated from their readers through the desire for applause which their readers cannot share, and that they nonetheless need the readers to supply it.

He repeats his message about dependence on an audience in *Idler* 75, which he wrote with his own life 'in his eye'. Gelaleddin, planning to revisit his native place, as Johnson had just done, says: 'I shall see the eyes of those who predicted my greatness sparkling with exultation, and the faces of those that once despised me, clouded with envy, or counterfeiting kindness by artificial smiles' (Y, II, 233). Gelaleddin's dual expectation, the delight of his friends and discomfiture of his enemies, echoes the general statement of *Rambler* 203: the scholar raised 'from obscurity, looks round in vain from his exaltation for his old friends or enemies, whose applause or mortification would heighten his triumph' (Y, V, 293). Paradoxically, the desire to rise above the common herd links people in two ways with their fellows: in the deadly relationship of rivalry, and in courtship of those who may adjudge and testify success. Johnson writes sardonically in *Rambler* 106: 'An assurance of unfading laurels, and immortal reputation, is the settled reciprocation of civility between amicable writers' (Y, IV, 200). No-one can attain superiority on his own, but needs 'the concurrence of those, who are for a time content to be counted his inferiours'. The possessor of superiority is far from exempt from dependence on others (Sermon 12: Y, XIV, 134); as royalty requires subjects and authors require readers, excellence requires people to be excelled.

Throughout his writings, Johnson mentions competition in conjunction with community. Success and failure, he writes sorrowfully in the preface to the *Dictionary*, lose their meaning in the absence of people to please (*Works*, V, 51). He does not usually, though he may occasionally, imply that competition is the harsh fact, community the unattainable ideal. What I call community, the dependence of human beings on each other for their most important satisfactions, is in his view as inescapable a truth as competitiveness. It is this fact, rather than a moralistic desire to show them punished, that causes Johnson to represent most of his successful competitors as unsatisfied with their success.

To recall this truth may throw some light on one of the most puzzlingly ambivalent of all Johnson's moral essays, *Adventurer* 81, which tells the story of the Admirable Crichton.[15] It has affinities with narratives to be discussed later under the headings of heroism or greatness, but it is pre-eminently an exemplum of the competitive drive in action.

Johnson modelled his tale of Crichton's life chiefly on George Mackenzie's *Lives and Characters Of the most Eminent Writers of the Scots Nation*, III (1722). Behind Mackenzie (among other sources which he details with scholarly precision) lies Sir Thomas Urquhart's *The Jewel* (1651), which he calls 'fustian and bombastick' and which reads farcically though framed as heartfelt adulation. There seems to be no evidence that Johnson had read Urquhart except for passages quoted by Mackenzie (if he had, his natural combativeness might well have impelled him to condemn Crichton outright). He performs on Mackenzie his usual masterly job of tidying and condensing; he removes tedious reiterations of praise (as well as a reported suggestion that Crichton might have been Antichrist), and he produces an effect of blankness and amaze quite different from Mackenzie's enthusiasm.[16]

The first eight paragraphs of the essay, which introduce the actual biography, lead us to expect a story of different and less intensely competitive greatness. Horace's *Nil desperandum* stands as a motto; it prepares us to see Crichton's achievements as proving 'that there are few things above human hope' and encouraging us to 'imagine ourselves equal to great undertakings'. The germ of Johnson's essay, in fact, probably lies in the desire to confute Joannes Imperialis, as quoted by Mackenzie, who called Crichton 'rather a shining Particle of the divine Nature and Majesty, than a Model of what humane Nature and Industry can attain to'. Johnson sets out to vindicate human potential. He argues that while one who underrates his own abilities is uncompetitive and inoffensive, and one who overrates himself *in comparison with others* 'must be always invidious and offensive', the desirable option is to rate one's own powers highly in relation *not* to the powers of others but to 'great attempts and great performances'. To adopt a less competitive, more nearly absolute scale, he says, gives the best chance of succeeding, or at the very least of failing 'with honour' (each of which things Crichton does in an unusual degree). 'Every man should, therefore, endeavour to maintain in himself, a favourable opinion of the powers of the human mind', which may be exemplified by Crichton's 'various endowments, and contrarieties of excellence', but which are in *everyone* 'perhaps . . . greater than they appear'.

Crichton is introduced as a marker on the scale of human potential, as one whose prowess may spur us on to 'honest emulation' (though not to competition) and clinch the argument that we do well to think well of our powers. His 'extensive abilities', Johnson says, have dignified humanity in general. This discussion implicitly differentiates him from the friendly uncompetitive under-rater of himself and, we might suppose, from the offensive challenger of the claims of others. Yet he emerges, in the story to come, as nothing like a non-competitor, nothing much like a benefactor of humanity, but as very much like the 'invidious and offensive' self-booster. He is, it turns out, one who consistently measures himself against rivals rather than against 'great undertakings'.

The 'appellation of the Admirable Crichton' is one that already implies such superiority as we might expect, from *Ramblers* 2 and 3, to be not willingly indulged. It is possible that Johnson found this appellation provoking. We should not, like Hawkins with his criticism of Shakespeare, be too quick to diagnose an attitude of rivalry, but an attitude of admiration comes hard to Johnson. 'Contempt and admiration are equally incident to narrow minds' (*Adv.* 67: Y, II, 386). Ambivalence accompanies Johnson's final sinking of criticism in admiration before the style of *Paradise Lost*, and, more pertinently here, his designation of Milton as 'like other heroes . . . to be admired rather than imitated'. Horace's *nil admirari* was a maxim with him – and could have been linked in his mind with the *nil desperandum* which heads this essay.[17]

For those who have not read the adulation of Urquhart, Johnson gives the fullest credit possible to what is admirable in Crichton. Leaving incredible reports aside, he says, we must allow this Scotsman to have been among 'the favourites of nature', a prodigy, 'eminently beautiful' as well as athletic, brilliant, and a master of 'stupendous' learning. He asserted his superiority in every 'accomplishment in which it becomes a gentleman to excel', dancing, 'drawing and painting . . . both vocal and instrumental music'; 'at a public match of tilting he bore away the ring upon his lance fifteen times together'; he played fifteen parts 'in an Italian comedy composed by himself'. More crucially, he vanquished a hitherto undefeated and homicidal gladiator who was, in a rare comment added by Johnson to Mackenzie's facts, travelling the world, 'according to the barbarous custom of that age, as a general challenger'.

Crichton, however, sallies forth to his specifically intellectual exploits in a championship spirit precisely analogous to that of tilting or duelling. Arriving in Paris from Scotland at the age of twenty he

affixed on the gate of the college . . . a kind of challenge to the learned . . . to dispute with him on a certain day, offering to his opponents, whoever they should be [as a duellist offers choice of weapons], the choice of ten languages and of all the faculties and sciences. On the day appointed three thousand auditors assembled, when four doctors of the church and fifty masters appeared against him.

Having defeated them all to 'repeated acclamations', and notched up similar victories at Padua and Rome 'in the presence of the pope and cardinals', he initiated a new class of contest:

He afterwards published another challenge, in which he declared himself ready to detect the errors of Aristotle and all his commentators, either in the common forms of logic, or in any which his antagonists should propose of a hundred different kinds of verse.

The phrase 'according to the barbarous custom of that age' seems to apply as well to Crichton's own career as peripatetic challenger as to that of the gladiator, who in his course of victory appears almost as a sinister alter-ego of Crichton.[18] Like Mackenzie, Johnson places the intellectual combats before the gladiatorial one, so that any allusions must be retrospective; unlike Mackenzie he uses the word 'masters' for beaten pugilists as well as beaten scholars. The obvious difference is that the fighter has killed three men and made three widows; Crichton looks 'on his sanguinary success with indignation' (Johnson's addition), and after killing him divides the prize money among the widows. This victory, Crichton's only sanguinary one, is also the only one in the story which approximates to those of traditional heroes, like Hercules or the knights-errant, in ridding the world of a menace and avenging the downtrodden.

But the effect of heroic benevolence is contaminated by the prize-fighting comparison; and Crichton's bloodless victories in dispute come in Johnson's account (quite unlike those of his predecessors) to look doubly purposeless, increasingly unlike 'great undertakings' or those exploits which serve one's country, as the double comparison is retrospectively set up, with the destructive triumphs of the prize-fighter and with Crichton's heroic triumph over him. Johnson preserves several extravagant grace-notes. One of the defeated antagonists says that 'a hundred years, passed without food or sleep, would not be sufficient for the attainment' of Crichton's learning; what Johnson calls his 'performance' at Padua concludes 'with an oration . . . in commendation of ignorance'; he spends so much time 'in the interval between his challenge and disputation at Paris . . . at cards, dice, and tennis' as to cause scandal. In Johnson's spare and non-explanatory account, such details no longer suggest childish delight in legendary flamboyance, but rather ironic amusement at a sportsman for whom the ultimate sport is one-up-manship. To see Crichton as driven by the rage for superiority would be not a necessary but an entirely natural consequence of his epithet and his legend, especially for one who, like Johnson, both deeply respected and feared the competitive instinct.

Crichton's meeting with the final challenge of death must be considered before we can either draw conclusions or say there are none to be drawn, according to the advice of Solon to Croesus which Johnson more than once quoted or cited.[19] Johnson here is close to Mackenzie and in complete contradiction of Urquhart. His Crichton, by now tutor to the Duke of Mantua's son, is ambushed by six masked men during a Carnival night:

Neither his courage nor skill in this exigence deserted him; he opposed them with such activity and spirit, that he soon dispersed them, and disarmed their leader, who throwing off his mask, discovered himself to be the prince his pupil. Crichton falling on his knees, took his own sword by the point and presented it to the prince; who immediately seized it, and instigated as some say by jealousy, according to others, only by drunken fury and brutal resentment, thrust him through the heart.

One may feel it would take a Solon to trace the implications of this ending. Its circumstances are both as petty and as dubious as those Johnson gives to Charles XII's death in *The Vanity of Human Wishes*. Crichton loses none of his old, swashbuckling, film-star skill; he would have conquered in this vulgar brawl as in the great arenas if only he had not behaved like an ideal sportsman, like one belonging in a more chivalrous world. Johnson leaves in utter obscurity the prince's motives and the question of whether he had recognized his tutor, where Mackenzie specifies possibilities: fancied insult, or sexual jealousy, or unrecognizing drunkenness. It is consonant with Johnson's usual practice in biography to remind us that 'actions are visible, [but] motives are secret' (*Lives*, I, 15), but it makes evaluation difficult. If the prince never recognized his antagonist then Crichton's death outgoes his earlier triumphs in purposelessness; if he was jealous, then he acted as representative of all those malicious defeated rivals with whom Johnson generally surrounds and 'dogs' conspicuous success, and as representative even of Johnson and his reader, in so far as the former expresses or the latter shares any annoyance at Crichton's persistent superhumanity.

Johnson annexes to the manner of Crichton's death large cloudy suggestions of irony, futility and pathos. It leaves the reader unsatisfied, seeking for causes or meanings which are not offered. But all these effects are subordinated to the irony, futility and pathos of the fact of death itself, whose meaning Johnson makes clear and explicit. He sandwiches the account of the masked ambush between two paragraphs which read as follows (only the second incomplete):

> The death of this wonderful man I should be willing to conceal, did I not know that every reader will inquire curiously after that fatal hour which is common to all human beings, however distinguished from each other by nature or by fortune. . . .
> Thus was the Admirable Crichton brought into that state, in which he could excel the meanest of mankind only by a few empty honours paid to his memory.

The first of these paragraphs has no parallel in Johnson's predecessors; the material for the second comes from Mackenzie modifying Urquhart, and treating the posthumous honours as far from empty. Here as nowhere else in his essay Johnson transforms the perspective of his source, even though his words about the pictures of Crichton with book and lance descend to him through Mackenzie from Urquhart. The periphrasis which he uses for death ('that state, in which he could excel the meanest . . . only by . . . empty honours') has parallels in neither of them but in many of his own writings, particularly sermons (see above, pp.9–10). Crichton's superiority is here brought into vain combat with extinction. Johnson implicitly measures the honours as he specifies them: court mourning (but no mention of either punishment or grief for the prince, whom Urquhart makes remorseful even to attempted suicide), 'profuse . . . encomiums' from erstwhile competitors (who are not likely to be the sincerest of mourners), the statues which encapsulate his achievements as book and lance. Johnson is assessing the precise degree of eminence available after death to a 'name, at which the world grew pale'. The essay moves through romance to anti-romance, if we accept what Northrop Frye says of romance's close relationship with 'the wish-fulfilment dream' and its ending with the hero's exaltation even in death (which is the essence of Urquhart's Crichton).[20]

The reader will perceive that Johnson shares his or her own curiosity about the fatal, levelling hour of Crichton's death, and may well doubt the sincerity of his desire to conceal it. Johnson later uses almost the same formula about the equally unnecessary and comically grotesque end of the dramatist Otway; but whereas he expresses himself unwilling to mention the *manner* of Otway's death (though he does so anyway), it is the *fact* of Crichton's death which he professes himself willing to conceal. We must suspect irony in this profession as in the same sentence's epithet 'this wonderful man' – an epithet which Johnson also applied ironically to Miss Pond in *Idler* 6, who is another equally successful though less prestigious competitor, also to be immortalized in a statue. The fall of Johnson's Crichton, like that of his Charles XII, disappoints expectations that it will be grand and apocalyptic.

The story of Crichton, though conceived on such a different scale from that of, say, Nugaculus, in the end moves unexpectedly in the same direction. Having professed its intention of enlarging our ideas of human potential, it reverses itself to a sharp reminder of human limitations. Despite the attractiveness of Fussell's suggestion that Johnson, making up his essays impromptu, often allows his end to contradict his beginning for lack of foreseeing where his argument would lead him,[21] we do not really need to invoke it to explain the apparent contradictions here. Johnson's introductory paragraphs advocate estimating our abilities highly in relation to 'great undertakings' rather than to possible rivals; Crichton on the contrary has his eye always on the competitors who figure prominently in all his exploits. Whether or not he inspires us to 'honest emulation', we are bound to turn back from the account of Crichton's death with a modified view of Johnson's early statement that 'none seems to have been more exalted above the common rate of humanity'. If none can be exalted further than this, none can *in the end* be exalted above the common. Crichton's story illustrates the insufficiency of the competitive struggle to both our desire and our capacity for achievement. He mounts, shines, evaporates and falls; likely though he seems to do so, he cannot escape 'the doom of man',[22] 'the common fate of humanity'.

Some readers may see Crichton as a typical Johnsonian example of limited greatness or failed heroism; but his affinity with Charles XII should not entirely obscure that with Miss Pond. He judges and is judged by a scale of competition rather than one of greatness. Johnson was, as so often, pursuing a theme from one paper to another, and doing so with deliberate bathos, when he devoted his next *Adventurer*, no. 84, to the antics of a stage-coachload of passengers jockeying for superiority. Crichton, the man absolutely competitive and triumphant, who only once in his life performs an action of any value to his fellow-men, cannot be made to reveal his common humanity except in death. This sombre essay expresses Johnson's considered, complex view of competitiveness, with only the merest hints of that relish for the fray which sometimes emerged in his talk.

7
COMMUNITY

No degree of knowledge attainable by man is able to set him
above the want of hourly assistance, or to extinguish the
desire of fond endearments, and tender officiousness.

(Rambler 137)

———

To receive and to communicate assistance, constitutes the
happiness of human life.

(Adventurer 67)

JOHNSON EMPHASIZES Crichton's isolation at every stage of his career.
The Crichton essay was preceded by several expressing Johnson's 'strong
feeling for human solidarity'. He emphatically does not believe with Pope
that 'SELF–LOVE and SOCIAL are the same'; but it seems clear that as an
observer he recognized in human beings an instinct of community, the
counterpart of the equal and opposite instinct of rivalry, and that as a
moralist he supported an ideal of community which can tame the
competitive struggle and compensate for individual pettiness, transience
and insufficiency. In this as in many things Johnson is very much a mind of
the early eighteenth century. Though he sees social bonding differently
from Pope, and though he is writing later, they both exemplify the
operating principle which Eric Rothstein finds in poetry from about the
1690s to the 1740s, 'that of interaction, interconnectedness'.[1]

In *Adventurer* 67, well known for its rhapsodic praise of London, Johnson
ascribes the functioning of the city (which Max Byrd calls the largest
man-made thing to exist) to 'the secret concatenation of society, that links
together the great and the mean, the illustrious and the obscure', which he
'cannot but admire'. Reciprocation of help is 'the great end of society',[2] and
eighteenth-century society is for Johnson an improvement on that of
Crichton's middle ages in so far as it makes fuller provision for this end.

As a Christian moralist, Johnson also regularly urges the supreme importance, on a more personal level, of the exchange of brotherly love. A.T. Elder distinguishes among the central themes of his essays both that of fitting into life as a social being and that of contributing to the welfare of one's fellows. The latter, he says, is the favourite theme of all, 'the connective tissue of the essays', more important even than that of the seeking and promotion of virtue.³ To interact with one's fellows and to contribute to their good, the two vital elements in Johnson's concept of community, demand a self-emancipation from the competitive struggle just described. Johnson, so vividly aware of the pressures of competition, sees mutual assistance, either public or personal, as a frail achievement of civilized, moralized humanity; but it rests on a foundation of mutual dependence which is, as much as competition, an inescapable condition of our being. On these matters the instruction Johnson gives is identical with that of orthodox Christianity: love one another, be 'members one of another'.⁴ Johnson's thought is differentiated from orthodoxy, however, in several ways: in the urgency with which he invokes community as an antidote to competition, a goal to set against that of greatness; in the degree to which he sees it as a requirement not specifically Christian (like repentance) but as made in every area of life, personal, intellectual, political, social; and in the paradox which makes it both a dictate of our nature and a hard achievement of our moral will.

Although Johnson had only qualified respect for the concept of the Great Chain of Being, a chain is, as Robert Voitle remarks, his favourite image for reasoning or discourse, as well as for the interconnectedness by which petty detail is given value. *Concatenation* and *reciprocation* are much-used terms in his vocabulary.⁵ He uses *avenues* or *passages* to the heart to signify participation in the feelings of others, and the stopping-up of such avenues becomes a disturbing image for emotional isolation (often associated in Johnson's thought with the other perils of climbing too high or reaching too far).

Johnson's view of human interconnectedness has something in common with the popular concept of the Great Chain, and something also with the ideas of the sentimentalists. He sees the human race as necessarily, involuntarily interconnected in the same way that the Chain connects it with the rest of creation, and like the sentimentalists he sees benevolent connection with other people as life's most urgent objective. But there resemblance ceases. Believers in the Chain subscribed to a scientific theory which Johnson did not accept. The sentimentalists, not laying his emphasis on the underlying fact of natural, unchosen community, correspondingly aggrandized the feeling individual. Johnson would have subscribed on the whole to Thomson's enthusiasm for the love 'Of human race; the large ambitious wish/To make them blest' and revulsion from 'a listless unconcern,/Cold, and averting from our neighbour's good'.⁶ Johnson would have agreed with Thomson in perceiving the ambition but he would have been more inclined than Thomson to see this as a threat – as it is, for instance, to the astronomer in *Rasselas*. Johnson's ideal of community emphasizes mutuality ('the reception and communication of happiness' in 'the universal league of social beings'),[7] and so avoids both the isolating and the self-dramatizing aspects of the sentimental urge to beneficence, by focusing on the point of view of recipients as well as benefactors. From the 'one vast republick' of humanity 'none have a right to withdraw' (*Idler* 19: Y, II, 59). Johnson is alert to the way the doing of good can become a self-satisfying luxury – what in connection with the giving of advice he calls 'a visible sense of their own beneficence' – and he sees this as an alternative to, rather than a feature of, true friendship (*Ram.* 87, 64: Y, IV, 96; III, 344). Achieved community or mutuality in his view requires two conditions: that we act to benefit others, but that we do not claim the credit – the sense of superiority – which such action makes available. It is obvious that these two conditions are likely to work against each other.

As competition is associated with self-aggrandizement, so community is associated with a diminished view of the individual. Johnson maintains that Providence has decreed out of kindness 'that no individual should be of such importance, as to cause, by his retirement or death, any chasm in the world'. He says this in *Rambler* 6, about the retirement of Cowley, who doubly underestimated the principle of community: he thought that the world would miss him, and that he could do without the world (Y, III, 33–5). 'It is long before we are convinced of the small proportion which every individual bears to the collective body of mankind' (*Ram.* 146: Y, V, 15).

Johnson regularly celebrates the achievement of community, in personal, intellectual and political relationships, even while emphasizing its difficulty. Many of the traditional, familiar moral points which he makes are not so much recommendations of community as statements of the basis on which it rests. He devotes a whole *Rambler*, no. 151, to the fact that people all develop in the same way, the individual following the path which others have followed. He condenses the same thought into a whole collection of pithy summaries: 'We have all been born; we have most of us been married; and so many have died before us . . .'; 'We are all naked till we are dressed, and hungry till we are fed'; 'We are all prompted by the same motives, all deceived by the same fallacies,' all variously played on by the same passions.[8] In *Rambler* 135 (on the annual migration of fashionable society to the countryside) he remarks that the principle of imitation, of following the beaten track of one's fellows, governs even the choice of pleasure (Y, IV, 350). Unchosen adversity and even death are, equally, useful reminders of our common humanity. Nothing 'endears men so much as participation of dangers and misfortunes'; 'disease generally begins that equality which death completes; the distinctions which set one man so much above another are very little perceived in the gloom of a sick chamber' (*Ram.* 200, 48: Y, V, 278; III, 260). In the *Lives* the deaths of great and would-be great poets alike incorporate ironical circumstances which diminish the pretensions of the gifted individual:[9] Otway is choked by a charitable gift (I, 247); Pomfret's promotion is delayed by malicious allegations, which can be easily contradicted, but not before the delay occasions his death (I, 301–2); Dryden's funeral allegedly becomes a farce (I, 389–92); Smith kills himself by 'swallow[ing] his own medicine' (II, 17–18); success comes too late to Hughes (II, 163–4); Pope has his last wishes betrayed by the man who had wept over his sickbed. These things, like Pope's experience of delirium, are 'a sufficient humiliation of the vanity of man' (III, 190–4), a reduction to common 'imbecility'.

In chronicling such reminders of our comparative equality, Johnson the biographer of individuals shifts for a moment to the employment of a larger scale, a more distant view which obliterates or minimizes individual differences. *The Lives of the Poets* is a kind of composite portrait, an evocation of that continuing literary community or timeless intellectual co-operation which swallows up the achievements of individuals. It is the culminating statement of a theme Johnson had often touched. The works of those who advance knowledge 'are always lost in successive compilations, as new advances are made' (*Ram.* 106: Y, IV, 203); a 'writer who obtains his full purpose loses himself in his own lustre. . . . Of an art universally practised, the first teacher is forgotten' ('Dryden': *Lives*, I, 411).

> Providence has given no man ability to do much, that something might be left for every man to do. The business of life is carried on by a general co-operation; in which the part of any single man can be no more distinguished, than the effect of a particular drop when the meadows are floated by a summer shower. (*Adv.* 137: Y, II, 489)

Despite the self-abnegation which it entails, Johnson valued intellectual sharing highly. *Rambler* 9 expresses delight in such 'successive labours of innumerable minds' as have gradually evolved the arts of ship-building and navigation from the hollowing of a tree-trunk, and puts this communal evolution forward as a specific against competition and malignity. Since we build on our predecessors, since the theoretical scientist and the practical workman each needs the other, each 'ought to endeavour at eminence, not by pulling others down, but by raising himself' to a kind of reciprocal superiority (Y, III, 49–50). *Rambler* 41, written four months later, again contemplates a ship (this time in contrast with a bird's nest, the once-for-all product of instinct) as 'exhibit[ing] the collective knowledge of different ages, and various professions' (Y, III, 223). The ship symbolizes the achievements of co-operation, as does the social and mercantile reciprocation of London compared with enforced and irksome self-reliance like that of the Hebrides (Y, II, 387; IX, 130).

Johnson's trust in the collective literary verdict of the common reader, and the moral verdict of the people at large, is well known, as is his fine praise of Gray's *Elegy* for expressing what is common to us all.[10] In conversation he expressed approval of classical quotation as 'the *parole* of literary men all over the world', having in it 'a community of mind' (Boswell, IV, 102). Writing about literary imitation, he says cautiously that only a few may hope to add 'some small particle of knowledge, to the hereditary stock devolved to them from ancient times, the collective labour of a thousand intellects' (*Ram*. 121: Y, IV, 282). A month later he touches the same subject more encouragingly: everyone ought

> to endeavour that something may be added by his industry to the hereditary aggregate of knowledge and happiness. To add much can indeed be the lot of few, but to add something, however little, every one may hope. (*Ram*. 129: Y, IV, 325)

It is good to think 'that almost every understanding may by a diligent application of its powers hope to enlarge' our knowledge, even though that shows how scanty it is at present (*Adv*. 137: Y, II, 491).

Johnson introduces the theme of intellectual concatenation in the third paragraph of *The Lives of the Poets*, saying that Spenser made Cowley a poet as Jonathan Richardson made Reynolds a painter; he carries it on in further frequent references to the part in the poets' achievement that has been played by their teachers (notably Addison's: II, 79–82) and by their reading. His final word on Pope's greatness (III, 252) is a word as to what Homer *would* have said of him. He takes a progressive view of English poetry which has something in common with his view of ship-building: Cowley, the first poet treated, belongs to a school whose aims are in important respects mistaken; Denham, the second, writes one of his best poems on Cowley's death, deserves high praise for inventing 'a new scheme of poetry' (the topographical), originates a more imaginative approach to translating the works of the past (which, though he cannot make much of it himself, 'taught Dryden to please better'), and claims the regard of posterity for 'his improvement of our numbers'. Through his channel the stream of poetry flows. He affords us the pleasure of watching him 'forsaking bad copies by degrees and advancing towards a better practice', a pleasure which Johnson passes on to his readers with earlier and later examples (I, 77, 79, 80). This life concludes with a vista forwards: 'He is one of the writers that improved our taste and advanced our language, and whom we ought therefore to read with gratitude, though having done much he left much to do' (I, 82). Johnson's concluding judgments on Waller, and several passages in the lives of Dryden and Addison, similarly dwell on their transitional position: each, in his way, an improver who is yet to be improved on (I, 293–6, 386, 419–22, 469; II, 146). Pope, himself a negligent editor of Shakespeare, 'taught others to be more accurate' (III, 139). By this means the reader's impression of literary rivalry, of the envy and mutual ill-will that mars the poets' lives, is balanced and lightened by a different impression: of all the successive individuals working together, like coelenterates in coral, to form the great branching structure of English poetry. Few later judgments on Johnson would have pleased him more than that of J. Churton Collins – though mixed with much carping – that *The Lives of the Poets* 'has added importantly and permanently to the common stock of intellectual wealth'.[11] This is a more fruitful approach to the *Lives* than that which sees them as a great individual's celebrating individual greatness, or failing to.

Johnson closes his literary account of Pope with an extraordinary example of literature as communal achievement. Pope is represented as incorporating into his Homer translation many favourite gleanings from earlier English authors. This unusually extreme example of the poet gathering his honey from other men's flowers is eclipsed in interest by the remark immediately following:

New sentiments and new images others may produce, but to attempt any further improvement of versification will be dangerous. Art and diligence have now done their best, and what shall be added will be the effort of tedious toil and needless curiosity. (III, 251)

What is wrong with this pronouncement is not that it sees literary history as progressive but that it sees it as ceasing to be so. Johnson envisages no continuance for the poetical concatenation which he has traced as far as his own time.

Intellectual co-operation occurs even without the intention or awareness of some of the partners. In social and political matters, where the principle of community is just as important, it has to be achieved and maintained by effort and care. Johnson regards political systems based on this principle not as a primitive ideal from which more complex societies move away, but rather as the outcome of sophisticated development. Though in the haphazard skirmishing of conversation he may speak tenderly of feudalism, he presents it as more like a fantasy of interdependence than a fact, even a vanished one. The reality of Highland life is painful self-sufficiency and separation. Johnson's model for economic co-operation is not community of possessions, a system which he thinks impossible or absurd (*Ram.* 131: Y, IV, 334), but the intricate interacting urban community of London. In *Taxation no Tyranny* he maintains that since the distant days of power wielded competitively by many petty leaders, it has been 'found that the power of every people consisted in union', until now everyone 'has consented to throw his atom of interest into the general mass of the community' and 'is taught to consider his own happiness as combined with the publick prosperity'. From the discovery of the power of union, 'independence perceptibly wasted away' – an argument which prepares for Johnson's later calling the colonies' aspirations the 'madness of independence' (Y, X, 419–20, 430, 438). More important in the present context is the reason he gives for our placing any confidence in the representatives who govern us: 'that they must share in the good or evil which their counsels shall produce' (more, one might say today, like airline pilots than like doctors). A government is to be praised for willingness to 'stand on a level with their fellow-subjects' (Y, X, 434, 398). The principle of sharing is the foundation of political stability as well as of personal fulfilment and intellectual and technological progress.

In every sphere, however, community stands opposed to competitiveness, and in none is it easy for it to make headway. Johnson's fine sermon on brotherly love, no. 11, points out the need to combat our innate 'desire of superiority'; no. 23 draws attention to the fragility of the ties of society, the fact that 'instead of hoping to be happy in the general felicity, every man pursues a private and independent interest'. It is so hard for people to act for the general good, 'in hopes only of happiness flowing back upon [them] in its circulation through a whole community', that failure to do so is 'the natural condition of human life' (Y, XIV, 120, 238). For someone newly rich to snub an old friend who had expected him to 'desire to communicate his happiness' is behaviour no worse than most (*Ram.* 200: Y, V, 278–81). It is against this background that Johnson's sermons regularly urge, in opposition to the ambitious struggle, not an offensively detached immunity but rather acceptance of our 'one common nature and one common father' (no. 27: Y, XIV, 290–1, 296).

Johnson's essays, devoting more space to snares and dangers than to ideals, teem with individualists whose resistance to community is carefully noted. Polyphilus of *Rambler* 19, who is always switching from one career to another, regularly selects his new line for the sake of avoiding too close contact with his (inferior) fellow-creatures. Giving up medicine will free him from 'melancholy attendance upon misery, mean submission to peevishness', giving up the law from 'the absurdities of attorneys, and misrepresentations made by his clients of their own causes . . . the useless anxiety of one, and the incessant importunity of another', besides the 'barrenness of his fellow-students'. Polyphilus, the man of many interests, finds other people's emotions irritating, and seeks to escape community (Y, III, 104, 106–7). In *Rambler* 24 Johnson paints a chilling picture of the scholar Gelidus,[12] who lives shut away from his family and impervious to human sorrow, ignorant of the elementary fact 'that men are designed for the succour and comfort of each other'. Gelidus may strike the reader as improbably dehumanized; but Johnson presents him as typical of the 'great fault of men of learning', who choose to remain with all their qualifications 'unqualified to perform those offices by which the concatenation of society is preserved, and mutual tenderness excited and maintained'. Such people reject social or personal ties for the sake of different ones: the 'intricate combinations' and 'longest chain of unexpected consequences' of science. Their crime carries its own punishment, to 'be justly driven out from the commerce of mankind' (Y, III, 132–4). Willed separation from the rest of humanity characterizes one *Rambler* figure after another (see above, pp.89ff.) and one writer after another in *The Lives of the Poets*: Cowley in his rage for retirement (I, 15–16; *Ram*. 6: Y, III, 32–5), the Metaphysicals in their neglect of 'uniformity of sentiment' and the sympathy it can tap (*Lives*, I, 20), Edmund Smith in arrogant contempt (II, 17–18), Addison in bashfulness (II, 123), Swift and Pope in assumed disdain for the world beyond their immediate circle (III, 61, 212), and so on.

Johnson himself finds it hard to distinguish consistently between genuine approaches towards other people and the search for others to confirm one's own superiority. His appeals for community are frequently directed at those who have some cause to think themselves superior; but their withdrawal is generally seen as in itself an inferiority. It is the man who can converse *merely* 'upon questions, about which only a small part of mankind has knowledge sufficient to make them curious', who 'must lose his days in unsocial silence, and live in the crowd of life without a companion'. Johnson represents the self-inflicted punishment of withdrawal as more debilitating even than the lacerating struggle for achievement. Nor is it a price necessary to be paid: the arts of friendship are open to all as 'abstruse researches and remote discoveries' are not (*Ram*. 137: Y, IV, 364, 363). *Rambler* 72 uses two significantly non-human images for isolated greatness:

> Without good humour, learning and bravery can only confer that superiority which swells the heart of the lion in the desart, where he roars without reply, and ravages without resistance. . . . A man whose great qualities want the ornament of superficial attractions, is like a naked mountain with mines of gold, which will be frequented only till the treasure is exhausted. (Y, IV, 13, 17)

Johnson is not referring here to the envy which superiority naturally or necessarily provokes; it is not the great qualities which leave their possessor 'without reply', without visitors, but the failure to leaven them with 'the will to please' or with admission of natural individual insufficiency (Y, IV, 16). Good humour might supply the humanity which is more valuable than an artificial lion or mountain. Three weeks later Johnson enforces the horror of isolation by appeal to the end of life:

> that desire which every man feels of being remembered and lamented, is often mortified when we remark how little concern is caused by the eternal departure even of those who have passed their lives with publick honours, and been distinguished by extraordinary performances. It is not possible to be regarded with tenderness except by a few. That merit which gives greatness and renown, diffuses its influence to a wide compass, but acts weakly on every single breast; it is placed at a distance from common spectators, and shines like one of the remote stars, of which the light reaches us, but not the heat. The wit, the hero, the philosopher, whom their tempers or their fortunes have hindered from intimate relations, die without any other effect than that of adding a new topic to the conversation of the day. (*Ram*. 78: Y, IV, 48)

Paradoxically, the individualistic desire to be remembered and lamented propels people into the pursuit of fame, that in turn into choosing a public, a remote, instead of a private life, and that in the end to being not remembered and not lamented, stellar instead of human. The value which Johnson places on intimate relations, the tenderness of a few, is closely related to his ideal of broader community; it is also a counterforce to the attractions of greatness.

Johnson repeatedly urges people of merit or renown to participate in daily littleness, as specific against the sense of superiority that may spring from either surpassing or benefiting others. The essays in which he does so generally present the sphere of social, personal, emotional relationships as a lower one than those of study and science in which would-be 'benefactors of posterity' hope to make their mark. When Johnson tells us that 'if our superiors descend from their elevation, we love them for lessening the distance at which we are placed below them', he has in mind a descent *into* the purely personal. The contrast of singleness and community is regularly combined with that of high and low, as Johnson maintains that the lower, less lonely position is preferable. Descent 'from the pinacles of art' is 'always overpaid by gratitude'; Gelidus 'spends his time in the highest room of his house', from which his family are debarred, and is restless and uneasy when he comes *down* to dinner. The sphere of the puny individual, in which it is most necessary to renounce competition and superiority, ranks lower than those which deal with the affairs of the community and the species. Yet in this matter too, it seems, our standards of judgment need adjustment, for the humble individual enjoys a spiritual advantage which the wielder of public influence misses. It is love which 'always implies some kind of natural or voluntary equality', and love takes the highest place of all in the scale of Christian values (*Ram*. 89, 137, 24: Y, IV, 108–9, 364; III, 132–4). The statement about love and equality is foreshadowed in *Rambler* 72's 'We are most inclined to love when we have nothing to fear' (Y, IV, 15), which in turn echoes St John's 'There is no fear in love; but perfect love casteth out fear'.[13] In the Bible these words convey a sense of restful reassurance; but for Johnson voluntary equality is as much a matter for effort and struggle as the most ambitious eminence. It is far easier to seek eminence by urging community than it is to seek community.

Johnson consistently presents community as beleaguered. Characteristically, he places some fine praise of 'the natural contagion of felicity, by the repercussion of communicated pleasure' in an essay on parental cruelty (*Ram*. 148: Y, V, 24); tribute to 'the gentle pleasures of sympathy and confidence' – 'those honest joys which nature annexes to the power of pleasing' – appears in an essay on the pain of loss (*Ram*. 47: Y, III, 256); and probably his fullest statement of the inevitability and even desirability of mutual dependence opens an essay whose body is devoted to undesirable dependence, the kind of flattering and parasitical relationships discussed above.

> The apparent insufficiency of every individual to his own happiness or safety, compels us to seek from one another assistance and support. The necessity of joint efforts for the execution of any great or extensive design, the variety of powers disseminated in the species, and the proportion between the defects and excellencies of different persons, demand an interchange of help, and communication of intelligence, and by frequent reciprocations of beneficence unite mankind in society and friendship. (*Ram*. 104: Y, IV, 190)

Johnson has here sounded the themes for his coming essay. He does not, like most Christian moralists, simply recommend helping and benefiting, but exchange of help, reciprocation of benefit. In a relationship of patronage, the essay continues, only one side admits the need of assistance; respective defects and excellencies do not remain static but are changed for the worse by the nature of the relationship; beneficence becomes impossible on either side, for lack of 'voluntary equality'. The 'great community of mankind' exists as a law of nature whether we like it or not, but the choice of more intimate community within it must be made in the teeth of natural inequality and the natural desire to increase, not lessen, that inequality. *Rambler* 64, which tells us how difficult it is to maintain friendship in circumstances of rivalry, also applies to *any* continued friendship the language of achievement: 'a constant and warm reciprocation of benevolence' is 'elevated excellence' based on 'superior motives' (Y, III, 343, 340). That community which may supersede competitive struggle is itself an object of struggle; that equality which provides an alternative to greatness is itself a kind of greatness.

It is one of Johnson's aims as a moralist to expose competitiveness which disguises itself as community: flattery and sycophancy, which we have met as weapons of competition, may also be simulacra of benevolence. *Rambler* 188 (Y, V, 220–4), on conversation, opens with a familiar statement of our mutual dependence: 'no man can live otherwise than in an hermitage, without hourly pleasure or vexation, from the fondness or neglect of those about him'. It proves, however, to be another puzzling essay, in which what looks at first like an ideal to be followed turns out to be, like Crichton, an awful warning. Since one needs affection, Johnson says, it is necessary to please those about one, and since few 'spend their time with much satisfaction under the eye of uncontestable superiority', it follows that anyone 'that would please must rarely aim at such excellence as depresses his hearers in their own opinion'. These quotations, taken from the third and fourth paragraphs, might appear designed to set up an opposition now familiar to us: that between excellence or superiority on the one hand and 'pleasing' on the other. The situation, however, turns out to be much more complicated. From its first sentence the essay addresses itself to the desire (a desire entirely natural, but also competitive) 'of being *distinguished* for the arts of conversation'.[14] The second paragraph begins with the particular qualifications necessary 'to *excellence* in this valuable art'. The opposition between excellence and pleasing evaporates; it seems that Johnson can find no other vocabulary than that of excellence and distinction to apply to the art which consists in renouncing those things.

In fact the conversational art he describes here only pretends to substitute community for competition. The 'art of *procuring* love' excludes mutuality as surely as does that of '*forcing* attention'. Of the former, Johnson says that it may be attained by those who do not by excellence awake envy; of the latter, that once attained it will be envied. To please, this essay gradually reveals, is not the same as to make any kind of exchange with others.

The second paragraph provides a different slant on the relation of love and equality: 'we have all, at one time or another, been content to love those whom we could not esteem'. In case this phrase has not conveyed sufficient distaste, it then elaborates those we cannot esteem into the ignorant or treacherous. The body of the essay describes, with inverted commas, the 'merry fellow', 'good-natured man' and 'modest man' (the last being what we should call a 'good listener'), companions of first, next and 'yet lower rank', who will be the successful ones in the competition for conversational popularity. We are back in a familiar *Rambler* world of patronage and dependence. The essay's last two paragraphs, using the word *art* three times, and *performance*, *pretending* and *contriving* once each, drive home the point already made in *procuring* and *forcing*: this distressing parody of mutual benevolence is both petty and self-serving. The moral on which the essay closes, that 'those who despise them should not rigorously blame' these arts of endearment, 'for it is always necessary to be loved, but not always necessary to be reverenced', does nothing to mitigate or reconcile the bitterness of 'such is the kindness of mankind to all, *except* those who aspire to real merit and rational dignity, that every understanding may find some way to excite benevolence'. We might accept the advice against aspiring to be reverenced, as coming from a straightforward moralist; we can only take the advice against aspiring to real merit or rational dignity to be that of a cynic or an angry ironist. This essay uses *love, kindness, benevolence* in as slippery a manner as its other key words. It carries to an extreme the ambivalence admitted by the correspondent of *Rambler* 72: 'You may perhaps think this account of those who are distinguished for their good humour, not very consistent with the praises which I have bestowed upon it' (Y, IV, 15). The desire to win approval for oneself is too one-sided to be confused with community; it encourages the exercise of those little arts which have hardly the dignity of ambition but which reproduce, on their own small scale, all the mean stratagems of competition for superiority.

Johnson finds human co-operation, like other ideals, less plentiful than failed attempts at it and false pretenders to its title. *Rambler* 188 describes some means 'to excite benevolence' towards oneself, not to exercise it towards others or exchange it with them. The second project also may be infiltrated and undermined by the desire to distinguish oneself. The astronomer in *Rasselas* and the naturalist in *Idler 55* (Y, II, 171–4) each entertains the fantasy that the human race depends on him for an unimaginably valuable benefaction. Each cuts himself off from normal intercourse with humanity (the naturalist spends seven years in strenuous solitary collecting and one 'in mines and coalpits', and breaks off communication with his friends when they criticize his work). In each the desire of benefiting others has enlarged itself into madness; in each the desire for the *reciprocation* of benefits with the rest of humanity has been suppressed. The astronomer, whose case is treated in more detail, is cured by abandoning the role of solitary, superhuman benefactor for that of equal member of a social group.

The role of unparticipating benefactor merges naturally into that of the moralist or sage. Johnson's often noticed retreat from satire amounts to a refusal to carry through the satirist's (or preacher's) usual separation of himself from his subject-matter, the object or person satirized or exhorted: 'his own intimate and honest participation' in what he describes.[15] He involves not only himself but also his reader. When Swift's *Tale of a Tub* persona, after cataloguing the various manifestations of madness, admits that his own 'Imaginations are hard-mouth'd, and exceedingly disposed to run away with his *Reason* . . . upon which Account, my Friends will never trust me alone',[16] the reader shifts from aligning himself with the hack as spectator of the assorted lunatics, to standing as lone spectator of the hack and other lunatics together. When, on the other hand, Johnson ends his life of Savage by reminding us not to think we could have lived better in his circumstances, or follows the risible letter of Quisquilius with a denial that the virtuoso is either blamable or wholly useless; or when he makes Imlac sternly reprove Nekayah and Pekuah for finding the astronomer's delusions funny; or when he reminds us how gladly the moralist turns from self-examination to recommending self-examination to others —[17] in these cases, as in many more, he is shifting his ground in order to associate both himself *and* his reader with the follies and mistakes he has exposed, asserting both his *and* our community with his satiric butts. It is the very reverse of the distancing technique which reports from a secure vantage-point the similarity of human beings to each other.

In *The Vanity of Human Wishes* the early exemplars (Wolsey, the scholar, Xerxes, the military Charleses) operate in a position of almost inhuman isolation. The dreadful old man and the unhappy beauty are beset by people, but people in unequal, exploitative relationships, for one 'the fawning niece and pamper'd guest', for the other the equally destructive lover and rival, for neither the 'sweeter musick of a virtuous friend' (lines 276, 332, 272). For these characters abandonment of community is the opposite face of the competition for superiority which drives them. The poem's only good character is also the only one to enjoy human affection, the 'gen'ral fav'rite as the gen'ral friend' (although Johnson makes this in itself a source of sorrow to the long-lived, in accordance with his brief to prove the vanity of *all* wishes: lines 297, 302).

It is, however, divine love and connectedness, not human, which this poem opposes to the isolations of ambition. Whatever the precise significance of 'love, which scarce collective man can fill',[18] Johnson, in including it among things we may safely pray for (line 361), has indubitably broadened his view to something even wider and more communally shared than simply the love of God for the individual or of the individual for God.

8

MALIGNITY

he that has given no provocation to malice, but by attempting
to excel, finds himself pursued by multitudes whom he never
saw with all the implacability of personal resentment.

(*Rambler* 183)

He that burned an animal with irons yesterday, will be
willing to amuse himself with burning another to-morrow

(*Idler* 17)

WE HAVE ALREADY SEEN (above, pp.104, 108ff) how closely Johnson
associated competition with envy and envy with malice. Hatred is only to
be expected between rivals for what many desire and only few can obtain,
and to overcome it is a rare victory. But beyond this Johnson distinguishes
in human nature a further degree of malice for which rivalry seems not fully
to account. The ill-will of rivalship reaches to envious malignity, but
absolute malignity defines itself as the desire to do harm to others without
reference to oneself, without hope of profit, as end not as means. This
quality presents itself as an inescapable spectre in Johnson's thinking. He
sees it sometimes as an instinct, sometimes as an aberration. It is not an
element in human nature generally stressed by anti-benevolist theorists of
the time. Hobbes and his followers emphasized competition, self-seeking,
absence of altruism, rather than gratuitous pleasure in others' harm; their
system gave less scope to the idea of absolute malignity than did the
orthodox Christian doctrine of the depravity of the human heart since the
Fall.[1]

Investigation of the idea in Johnson might seem to lead further from, not
closer to, his measuring the scale of human actions and his ascribing these
actions to aspiration after greatness. But the connection, though less logical,
is still crucial. Johnson's judgment of actions and motives cannot be
properly understood without some reference to the malice which, he

believes, lies on the far side of tactical rivalry. In his psychological analysis it is just that person whose malevolence strikes us as shockingly gratuitous who is necessarily denying community or mutuality – claiming not to belong on the same scale as the victim.

Johnson's recognition of human malevolence in his talk evoked horrified comparison with Swift. In *The Rambler* the same recognition evoked the same horror, most memorably of all from William Mudford. Having praised both Addison and Johnson as moralists, and compared Addison's picture of human nature to 'a lovely garden', Mudford complains that the *Rambler*'s picture of it is 'a frightful desert':

> the heart is appalled; terror hovers over us; the ears are filled with dismal cries; nothing is to be seen but vice, deformity, treachery, and ingratitude; the eye recoils back, startled and disgusted; and the mind refuses to recognize the dreadful picture![2]

Not many of us are so shaken by Johnson's essays as Mudford, but many readers notice the way the words *malevolence*, *malice*, *malignity* recur there with a haunting persistence. They and their derivatives take up a lot of space, too, in the *Dictionary*.[3] Their force challenges investigation. Too much is left out (about the *wickedness* of mankind) in Maurice J. Quinlan's view that Johnson 'believed man to be a frail creature, morally weak, and intellectually unstable', and in Robert Voitle's that 'Johnson's strictures on the malevolence of some individuals toward others are the sort of reaction we might expect from any compassionate person'.[4] Johnson's strictures are more peculiar than these remarks would suggest, more closely related to the whole cast of his personal thought and to his unique literary productions.

When Johnson's *Dictionary* treatment of these words is compared with that of Benjamin Martin (*Lingua Britannica Reformata: Or, A New English Dictionary*, 1749), two general points emerge clearly from the confusing mass of material. One is that Johnson takes these concepts seriously and weightily, the other that he lays strong emphasis on intention. Martin has no entries for some of the less obvious words of the group: he omits *malevolently*, the verb to *malice*, *malignantly*, *maligner*, *malignity* and *malignly*. His definitions make frequent use of words which are belittling or dismissive, such as *spite* and *grudge*. He uses *mischief* five times to Johnson's seven; but *mischief* was at this date a more ponderous word than *spite*, without its present-day connotations of roguishness. The words *will*, *disposed*, *intend*, *inclination*, *deliberate*, *design*, *desire*, etc. occur seventeen times in Johnson's definitions of this group of words; Martin uses no such words except *ill-will* and *wish*.[5]

Johnson's *Dictionary* resembles Martin in emphasizing the kinship of malice with envy. It uses *envy* or its derivatives in three definitions to Martin's four; its illustrative quotations use them much more. It is no surprise to find Satan and Macbeth among the quotations' exponents of malice. Johnson's lexicography here reflects his writings: many *Rambler* essays bracket envy and malignity without special emphasis, as a matter of course.[6]

The *Dictionary* does less to bring out the leading element in what I call absolute malignity: its lack of visible motivation, its gratuitousness. Johnson's works do not limit the word *malignity* to the absolute kind: he uses it, for instance, three times on a single page of *Rambler* 185 (on revenging injuries) in senses which imply some degree of provocation (Y, V, 208). But it was gratuitous ill-will which drew his most fascinated attention, as it did that of Fielding, who regularly takes pains to make his good characters discover, with sorrow and astonishment, that people can take pleasure in doing evil to others *without* either provocation or expectation of advantage.[7] Fielding's novels provide various examples. In *Joseph Andrews* one land-owner tricks the travellers with all kinds of generous offers aimed at nothing else but to cause them disappointment when the offers do not materialize, a species of cruelty which Johnson analyses in *Rambler* 163 as 'encouragement of expectations which are never to be gratified' (Y, V, 100ff.). Another of Fielding's squires wilfully, with 'no motive but ill-nature', shoots a little girl's lap-dog which represented no threat at all to his sport. Parson Adams, who has never noticed the inborn 'malignity in the nature of man' to which Mr Wilson calls his attention, withholds belief for as long as possible both in widespread malignity and in the land-owner's trick, 'for what a silly fellow must he be who would do the devil's work for nothing! and canst thou tell me any interest he could possibly propose to himself . . . ?' (II, xvi; III, iii and iv). At the opposite pole from Adams, the Man of the Hill in *Tom Jones* has found that the fact of malignity makes the ideal of community impossible: hatred of vices 'of a relative kind; such as envy, malice, treachery, cruelty, with every other species of malevolence' makes even a true philanthropist choose to avoid 'society itself' (VIII, x). The Man of the Hill is an aberration, his doctrines not those which Fielding wishes to leave with his readers; yet Fielding shows the world as being such that the Man of the Hill's position is not unreasonable.

Johnson resembles Fielding in associating the malicious with the devilish. Sermon 27 warns that the damned will spend eternity in the company of 'those beings, whose depravity incites them to rejoice at the destruction of mankind' (Y, XIV, 292). He too believes that much of the devil's work *is* done for nothing; he tells us so directly, and he forces his characters, like Parson Adams, reluctantly to discover the painful fact. A speaker in his parliamentary debates reminds the House: 'It is well known, my Lords, that there is, in a great Part of Mankind, a secret Malignity, which makes one unwilling to contribute to the Advantage of another, even when his own Interest will suffer no Diminution.' He adds that he hopes this opinion is mistaken, that more experienced Lords will say he is wrong; but Johnson produces no-one to deny it.[8] When Imlac relates how in his youth some travelling merchants exposed him to theft and fraud 'without any advantage to themselves, but that of rejoicing in the superiority of their own knowledge', he instantly provokes Rasselas to interrupt. 'Stop a moment, said the prince. Is there such depravity in man, as that he should injure another without benefit to himself?' Assured by Imlac that there is, he is gracious but not convinced. 'Proceed, said the prince: I doubt not of the facts which you relate, but imagine that you impute them to mistaken motives.' The experienced Imlac makes no further attempt to disabuse him (*Rass.* IX).

Nonetheless, such depravity continues to cause Johnson himself the same astonishment as Adams and Rasselas.[9] Boswell describes him as saying 'I . . . once knew an old gentleman who was absolutely malignant. He really wished evil to others, and rejoiced at it' (III, 281). Johnson's reported words – *once, really* – present this old gentleman as a portent in his absolute malignancy, as if to have known him was an exceptional experience. Yet his writings frequently present such experience, and increasingly present it as commonplace. In 1744 he assumed that Savage's mother rejoiced in doing evil to her son; in 1756 he declared that the 'power of doing wrong with impunity seldom waits long for the will'.[10] He wrote on cruel parents in *Rambler* 148, and populated his later political pamphlets with villains to whom are ascribed 'airy bursts of malevolence' and elaborate continuance of harm.[11]

The essays enunciate the apparent inconsistency that malevolence is common and yet remarkable. On the one hand, it cannot surprise any but the pathologically innocent. 'The depravity of mankind is so easily discoverable, that nothing but the desert or the cell can exclude it from notice. The knowledge of crimes intrudes uncalled and undesired' (*Ram.* 175: Y, V, 160). On the other hand, the intrusive knowledge always surprises. Johnson counts it as something that 'might be expected that no man should suffer his heart to be inflamed with malice, but by injuries . . . that the armies of malignity should soon disperse, when no common interest could be found to hold them together' (*Ram.* 144: Y, V, 3). But what might be expected is of course stated only that the expectation may be contradicted.

Rambler 183, on interest and envy, presents, with fervent condemnation, the degrees by which envy shades into absolute malignity. It makes much of our recurrent, instinctive belief that the devil's work will be done only for wages, that self-advancement must be more of a temptation than disinterested malice. This 'seems probable at the first view . . . is easy to conceive'; the opposite 'surely . . . cannot' be true. 'It must be more natural to rob for gain, than to ravage only for mischief.' Yet Johnson goes on to prove that what we find probable or easy to conceive is not so, that ravaging for mischief is yet more popular as well as more pernicious than robbing for gain (Y, V, 196–200).

So the one old gentleman who really wished evil to others joins hands with all those who provoke the repeatedly intrusive, unwelcome discovery: with Lady Macclesfield, mother of Richard Savage,[12] and with the purveyors of hate and insult who flourish in *The Vanity of Human Wishes* (line 78) and in the essays and pamphlets. McIntosh observes that Johnson gives us no evil protagonists, and ascribes this fact to his being 'deficient in negative capability'.[13] A more plausible explanation is that he could not reconcile the position of protagonist with his need to express astonishment at the very existence of such a person. Such characters as Nugaculus certainly *do* evil, but neither malignantly nor incomprehensibly. Lady Macclesfield, the imaginary beings of the Soame Jenyns review, and the patriots of the 1770s, are, if not protagonists, at least portents who occupy prominent positions and deserve examination.

The life of Savage has been much discussed, and so have the sources of Johnson's view of Lady Macclesfield (presumed by him though not admitted by herself to be Savage's mother) as a monster of evil. This view, which had been committed to print by Aaron Hill and others before Johnson, presumably derived from Savage himself, who must have had his own psychological reasons for needing to believe himself the victim of staggering maternal cruelty. Presumably Johnson simply took his friend's word for it; but where Savage was inconsistent, fiercely blaming his mother yet insisting on her tender heart, Johnson reflected only one side of this inconsistency.[14] His reasons for painting this portrait, and the question of its accuracy, need not detain us here. What is relevant is the way it exemplifies his concept of absolute malice.

The first essential component is its shock effect, its incomprehensibility. 'It is not indeed easy to discover what motives could be found to overbalance that natural affection of a parent, or what interest could be promoted by neglect or cruelty', Johnson writes, interrupting the narrative of his sources to insert his own comment.[15] Earl Rivers, lover of Lady Macclesfield, 'probably imagined' that she would be good to the child which had been instrumental in setting her free from her husband: 'It was . . . not likely that she would be wicked without temptation, that she would . . . delight to see him struggling with misery' (*Lives*, II, 323–4). Johnson represents even Savage himself, after long experience of his mother's vindictiveness, as failing to anticipate to what lengths she would go (II, 351). It is one of the touchstones of such malice that it should be almost unbelievable. This works sometimes to increase its power, as when Lady Macclesfield perpetrates 'an act of wickedness which could not be defeated, because it could not be suspected: the Earl did not imagine that there could exist in a human form a mother that would ruin her son without enriching herself' (II, 327). Gratuitous malignancy ('without temptation', 'without enriching herself') produces astonishment in others and intense pleasure for the malicious person ('delight to see him struggling'). This delight is the closest thing to motive which Johnson can find for what is otherwise causeless.[16] It is entirely characteristic that he should describe this as pleasure in *seeing* the struggles of a victim (see below, pp.152–3).

Johnson himself, unlike Earl Rivers, has no difficulty in crediting the existence of this kind of mother. He twice disavows understanding of her motives, though this is no more than he frequently does with other biographical subjects (*Lives*, I, 15). He omits from this life any such insights as his later remarks that a person whose sight arouses pain will also arouse hatred, or that the 'world will never be long without some good reason to hate the unhappy' (*Adv.* 99: Y, II, 429–30). Either of these would have helped to account for Lady Macclesfield, but Johnson never attempts to *explain* her behaviour. What he does, surprisingly, is to *invent* motives for her without a shred of evidence. He tells us he does not know why *her* mother, Lady Mason, involved herself with the child: she might have had either of two possible intentions. But he offers no such latitude in interpretation as to why the daughter wanted her mother involved; instead, he bluntly assigns a reason. 'As it was impossible to avoid the inquiries which the curiosity or tenderness of her relations made after her child, she was obliged . . .' (*Lives*, II, 324). Similarly, Johnson explains away a gift of money to her unacknowledged son, recorded in his sources, by a 'prospect of sudden affluence'.[17] He also identifies her motive in trying to send Savage to America simply and certainly as the 'same cruelty', though he speculates, admitting uncertainty, as to Lady Mason's motives for co-operating, and even as to the probable recoil of hardened accomplices from such unparalleled maternal malignity (II, 327).

Johnson, as Clarence Tracy has pointed out, resembled his contemporaries in never considering the possibility that Lady Macclesfield believed, either rightly or wrongly, that Savage was not her own child but an impostor. Nor does he consider whether she might have believed, reasonably or unreasonably, that his entry into her house at night really was an attempt to harm her.[18] Johnson's two paragraphs of magnificent denunciation begin with the point that it is 'natural to enquire' into her motives; but they make no such enquiry. What purports to be enquiry is really a repetition of the previous accusations with the previous techniques:

> It is natural to enquire upon what motives his mother could
> persecute him in a manner so outrageous and implacable; for what
> reason she could employ all the arts of malice, and all the snares of

calumny, to take away the life of her own son, of a son who never injured her, who was never supported by her expence, nor obstructed any prospect of pleasure or advantage; why she should endeavour to destroy him by a lie – a lie . . . of which only this can be said to make it probable, that it may be observed from her conduct that the most execrable crimes are sometimes committed without apparent temptation.

    This mother is still alive, and may perhaps even yet, though her malice was so often defeated, enjoy the pleasure of reflecting that the life, which she often endeavoured to destroy, was at least shortened by her maternal offices; that though she could not . . . hasten the hand of the publick executioner, she has yet had the satisfaction of imbittering all his hours, and forcing him into exigences that hurried on his death. (II, 353)

Johnson's enquiry stops short without uncovering reasons or even facts. Savage's mother 'may perhaps' still take pleasure in the harm she has done; any doubts are limited to the question whether she still takes such pleasure, not whether she ever did. Johnson uses the sporting image of 'snares'; he devotes three parallel clauses to insisting that these injuries were unprovoked; he identifies the malicious person's pleasure as that of 'reflecting' if not directly observing; and – another recurrent element in his accounts of malice – he compares the damage she does with the worse damage which she wished to do, but could not. Her conduct is said to prove that absolute malignity does exist, and its existence is then said to be the only thing that makes her conduct probable. Johnson carefully avoids discussion of the ways in which Savage could have provided a motive by threatening her self-interest. The gratuitous quality of her wickedness is matched only by that of the attempted matricide of which she accuses her son; nothing could be so improbable as her wishing him dead except the reciprocal wish which she attributes to him.

    In its symmetrical paradoxes, its forensic oratory, its refusal to look for motives, its absence of any sympathy for or self-identification with the person described, the passage differs markedly from almost all Johnson's writing about individuals. Lady Macclesfield, though appearing in a biography, remains a fiction,[19] a richly imaginative realization of a fantasy, like an allegorical representation of malice or a philosophical demonstration of its existence, or like Johnson's horrific postulation, in his review of Soame Jenyns, of superior creatures who take delight in human suffering. (Indeed these imaginary beings, through the way Johnson's language converts them into sportsmen or ringside spectators, are less remote from the manageably human sin of self-interest than is Savage's still living, actual mother.)

Johnson portrays in detail no other human figure who really wishes evil to others with so little psychological explanation. Between absolute unmotivated malice, however, and practical self-interested ill-will, lies a broad spectrum. Its range can be demonstrated from his treatment of a single group, the so-called patriots who in *Falkland's Islands* 'sat wishing for misery and slaughter' but were 'disappointed of their pleasure', who 'fixed their hopes on publick calamities', who when 'they found that all were happy in spite of their machinations . . . felt no motion but that of sullen envy'. Johnson compares them to Milton's Satan, only to find them yet worse than he (Y, X, 375, 384).

The first level of evil we encounter in this pamphlet is simply deficiency in goodness. Johnson early observes that 'every man, either good or wise' is opposed to war (Y, X, 353), and his later argument addresses itself to lack of wisdom before lack of goodness. The astonishing 'coolness and indifference' with which 'the greater part of mankind see war commenced' stems from ignorance, not malignity. 'Those that hear of it at a distance, or read of it in books, but have never presented its evils to their minds, consider it as little more than a splendid game' (Y, X, 370). Such ignorance may be overcome by education. A different kind of book can present those evils to their minds, as Johnson fiercely sets out to do, in such a way as to produce 'sorrow for the . . . calamities of others . . . by an act of the imagination, that realises the event' (*Ram*. 60: Y, III, 318). Even those who lack goodness rather than wisdom, the 'paymasters and agents, contractors and commissaries' – who rejoice at the prolonging of slaughter 'and laugh from their desks at bravery and science, while they are adding figure to figure, and . . . computing the profits of a siege or tempest' (Y, X, 371) – even these have something reassuringly human in their selfish profiteering. Their wickedness poses no problems of credibility or comprehension: they stand to gain. Already, however, Johnson is stressing their pleasure as well as their profit; and beyond the financially motivated there remain those whose interest, being political, is less straightforward. While historically they had aims in view which could be (and were) argumentatively defended, Johnson ignores these as far as possible (even the ignominious aim of acquiring power), to suggest instead absolute malice. Of those who 'wish for war, but not for conquest', who hope to 'diffuse discontent and inflame malignity' he alleges that their 'hope is malevolence, and their good is evil' (Y, X, 374–5). In *The Patriot*, a man who claims that name is one who 'raises false hopes' purposely to cause 'disappointment and discontent', whose design 'is not to benefit his country, but to gratify his malice'. Although Johnson again mentions 'counting the profits', he seems to dissociate those profits, though in the same sentence, from the pure disinterested delight of malevolence as it 'enjoyed the patriotic pleasure of hearing sometimes, that thousands had been slaughtered in a battle, and sometimes that a navy had been dispeopled by poisoned air and corrupted food' (Y, X, 394, 391, 396). Here the patriot is to his countrymen as Savage's mother to her son, and the contempt expressed in these pamphlets gives way to disgust and fear.

For comparable literary representations of wholesale destructiveness we must turn away from the age of enlightenment, to Marlowe's Tamburlaine or Barabas, to Dryden's Muley Moloch, or to Beckford's Vathek. Johnson's malignants, though their setting is actuality and the style in which he describes them is restrained, have a touch of nightmare which allows comparison with these. The creatures of his Soame Jenyns review are as fantastical as Vathek himself.

Johnson's presentation of evil, with its emphasis on the infliction of pain, reflects his sensitivity. Thomas Tyers reported him as saying 'he would not sit at table, where a lobster that had been roasted alive was one of the dishes'.[20] He reacted as strongly to literary as to culinary cruelty, recording his outrage at John of Lancaster's treacherous killing of the confederates in *Henry the Fourth, Part II*, at Gloucester's blinding in *King Lear*, and at the animal experiments in *Cymbeline*. He found the death of Cordelia too painful to be ever voluntarily read through, the speech in which Hamlet declares his determination to destroy Claudius in soul as well as body 'too horrible to be read or to be uttered', and the scene in which Othello kills Desdemona a 'dreadful' one, 'not to be endured'.[21] When he writes of the phenomenon of cruelty, of pleasure in others' suffering, he both records and communicates such pain.

This phenomenon occupies a prominent place in many of Johnson's general essays on human life. Though it is more conspicuous and shocking than simple competition, it is not unrelated to the system of thought considered here. While its absolute form is a monstrosity to cause amazement, there is nothing surprising, for Johnson any more than for Swift, in the twin propositions that we hate those who outdo us and draw comfort from those who drop behind. That 'when you sink, I seem the higher' may be 'thought too base for human Breast',[22] but it is nonetheless a truism to be reiterated, not discovered. Malice, even absolute malice, can hardly be separated on one hand from the frustration of inferiors who feel themselves out of the running, or on the other hand from a superior's sense of exemption and apartness. In both these forms it is pandered to by those mistaken scales of judgment which mark us off from others as either grander or pettier; in both cases an allegiance to the ideal of greatness becomes distantly implicated in the fostering of absolute evil. While great suffering may evoke compassion, 'Petty mischiefs . . . are always seen with a kind of malicious pleasure' (*Ram.* 176: Y, V, 164), and so are mischiefs happening to the great, or to those inaccurately seen as great. Since malignity becomes aggravated as the element of self-advancement or self-protection decreases, malice towards inferiors (who do not even appear to threaten our position) is the more hateful and the harder to credit.

Johnson's essays subject the mysterious sources of malignity to analytical consideration. In *Rambler* 56 (Y, III, 299–304) he writes of the possible ill-feeling being fostered against him by those correspondents whom he has ignored. Acquitting himself 'of *malice prepense*, of settled hatred or contrivances of mischief', he nevertheless suspects himself of 'too much indifference to the happiness of others'; and he points out how from such slight causes out-and-out malice may reciprocally arise. The essay, reasonable, balanced and conciliatory in tone, investigates the murky boundaries between resentment, envy and *malice prepense*; it seems a far cry from the passionate intensity of Savage's mother. Its ending, however, returns to the notion of actual malice – not settled hatred but a disposition to enjoy a neighbour's trouble – and finds it to be universal. Johnson advises his potential contributor to 'observe the cautions of Swift, and write secretly in his own chamber, without communicating his design to his nearest friend, for the nearest friend will be pleased with an opportunity of laughing'. A footnote in the Yale edition points to Swift's habit of anonymity as the reference here, but surely Johnson was also glancing at Swift's famous endorsement of La Rochefoucault's maxim that we find pleasure

> In all Distresses of our Friends. . . .
> What Poet would not grieve to see
> His Brethren write as well as he?

(Johnson later commended Swift's knowledge of the world as shown in this poem; he frequently alluded to it or the maxim or both.[23]) Malignity, which this essay has carefully argued out of the relationship between correspondent and periodical writer, flows back into that between correspondent and nearest friend.

The blend of envy and malignity – not directly self–interested but not divorced from feelings of rivalry – is enough to provoke in Johnson a feeling related to incredulity: to avoid this vice 'it is not necessary that any one should aspire to heroism or sanctity, but only, that he should resolve not to quit the rank which nature assigns him, and wish to maintain the dignity of a human being'. The same essay (*Rambler* 183) defines envy as including 'the satisfaction of poisoning the banquet which they cannot taste' and 'the pain of seeing others pleased' (Y, V, 196–200). This and no. 143 delineate the relationship and the distinction between competitiveness and envy. An author balked of recognition for himself, says no. 143, progresses smoothly to denying it to others:

> When the excellence of a new composition can no longer be
> contested, and malice is compelled to give way to the unanimity of
> applause, there is yet this one expedient [the accusation of

plagiarism] to be tried, by which the author may be degraded, though his work be reverenced; and the excellence which we cannot obscure, may be set at such a distance [traced to its source in an earlier writer] as not to overpower our fainter lustre. (Y, IV, 394)

Johnson sometimes takes steps to prevent us from thinking this satisfaction or this pain alien to ourselves. The almost offensively clear-sighted lovers Hymenaeus and Tranquilla imply that Mr Rambler himself may be subject to the temptation elsewhere described as that of wishing 'to destroy that reputation which [he has] no hopes to share' (*Ram*. 167, *Adv*. 85: Y, V, 120–1; II, 412). Shortly afterwards Johnson implicates himself and his readers in competitive envy through use of the first person plural. 'Of them, whose rise we could not hinder, we solace ourselves by prognosticating the fall' (*Ram*. 172: Y, V, 147. Cf. above, p.108). At other times, however, he unleashes against such malignity the full force of righteous condemnation. Only a few days after describing how *we* solace *ourselves*, he characterizes, in *Rambler* 175, those who prey on others as 'indeed the meanest and cruelest of human beings' before, remembering his undesired but intrusive knowledge of human baseness, he corrects himself: 'Others, yet less rationally wicked, pass their lives in mischief, because they cannot bear the sight of success, and mark out every man for hatred, whose fame or fortune they believe encreasing' (Y, V, 163).

Johnson's stunningly energetic and figurative accounts of this 'mischief' eclipse even those of purposeful competitiveness. They recur throughout *The Rambler*, with, for whatever reason, a special concentration in August 1751:

When once a man has made celebrity necessary to his happiness, he has put it in the power of the weakest and most timorous malignity, if not to take away his satisfaction, at least to withhold it. His enemies may . . . gratify their malice by quiet neutrality. (Y, V, 13)

This summary, in no. 146, follows on no. 143, which investigates writers as typical of the excellence-envy struggle, and no. 144, which, though mainly devoted to a *Spectator*-like series of group character sketches, is chiefly remarkable for its extended and chilling account of malignity against greatness. The first appearance of excellence 'unites multitudes against it'. Johnson firmly distinguishes malice from competition here, if only because more people are capable of the former than of the latter.

The hazards of those that aspire to eminence would be much diminished if they had none but acknowledged rivals to encounter. . . . Yet such is the state of the world, that no sooner can any man emerge from the crowd, and fix the eyes of the publick upon him, than he stands as a mark to the arrows of lurking calumny, and receives, in the tumult of hostility, from distant and from nameless hands, wounds not always easy to be cured. . . . when war is once declared, volunteers flock to the standard, multitudes follow the camp only for want of employment . . . so pleased with an opportunity of mischief that they toil without prospect of praise, and pillage without hope of profit.

When any man has endeavoured to deserve distinction, he . . . will find the utmost acrimony of malice among those whom he never could have offended. . . . Nothing is too gross or too refined, too cruel or too trifling to be practised; very little regard is had to the rules of honourable hostility, but every weapon is accounted lawful.

Johnson carefully avoids any images of lists or duels, which would suggest the more regulated, less hazardous encounters of acknowledged competitors for actual prizes. He avoids also the terms of covert assassination and of hunting, although 'blows of invisible assailants' and 'arrows of lurking calumny' hint at cloak-and-dagger or sporting violence. Instead, he chooses mainly the terms of full-scale war: armies, volunteers flocking to standards, flying squadrons, pillage. The metaphor is drawn out through six paragraphs; it probably expanded beyond expectation in the writing, since it has no bearing on the characters which follow and which cannot be seen in its terms; in revision Johnson deleted subsidiary figures of speech which might distract attention from the central one.

The pell-mell vigour of the passage owes some of its disturbing quality to a certain deliberate inappropriateness. The armies, vividly realized, are all on one side: the apparently lone contender on the other side remains unimaginable, a Hector or Achilles confronting a host instead of a single opponent. In *The Vanity of Human Wishes* Johnson depicts Charles XII alone, like the candidate for renown in this essay, rushing to the battlefield to challenge 'surrounding kings' or 'hostile millions' (lines 198–9, 218). The reader knows that Charles marched in fact at the head of an army, but in the poem he is the solitary figure on his own side to draw attention. In both poem and essay Johnson must have deliberately created the discrepancy, in the 'original' sense of the image, between surrounding armies and single champion. For in the 'secondary sense' the discrepancy exactly represents the way things are. An individual who has climbed to eminence *does* find himself confronting hostile multitudes of opponents though not competitors. Johnson, who valued exact parallelism in a metaphor, and feared that 'the mention of particulars' might reduce its force by turning the mind 'more upon the original than the secondary sense, more upon that from which the illustration is drawn than that to which it is applied' (*Lives*, I, 45), has here produced an image which *does* turn the mind quite thoroughly upon the circumstances of actual war; but the impossible onesidedness of the war as described turns the mind back to the figurative sense. In this way the remarkably detailed and realistic image nevertheless adds a touch of nightmare unrealism to the vision of envious malignity.

In *The Lives of the Poets* the malice directed against success becomes a theme yet more vital than in Johnson's earlier biographies; its recurrence is an organizing and unifying factor in the collection. It is announced early: not in the first life, where Johnson's most important general theme is that of scale, but in the second. The life of Denham accumulates three striking instances of malice between rival writers (as formulated by Swift, who says a poet, 'rather than they should excel, /[would] wish his Rivals all in Hell').[24] First, *Cooper's Hill* 'had such reputation as to excite the common artifice by which envy degrades excellence': it was rumoured to be not Denham's own. Secondly, Johnson presents Butler's 'malignant lines' on Denham's madness as an example of absolute, unmotivated malice: 'I know not . . . what provocation incited Butler to do that which no provocation can excuse.' Thirdly, he quotes Denham's comparison of the mutual malignancy of authors to the Turkish sultan's liquidation of close relatives; Johnson emphasizes the truth, not the uniqueness, of this insight by quoting along with Denham's image the similar ones of Orrery and Pope (*Lives*, I, 72, 75, 76). The life of Denham establishes the commonness of literary malignity. It prepares the ground for Johnson himself to ascribe Turkish malignity to great men like Milton and Addison (I, 104; II, 120), besides innumerable instances of envious malignity in little men (I, 317, 346, II, 182; III, 215). In all these cases actual rivalry, which could have been pointed to as motive, is ignored or minimized.

Johnson assumes that his readers will share his views. He offers no comment on phrases like 'conspicuous enough to excite malevolence' and 'such excellence as to raise much envy', or on equating praise of liberty with 'an envious desire of . . . degrading greatness' (II, 236, 318; III, 411–12). Not only writers but the general public, he suggests, not only the public but *we* (again associating both himself and his readers in this fault common to humanity) may be glad to see excellence brought lower (I, 290). The *Lives*' most characteristic attitude to envious malice is a resigned acceptance which in the essays appeared only as an infrequent alternative to vigorous indignation.

Malice towards *inferiors*, on the contrary, powerful malice, drew from Johnson a series of denunciations which never slackened in force; it might become less astonishing with the passage of time, but never less shocking. In the life of Savage he uses it as a key to the reader's sympathy. Ironically, Savage suffers malice from both directions. His weakness attracts cruelty from his mother, from whom he might have expected parental protectiveness. His purely notional eminence attracts a hatred which is real.

Page (a 'hireling judge' like the one in *The Vanity of Human Wishes*, line 26) tries to get him convicted for homicide with a direct appeal to envious malignancy: 'Gentlemen of the jury, you are to consider that Mr. Savage is a very great man, a much greater man than you or I, gentlemen of the jury' (*Lives*, II, 349). Savage, who is in many ways a representative of struggling humanity, and with whom Johnson associated himself, is one whose vulnerability makes him a classic victim of powerful malice, while at the same time the hollowness of his triumphs might have been expected to protect him from envious malice, but does not. He stands as exemplar not only of the fact that 'the summits of human life' are unreasonably envied, but also of all the cruelty to which those of 'a lower station' can be subjected (II, 321).

Malice from a superior position may sometimes be explained, like the envious sort, through a tenuous relationship with competitiveness; but in this case to explain is not to excuse. When Johnson appears to find excuses for it he does so in a spirit of bitter sarcasm (note that in order to opt for powerful malice one must reject community):

> It is so little pleasing to any man to see himself wholly overlooked in the mass of things, that he may be allowed to try a few expedients for procuring some kind of supplemental dignity. . . . He may by a steady perseverance in his ferocity fright his children, and harrass his servants, but the rest of the world will look on and laugh; and he will have the comfort at last of thinking, that he lives only to raise contempt and hatred. (*Ram.* 11: Y, III, 59–60)

In *Adventurer* 50 he singles out for chastisement a writer of false newspaper reports, one of those 'whose pride is to deceive others without any gain or glory to themselves'. This journalist's disinterestedness is qualified only by the word *importance*, which hints at some advantage to his own competitive self-esteem. He is debarred from the malicious pleasure of witnessing the pain he causes, but 'to have done mischief, is of some importance. . . . he may . . . please himself with reflecting, that by his abilities and address, some addition is made to the miseries of life' (Y, II, 365–6).

In *Rambler* 148 (Y, V, 22–7) Johnson excoriates cruel parents in terms which recall his life of Savage. He represents parental tyranny as shocking all our expectations (the early Romans apparently disbelieved in it; our slowness to suspect it, like that of Earl Rivers, actually helps it to 'wanton in cruelty without controul'); but this time he moves further towards a psychological explanation of its development. The result is a progressive deepening of resonance in an equally outraged and condemnatory passage.

> If in any situation the heart were inaccessible to malignity, it might be supposed to be sufficiently secured by parental rela-

tion. . . . To see helpless infancy stretching out her hands . . . without any powers to alarm jealousy, or any guilt to alienate affection, must surely awaken tenderness in every human mind; and tenderness once excited will be hourly encreased by the natural contagion of felicity, by the repercussion of communicated pleasure, and the consciousness of the dignity of benefaction.

A reader who has perceived the pattern of Johnson's comments on malignity will recognize that the phrases 'it might be supposed' and 'must surely' herald their own contradiction.[25] The images of contagious felicity invoke the ideal of community, mutuality and interdependence; but that of 'the dignity of benefaction' circles back to the earlier part of the paragraph, being relevant solely in *un*equal relationships.

Consciousness of one's own dignity as benefactor is a quality one would expect Johnson the moralist to view with suspicion, and sure enough at the beginning of his next paragraph he diagnoses behind this consciousness the more sinister 'pride of superiority'. This may choose to gratify itself not through benefaction but by 'another method':

with exciting terror as the inflicter of pain; he may delight his solitude with contemplating the extent of his power . . . with . . . multiplications of prohibition, and varieties of punishment; and swell with exultation when he considers how little of the homage that he receives he owes to choice.

Comparing the tyrannical father with the tyrannical ruler, Johnson finds the difference between them to be that between gratuitousness and interest. A prince may have a variety of politic reasons for oppression; on the other hand, though no one will confess that 'he delights in the misery of others . . . yet what other motive can make a father cruel?' Johnson has devised a steady degradation: from 'consciousness of the dignity of benefaction' to 'pride of superiority', from pride of superiority to delight in others' misery: a moral decline and fall from an initial position also occupied by the astronomer in *Rasselas*.

This gradual choice of homage, power and solitude in preference to love is the most alarming possible consequence of success in the struggle to excel. The superiority of a parent, however, is not achieved but temporary and accidental. Johnson's final and practical argument against persecuting one's children is an appeal to inescapable community: one will in turn be dependent on them.

Many of Johnson's essays pillory the insulting malignity of those who consider themselves superior: prospective employers, good-looking women who draw attention to smallpox scars, a squire who settles for being hated in order to be feared, rich relations who inflict on dependants innumerable modes of insult, and tokens of contempt, for which it is not easy to find a name, which vanish to nothing in an attempt to describe them, and yet may, by continual repetition, make day pass after day in sorrow and in terror.[26]

He tells us that the 'lady who is hastening to the scene of action [London] . . . is sure to' triumph over her friends left behind: not that she might, not that some would in her situation, but that she is *sure* to. 'Her hope of giving pain is seldom disappointed; the affected indifference of one . . . and the silent dejection of the rest, all exalt her opinion of her own superiority' (*Idler* 80: Y, II, 249–50).

Pleasure in oppression is as insidious a tendency as envy of superiors, no matter how astonishing it seems to inexperienced people like the young Rasselas. The early Romans may have hesitated to admit that a father can be cruel to his child; twenty-eight years after writing that of the Romans, Johnson expressed himself unsurprised at the rigour of nurses towards their charges. A

Nurse made of common mould will have a pride in overpowering a child's reluctance. There are few minds to which tyranny is not delightful; Power is nothing but as it is felt, and the delight of superiority is proportionate to the resistance overcome. (*Letters*, no. 636)

This malice directed *from* a position of superiority, and psychologically explained, has its own particular horror to match that of the unexplained malice of Savage's mother. In his last years Johnson no longer saw delight in tyranny as an aberration, but as something to be expected in most minds, perhaps in all not of uncommon mould.

Having tracked Johnson's thought this far we may now consider his review of Soame Jenyns's *Free Enquiry into the Nature and Origin of Evil*, with its hypothesis about 'some beings above us' (*Works*, VI, 64) who take pleasure in human suffering. Johnson does not, like Jenyns, think the postulation of such beings makes human pain easier to bear; he does not, like the young Thomas Hardy, consider he would be even half eased by the revelation that 'some vengeful god' takes satisfaction in human sorrow. Johnson's mind did, however, play with the idea of such a vengeful god's existence.[27] Here on earth 'the quiver of Omnipotence is stored with arrows' against the guilty and innocent alike (*Adv.* 120: Y, II, 468). *If* 'God were a power unmerciful and severe', His creatures would have no reasonable alternative but 'to abstract the mind from the contemplation of him'. Here, in his second sermon, reminding the congregation of God's ultimate mercy, Johnson finds it expedient to allow them for a moment to imagine what it would be like if He were *un*merciful (Y, XIV, 18–19).

When, however, Soame Jenyns imagined something similar of hypothetical beings placed between God and man, Johnson reviewed him with an indignation even greater than that which informed his accounts of Savage's mother and of cruel fathers.[28] Here, however, he rebukes not a malicious individual, not the non-existent 'beings above us', but Jenyns, who has conceived of them. In carrying further Jenyns's 'analogy' between the use of animals by man for food and 'diversion' and the use of man by these postulated beings, Johnson has in mind also Jenyns's description of his own idea as 'impossible to be conceived' (*Works*, VI, 64). In Johnson's hands it becomes inconceivable in a looser sense: not to be imagined without resistance and pain; demanding, like the fate of Gloucester's eyes in *Lear*, the relief of incredulity. He therefore wishes to convey, not anger triumphing over incredulity as in his descriptions of actual malignity, but rather the other way round.

Johnson first provokes us to relieve our minds by incredulity in a part of his review where he is dealing not with malignity as such but with Jenyns's view of poverty. Here he uses an *image* of staggering impersonal malignity, that of torture. The poor, he says, are 'insensible of many little vexations' of the rich, but only as 'a malefactor . . . ceases to feel the cords that bind him, when the pincers are tearing his flesh' (*Works*, VI, 55). This was a common analogy in Johnson's own and the previous century: the *Dictionary* quotes from Jeremy Taylor under *rack* ('1. An engine to torture'), 'Did ever any man upon the *rack* afflict himself, because he had received a cross answer from his mistress'; Locke and Hume both use, as example or as image, the way the pain of the rack obliterates other considerations.[29] It seems to me likely that in comparing the pain of binding with that of torture Johnson had also in mind the scene in *Lear* which he found 'too horrid to be endured in dramatick exhibition', when Cornwall, anticipating the 'extrusion' of Gloucester's eyes, cries gloatingly, 'Bind fast his corky arms'.[30] One reason why torture seems an extreme or exaggerated simile for poverty is that it implies a human agent deliberately inflicting it, like Cornwall, or perhaps watching it with enjoyment, like Regan. Johnson manages to suggest that Soame Jenyns and like-minded people, though they do not actually produce the pain of poverty, do observe it with the culpably unmoved superiority of a paid executioner. He here takes an idea unacceptable to him (that poverty *luckily* exempts from certain pains felt by the rich) and renders it so distressful to us that we are bound to reject it; he 'compel[s] the mind to relieve its distress by incredulity', as he says of spectators of *Lear*. He performs in little, with this idea about poverty, the same strategy which he applies to Jenyns's notion of superior beings.

Several pages later, Johnson comes to Jenyns's suggestion that human miseries are somehow of service to these beings, for *either* pleasure or utility. Johnson quickly tips the balance to make them not self-interested but absolutely malicious, motivated not by utility but by pleasure. Being apparently immune from suffering themselves, they have not even the human excuse which Imlac suggests when he mentions 'the natural malignity of hopeless misery' (*Rass.* XII). What they seek is sport, a word which occurs five times in Johnson's key passage, and which implies both the agents' amusement and their human victims' animality.

In *Rambler* 176 Johnson wrote of irresistible 'merriment' at others' petty troubles (Y, V, 164). He twice referred to European colonists slaughtering more primitive people in 'mirth' or 'wanton merriment'.[31] The link between malignity and mirth or sport, which is of paramount importance in this passage of the review, shows itself also in the pages of the *Dictionary*, published only the year before. It too may be connected with Shakespeare's Gloucester, whose despairing comment on hypothetical superior tormentors recalls his recent ordeal: 'As flies to wanton boys, are we to th' Gods;/They kill us for their sport' (IV, i, 36–7). This Johnson quotes twice in the *Dictionary*: under *sport* and again under *wanton*. Other quotations under *sport* and similar words give them an extremely sinister turn. Under *sport*, noun ('1. Play; diversion; game; frolick and tumultuous merriment', which precedes '2. Mock; contemptuous mirth'), Johnson quotes, besides Gloucester, from Ford in *The Merry Wives of Windsor*, offering to become a sport and jest should his jealous suspicions prove unfounded, in ignorance that he is being made a sport and jest already (III, iii, 139). To these he adds three threatening usages from the Bible: on the sport of fools 'in the wantonness of sin', on the man (kinsman to one of Fielding's practical jokers) who destructively 'deceiveth his neighbour, and saith, am not I in *sport*',[32] and on Samson cruelly called to make sport for the Philistines when 'their hearts were merry', and soon to exact his terrible revenge.[33] Only one quotation (from Sidney) uses *sport*, noun (1), in an urbane and happy context.

Again, under *sport*, transitive ('1. To divert; to make merry'), all five examples are sinister. They include Sidney, this time on people sporting themselves with a poor man weeping and bleeding, and Leontes in *The Winter's Tale* replying brutally to his rejected wife's attempt to believe that his persecution of her is in sport (II, i, 58–61). Under *jest*, '1. Any thing ludicrous, or meant only to raise laughter', Johnson quotes first from *The Taming of the Shrew*, Vincentio's question whether Petruchio is speaking truth or only playing 'Like pleasant travellers to break a *jest*/Upon the company you overtake' (the answer being that Petruchio, though he now speaks truth, *has* been jesting in a wild and baffling manner, backed up by the sportfully but thoroughly disciplined Kate: IV, v, 72). The next three quotations suggest that certain subjects *ought* not to be matter for jest.

Under *merry*, '2. Causing laughter', Johnson quotes (solely) Shakespeare's Titus Andronicus, enumerating his wrongs preparatory to cutting the throats of enemies who had made the cutting-off of *his* hand into 'a *merry jest*' (V, ii, 175). Under *game*, '3. Insolent merriment; sportive insult', he quotes the story of Samson again, this time in Milton's poem, 'make a *game* of my calamities' (line 1331). Under *amusement*, two out of three examples are cruel: from Swift (see above, p.39) and from Pope: 'his *amusement* was to give poison to dogs and cats, and see them expire by slower or quicker torments'.[34]

In a high proportion of these *Dictionary* examples, the cruelty includes deception. To be kept in the dark, with a deluded or inadequate concept of what is going on, is an aspect of the victim's role which Johnson consistently emphasizes. To a malignant superior an uncomprehending sufferer is especially funny, as witness the practical jokers of eighteenth-century novels.[35]

There is nothing remarkable in the fact that Johnson's *Dictionary* should recognize that these potentially cheerful words are also applied to amusement at pain which others suffer, either accidentally or by express arrangement of the person amused. The society in which he wrote was one that relished such amusement, as readers of its novels know, and his chosen illustrative quotations show that earlier generations had shared this relish.[36] What is remarkable is that a lexicographer so full of 'fun, and comical humour, and love of nonsense'[37] should weight his examples under *game*, *jest* and *sport* so heavily towards the sadistically as distinct from the harmlessly playful – and this despite his desire to make his examples 'pleasing or useful', and wherever possible even 'verdure and flowers' to relieve 'the dusty deserts of barren philology' (*Works*, V, 38). It shows, at least, that his sense of the connection between sport and cruelty was considerably more vivid than most people's is.

The superior beings of the review see mankind as animals: not the domestic animals whose dependent relationship, says *Rambler* 148, endears them to us their protectors, but as victims for blood-sport or vivisection, which two activities (sportful rather than useful) hold a special place in Johnson's imagery of malice. The animal experiments in *Idler* 17 – 'to nail dogs to tables and open them alive' for amusement – have the gratuitousness of pure malevolence. By this sport 'knowledge is not always sought, and is very seldom attained' (Y, II, 55–6). McIntosh writes that Johnson 'compares man to animals when he wants to describe pitiless cruelty or inexplicable suffering'.[38] He thinks that Johnson does this rarely, but I disagree. In *The Vanity of Human Wishes* (lines 5–6) snares are set for mankind by the personified passions Hope and Fear, Desire and Hate, which therefore share certain important characteristics with the imaginary beings of the Soame Jenyns review. *Rambler* 175 is only one of many essays employing sporting imagery: it describes innocent people, animal-like, as liable to be 'intangled' in 'the snares of artifice' and 'the pitfals of treachery';

the predators seem human as they set such devices, but bestial as they are 'lured . . . by the scent of prey; and . . . hope for some opportunity to devour' (Y, V, 162, 161).

Johnson also uses sporting imagery light-heartedly. In 'A Short Song of Congratulation'

> All that prey on vice and folly
>   Joy to see their quarry fly,
> Here the gamester light and jolly
>   There the lender grave and sly. (Y, VI, 307)

Rambler 176 maintains that the

> diversion of baiting an author . . . is more lawful than the sport of teizing other animals, because for the most part he comes voluntarily to the stake, furnished, as he imagines . . . with resistless weapons, and impenetrable armour, with the mail of the boar of Erymanth, and the paws of the lion of Nemea. (Y, V, 165)

Here the author who imaginatively identifies himself with the powerful monsters instead of the baited bull or badger unintentionally transforms his critics from mob torturers to the champion Hercules, out to rid the world of evils. But light-hearted examples do not dispel the sinister associations which this imagery generally carries.

In the famous passage in the Jenyns review, Johnson deploys all the key concepts and images which he associated with malignity: the superiority indicated by looking down from a height, the spectatorial detachment (see below, pp.164ff.), the laughter, the delight as in a sport, the equation of the puzzled victims with tormented animals, immeasurably unimportant and petty. If Johnson's essays have correctly diagnosed the psychological springs of superior malevolence, then his review of Jenyns provides a vivid metaphorical, almost allegorical, account of that syndrome.[39] I shall quote from it using italics to pick out the vital images. These beings

> have many *sports* analogous to our own. . . . they *amuse themselves*, now and then, with sinking a ship, and *stand round the fields of Blenheim, or the walls of Prague* [a city which in the previous war had been three times besieged], as *we encircle a cockpit.* . . . Some of them, perhaps, are virtuosi, and *delight* in the operations of an asthma, as a human *philosopher* in the effects of an air pump. To swell a man with a tympany is as *good sport* as to blow a frog. Many a *merry bout* have these *frolick beings* . . . and *good sport* it is to see a man *tumble* [like a clown] with an epilepsy, and revive and *tumble* again, and all this he *knows not why*. As they are *wiser and more powerful than we*, they have more *exquisite diversions*; for we have no

way of procuring *any sport so brisk* and so lasting, as the paroxysms of the gout and stone, which, undoubtedly, must make *high mirth*, especially if the *play* be a little diversified with the *blunders and puzzles* of the blind and deaf. *We know not how far their sphere of observation may extend.* Perhaps, now and then, a *merry* being may place himself in *such a situation, as to enjoy, at once, all the varieties* of an epidemical disease, or *amuse his leisure* with the *tossings and contortions* of every possible pain, *exhibited* together. (*Works*, VI, 64–5)

In the second paragraph Johnson's mood shifts from the darker to the more playful as he moves from Jenyns's conception to Jenyns himself as a poor floundering animal tormented by his own fictional beings – but not until the various elements have fused into a single searing image of what malignant power can be. From pleasure in others' inferiority the way leads plain to amusement at their suffering. This image haunts the remoter reaches of Johnson's mind, casting a shade over more acceptable, even over the most coveted, versions of superiority.

9

SUPERIOR
OBSERVERS

But much more sweet thy lab'ring steps to guide,
To Vertues heights . . .
From thence to look below on humane kind,
Bewilder'd in the Maze of Life, and blind.

(Lucretius, *De rerum natura*, II:
Dryden's translation, lines 7–11)

---

the above-seated Gods . . . place themselves on the ascent
of some Promontory in Heaven, and from thence survey
the little mole-hill of Earth. And trust me, there cannot be
a more delightsome prospect.

(Erasmus, *The Praise of Folly*,
translated by White Kennett)

[The poet] must . . . observe the power of all the passions
in all their combinations. . . . and consider himself, as
presiding . . . as a being superiour to time and place.

(Imlac in *Rasselas*, chapter X)

A POPULAR IMAGE of greatness for Johnson's age was that of the distant
watcher, placed high up, observing scenes of struggle, passion and misery,
and remaining uninvolved and dispassionate. To Johnson this image
suggests a peculiar kind of threat, a peculiar kind of negation of community
and potential for evil. This is so despite its connection with achieved
greatness, and despite particular aspects of Johnson's thought: the value he
set on broad observation of life and his association of height with excellence.
His treatment of the watcher from on high relates to several traditions in
literature, which will be discussed here under the categories of writer as
observer, God and other rulers as observers, and good man as observer. In
each of these the observer enjoys a different kind of superiority over those

he observes. Johnson's handling of each of these motifs is affected by his concern for adjustment of scale and his ambivalence about greatness.

The writer, to Johnson as to many others before and since, is before everything an observer of life. This idea sustains Johnson's optical imagery discussed above (pp.29ff.). He praises Shakespeare for having 'looked through life', identifies 'the power of presenting pictures to the mind' as one of 'the great sources of poetical delight', and 'acknowledged, that "The Spectator" was the most happily chosen of all' titles for periodical essays.[1] He certainly saw his own literary role as one of observation, but as W.J. Bate writes he 'was unable merely to observe, but had to participate and share' (Y, III, xxix).

All this was part of a long tradition. When Homer introduces his hero at the beginning of the *Odyssey*, nothing said of him is more important for the coming poem than that he has seen much. Johnson several times cites these lines. He quotes them with Pope's translation in *Rambler* 158 as part of the 'eminently adorned and illuminated' opening of Homer's poem (Y, V, 79). In the *Dictionary* he quotes Pope's version under *observant* ('1. Attentive; diligent; watchful'). In a letter (see above, p.72) he humorously alludes to Horace's allusion to this passage.

English poets also laid claim to vision. Milton in lines 27–8 of *Paradise Lost* besought his 'heavenly Muse': 'Say first, for Heav'n hides nothing from thy view/Nor the deep Tract of Hell . . .'. His Christian epic laid stress on far-reaching cosmic views, as enjoyed by his superhuman characters and as displayed by Michael to Adam in book XI. Pope must have remembered Milton's confident invocation of heavenly seeing as he pursued his own more dubious notion of sight through the windings which open *An Essay on Man* (lines 3–32).

> Let us (since Life can little more supply
> Than just to look about us and to die) . . .
> The latent tracts, the giddy heights explore
> Of all who blindly creep, or sightless soar;
> Eye Nature's walks. . . .

Pope speaks ostensibly as representative of a strictly limited vision: 'Of Man what see we, but his station here . . . ?' For him, only the non-existent being

> who thro' vast immensity can pierce,
> See worlds on worlds compose one universe,
> Observe how system into system runs,

could be competent, like Milton's heavenly Muse, to tell us about causes. But the poet is not that being, and he reminds his readers aggressively that we too are incapable of seeing into the intricate cosmic system. He mentions our blindness or imperfect sight again in lines 36, 38, 60, 77, 85, 193–6, and 239–40 of the first epistle.[2] A comparison with Milton suggests that it is the new cosmology more than anything that has produced the poets' plunge from penetration into obscurity (cf. above, pp.23ff.). In *The Temple of Fame*, following Chaucer, Pope had allowed himself a comprehensive view which is absent from *An Essay on Man* and *The Dunciad*. (Although Soame Jenyns drew on *An Essay on Man* for his great-chain explanation of human suffering, there is a marked difference between the poem's confused seeing and the unimpeded spectacle enjoyed by the beings whom Johnson developed from those of Jenyns.) Pope has abdicated the position of seer, and satirizes any claim to thoroughly superior vision, though, in this as in other matters, his modest air cloaks an actually ambitious programme. He tells us how little he sees, but presents detailed and authoritative observation; he both decries and adopts the role of privileged spectator.

Not surprisingly, seeing is as important an organizing concept in Johnson's writings as in Pope's. The original edition of *Rambler* 57 (quoted above, p.66) used the verb to *see* three times in its first two sentences (Johnson, revising, altered words but retained the meaning: Y, III, 305). *Rambler* 103 describes curiosity, 'one of the permanent and certain characteristicks of a vigorous intellect', almost entirely in terms of seeing (Y, IV, 184–5). This desire to see, representative of the desire to know, is by no means invariably productive of good (the passage about curiosity prefaces Johnson's account of Nugaculus: see above, pp.88–9) but it may be so. The prostitute Misella is certain that if the secure and fortunate could *see* the miserable condition of fallen women, their hearts would be softened into a desire to rescue (*Ram.* 171: Y, V, 144–5). This kind of seeing, 'that realises the event' (*Ram.* 60: Y, III, 318), is what Johnson's writings aim to produce. *The Lives of the Poets* is a constant struggle against obscurity: bemisting panegyric, the blanket of forgetfulness which enwraps alike a Pomfret, a Dryden, and an Edmund Smith, the secrecy in which Pope and Swift deliberately involve themselves.

Johnson's several dream-visions (*Ramblers* 67, 102, 105, 'The Vision of Theodore') present the same sort of comprehensive view as *The Temple of Fame*: boundaries are set to the field of sight in 'Theodore' where mists intervene, but on the whole the convention of the dreamer's comprehensive sight prevails. Johnson's other periodical essays, too, make much of seeing as perception; but they also, as the aptly-named *Spectator* does not, make much of the difficulties of seeing accurately (something with which Johnson was, in life, all too familiar). His second *Rambler*, for instance, presents humankind in general averting their gaze from what is present towards what is still invisible, and even their advisers and censors only imagining that their surveys are more comprehensive and revealing (Y, III, 9–11).

Johnson's discussions of how to attend to both things vast and things minute (see above, p.32) characteristically stress the problems of each kind of seeing: long and large views are hard to combine with precision; the distractions of the distant make us liable to miss what is before our eyes. *Rambler* 28 (which employs the analogy of an optical instrument and which keeps up the idea of seeing in *turn our view*, *blinded*, *cloud* and *observers*) warns us against negligence in examining ourselves, and connects such examination with entering 'his presence who views effects in their causes, and actions in their motives' (Y, III, 153–6). *Rambler* 63 and *Adventurer* 137 voice related warnings: 'To take a view at once distinct and comprehensive of human life' requires 'a wider survey of the world than human eyes can take'. 'Of the state with which practice has not acquainted us, we snatch a glimpse, we discern a point' (Y, III, 336; II, 488–9). These remarks show less confidence even than Pope, who is willing to view and pronounce freely on 'all this scene of Man',[3] though not on the universe. 'Irresolution and mutability' are identified in *Rambler* 63 as characteristic faults of those whose wide views 'are continually ranging over all the scenes of human existence' (Y, III, 337). Sermon 8 says baldly that of human life 'to judge only by the eye, is not the way to discover truth' (Y, XIV, 85).

Yet, despite his own message that a view of human life both distinct and comprehensive is impossible, Johnson repeatedly attempts such a view. In a particular and personal manner in *A Journey to the Western Islands*, and more broadly in *Rasselas* and *The Vanity of Human Wishes*, he carries out what McIntosh calls 'the Augustan survey, which examines the various scenes of human life to gain wisdom through broader perspectives' or the 'Johnsonian survey', which 'relies on an encyclopedic structure',[4] even though each survey ends in a confession of limitations. Johnson has been accused of observing from too great a distance in each of these works, but undoubtedly he aimed at distinctness as well as comprehensiveness, at discovering 'petty discriminations . . . by a close inspection' (*Adv.* 84: Y, II, 406).

The *Journey*, like most travel books, makes much use of the vocabulary of *sight-seeing*: it fully reflects Johnson's pleasure in this process. To the girl to whom he gave Cocker's *Arithmetic*, at the beginning of his passage across the Highlands, he spoke of surveying, of contemplating appearances, and of comparing the effect of mountains to the eye with their effect on the life lived among them (Y, IX, 36–40). He brings his book to its end on his 'opportunity of seeing, and . . . the reflections which that sight has raised'. But it has never allowed us to forget the limits of observation: Johnson began to write it after experiencing a hampered prospect,[5] and much of his search has been for the vanished past, which in the absence of written records, 'once out of sight is lost for ever' (Y, IX, 164, 40, 65). His concluding words, that he has 'seen but little', decline the role of superior observer.

Words of seeing and showing abound in *Rasselas* too. Of the central characters, Imlac corresponds to the authorial observer of the *Journey*; the others fulfil the expectation of *Rambler* 63 that such wide views will result in irresolution and mutability. They escape from a valley (common emblem of restricted sight) in which they are themselves subject to close surveillance (see below, p.163): the early chapters are dominated by the desire to see – the image of expanding horizons – and the later chapters by the difficulties of the skill of seeing. In the valley Rasselas' 'chief amusement was to picture to himself that world which he had never seen' (IV). Having 'no prospect' of escape, he singles out Imlac (the least dissatisfied valley-dweller on account of his 'mind replete with images') for skill in painting 'the scenes of life', and finds that Imlac when young had also been keen on seeing what he had never seen before (VII-IX, XII). Rasselas has his views figuratively 'extended to a wider space' while his actual looking or surveying is still severely restricted (IV, V, VII). On his emergence he is 'delighted with a [literally] wider horizon' (XIV).[6]

The travellers choose Cairo because it offers the chance to 'see all the conditions of humanity' (XVI). Nekayah, having overcome some difficulty in adapting to literally wide prospects, now confronts a difficulty of the figurative kind. When Rasselas attacks her conclusions on marriage, she replies that 'To the mind, as to the eye, it is difficult to compare with exactness objects vast in their extent, and various in their parts' and that we cannot always 'perceive the whole at once' (XXVIII). By the end of the story she has become an observer equal to Imlac in his youth, eager to inspect the pyramids 'within and without with my own eyes', and led to the catacombs by her desire to 'see something to morrow which I never saw before' (XXX, XLVII). Imlac, from his different vantage-point of age, expects different benefits from this 'survey' (XXXII).

The travellers in *Rasselas* work strenuously at accurate observation, while around them Johnson deploys various examples of observers either prying or remote, to emphasize still further how rare and difficult is accuracy. The story presents its central characters with opportunities of privileged observation, but draws from these no privileged insights. The survey of human life in *Rasselas*, both detailed and extensive, is more adequate than most offered in Johnson's fictions, but it remains, of course, inconclusive.

Observation in *The Vanity of Human Wishes* is less closely identified with personal experience, but even more subject to limitation than in *Rasselas*. Johnson begins by invoking Observation almost as Milton invokes his heavenly Muse: with her 'extensive view' she is to 'Survey . . . Remark . . . watch the busy scenes of crouded life;/Then say' what all that activity signifies.[7] Critical opinion is divided as to the way in which her 'extensive view', with its superhuman scale, operates. Arieh Sachs says that the opening couplet invites us as readers 'to widen our horizon' and comprehend each detail of the whole; Lawrence Lipking that on the contrary it demonstrates the untrustworthiness of sight; Frederick W. Hilles that it puts us in precisely the position ('above the world, looking down' so that even 'the greatest of men dwindle') which I feel Johnson generally disliked and distrusted (see below, p.164ff.). Hilles goes on, however, to argue that the end of the poem reverses the viewpoint, so that we look up to heaven.[8] There is fairly wide agreement that the body of the poem proves the apparent smoothness and ease of observation to be delusive. W.B. Carnochan believes that the poem 'ferrets out the impulses to grand prospective views and subjects them to a critical reading', D.V. Boyd, more sweepingly, that its 'concluding appeal to faith . . . signals the ultimate bankruptcy of its initial appeal to observation'.[9]

Whereas Milton's heavenly Muse could tell the causes of the Fall, since Heaven and Hell were open to her sight, Johnson's Observation soon runs into difficulties. 'But scarce observ'd, the knowing and the bold/Fall . . .' (lines 21–2). Johnson surely intends us to notice his repetition in *observ'd*. As he says in his essays, there is too much going on for the most extensive view to take in every casualty. Observation having failed him, he turns to other sources of intelligence: first in 'Let hist'ry tell' (line 29, which calls on a resource not open to him in the Hebrides); then in summoning Democritus to 'See. . . . descry . . . pierce each scene with philosophic eye', and reveal it to be 'empty shew' (lines 49–68); and finally in requiring of the reader to weigh the testimony of Democritus' 'glance' on the basis of his or her own survey: 'How just that scorn ere yet thy voice declare, Search every state') lines 70–2: see below, p.243, n.27).

When, after his 98 introductory lines, Johnson moves into his series of examples, he continues to stress that he is presenting a survey to the reader's eyes: we are to *see* the picture of Wolsey (line 99), to *behold* the triumphs of Charles XII (line 199); 'blushing Glory', like an aerial figure in an allegorical painting, is to *hide* the sight of the hero's shameful defeat (line 210); the fates of Xerxes and Charles Albert of Bavaria figure as *scenes* of 'pompous woes', those of Marlborough and Swift as 'life's last scene' (lines 223–4, 315).

For the poem's characters as well as for its reader, seeing is uncertain. The swarming crowd in the opening paragraph endures inadequate light in cloud and mist (lines 6–9); the traveller with something to lose fears darkness, though he also fears light (lines 42–4). The exemplary characters are presented as failing to observe either the world or themselves. The scholar is urged to turn his *eyes* on the world, to *see* the undervaluing of learning and the victimization of Laud (lines 157, 161–2, 167–8). The 'triumphal show' and 'martial show' (lines 175, 235) deserve to be seen *through*. The successful suppliant for long life 'views' plenty or riches with 'listless' or 'suspicious' eyes, but 'Hides from himself his state' (lines 263–4, 289, 257).

The survey structure provides the poem with its opening but not its close. As Johnson suggested in *Rambler* 63 and *Adventurer* 137, any evidence that human observation can present will remain inconclusive. The attempt to 'Search every state', encyclopaedic as it seems, leads not to any satisfactory assessment of Democritus, but to further questions: 'will not . . . ? why did . . . ? What gave . . . ? did not . . . ? who shall . . . ? Where then . . . ? Must . . . ? Must . . . ?' (lines 91, 125, 129, 215, 298, 343–5), and as in *Rambler* 28 and in *Rasselas*, to admitting failure and to calling instead on the keener sight of God:

> Safe in his pow'r, whose eyes discern afar
> The secret ambush of a specious pray'r.
> (Lines 353–4)

More emphatically than Pope, Johnson takes up the old image of writer as seer (that is, one who offers the reader superior insights) only in order to expose its limitations.

The discerning God who succeeds to Observation at the end of *The Vanity of Human Wishes* reminds us of another tradition which, with that of writer as seer, lies behind the surveys of Milton and of Pope. It is that of the Bible and later Christian writings. As in the *Iliad* the gods watch from mountain peaks (like Zeus and Poseidon at the opening of book XIII), so in the Old Testament God's height and watchfulness are often associated. They are often ambivalently regarded by His sinful creatures. Adam and Eve after the Fall hide themselves from the eye of their Maker, vainly of course. The question, 'Is not God in the height of heaven? and behold the height of the stars, how high they are!' forms part of Eliphaz the Temanite's reproach of Job for underestimating God's watchfulness; he goes on, 'And thou sayest, How doth God know? can he judge through the dark cloud?'[10] To think the clouds intercept the divine sight is of course a serious mistake. Psalm 139 puts the case most eloquently of all:

> O Lord, thou hast searched me out and known me: thou knowest
> my down-sitting and mine up-rising, thou understandest my
> thoughts long before.
> Thou art about my path, and about my bed: and spiest out all my
> ways. . . .
> Whither shall I go then from thy Spirit: or whither shall I go
> then from thy presence? . . .
> If I say, Peradventure the darkness shall cover me: then shall my
> night be turned to day.[11]

Milton both emphasizes God's watchfulness from on high and gives the same attribute to malevolent power. His God in His stronghold of Heaven looks securely down on angelic wars and mortal sins; Satan also gazes down at the earth he will corrupt or the kingdoms with which he hopes to tempt Christ.[12] Unlike the observant, exploring human agents in the *Journey* and *Rasselas* and *The Vanity of Human Wishes*, they combine their height with stillness; they do not have to move in order to see everywhere. Johnson quotes from Satan's observation of the earth, 'Round he *surveys*, and well might where he stood,/So high above', in the *Dictionary* under *survey* ('1. To overlook; to have under the view; to view as from a higher place'). Under *distinct* ('3. Clear; unconfused') he gives as the only example Eve's deluded and intoxicated speech on tasting the apple:

> Heav'n is high,
> High and remote, to see from thence *distinct*
> Each thing on earth.

Being now sinful, she is afraid of God's observation: she goes on to picture Him at 'continual watch/. . . with all his spies/About him'; she hopes His sight will share the limitations of the distant human observers of Johnson's essays, and tries, in fact, to deny His vigilance as Job unsuccessfully tried.[13]

The impossibility of concealment from 'the Eternal eye, whose sight discernes/Abstrusest thoughts' was a popular theme with Christian writers aiming to arouse salutary guilt. Isaac Watts provides a representative example in a hymn called 'The All-seeing God', of which the first and last stanzas read:

> Almighty God, thy piercing Eye
>   Strikes thro' the Shades of Night,
> And our most secret Actions lie
>   All open to thy Sight. . . .
>
> O may I now for ever fear
>   T'indulge a sinful Thought,
> Since the Great God can see, and hear,
>   And writes down ev'ry Fault![14]

Johnson showed what he could do in this vein himself in a Latin prayer (one of the last two he composed), based on the collect for the Communion service, which translates:

> Greatest God, to whom the hidden interior of the heart lies open; whom no anxiety, no lust escapes; from whom the subtle craftiness of sinners keeps nothing secret; who, surveying all things, rulest all everywhere. . . .[15]

This is the far-discerning, ambush-watchful God of *The Vanity of Human Wishes*. In the earnest Christian submission of his prayer, Johnson accepts and even welcomes the divine scrutiny. In conversation he referred to it with some vehemence as a fact not to be forgotten (Boswell, II, 104). His second sermon assures the congregation of its traditional benevolence. His tenth is less comforting. We live and act, it says, 'under the eye of our Father and our Judge, by whom nothing is overlooked' (Y, XIV, 17, 107). Since his subject is that of rewards and punishments after death, we sense a threat as well as a reassurance.

The *Dictionary* hints at the threat of investigative power in its treatment of *observer* ('1. One who looks vigilantly on persons and things; close rema[r]ker'), though not in that of *observe* or any other of its derivatives. Its first two examples for observer (1) come from Shakespeare: Johnson quotes lines from the first acts of two plays, in each of which a powerful man retails observations on the character of another. Caesar expresses apprehension about Cassius:

> He reads much;
> He is a great *observer*; and he looks
> Quite thro' the deeds of men.

The Duke in *Measure for Measure* expresses perfect confidence that Angelo's life 'to th'*observer* doth thy history/Fully unfold'. Of the observers mentioned in the quotations (by no means the only ones in these plays, where Cassius, Angelo and the Duke are all spiers out and draconian punishers of secret sins), the hostile one (Cassius) proves to be malevolent and murderous; the benevolent one who might think he understands Angelo (whether or not we equate the Duke himself with this hypothetical person) proves to be dreadfully deceived.[16] As with the *Dictionary* examples under *sport*, etc., we cannot safely pronounce as to how fully these dark and intricate contexts were present in Johnson's thoughts when he picked the lines to illustrate *observer* (though we know that *Measure for Measure*, and the threatened consequences of Angelo's rigour, were often in his mind).[17] But his choice of these quotations in preference to any others does suggest a strong connection in his thinking between the notion of the observer and the notion of power and punishment. God's distant discernment without God's mercy is a threat indeed.

In Johnson's imagination, real or invented lesser beings sometimes participate in the divine scrutiny. In his first literary work, the preface to his translation of Lobo's *Voyage to Abyssinia*, he chooses to present the strife between Christian churches in terms of the frustrated expectations of 'an inhabitant of some remote and superiour region' coming down on investigation (Y, XV, 4). Sermon 6 imagines a similar case: 'A superiour being that should look down upon the disorder, confusion and corruption of our world', and all our imperfections, 'would hardly believe there could be among us such a vice as pride'.[18] Johnson amplifies 'God's spies' in the last scene of *King Lear* into 'angels commissioned to survey and report the lives of men, and . . . consequently endowed with the power of prying into the original motives of action and the mysteries of conduct' (Y, VIII, 700).

All these superior beings are benevolently vigilant, and so, often in Johnson's view, are more ordinary superiors. His Sermon 26, on a text from *Proverbs*, 'A king that sitteth in the throne of judgement, scattereth away all evil with his eyes', extols the observation of kings and governors: 'The king is placed above the rest that he may from his exalted station survey all the subordinations of society, that he may observe and obviate . . . vices and corruptions'; others entrusted with public office must emulate this vigilance, which was also beneficial in primitive Highland society (Y, XIV, 273–4, IX, 91). An *Adventurer* character goes to the bad because he is 'removed too early from the only eye of which he dreaded the observation' (no. 62: Y, II, 380).

Often, however, Johnson finds surveillance over others more dubious. Even benevolent human scrutiny is generally unwelcome to its objects. Virtue depends on 'witnesses of . . . conduct': it is maintained by 'exposing . . . manners to the public eye, and assisting the admonitions of conscience with the fear of infamy' (*Adv.* 126: Y, II, 475). Yet people squirm under each other's observation, 'employing every art and contrivance to . . . hide their real condition from the eyes of one another' (*Adv.* 120: Y, II, 468). It is 'captiousness' to employ our faculties 'in too close an observation of failings and defects' (*Adv.* 126: Y, II, 473). The contexts of these remarks recognize that our unwillingness to be watched generally results from consciousness of faults, yet many of Johnson's mortals who imitate the watchfulness of God are downright sinister. He refers in Sermon 11 to the heathens watching the conduct of the early Christians in their midst 'with suspicious vigilance' (Y, XIV, 117). He presents an almost totalitarian surveillance in the Happy Valley, where Rasselas, observing fish and animals, is in turn kept under observation by his attendants and secretly shadowed by the Sage; where the gate to the outside world 'was always watched by successive sentinels, and was by its position exposed to the perpetual observation of all the inhabitants'; and where Nekayah on her first appearance in the story has to explain that she is not a spy (II, V, XIV).

An oppressive degree of supervision can be maintained in the artificial environment of the valley, although, as Imlac remarks, even a desirable degree of it is not practicable in the wider world (VIII). Rasselas at the end of the story is developing towards exercise of the paternal vigilance which he once escaped – further evidence that the structure of *Rasselas* tends to circularity. Having begun with a passionate desire for the extension of prospect, while Nekayah still feared it, he longs at the end for inclusiveness, and is willing to renounce the 'wider compass' that exposes one to enemies and to chance. His new desire for a clear though limited field of vision persists whether his mood leads him to wish for a private station (where he would see 'with his own eyes the whole circuit of his influence') or 'a little kingdom' (where he would 'see all the parts of government with his own eyes': XXVII, XLIX). As so often in Johnson's moral writings, the reader is left in doubt whether to give or withhold moral approval. Should we look on Rasselas' desire for watchfulness with the approbation of the *Book of Proverbs* and Johnson's Sermon 26, or with the unease which we felt when that same watchfulness was exercised by Rasselas' father? The reduction of the expanded scale is clear, an important and inescapable element in the prince's growth in years; the moral implications are intentionally obscure. Obviously Rasselas, when he longs to become all-seeing, aims at participating in the care of a paternal monarch to prevent evil, without malignity or oppressiveness. Nevertheless the opening chapters of his story entitle us to look on this last impossible desire with some apprehensiveness.

A similar strand of images of watchfulness runs through *The Vanity of Human Wishes*, quite distinct from the working of Observation, and from exhortation to the reader to see clearly. The people in the poem, like those in the Happy Valley, find themselves the cynosure of unfriendly eyes. The wealthy traveller fears to be exposed to daylight (lines 43–4). When at length Wolsey's sovereign frowns,

> the train of state
> Mark the keen glance, and watch the sign to hate.
> Where-e'er he turns he meets a stranger's eye. . . .
> (Lines 109–11)

When Charles XII marches on Moscow 'nations on his eye suspended wait'; vanquished, he *shows* his miseries, while the vanquished Charles Albert *steals* to death as if away from exposure (lines 206, 212, 253–4). The aged miser finds himself surrounded by *watchful* guests (line 279); even virtuous old age is exhibited on a public *stage*, awaiting leave to retire (lines 291–2, 297, 308–10). Publicity comes to the beauty when 'hissing Infamy' proclaims her fall (lines 341–2). After such a multitude of hostile watchers, after the whole human race has been made a show of by Democritus, it is natural to feel something of a threat in the eyes of God from afar discerning secrets and hidden hostilities against Him (lines 353–4). The whole poem is an intricate blend of observation for good purposes (searching for knowledge and understanding) and observation for bad purposes (watching for chances to mock, to insult, or to profit from the downfall of others). At the close of the poem, God takes over from humanity the task of observation; the sense of being a target for the divine vigilance is an important part in the unease which this close produces.

The third tradition of lofty observer which Johnson had to reckon with, one which appealed to many of his contemporaries, was that of the looker-down not as explicator, not as judge, but simply as indifferent. It is one that seems to stress the inferiority of the spectacle even more than the superiority of the spectator, yet it has made its mark among the *Dictionary*'s definitions of *superiour*: '1. Higher; greater in dignity or excellence; preferable or preferred to another. 2. Upper; high locally. 3. Free from emotion or concern; unconquered', to which he later added 'unaffected.'[19] The tradition of linking superiority with unconcern has roots in classical literature, owing something to Horace's picture of the just man unmoved by apocalypse.[20] But for Johnson among others a more important source was the Epicurean philosopher Titus Lucretius Carus (d. *c*. 50 BC).

Lucretius' system has been summed up as consisting of four important parts (none of them calculated to appeal to Johnson): a theory of matter as made up of atoms, identification of pleasure as the *summum bonum*, denial of immortality, and a belief that the gods are distant from humanity and indifferent to it. The passage that most closely concerns us here is the opening of *De rerum natura*, book II, which is associated with the last of these points. It describes the philosophical pleasure of watching the turmoil of life from a safe height. Johnson, when he described the Metaphysical poets as beholders rather than partakers of human nature, compared them to 'Epicurean deities . . . without interest and without emotion', whom Leopold Damrosch further identifies as 'an intellectual abstraction against which Johnson often vented his wrath'.[21] There can be no doubt that these deities, and more especially the human sage whom Lucretius at the beginning of his second book imagines as sharing their indifference and superiority, lie behind Johnson's various descriptions of unmoved observers.

Despite the gulf between the Epicureans and their rivals and adversaries the Stoics (which Johnson understood perfectly well), their joint categorization of detachment as a virtue gave them, for him, one important point in common. Therefore his attitudes to the Stoics are also relevant here.[22] Occasionally (e.g. *Ramblers*, 2, 17: Y, III, 13, 93), he quoted with some approval the advice of Stoic philosophers on cultivating detachment. More often, however, even while mentioning their opinion with respect, he inculcated at most a heavily modified Stoicism and more often an engagement which is the very reverse of it (*Ram*. 47, 52, 66, 89; *Idler* 19). Also he seems to have found it hard to voice his qualified regard for the Stoics without, like Swift,[23] an accompanying touch of satire. They are 'that lofty sect', advocating (with 'such extravagance of philosophy') an 'exalted state', 'heights of wisdom which none ever attained, and to which few can aspire' (*Ram*. 6; *Idler* 11: Y, III, 30; II, 39). With 'wild enthusiastick virtue' they 'passed, in their haughty stile, a kind of irreversible decree' that 'pain, poverty, loss of friends, exile, and violent death' were no longer to be considered evils; but this 'edict was, I think, not universally observed' (*Ram*. 32: Y, III, 174–5).

The metaphor running through *lofty*, *exalted*, *heights* expresses Johnson's reservations about an ideal similar to that with which Lucretius opened *De rerun natura*, book II. In the Loeb Library translation the passage runs like this:

> Pleasant it is, when over a great sea the winds trouble the waters, to gaze from shore upon another's great tribulation: not because any man's troubles are a delectable joy, but because to perceive what ills you are free from yourself is pleasant. Pleasant is it also to behold great encounters of warfare arrayed over the plains, with no part of yours in the peril. But nothing is more delightful than to possess lofty sanctuaries serene, well fortified by the teachings of the wise, whence you may look down upon others and behold them all astray, wandering abroad and seeking the path of life: – the strife of wits, the fight for precedence, all labouring day and night with surpassing toil to mount upon the pinnacle of riches and to lay hold on power. O pitiable minds of men, O blind intelligences! In what gloom of life, in how great perils is passed all your poor span of time![24]

Johnson quoted from Dryden's version (see above, p.154) in *Rambler* 117, and probably had its phraseology in mind both in the opening of *The Vanity of Human Wishes* and in the Soame Jenyns review. Besides this key passage in Lucretius, a further one seems to have contributed something to *The Vanity of Human Wishes*. Johnson describes warfare from what amounts to a birds'-eye view ('the rapid Greek o'er Asia whirl'd,/. . . the steady Romans shook the world': lines 179–80); Lucretius, three hundred lines further on, comes back to the image which opened his second book:

> Besides, when great legions cover the outspread plains in their manoeuvres, evoking war in mimicry . . . and horsemen gallop around and suddenly course through the midst of the plains, shaking them with their mighty rush, yet there is a place on the high mountains, from which they seem to stand still, and to be a brightness at rest upon a plain.[25]

Johnson as an undergraduate had a copy of Lucretius in his personal library culled from his father's bookshop; he later owned an edition which still survives, as well as Creech's translation.[26] He called Lucretius a poet 'unreasonably discontented at the present state of things' (Y, IV, 210), but his several references to him reveal mixed though strong feelings. The first introduces a quotation of the opening of book II which approves and endorses it (*Ram.* 52: Y, III, 281–3): to behold the evils under which others groan, Johnson says here, will indeed teach us a more accurate estimate of our own lot. When he next quotes Lucretius (*Ram.* 108: Y, IV, 210) it is a passage from book V, describing the habitable earth, which resembles both the opening of his second book and, more strikingly, the pronouncements of Cicero's Scipio Africanus 'from the celestial regions', which Johnson was to quote, analyse and question about a month later – immediately after making a third reference to Lucretius, his second to book II (*Rams* 117, 118: Y, IV, 260–1, 265ff.; see above, pp.25–6). We may safely suppose, from two *Rambler* discussions of it and one of a related passage, that the famous paragraph about the calm and lofty observer interested Johnson deeply. *Rambler* 117 treats it with the levity of some of his remarks on the Stoics: a crazy correspondent presses the lines into service as classical authority for belief in the medical and intellectual benefits of garret-dwelling. The famous passage, Hypertatus says, comically associating ancient philosophy with modern pseudo-science, makes it 'impossible not to discover the fondness of Lucretius, an earlier writer, for a garret' (Y, IV, 260).

Twenty-two years later, on his way to the Hebrides, Johnson again remembered the passage in a manner combining respect, criticism and a hint of mockery. Describing how from a high cliff he overlooked the sea, he comments, 'I would not for my amusement wish for a storm; but as storms, whether wished or not, will sometimes happen, I may say, without violation of humanity, that I should willingly look out upon them from Slanes Castle' (Y, IX, 19). Comparing himself to Lucretius' elevated, unmoved observer, he clearly implies a feeling that *that* observer violated humanity.

Lucretius dissociates himself in the first sentence of his second book from the idea of enjoying the *pain* of others, which was to provoke outrage when voiced by La Rochefoucault and Swift. His idea of the calm good man enjoying thé spectacle of others' *struggles* does not seem to have struck anyone but Johnson as either ludicrous or inhumane. (It was, of course, a milder notion than that the redeemed would enjoy watching the tortures of the damned in Hell: see below, p.252, n. 28) It was a favourite idea of the influential Stoics; and Lucretius after all uses his storm-watcher less literally than as an image of philosophic equilibrium. Denham, Cowley and others of their century and the next subscribed to this equation of local with moral superiority and of impassive looking-on with virtue; it contributed both to one version of the great-man ideal and to that vogue for country retirement which Johnson so tirelessly opposed. Denham in an early version of *Cooper's Hill* wrote 'from thy lofty topp my Eye lookes downe', 'Secure from danger & from feare', on 'men like Ants' – on which W.B. Carnochan cites the Epicurean gods, and comments, 'those raised in body or in thought, for all their apparently mortal origins, are more like gods than men'.[27] Addison in *Spectator* 418 and Hume in his *Treatise of Human Nature*, as well as innumerable poets, cited or copied the opening of *De rerum natura*, II, and assented fully or in part to its position.[28] The notion of the good man as above all things calm and passionless may have affected, for the worse, *Sir*

Charles Grandison. Sir Charles continually makes others feel little and low; Harriet feels soon after meeting him that she is raised above the world and triumphantly looking down on it, and later that he shows 'that goodness and greatness are synonymous words'. The year after Johnson's death, Cowper produced a singularly pure expression of Lucretian superiority, from 'more than mortal height', to human turmoil, especially war.[29]

It is not necessary to stress how alien to Johnson these sentiments are, even though they had entered deeply into Christian thought: Isaac Watts, for example, in 'True Monarchy' (1701) urges the 'rising Soul' to 'sit above the Globe', to

> climb the Height
> Of Wisdom's lofty Castle, there reside
> Safe from the smiling and the frowning World.
>
> Yet once a Day drop down a gentle Look
> On the great Mole-hill, and with pitying Eye
> Survey the busy Emmets round the Heap.[30]

Johnson by implication reproves Pope for his contempt of the world, for 'looking on mankind . . . with gay indifference, as on emmets of a hillock below his serious attention' (*Lives*, III, 210).

The widely-used vision of mankind of emmets or ants, which brings out the scale distortions implicit in distance, derives not from Lucretius but from Lucian, a satirist who flourished in the second century AD, whose works Johnson owned in three editions, and learned from in a manner which has been discussed by James F. Woodruff.[31] Lucian makes less of the moral superiority and more of the satirical amusement of his looker-down from above, but also stresses the pettiness of what is observed. His *Icaromenippus, or the Sky-Man* features Menippus recounting his flying adventures: how, having discovered the vanity of wealth, power, and philosophy, he exits upwards from earth, provided with one eagle's wing and one vulture's. Then,

> perching on the moon, I rested myself, looking down on the earth from on high and like Homer's Zeus, now observing . . . Greece, Persia and India; and from all this I got my fill of kaleidoscopic pleasure. . . . the earth you see is very small, far less than the moon, I mean. . . . the whole of Greece as it looked to me then from on high was no bigger than four fingers. . . . I thought, therefore, how little there was for our friends the rich to be proud of; for it seemed to me that the widest-acred of them all had but a single Epicurean atom under cultivation.[32]

This passage, in which Lucian mocks both Homeric and Epicurean deities, is full of details which reappear in a whole range of Johnson's writings. Like

The Vanity of Human Wishes and *Falkland's Islands*, this Menippus notes the inadequacy of the rewards of war: 'what a tiny region, no bigger in any way than an Egyptian bean, had caused so many Argives and Spartans to fall in a single day'. Like Johnson's Democritus he judges life a risible show; like Cicero's Scipio Africanus he pronounces from on high that the earth's littleness proves its insignificance. The passage quoted leads directly into one about the variety of human experience ('In one place there were banquets and weddings . . . in a different direction a man was offering sacrifice, and close at hand another was mourning a death'), which draws on Homer's description of the shield of Achilles in just the same way as Johnson does in his defence of tragi-comedy (which therefore unites Lucretius, who also juxtaposes mourning with celebration, with Lucian).[33] The latter's comment on this variety is a simile about human beings as stage performers, all at odds 'until the manager drives each of them off the stage – a remark which Johnson probably remembered, as well as a line from Pope, in his own image of death as leaving a stage.[34]

Lucian moves on from boundary disputes to comparing cities with ant-hills, and this image later recurs, naturally enough, in contexts of superior observation. Erasmus drew on this passage in *Icaromenippus* (which he also translated) for his account of the gods' intense enjoyment, their carefree and tipsy laughter, at the spectacle of human suffering and folly, which looks to them like 'thick swarms, as it were, of Flies, and Gnats, that were quarrelling with each other, justling, fighting, skipping, playing'. Johnson, who owned Erasmus's works in Latin, must have taken note of this passage, which brings one step nearer the superhuman watchers of the Soame Jenyns review.[35] Erasmus introduces his account of the spectator gods with a remark that the present needs a thousand Democrituses to laugh at it (and one more to laugh at the thousand). The parallel with Johnson's Democritus, who laughs at the *scene* or *show* until himself put under judgment, is striking.[36]

Few of Johnson's detached observers are malicious and amused; few are vigilant power figures like the king in *Proverbs* or the servants of Rasselas's father; most have more in common with philosophic students and moralists like Democritus or Imlac. They are the contrary of the good man Serenus (ironically named) in *Adventurer* 62, 'who might have lived in competence and ease, if he could have looked without emotion on the miseries of another' (Y, II, 378). They include all those 'persuaded to imagine that they have reached the heights of perfection', who contemplate 'their own superiority' and 'look unconcerned from their eminence upon the toils and contentions of meaner beings' (*Ram.* 127: Y, IV, 315), like Scipio Africanus, Dick Shifter in *Idler* 71 (Y, II, 221), and the Metaphysical poets.

Such watchers play an important part in *Rasselas*, where McIntosh has noted the fusion of Lucretian and Lucianic elements.[37] In different ways one character after another – the would-be flier, the poet Imlac, the philosopher and the astronomer – aspires after these tranquil heights, but is forced to relinquish them. The first exemplar enthusiastically anticipates both security and amusement in watching the world below, including 'fields of battle', and confidently expects to 'leave vultures and eagles behind him' (VI). His expected superiority is to be made easier by his expected remoteness: as well as Lucretius and Lucian, he recalls Swift's Gulliver when flown with the prospect of temporal rather than spatial elevation above others (see above, p. 38).

The flier's path to superiority proves no more possible than Gulliver's. Rasselas, chafing in the 'seat of tranquillity' though lacking facilities as a spectator, entertaining fantasies of action as a chivalric rescuer, is the very opposite of the man who retreats to a philosophical mountain-top. (Rothstein points out that 'with a Johnsonian touch', he escapes at last by 'imitating not an eagle but a coney', a lowly creature with confined views.)[38] Yet Johnson's story allocates him and his friends little part in the struggle of life after the initial escape and connects them only loosely with the world they observe. It is therefore important for Johnson to present instances of *more* distant observation, even less engaged and therefore less satisfactory than theirs. Each instance constitutes a bid to be distinguished and exceptional, conveyed through the image of detached onlooking.

This image is instrumental when Imlac in his 'enthusiastic fit' about the profession of poetry becomes the butt of Johnson's sympathetic satire;[39] the manner of seeing which he arrogates to the poet has much in common with that of the 'pendant spectator', the 'philosopher furnished with wings' to whom the world displays itself in panorama. In *Rambler* 36, writing of pastoral poetry, Johnson had mapped out two complementary scales for applying to the works of nature: they are simultaneously 'obvious to the most careless [in his first version 'careless and superficial'] regard, and more than adequate to the strongest reason, and severest [at first 'most assiduous'] contemplation'. It is the careless eye which is open to 'that simplicity of grandeur which fills the imagination'. To dwell on 'minuter distinctions' may threaten our perception of the grander scale; but Johnson is advocating use of each scale, not a choice between them (Y, III, 196, 197; cf. above, p.32). Imlac is far less successful than *Rambler* 36 in mapping the relationship between the minute and the grand, either by choice or combination.

He begins with minuteness, even with a claim to comprehensiveness: that he has studied *all* 'the appearances of nature'. When Rasselas objects, on the basis of his own experience, against the claim to have achieved comprehensiveness, Imlac shifts to invoking 'general properties and large appearances', in a 'brilliantly overstated rejoinder' which Robert Folkenflik calls an outstanding example of talking for victory.[40] When his talk moves from nature to human nature he claims combined comprehensiveness and minuteness: the poet must not only observe *all* 'the passions in all their combinations', but observe them worldwide, 'divested' if not of emotions at least of 'prejudices' and of care for praise or neglect, 'presiding . . . as a being superiour to time and place'. This is to attempt those views which *Ramblers* 28 and 63 tell us are possible for God but not for us; it is to verge dangerously on Lucretius. No wonder he convinces Rasselas 'that no human being can ever be a poet' (XI).

We see the delusion of superiority fully indulged by the sage in chapter eighteen, a man 'raised above the rest' who advocates and apparently knows how to achieve the substitution of indifference for emotion. This philosopher is generally identified as a Stoic,[41] but as Rasselas perceives him he could also be an illustration of *De rerum natura*, II. 1ff.: 'a superiour being. . . . who, from the unshaken throne of rational fortitude, looks down on the scenes of life changing beneath him.' When he has proved himself a member of humankind in the normal path of calamity and grief (in an episode strikingly parallel to that which befalls Fielding's Parson Adams, who talked Christian Stoicism though he never practised it),[42] he *feels* for the first time the deprivation which his earlier philosophical position had already implied, of being 'a lonely being disunited from society'. The astronomer's malady attacks him as he watches the heavens alone in 'the turret of his house'; but we know from the beginning that he is curable, being glad of interruption from Imlac, who brings him down 'for a moment into the lower world', or from those who 'want his assistance' (XLI, XL). Unlike Gelidus in *Rambler* 24, whose retreat remains unviolated, he achieves a permanent descent from the heights of solitary philosophic observation. Indeed, the *Rasselas* characters are never passionless: they only mistakenly aspire to be so.

Imlac claims greatness as a poet, not as an individual. These lofty observers assert a superiority imaged as a really or figuratively elevated position, which is different from greatness imaged as size. In fact unfeeling detachment, if they could achieve it, would be a moral failing, a deprivation, as are other undesirable characteristics – isolation, malignity – sometimes associated with greatness. Even the theatregoer who takes the spectacle for reality 'is in a state of elevation above the reach of reason, or of truth, and from the heights of empyrean poetry, may despise the circumscriptions of terrestrial nature' (Y, VII, 77). A different critic might interpret this state as participation in the fable; Johnson chooses to see it instead as superior non-participation in reality, a position from which one must descend to see without distortion of scale.

To remain emotionless in a high place may have carried a special meaning for Johnson if, as seems likely, it was physically an ordeal for him to look down from a height. It would be futile, he says, to advise someone 'who has always lived upon a plain to look from a precipice without emotion' (*Ram.* 159: Y, V, 83). In *A Journey* he describes

> the Buller, or Bouilloir of Buchan, which no man can see with indifference, who has . . . sense of danger. . . . He that ventures to look downward sees, that if his foot should slip, he must fall from his dreadful elevation. (Y, IX, 19–20)

Elsewhere in Scotland he reported 'a very steep descent, of such dreadful depth, that we were naturally inclined to turn aside our eyes'; elsewhere again there was 'more alarm than danger' in what the eye would see if it ventured to look down (Y, IX, 34, 53). His commentary on *Lear* identifies looking from a cliff with 'one great and dreadful image of irresistible destruction – an image that *assails* (Y, VIII, 695). 'The Vision of Theodore' also emphasizes the terror of looking down. (Geoffrey Tillotson, discussing Johnson, quotes from Burke's *Enquiry*, 'I am apt to imagine . . . that height is less grand than depth; and that we are more struck at looking down from a precipice, than at looking up at an object of equal height', and adds, 'Burke ought to have linked this sensation with fear'.[43]) Johnson's fondness for gulf and precipice images is relevant here, and also the images of physical insecurity – of sinking and falling – in *The Vanity of Human Wishes*.[44] Perhaps exemption from the human weakness of physical fear was for him another deprivation of the complacent lofty observer.

There is one more among the complex of associations with which Johnson invests this image: not only superiority, indifference, distortion of scale, but also approaching devastation: a sudden, hostile descent not to participate in but to add to the pain and bewilderment below. To 'hover' with no solid support he makes a threatening action, implying a coming vulture-like pounce. 'Time hovers o'er, impatient to destroy'; 'hov'ring death prepar[es] the blow'.[45]

Most of Johnson's lofty observers, like those of both Lucretius and Lucian, observe war. He takes occasion in many genres of writing to dwell on detached watchers of actual battlefields: in his parliamentary debates, in notes on Shakespeare, and in criticism of war poems. The projector in *Rasselas* foresees aerial attack as unprecedentedly devastating (while Benjamin Franklin imagined it, in a now familiar view, as likely to transform human affairs for the better by convincing rulers of 'the Folly of Wars').[46]

Johnson describes the wars of the 1750s through their observers: Indians in Canada, vultures in Europe (*Idlers* 81 and rejected 22). His 1770s pamphlets revert again and again to the astonishing 'coolness and indifference [with which] the greater part of mankind see war. . . . at a distance'. Such indifference is a distortion of Lucretius – and those who 'laugh from their desks', those who wait like vultures for the spoil (Y, X,

370, 371, 384), have at least something in common with Lucian's merry, half-vulture-winged Menippus.

Indeed, the battle-watcher naturally shades into the vulture, that sinister and repellent relative of the eagle which traditionally (as in Johnson's remarks to Fanny Burney: see above, p.103) symbolizes the highest and greatest. The vulture's own symbolism is more miscellaneous. Apart from Lucian, we have Ben Jonson giving its name to a character in the dog-eat-dog world of *Volpone*, Milton likening Satan to it, when he walks high in air 'bent on his prey', Addison connecting it with envy, and Swift with nations at war.[47] Its image implies, unlike that of the ants, connection between watcher and watched – but certainly not community.

Johnson drew on all these possibilities. His reports on wars use the Swiftian vocabulary of watching, hovering, dismembering; so do his reports on petty exploitations, in essays which teem with descendants of Ben Jonson's Voltore. The vultures which hover in *The Vanity of Human Wishes*, signifying Crown confiscation, also evoke the civil war which had, historically, preceded it.[48]

Johnson's most extended and most puzzling use of the vulture image is the *Idler* essay which he subsequently rejected from the collection (Y, II, 317–20). This reports the 'earnest and deliberate' talk of a vulture family who in themselves, in their domestic affections and their practical approach to the skills of their *métier*, are attractive rather than repulsive. Though they look forward to revelling in human blood, though one has 'fed year after year on the entrails of men', yet they kill only from necessity, not malice, which makes them morally superior to the human race as this essay presents it, which regularly gets together in numbers for the purpose of 'destroying one another'. The goriness of Johnson's battlefield description, which is rare in his writings, administers the kind of shock we associate with the last book of *Gulliver's Travels*, and like that it makes us see our own race exchange moral positions with one we are accustomed to despise. Vultures are better and people worse than we had supposed.

Johnson's exclusion of this essay from the collected *Idlers* is often seen as disowning the views it expresses. More likely, he may have suspected a failure to convey the full interlocking range of his complex attitudes, an expression of horror at the expense of thought. His vultures perceive baffling malignity in human beings, but 'the most subtile bird of the mountain' cannot guess at human motivation. They know nothing either of human passions and the rage for superiority, or of those 'laws by which the rage of *war* is mitigated' (of which the first Vinerian lecture part-written by Johnson speaks[49]), or of any of the good in human nature. Johnson stresses their limitations as observers. Watching from above, doubting, speculating, they are at a loss about us exactly as the human naturalists earlier in the essay are at a loss about the language of beasts. The learned vulture's conclusion that men are automata is only as satisfactory as the naturalists' that birds can speak. From their position of height, distance and absence of sympathy, they see what undoubtedly exists, but everything of value they overlook, not, the satire insists, because they are wicked, but because of the position they occupy. They are, however, a more logical development from the habit of superior observation than a luminous philospher would be.

Both the unmoved observation of Lucretius and the frankly deflating mockery of Lucian were attitudes regularly used by writers, but with which Johnson's Christianity, his view of the writer's responsibility, his commitment to the ideal of community, all forbade him to associate himself. Indeed, he saw them as stages on the way to positive malignity. To opt out, 'to stand a lazy spectator' (*Adv.* 67: Y, II, 386), is, like the excesses of competition, an attempt to assert superiority, and it is equally unjustified. Some critics nevertheless have seen Johnson, as James T. Boulton sees him in the 1770s pamphlets, as sitting above the fray and looking down with philosophic calm, taking a viewpoint 'indeed, *sub specie aeternitatis*' against which human activities are diminished. If there is truth in this interpretation of these pamphlets (there is some, I think, though the calm is far from total, and though they offer a scarifying picture of other calm onlookers) then this makes one more point of contrast between them and most of Johnson's work. Ian Watt gives a more generally accurate verdict in mentioning Johnson's 'refusal to locate himself permanently on the Parnassian eminence, above and beyond the mob, from which Pope and Swift had looked down'.[50]

His positioning of himself as a writer is often more complicated than a simple refusal of eminence. Donald T. Siebert, Jr, remarks that Johnson in his life of Shenstone distinguishes himself from the 'sullen and surly speculator' or 'most supercilious observer', yet manages nonetheless to express their point of view.[51] Typically, Johnson first tries out the role of supercilious observer, then ultimately rejects it. Having made the observation, he relinquishes the post which might make him impervious and inhuman. In *Rambler* 67, a dream allegory, he describes himself as having 'mounted an eminence, from which I had a more extensive view of the whole' Garden of Hope, but before he woke he was wandering among the other people in the vale of Idleness (Y, III, 356, 358). The inactive Lucretian onlooker has something of the Observation upon whom Johnson calls at the opening of *The Vanity of Human Wishes*, whose brief he altered from 'O'erlook' in manuscript to 'Survey'. The poem's coda, however, makes its suggestions from no point of extensive view: from a position *sub specie aeternitatis* indeed, but also under the eye of God, a position not high but deliberately low.

The action of surveying, in Johnson's vividly physical imagination, implies looking down; to look down on others inhibits sympathy, even humanity. I have already mentioned Johnson's various techniques for participating, as a writer, in the scenes he describes (see above, pp.131–2). Such techniques are especially necessary to keep in check the writer's necessary function of observing as from above. Again and again we find Johnson first assuming but then descending from the twin elevations of detached and lofty satirist, detached and lofty sage.

10

GREATNESS AND
HEROISM

A frame of adamant, a soul of fire.

(*The Vanity of Human Wishes*, line 193)

THIS CHAPTER considers the workings of Johnson's thought about achieved greatness: an aspect of identity arising from experience, not an attitude or position assumed *vis–à–vis* the rest of the world. This concept, when seen in relation not to himself but to some other individual, naturally blends with that of heroism, the name which human beings have given to active greatness (an ideal remote from that of Lucretius) when their astonishment and admiration have been strongest.

The concept is a slippery one. While goodness can be simply defined as that which is pleasing to God, whether important or unimportant, greatness has to be assessed by purblind humanity in relation to other examples of greatness and littleness, and is therefore always subject to misapprehension. Further, it depends for recognition on the vagaries of prosperity and publicity, chance and fame, both key elements in tales of heroes.

While goodness is unmistakably commanded as an aim for all humanity, and must therefore be at least in some degree attainable, greatness (however hard to define) is by definition beyond the norm. Those who seek it aspire through competition and rivalry; those who achieve it are likely to look down from its height with coldness or even malignity, demeaning qualities which will inevitably drag them down again. All this suggests that greatness can no more be stable than can other human qualities.

So far in this study we have seen Johnson measuring and judging, calling attention to the inescapable littleness of the human scale, charting the deplorable consequences of the drive to excel others, and investigating and rejecting several popular myths of superiority. We might expect him to conclude that the quest for greatness is impossible, and its recognition always an error to be exposed by correcting the scale of vision. We might expect him as a moralist to recommend goodness as the surer goal of action.

The image of greatness, however, never loses its hold on Johnson. His assumptions and vocabulary as a moralist are deeply imbued with those tales of chance and fame. He loves to celebrate any fulfilment of a larger potentiality than that of most of us, any pushing back of those limits which can never be entirely transcended. Even goodness in its most impressive form, that 'idea of perfection' which we must propose to ourselves as an absolute, he images strenuously as 'the summits of speculative virtue' (*Ram.* 14: Y, III, 76), which in the end we must always rest beneath. His respect and admiration seem to be called forth more immediately and more fully by the effort to achieve wisdom and virtue than by those qualities as achieved; the effort to achieve greatness, as we have seen, both delights and alarms him. Excellence continually engages him: not only achievement high on the scale of what others may reach, but also or particularly attempts to do more than is possible, the aspiration beyond humanity towards heroism. His 'notorious disdain for imperial tragedy and martial heroics' co-exists with stubborn loyalty to 'the heroic ideal'.[1]

Johnson more than most moralists remains always conscious of the pressure of contingency: virtue, wisdom, greatness, are qualities that need to be fulfilled in action, in process; they have no being apart from what we do, or say, or write. 'What might have been is an abstraction',[2] not at all the kind of abstraction with which Johnson concerns himself. He sees achieved greatness, therefore, as far rarer than great talent or great potential, and always to be distinguished from those things (the gifted Savage and Polyphilus in *Rambler* 19 actually accomplish little). Because of his acute awareness of the difficulty of working things out in practice, and of the limited time and space to which any human endeavour extends, it is much easier to discover from Johnson's works what he thinks does not constitute human greatness than what he thinks does. Failed attempts and false claims abound. Yet the whole bent of his mind towards measuring and assessment, his whole view of human life as inherently, essentially involved in the ceaseless competition to excel, reserves his most sympathetic attention for approaches towards that combination of fulfilled potential which for convenience we may call greatness or even heroism. Humanity's developing ideas of the hero reflect our changing concepts of what constitutes exceptional achievement; the word conveys the element of glamour and dazzlement which such people exert over their fellows. Such amazing greatness engages Johnson's concern as much as exploded greatness on the one hand or vindicated littleness on the other.

In scattered phrases, but with a compelling vividness of language, Johnson recognizes this glamour: 'those qualities which have a claim to the veneration of mankind', 'that ardour of enterprize, by which every thing is done that can claim praise or admiration . . . that generous temerity which often fails and often succeeds', 'prodigies of excellence . . . when . . .

magnanimity breaks the chains of prudence' (*Idler* 51, 57: Y, II, 160, 178). Each of these phrases sets the great achievement in relation to things outside itself: it surpasses but also benefits others; it risks failure; it claims applause.

The *Dictionary* definitions of *greatness* include several which reflect glamour and at least one which may claim veneration as well as some which do not even claim approval. After the first three, which have to do with mensuration or 'Comparative quantity', comes the tempting but morally suspect 'High place; dignity; power; influence; empire', with its first quotation from Shakespeare's Wolsey bidding his long farewell.[3] The sense closest to that of heroism ('Merit; magnanimity; nobleness of mind') is placed sixth, flanked by the less admirable 'Swelling pride; affected state' and 'Grandeur; state; magnificence', with a quotation about the Brobdingnagian architecture of Pope's Timon. This range of definitions recalls the opposition of *great* and *good*, and keeps admiration within bounds. The definitions of *hero* are broader and more open, erecting no bulwarks against misplaced veneration: '1. A man eminent for bravery. 2. A man of the highest class in any respect', to which the fourth edition adds 'as, a *hero* in learning'. The illustrative quotations attach the connotations of grandeur, repeatedly linking heroes with kings. The second definition of *heroick* elaborates: 'Noble; suitable to an hero; brave; magnanimous; intrepid; enterprising; illustrious'. Both quotations under this sense deal with fame.

To attribute to Johnson a strong interest in, let alone a veneration for, intrepidity and nobleness, may seem to be going against many of his own explicit statements. In both writing and talk he often represents the scale of heroism as at variance with that of humanity. To suffer, for instance, without complaint is 'most like a hero', but to complain is 'like a man, like a social being who looks for help from his fellow-creatures' (*Ram.* 59: Y, III, 318). 'Heroick Virtues' are unhesitatingly dismissed in favour of Words-worthian 'little, but continued Acts of Beneficence'.[4] The chief tendency of this book's argument so far has been to associate Johnson with anti-heroic, mock-heroic and even soberly levelling attitudes.

Yet Johnson's loyalty to the ordinary, the useful, the little and continuous in human nature is not to be separated from his longing for something more. His perception of littleness is perpetually qualified by his conception of greatness. He vindicates non-heroic humanity in the teeth of his own predilection. The language of *Idlers* 51 and 57, as well as the *Dictionary*'s second definition of *heroick*, suggest Yeats's 'wasteful virtues'.[5] Johnson does cherish intrepidity and nobleness more than mere merit, and he does associate those qualities with grandeur, dignity, empire, and with the heroic or chivalric (originally, therefore, military and aristocratic) code. The word *hero*, with its associations of superabundant, amazing excellence, of Achilles and Alexander, strongly attracts him, as do the places and fables of the heroes. His reverence for the saints of Iona is remembered more frequently than that for the heroes of Marathon whom he uses as their yardstick (*Journey*: Y, IX, 148).

William C. Edinger says that Johnson as a mature critic 'rejects mythological fiction categorically', but this is only half of the truth, for at the same time he harboured a lifelong susceptibility to its glamour. From his boyhood he was 'immoderately fond' of reading that kind of romance which the *Dictionary* defines as a 'military fable of the middle ages; a tale of wild adventures in war and love'. His most characteristic imagery leans heavily on the scenery and incidents of heroic romance: journeys, battles, enchantments, imprisonments. He judged that the best lines in Pope's 'Ode on St. Cecilia's Day' were 'Transported demi-gods stood round,/And men grew heroes at the sound'.[6] He enjoyed the implications of comparing himself in jest with Aeneas or Odysseus or Alexander.[7] When he writes that an Amazon heroine 'had at least the Honour of falling by no meaner Hand than that of *Achilles*, the great *Achilles*, by whom Hector had been slain', I cannot agree with John A. Dussinger in hearing any 'characteristically ironic, anti-feminist tone'. Far from summarily deflating heroism in either Achilles or Penthesilea, Johnson accepts it, unlike much of the Amazons' behaviour, at their own valuation.[8] On ancient battlefields, far removed from his readers' experience, 'prodigies of excellence' (even of a very specialized type of excellence) may be celebrated without scepticism.

Johnson's devotion to such heroes emerges occasionally in unexpected ways to take its place beside his devotion to the ordinary. In his essay on painting, *Idler* 45 (Y, II, 139–42), he first expresses a preference for domestic portraiture. To paint heroes is to paint 'empty splendor'; in painting as in life 'what is greatest is not always best'. Once he begins, however, to cast around for a topic suitable for the history painter, his imagination quickens, and he describes first the agonized and raging death of Hercules, 'which the deities behold with grief and terror from the sky', and then the disdain of Achilles when one of the least illustrious sons of Priam, held at his mercy, entreats elaborately for his life although he knows so many heroes are dead, and 'that the time must come when Achilles is to die'. The essay provides interesting testimony to the force – sometimes denied – of Johnson's dramatic and visual imagination. The latter scene would indeed make a striking canvas: the prostrate, unarmed, beseeching Trojan clutching the spear of the proud unmovable Achilles who, ready to deal death to another, is visited, just for a moment, by the thought of his own. Johnson cited this scene again in his preface to Shakespeare, and in conversation three months before he died he discussed literary treatments of the death of Hercules. Both scenes must have impressed him deeply, though he thinks them impossible to paint.[9] He might have said also that they 'flatter the imagination' purely because of the stature of the personages involved. That *even* Hercules, *even* Achilles, must be conquered by death, is an idea which simultaneously exalts their greatness and diminishes it.

Johnson goes on to suggest more feasible scenes to the historical painter, which are both fraught with complex emotion and directly communicative of 'irresistible instruction' as the scenes involving Hercules or Achilles are not.[10] But Johnson describes the less morally instructive heroes' deaths the most vividly of all in *Idler* 45: his account of them, like Homer's and Ovid's, 'cannot be read without strong emotions'.

The heroes' greatness combines with their mortality (denial of greatness) to arouse this emotion. Johnson made Latin translations of Greek epigrams – on Priam, Hector, Ajax, and obscure people – which present the confrontation of greatness with death (Y, VI, 317, 318, 320). Oddly enough the *Dictionary*'s definitions of *hero*, which recognize its warlike and competitive associations, include no parallel to Martin's 'demi-god or person partly of divine, and partly of human extraction',[11] and do not therefore reflect, even in less mythological terms, the sense which Johnson often elsewhere conveys of the heroic as more than human or *almost* more than human. Their status as demi-gods gives a special irony to the deaths of Achilles and Hercules. (We may compare the horror of Achilles' goddess-mother, in·Auden's poem, at what is to happen to her 'strong/Iron-hearted man-slaying Achilles/Who would not live long'.[12] For Johnson, since attempts to go beyond humanity must fail, the hero is pre-eminently the tragic hero. He has, as Mary Lascelles writes, a 'sense of a greatness whose authenticity is manifest in the very agony of *going off*', in the words of Shakespeare's Charmian.[13]

The eighteenth century rationalized earlier belief in demi-gods with the idea that exceptional human powers or the invention of new skills had won their exercisers the reputation of superhumanity. Lady Mary Wortley Montagu wrote that culinary improvements, among other discoveries, had 'first fram'd Goddesses' like Ceres. *Rambler* 145 supports this view, and in conversation Johnson observed that an earlier age would have made Newton a divinity.[14] Sir William Temple's 'Of Heroic Virtue' (1690), quoted by Johnson in his *Adventurer* 99, against heroes, had begun a re-definition of this quality, which it says, together with poetry, is the only human accomplishment to be called divine. Temple moved away from the code deriving from Homer (and therefore in fact from fierce, primitive Bronze Age tribesmen entirely lacking in the Christian or chivalric virtues of the heroes of romance) towards definitions of heroic virtue which play down the martial. For him it is 'some great or native excellency . . . transcending the common race of mankind in wisdom, goodness, and fortitude' and appearing more than moral.[15] The biographer of Temple's protégé and admirer Swift writes that in this 'finest essay, it was the Roman talents that he exalted – justice, government, prudence, and advances in the practical arts – not self-sacrificing magnanimity or sublime patriotism demonstrated on the battlefield'.[16] Temple, in fact, substituted a more 'civilized' code for the barbaric heroism which both drew and repelled Johnson.

Temple modified the old martial ideal; actual debunking of it was imminent. Within a few years Dryden called Homer's heroes 'those ungodly Man-killers' who owe their title to flattering poets, and Swift (in *A Tale of a Tub*, playing 'modern') apparently alluded sardonically to the title of his patron's essay, and in his next sentence suggested that 'those Antient Heroes, famous for their Combating so many Giants, and Dragons, and Robbers, were in their own Persons a greater Nuisance to Mankind, than any of those Monsters they subdued'. The most beneficial hero is therefore Hercules, who completed his purge of '*other* Vermin' by destroying himself. The supposed author of the *Tale* could hardly take a more different view of this event from *Idler* 45.[17] Fielding follows the line of Swift's modern writer in the opening chapter of *The History of the Life of the Late Mr. Jonathan Wild the Great*: to the statement that history consists entirely of the actions of great men, he adds, as it were, a footnote on *great*, which makes it the antithesis of *good*. Wild, famous thief and gangster, is given shared credit with Julius Caesar and Alexander for destructive greatness: their one or two good actions, Fielding says, tarnished their greatness with regrettable weak moments. Even when no longer tied to a rigid ironical framework he upholds the same opinion: the hero pursues glory 'over swelling tides of blood and tears . . . while sighs of millions waft his spreading sails'.[18] His *Covent Garden Journal* says that 'GREAT', when 'Applied to a Thing, signifies Bigness; when to a Man, often Littleness, or Meanness' (no. 4, 14 January 1752). Heroic greatness is mocked by equation with physical bulk or association with wild and gory fictions like those of nursery stories or crude ballads. Fielding celebrated the heroism of 'John the Great' (Jack the Giant-Killer) and of *Tom Thumb the Great* (1731).

Swift and Fielding were not alone in these views (which indeed go back as far as Erasmus).[19] Pope was equally disparaging of heroes: 'much the same, the point's agreed,/From Macedonia's madman to the Swede'. Richardson made Anna Howe comment on the improbability of heroes, and Lovelace on their wickedness. In a letter he wrote that 'the fierce, fighting Iliad'

> has done infinite mischief for a series of ages; since to it, and its copy the Eneid, is owing, in a great measure, the savage spirit that has actuated, from the earliest ages to this time, the fighting fellows, that, worse than lions or tigers, have ravaged the earth, and made it a field of blood.

This attitude persisted as far as Fanny Burney, who five years after Johnson's death equated the French revolutionary mobs with Hercules and Theseus.[20]

Johnson was as ready as any of these writers to subject 'the heroic image to the punishing presence of the commonplace'.[21] He too occasionally attacks military heroism. *Adventurer* 99 energetically expresses a wish to diminish, not vindicate, the reputation of 'heroes and conquerors' (Y, II, 433). His 1770s pamphlets mount a campaign against ignorant misapplication of the heroic ideal. 'The life of a modern soldier is ill represented by heroick fiction.' To employ the vocabulary of such fiction – 'bed of honour', 'joys of conquest', 'smile in death' – is to help to cover up the ugliness and futility of army deaths from disease and ill management, and to be guilty, therefore, of wilful moral evil. Even the word *hero* may misleadingly glamourize the facts of violence and disruption. Johnson often uses it, as he does *great* and *genius* (see below, pp.209–10), with a sarcasm designed to expose other people's misuse. Aristocratic young vandals, seducers, and citizens after rioting, fervent in the cause of law and order, are all 'heroes' in this way.[22]

Johnson takes a more serious historical view than Swift or Fielding of the ancient, prehistoric roots of the epic concept of heroism, even as he denies its applicability to his own age. He is more willing than they to accept martial heroism as a symbol for other kinds, and stops short of identifying the ancient heroes with modern bullies (though he does demean Alexander and Charles XII as 'projectors', and suggest a mercenary interpretation of the Argonauts' 'heroic ardour' for the golden fleece: *Adv.* 99; *GM*, XIX, 1749, p.393). But, sharing Temple's desire to detach the quality of 'heroic virtue' from its ancient, exclusively martial connections, he is consistently concerned to block any simple, backward-looking identification of the military with the heroic.

Such hankering for the supposed greatness of the past is for Johnson a regular present feature of human littleness. All nations believe their ancestors to have been giants (*Journey*: Y, IX, 126). A modern who tries on a suit of armour imagines that 'the heroes' our ancestors who fought and conquered under such a weight were bigger and stronger than ourselves (*Ram.* 78: Y, IV, 45). But no: just as custom was responsible for that physical capacity, it was responsible also for personal bravery and even extreme aggressiveness. The valour of the Norse heroes is not extraordinary in context: their religious beliefs and 'civil constitution' were such as 'would naturally produce pirates, adventurers, and invaders'.[23] To understand the causes which produce the physical heroism of other cultures enables us to see it with a disenchanted eye, to judge it by a scale not our own, and to reserve our admiration for something greater.

In celebrating the heroic, Johnson often diminishes the merely martial, but never without allowing its attraction. Every man, he believes, not just hearties below cultured consideration, still 'thinks meanly of himself for not having been a soldier'; consciousness of fear creates a sense of 'the dignity of danger' (Boswell, III, 265–6). He spins a complicated irony in a letter to Queeney Thrale (*Letters*, no. 585.1), who had failed to send him a long enough account of her visit to a military encampment. He calls the camp 'perhaps the most important scene of human existence, the real scene of heroick life'. 'Alexander and Darius . . . Charles, Peter and Augustus', he reminds her, passed their lives in tents, 'the lowest and most portable accommodation' human wit has contrived, though modern gentleman-officers may feel their dignity impaired there. Soldiers in peace should make her think of soldiers in war, snatching the scarce bread which they may not be granted time to swallow. He paints a memorably anti-heroic picture of the fear, inconvenience and powerlessness actually experienced in war, and also in life, by leaders and followers alike – yet he also sketches that dogged, daily endurance and courage in face of the eventual enemy which he admires as genuinely though not conventionally heroic. He is joking about the camp's supreme importance in the scale of human life, and about comparing the greatness of Alexander and of Sir Robert Cotton, yet he does bring out a significance and a non-pugnacious heroism in army life. The warrior remains for him the type of the human being attempting most, confronting most disadvantageous odds; this ideal continues to attract him despite his vigorous efforts to dispel belief in its actuality.

As its image receded into fiction, however, it left behind a vocabulary still useful, like that of romance, for the signalizing of quite different kinds of achievement. Military activities gave Johnson some terms of praise; the activities narrated in his life of Drake (see below, pp.195ff.) gave him many more. The composite work of navigators or astronomers, confronting the vast challenge of the ocean or the vaster one of the cosmos, is truly heroic. Though anybody can 'pursue a path already beaten', only 'the heroes in literature [can] enlarge the boundaries of knowledge by discovering and conquering new regions of the intellectual world' or venture 'into the unexplored abysses of truth' (*Ram.* 137: Y, IV, 362). To edit Shakespeare is to sail where other critical adventurers have been wrecked; to compile the *Dictionary* is not, despite all opinion, the sluggish pursuit of a beaten track but the invasion of a new province (Y, VII, 109; *Works*, V, 1–2, 21). Much of what Johnson most admires, he describes in terms of heroism.

Johnson stands historically midway between two opposite attitudes towards that glamourized greatness which constitutes heroism. Despite his ironical uses of the word *hero*, he does not share the eagerness of Swift, Pope or Fielding to shrink past exemplars of bravery into petty ruffians. Despite his emotional response to the heroic virtues, he has no desire to aggrandize them by hero-worship. This concept, although it was not to be fully adumbrated until Carlyle did so in 1840, was already taking shape, as not a few of Johnson's contemporaries began to place 'great men' in a different category from everybody else, almost equivalent to that of the demi-god.[24]

Some of Johnson's pronouncements read like warnings to his readers against this as yet imperfectly developed cult. During the course of his life he did not move away from satiric irreverence and towards veneration, but rather in the opposite direction, against the current of history. Whatever may be said of his early biographies (see below, p.192), the mature Johnson is no panegyrist. He seldom or never makes reference to heroes or great men purely in order to contribute to their glory. Though he may reinforce a particular piece of advice by appeal to the practice of some great name – Erasmus, say, or Socrates[25] – he may also use such people as examples of what to avoid. His famous biographics judicially balance the most dazzling excellencies with inevitable human failings. Though by a more sensitive process than the 'arithmetical' one which Hawkins (see above, p.16) attributed to him, he seeks to establish the greatness of heroes by comparing them with other people, and to limit it by comparing their actions with the time and space which they do not touch. Carlyle may perhaps stand, unchronologically, for the attitude Johnson opposes. His *Heroes and Hero-Worship* opens with a statement practically identical to that which opens *Jonathan Wild* (though not, like Fielding's, preparing for an ironic effect): that the whole world's history is 'at bottom' (a phrase to which Carlyle is curiously partial) the story of great men's deeds. It is a view of history which Johnson probably would not have disputed, though it omits his emphases on the importance of minute detail to full understanding, on the operations of chance, and on the dependence of each generation on the contributions of its predecessors.

Carlyle also believes, however, that mere exposure to a superior person will raise and illuminate inferiors. In the radiance of 'a natural luminary shining by the gift of Heaven . . . all souls feel that it is well with them'. Johnson's ideas about competitiveness and malignity, discussed above, prohibit him from any such confident belief. In his view, a lesser person *may* profit from meditating on heroic achievement, but will certainly not profit automatically, let alone 'feel that he is himself made higher by doing reverence to what is really above him', or subordinate his will to that of a greater, 'and loyally surrender . . . and find [his] welfare in doing so'.[26] He mocks the loyal reverence of government subordinates at the start of his writing career, and that of literary biographers at its close.

Carlyle may remind us here of Longinus: 'the soul is raised by true sublimity, it gains a proud step upwards, it is filled with joy and exultation, as though itself had produced what it hears'.[27] But the last clause quoted shows the difference between Longinean imaginative participation in another's greatness and Carlylean self-abasement before it. Johnson expects an emotional response contrary to Carlyle's: that to compare ourselves with the 'really and naturally great' will produce a disagreeable sense of degradation (see above, p.64). As he never tires of pointing out, it is 'every one' of us, not just the unusually self-centred, who prefers his or her own renown to that of others. Johnson is therefore inclined to anticipate from the ungenerous and guileful human heart some variation on one of two possible reactions to an illustrious superior: either base envy or a self-identification more delusive than that suggested by Longinus.

It might be suggested (in fact it was suggested by Hawkins, see above, pp.102–3) that Johnson debunks heroes because he anticipates discomfort from the contemplation of them; but I believe that this is not true. As moralist Johnson regularly urges his readers to emulate though not to envy (as well as warning us, sometimes even harshly, against false heroes and against expecting any hero to pass the limits of the human scale); as critic, he seeks an alternative to the false measures of heroism propagated by a collusion of writer and reader; as artist, he frequently offers us the disturbing sensation which he felt on reading the death of Hercules. This chapter will comment briefly on his critical views of the hero, and on his search for traces of the heroic age in the archaic Hebrides, before coming to his depiction of heroic individuals.

His comments in *Idler* 84, on autobiography, outline his own practice in that genre and others: the most useful narratives, he says, are those 'which are levelled with the general surface of life, which tell not how any man became great, but how he was made happy'. To elucidate the truth about any individual is to emphasize common humanity. 'Men thus equal in themselves will appear equal in honest and impartial biography.' It is the usual mistake of biographers (and, we may add, of moralists and even critics) to dwell 'most upon conspicuous events', to show their 'favourite at a distance decorated and magnified like the ancient actors in their tragick dress', to endeavour 'to hide the man' in order to 'produce a hero' (Y, II, 262–3). The costume image and the choice of definite and indefinite article are significant: the man who is hidden undoubtedly exists; the hero who is produced may not. Twice, in *Rambler* essays written only a month apart, Johnson had used this image in such a way as to suggest that greatness may be a mere illusion, a matter of stage properties. There exists 'an uniformity in the state of man, considered apart from adventitious and separable decorations and disguises'. In domestic hours the participant in great events 'shrinks to his natural dimensions, and throws aside the ornaments or disguises, which he feels in privacy to be useless incumbrances' (nos 60, 68: Y, III, 320, 360). The following essay, however, introduces 'the last scenes of the tragedy of life', in which all those who formerly took distinguished roles are reduced to playing the same one, that of unavailing struggle with 'one common distress' (Y, III, 363). This approximates the common mortal once more, unexpectedly, to the tragic hero. Johnson's image of the hero as someone in heroic costume reduces heroism not to mere illusion but to a role which can be played by any, but never continuously. It is therefore incumbent on the biographer to find out 'silent excellencies . . . soon forgotten' (*Works*, VI, 494) as well as the pettiness which appears when impressive panoply is laid aside. Some scenes in human life may reveal the heroic without denying the mortal.

Of course the equality or uniformity which Johnson invokes is not absolute, not such as to prevent one of any two people thrown together from at once acquiring an evident superiority (Boswell, II, 13). The superiority is that of a higher point on the same scale, not of a different standard. Johnson's emphasis on equality aims to prevent a Carlylean quasi-mystical view of greatness as inherent in a person's being. In real life, as opposed to epic or romance, achievement such as to evoke admiration comes not from semi-divinity but from human qualities backed by good fortune. He quotes Sir William Temple on this last essential quality of a hero, and comments how few – not even Temple – 'are able to separate the ideas of greatness and prosperity'. Johnson separates them himself here by telling us how different greatness appears with and without prosperity;[28] more frequently he does so by depicting greatness without prosperity or in the act of losing it.

Johnson's accounts of exceptional achievement recognize both that fortune plays a part in it, and that good fortune can hardly govern the *end* of any human achievement. The hero is a human creature engaged in great actions. Johnson never relinquishes the search for motive, the recognition of opposed or balancing tendencies, the necessity for interpretation of action. Where Carlyle reverently surrenders, Johnson independently scrutinizes; his observation is never so acute as when directed at those who stand on some elevation. When we have searched and canvassed, he finds, we may occasionally be able to call a particular person, and more often a particular action, great; this may be said without balking the offstage facts that Alexander the Great and other heroes sought oblivion in sleep and drunkenness, and that Milton worked as a schoolteacher.[29]

This analytical approach is the antithesis of the Carlylean concept of greatness as a quality which precedes and transcends individual character and particular event. Carlyle refuses to believe Cromwell guilty of lying, *because* of his greatness: 'Nay I cannot believe the like, of any Great Man whatever.'[30] To Johnson, accustomed to moralize on the drunkenness of Alexander, this would have been nonsense; Cromwell, whose noble eagerness to benefit mankind he had noted in 1741, may appropriately and without inconsistency serve him as an example of the undesirable passions in 1759.[31] For Carlyle in the fervour of his admiration 'at bottom the Great Man, as he comes from the hand of Nature, is ever the same kind of thing: Odin, Luther, Johnson, Burns . . . these are all originally of one stuff'.[32] For Johnson (whatever he might have made of the identification of himself with Odin or Luther) it was undeniably of first importance generally that identities should remain clear, that people should not confuse themselves with their heroes. What the heroes have in common, we others have in common too; it is the unique achievement of the individual that we admire and may desire to emulate.

On the whole Johnson attributes to humanity a strong degree of scepticism about the heroic. His literary criticism often pits it against the ordinary, and not only gives that the preference but assumes that others will do the same. The old romances amused their readers 'with heroes and with traitors, deliverers and persecutors, as with beings of another species . . . who had neither faults nor excellencies in common' with ourselves (*Ram.* 4: Y, III, 21), and heroic plays may maze the imagination of their audiences with phantoms. But of these 'delirious extasies' we may be cured by Shakespeare, who 'has no heroes' (Y, VII, 64–5), and the perusal of romances will not affect us for harm any more than for good. Johnson assumes that we share his own imperviousness when he writes that histories 'of the downfal of kingdoms, and revolutions of empires, are read with great tranquillity' or 'with the same indifference as the adventures of fabled heroes' (*Ram.* 60, *Idler* 84: Y, III, 319; II, 262). For the author 'nothing can be poorer' than writing 'Great He! but greater She! and such stuff' (Boswell, II, 210). What cannot be made close and familiar, as Shakespeare 'approximates the remote, and familiarizes the wonderful' (Y, VII, 65), is of no use or interest to us, either in life or literature. The reader will not covet either the 'enormous, wonderful, and gigantick memory' of Scaliger or Barthius, or 'the strength of Hercules, or the swiftness of Achilles. He that . . . has an equal share with common men, may justly be contented' (*Idler* 74: Y, II, 231). Milton's style, Dryden's tragedies, Addison's Cato and Young's Jane Grey, are all *too* heroic for a normal scale. Indeed, it is unreasonable of Dennis to criticize characters in *Cato* as unreasonable, since no principles of conduct are known for heroes and heroines, 'not beings that are seen every day'. Johnson's own *Irene* has been called 'a kind of moral tract directed against the false and distorted ideals of conduct depicted in the heroic play'.[33]

But these indictments of the fictional heroic are only one side of the account. Many of Johnson's writings may be regarded as records of a search for authentic heroism, begun in 1738 with *London* and the life of Sarpi, and gracefully relinquished in 1782 with his simultaneously noble and commonplace praise of Levet (see below, pp.236ff.): a search which, like his analogous one for evidences of the supernatural in earthly life, has little expectation of success. The act of renunciation by Thales in *London*, however variously regarded by the critics,[34] is certainly aimed at cutting himself off from the city of hireling senators, pensioned fools and corrupt Frenchmen and asserting some kind of despairing solidarity with the heroes and saints of the past,[35] and, more confidently, in the poem's concluding lines, with Pope's concept of the modern satirist as heroic wielder of a sacred weapon.[36] The potential environment for heroism, however, remains dubious and unrealized, while the anti-heroic city is vivid and actual, bursting with life. Here as later, the search for true heroism involves also the exposure of false or inadequate claims.

Thirty years after speculating about its being better to starve on 'the rocks of Scotland' than cringe and flatter in the Strand (*London*, line 10), Johnson travelled to the Highlands with the aim, among others, of seeking traces of the age of heroic warriors, 'a system of antiquated life' more recently existing there than elsewhere. He found, as is well known, that he was too late.

> The clans retain little now of their original character, their ferocity of temper is softened, their military ardour is extinguished, their dignity of independence is depressed, their contempt of government subdued, and their reverence for their chiefs abated. . . . there subsists no longer . . . much of that peculiar and discriminative form of life, of which the idea had delighted our imagination.[37]

Johnson shows himself alert to the heroic implications of his material by quoting from Homer early in his account of the Highlands and comparing explicitly with the mediaeval romances and with 'the Greeks in their unpolished state, described by Thucydides'.[38] Though the 'antiquated' characteristics of ferocity, independence, lawlessness, and the power of petty chiefs have declined, he finds plenty to say about them, but he carefully designs his language to neutralize any glamour attaching to them: to describe the heroic in terms of social history.

In the course of the detailed analysis headed 'Ostig in Sky', for instance, he gives a sympathetic account of the laird's more than regal power and of its sources, which are control of the land (the only means of subsistence), and 'the kindness of consanguinity, and the reverence of patriarchal authority'. Yet he later evaluates that reverence as 'a muddy mixture of pride and ignorance . . . a blind veneration', and describes the laird as 'a rugged proprietor of the rocks, unprincipled and unenlightened', 'a petty monarch, fierce with habitual hostility, and vigilant with ignorant suspicion' (Y, IX, 85, 89, 93, 156). He performs a similar devaluation of the romance investing the laird's ceremonial trappings:

> An old gentleman, delighting himself with the recollection of better days, related, that forty years ago, a chieftain walked out attended by ten or twelve followers, with their arms rattling. That animating rabble has now ceased. The chief has lost his formidable retinue. (Y, IX, 90)

These descriptions do not deny 'the kindness of consanguinity, and the reverence of patriarchal authority', but they redefine those phrases, widening the cultural gulf which separates the feudal lairds as they actually were from the kind of figure in which enlightened and civilized imagination might embody them. Johnson's account approximates the remote and familiarizes the wonderful, while insisting, nonetheless, on its remoteness as well as its wonder. His technique is gradually to replace one standard with another. He begins by apparently accepting the old gentleman's opinion of the old days as better days; the detail of 'arms rattling' belongs to the old gentleman's fond memory, but also provides the transition to Johnson's own estimate. The bodyguard was, to modern eyes, a rabble, however animating to the old gentleman – or, precisely, accurately, without prejudice for or against, a 'formidable retinue'.

Johnson achieves the same effect in his account of the Highlanders' high esteem for personal courage in general. He points out that 'with the ostentatious display of courage are closely connected promptitude of off-ence and quickness of resentment – and with these qualities are connected perpetual brawls, so that boys tag along after public processions hoping for a fight (Y, IX, 46). He conjures up for his reader the 'generous and manly pleasure to conceive a little nation' secure in the ready defensive swords of its pastoral people; then, however, he admits

> that a man, who places honour only in successful violence, is a very troublesome and pernicious animal in time of peace; and that the martial character cannot prevail in a whole people, but by the diminution of all other virtues. (Y, IX, 91–2)

First comes the generous pleasure of imagining a nation of heroes, then the reluctant recognition of the brute violence underlying the heroic code of honour.

Johnson devotes some attention to the workings of the code in actual pitched battle. In this passage (Y, IX, 113–14) he seeks by various means to debunk or at least qualify the extremes of 'all that has been said of the force and terrour' of the Highland 'glaymore, or great two-handed sword'. Firstly, it was not used with any unusual skill: the 'gentlemen were perhaps sometimes skilful gladiators [itself a term which equates them with the non-gentlemen of a more distant age], but the common men had no other powers than those of violence and courage'. *Violence and courage*, like *successful violence*, serves as a bald paraphrase of pre-Temple *heroic virtue*; it leaves nothing out, but it allows no unanalysed glorification to creep in. Secondly, the claymore's effectiveness against the English was due less to superior courage or even violence than to its novelty:

> New dangers are naturally magnified; and men accustomed only to exchange bullets at a distance, and rather to hear their enemies than

see them, are discouraged and amazed when they find themselves encountered hand to hand, and catch the gleam of steel flashing in their faces.

Johnson guards against romantic overestimate of the claymore, yet does full justice to the facts: its actual danger is not greater than that of guns; its terror is. On the one hand he provides a more rational reason than heroism for Highland success; on the other, he vividly brings out the thrill of hand-to-hand fighting.

Perhaps to counter this thrill, he goes on to a deliberately bathetic narrative of one of those opportunities for the exertion of personal courage given by 'single combats in the field; like those which occur so frequently in fabulous wars'. From this introduction we might expect a scene of passion and sentiment like that of Achilles and the Trojan (see above, pp.179–80), but no such expectation is answered by this account of combat between a Highlander and a dragoon. Johnson makes it clear that chance, not superior skill, obtains the victory, and also that the single combat is confusing and anticlimactic, not animating and heroic. The Highlander and the dragoon

> were both skilful swordsmen, and the contest was not easily
> decided: the dragoon at last had the advantage, and the Highlander
> called for quarter; but quarter was refused him, and the fight
> continued till he [the Highlander, despite his claymore] was reduced
> to defend himself upon his knee. At that instant one of the
> Macleods came to his rescue; who, as it is said, offered quarter to
> the dragoon, but he thought himself obliged to reject what he had
> before refused, and, as battle gives little time to deliberate, was
> immediately killed.

Instead of moving supplication, the dragoon has time only for a 'thought', a ridiculously heroic thought about some theoretical obligation of honour; and for this clearly mistaken thought he dies. He meets no fierce disdain like that of Achilles, but only the bald passive voice: 'was immediately killed'. The next paragraph treats, with only apparent irrelevance, the reduced scale of Highland funerals. What Johnson has done here is to take the heroism out of single combat while leaving the courage and violence their full force. He is concerned to forestall *too* great admiration for 'the soldier's virtues'.

To the Highlanders who fought in America he is willing to accord 'a very high degree of military praise'. The measured dryness of this phrase contrasts with the heroic 'bed of honour' or 'smile in death', but is itself revealed as almost a euphemism when Johnson spells out the manner in which such praise is acquired. 'Those that went to the American war, went to destruction. Of the old Highland regiment, consisting of twelve hundred, only seventy-six survived to see their country again.' Such odds are the stuff of heroic narrative. Johnson, however, strangely presents them as part of an argument against exaggerating the numbers of Highlanders in America. He seems more concerned to establish accurately how many did or did not fight there than how many died. He invokes as comparison not the Spartans at Thermopylae but the socially conditioned Norsemen, whose military rashness was automatic; and he insists on comparing the exaggeration of Norse and Highland numbers instead of their achievements (Y, IX, 98). Johnson is as concerned to dissipate such legends as he is the legend of the claymore, all in the interest of seeing things as they are. The *Journey* is of all his works the most closely involved with the idea of heroism, and also probably the most anti-heroic.

Although Johnson found no Achilles wielding the claymore, no Ulysses on the island of Raasay, he met a living legend in the person of Flora Macdonald, 'a name that will be mentioned in history, and if courage and fidelity be virtues, mentioned with honour'. This heroine of action was 'a woman of middle stature, soft features, gentle manners, and elegant presence'. Both her heroism and her ordinariness receive an emphasis in the *Journey* which Johnson's earlier, epistolary account, though detailing her actions, did not supply (Y, IX, 66–7; *Letters*, no. 329: I, 367). The reader is reminded of Fielding's introduction of his fictional heroine Sophia, when after pulling out all the stops (the ruler of the winds, Flora, the *Venus de Medicis*, fashionable beauties) he descends suddenly into 'Sophia then, the only daughter of Mr Western, was a middle-sized woman. . .'.[39] Fielding wishes to remind the reader of the humdrum physical normality underlying literary rhapsodies; Johnson also needs to insist on such normality on those occasions when he does recognize genuinely heroic courage and fidelity. The male heroes he encounters on his journey are equally unideal, not warriors but cultivators: young Col, who deserves equal praise with Peter the Great 'in the proportion of his dominions to the empire of Russia', and young Macleod of Dunvegan, of whom Johnson told Boswell, 'If he gets the better of all this [inherited debts], he'll be a hero'. (Macleod, as the Yale editor of the *Journey* puts it, found 'another sort of heroism' – conventional rather than Johnsonian – 'more feasible'. He pursued a distinguished military career on several continents while leaving the debts unpaid.[40])

Getting the better of handicap was Johnson's first requirement for personal heroism. Of the greatness of Lord Mansfield – with all the advantages of family, education, and backing – he is said to have observed: 'If his nurse had foretold it, you wouldn't have taken her for a witch.' But Lord Hardwicke was 'a son of the earth, with no education but what he gave himself, no friends but of his own making'; if *his* nurse 'had dared to foretell of him that he would rise to such a height, sir, she'd have swum for it'.[41] It is the self-made man whose life Johnson would like to write; he salutes that greatness which shows itself in struggle against odds, and whimsically imagines for it a supernatural manifestation such as marks a hero's birth. His lives, which investigate personal heroism as the *Journey* investigates the possibility of a 'heroic' social norm, consistently emphasize the obstacles which their subjects faced in their rise to eminence.

Johnson's earliest biographies, written for the *Gentleman's Magazine* between 1738 and 1742, deal with two groups whom he loved to compare as contenders for fame: thinkers and men of action.[42] They invest the thinkers with the same glamour that surrounds the soldiers and explorers, an aura of heroism unmatched in Johnson's later works.[43] The part played in this effect by extraneous causes needs to be fully recognized, but when all is said, to compare the earlier lives with the later is to demonstrate a radical shift in Johnson's attitudes. We cannot of course discount the influence on the early lives of the genre in which they were written, that of the account of a great man (maker of history, prodigy, or near-saint), a genre having its own traditions and expectations. Moreover they were based closely on earlier, mainly eulogistic sources. For Drake, Johnson drew on works intended in their day 'to stirre up all Heroicke and active SPIRITS' to emulation. He had to resort to a footnote when he wished to point out how Fontenelle's eulogy of Morin exalted the common into the wonderful.[44]

On the whole, however, Johnson seems energetically and voluntarily to endorse his sources' panegyrical estimates. Insertions of his own draw attention not to the common but to the wonderful in human nature, as scholars have noted. In the life of Father Paul Sarpi he makes a 'bare and colourless' phrase 'far more splendid and heroic'. When Sarpi enters a religious order at thirteen, Johnson comments 'a time of life, in most persons, very improper for such engagements': Sarpi is not like most persons. Johnson chooses to emphasize the greatness both of Drake's and Blake's behaviour and of the events of their lives.[45]

Richard Reynolds thinks that it took writing the life of Savage (who was a close friend, a complex character, and also an uneulogized figure of more notoriety than fame) to teach Johnson an approach different from the heroic.[46] Whether or not this was the cause, these early works are differently conceived from any later ones in almost every aspect of their presentation of greatness; and despite his sources, it seems safe to hold Johnson himself fully responsible for this presentation.

These men no sooner establish their distinction beyond doubt than they suffer the attacks of envy (all except Barretier, who dies too young); Johnson at least twice departs from his sources to enlarge on the attacks. Nevertheless they triumph over innumerable hostile forces: early poverty, or loss of parents, or both,[47] ill-health, and the hidebound methods and non-appreciation of the less gifted. So far they resemble Johnson's later biographical subjects; but another kind of triumph sets them off in sharp contrast. They experience death as a victory conferred almost without threat of defeat. Not content with enlarging the bounds of the humanly possible in their lifetimes, they assert their status as romance heroes by triumphing even in death.[48] Johnson, taking leave of Drake while some years of his life remain, refuses to believe the story which had made him die of discouragement.[49] His Sarpi dies with exemplary piety, more affectingly still than in Johnson's source; Boerhaave as he approaches death rises progressively above his 'exquisite tortures'; Barretier, Burman and Sydenham all endure extreme terminal pain with 'confidence and tranquillity', and without ceasing either from virtuous labours or from receiving their meed of veneration. Despite all the physical torments, these death-bed scenes avoid any impression of struggle, and avoid also the solemn irony of perspectives changed by approaching death, such as Johnson later supplied for his life of Hughes (*Lives*, II, 164; see above, p.9) and such as is particularly invited by the timing of Admiral Blake's death at a moment of yet uncelebrated victory. The genre of course forbids that exemplary figures should be represented as dying of arrogant self-sufficiency like Edmund Smith or of gourmandizing like Pope. But Johnson chose at this stage of his career to depict heroism as a matter of, comparatively, assured victory.[50]

Apart from the way they close, these narratives exalt greatness into heroism as Johnson never does again. They reverberate with the comparative words *eminent*, *superiority*, *distinguish*. The 'great Boerhaave' is 'one of those mighty geniuses, to whom scarce any thing appears impossible', 'a man formed by nature for great designs': the first and last phrases have no equivalent in Johnson's source.[51] Drake meets with 'heroick spirit' many occasions which demand 'all the qualities of an hero, an intrepidity never to be shaken, and a judgment never to be perplexed' (*Works*, VI, 323, 329); Johnson explicitly presents to readers the 'Importance of DRAKE's Expeditions, and the Greatness of his Reputation', to which 'his Country owes Reverence and Gratitude' (*GM*, X (1740), p.352). Blake, 'the great, the wise, and the valiant', is betrayed to his one blameworthy action by his own 'resistless ardour' and nobility. He fights in

> the memorable war . . . in which the greatest admirals that,
> perhaps, any age has produced, were engaged on each side; in
> which nothing less was contested than the dominion of the sea, and
> which was carried on with vigour . . . proportioned to the
> importance of the dispute. (*Works*, VI, 302, 297)

Johnson never again indulges, in his own person, in such advertisement of the grandeur of his subject (unless when discussing the story of *Paradise Lost*: *Lives*, I, 171–2). He gives this kind of language to some of his parliamentary orators, very soon after writing the life of Blake,[52] but their grandiloquence, as has been argued above (pp.47ff.), is presented tongue in cheek. The remarks about Boerhaave and Drake recall nothing in Johnson's later works so strongly as the terms in which aspiring *Rambler* characters voice their overestimations of themselves. In these biographies Johnson set out to substantiate claims which elsewhere he is generally wary of, and which indeed he explicitly denied in his life of Savage. There he points out that Savage's division of his last guinea with an old enemy would 'in some ages' have been seen as the action of a saint or hero, to be acclaimed and not analysed. To Johnson it is only 'an act of complicated virtue', not without its personal psychological causes: human, virtuous, but neither saintly nor heroic (*Lives*, II, 355).

In some respects the ideal of human greatness which the early lives present was never to change. It is like the later Johnson to be eager, and to expect his readers to be eager, for information, and to dwell on posterity's cause to be thankful to the great benefactors of mankind (*Works*, VI, 376, 339). These heroes suffer as remarkably from the onslaughts of malignity as his later subjects (cf. above, pp.141ff.). They exhibit that indifference to wealth (even when this meant adding to or subtracting from his sources[53]) which Johnson continued to believe a concomitant of greatness. Magnanimity is here the keynote. Hero after hero despises difficulties, pain, danger and personal reward, though they may hanker for fame: Johnson's Boerhaave has 'no ambition but after knowledge' (*Works*, VI, 279).

Johnson apparently held throughout his life a fairly consistent idea of what would, if attainable, constitute stature beyond that of ordinary humanity. His early heroes embody what he later continued to believe most admirable, but ceased to believe possible. In maturity (1756) he believed that in

> every great performance, perhaps in every great character, part is the gift of nature, part the contribution of accident, and part, very often not the greatest Part, the effect of voluntary election, and regular design. (*Works*, VI, 439)

In these early years he lays less stress on accident. He wrote in 1739 that people's 'ambition is, generally, proportioned to their capacity. Providence seldom sends any into the world with an inclination to attempt great things, who have not abilities, likewise, to perform them.' So Boerhaave attempts what 'would have been little less than madness in most men, and would have only exposed them to ridicule and contempt' (*Works*, VI, 275). In succeeding, he vindicates Johnson's comment – unlike subjects of later lives, whose misjudged attempts do expose them to ridicule and contempt, and in connection with whom no such comment could possibly be made. These early lives almost entirely lack the ingredient, so frequent in Johnson's later work, of failure either ironically undeserved or ironically unexpected. They also lay comparatively little stress on competitiveness – far less than the account of Crichton in *Adventurer* 81, for instance, or than the essays in general or *The Lives of the Poets*. Their pattern is one in which the central figure emerges early into eminence, after which only others, and not himself, address their wits to rivalry, producing therefore envy but not competition. They narrate a fulfilment of potential devoutly to be wished.

Johnson does not display here his later uneasiness about eminence. He declares again and again that his subjects stand above this or that human weakness without ever wondering how their accurate perception of their own humanity will weather this consciousness of superiority. He represents their greatness, too, as all of a piece, never to be shaken or perplexed, if not quite flawless still without serious flaws. When he finds Drake's humanity and presence of mind equal to his courage, and that he is superior to avarice as well as to fear, he calls this character 'consistent with itself' (*Works*, VI, 337), evidently *expecting* one form of superiority to accompany another. His later works on the contrary inure us to the expectation that someone proof against one passion or temptation may fall ignominiously victim to another. Indeed, they so frequently exploit the ironies which follow from this fact that a reader of these early lives may feel, by contrast, that their subjects have escaped human weakness: almost reversing the 'doom of man', these 'men grew heroes', as in the lines by Pope which Johnson admired (see above, p.179). Boerehaave and Drake even command a Carlylean response of reverence and submission (*Works*, VI, 288; see above, p.184). Nobody Johnson writes of later can command this response, not even Shakespeare or Milton. Johnson's mature view of veneration is more accurately expressed in *Idler* 99: the wise man 'lives with his own faults and follies always before him', having, unlike the rich, 'none to reconcile him to himself by praise and veneration' (Y, II, 303). The question of relation with oneself is never raised in the early biographies.

Johnson's attitude towards specifically martial heroism changes more radically than that towards greatness in general, as is suggested by comparing his lives of the soldierly leaders Drake and Frederick the Great, separated by sixteen years. In his 'Observations on the [Russian and Hessian] Treaties', written the same year as the latter life, Johnson deflates an example of English diplomacy not unlike Frederick's activities:

To arm the nations of the north in the cause of Britain, to bring down hosts against France from the polar circle has indeed a sound of magnificence, which might induce a mind unacquainted with public affairs to imagine that some effort of policy more than human had been exerted, by which . . : the influence of Britain was extended to the utmost limits of the world. But when this striking

> phenomenon . . . is more nearly inspected, it appears a bargain
> merely mercantile

– an exchange of unwanted troops on one hand for spare cash on the other (Y, X, 178–9). Johnson as he writes of Drake seems willing to believe in efforts more than human; but he subjects Frederick to the damaging close inspection which will reveal his true measure.

Before 'Drake', in 'The State of Lilliput', Johnson had already shown strong scepticism about colonial expansion in the present day, but still he presents it as a heroic activity in the past. Drake excels in both of *Adventurer* 81's terms, in comparison with other persons and in comparison with things (Y, II, 401). Johnson shows him as immensely superior to all around him: to his own men, who are timorous and slothful while he is intrepid even though badly wounded, and despairing while he is resolved; to his Spanish opponents; to the natives whose innocent and ignorant life Johnson indignantly denies to be preferable to a more enlightened one (*Works*, VI, 316–17, 334, 322, 363–4, 366–7). When Drake's behaviour needs defence, comparison supplies it. When he proves 'very little acquainted with policy and intrigue', he is opposed to people 'of narrow views and grovelling conceptions'; when he exercises a policy of secrecy or downright deception, this is contrasted with too much trust, or with destructive stratagems, or with the alarm and despondency which Drake's policy defeats (*Works*, VI, 338, 351–3, 319–21). When he acts cruelly he does so on carefully emphasized and brutal provocation from the other side. He is shown getting his first start in life by his own means (with a paragraph supplied additionally by Johnson to explain how little things provide 'the most successful introduction to greater enterprises'),[54] and rising superior to a whole series of crushing reverses. Every comparison works in his favour; he is never faced with a threat to success or reputation which he does not immediately dispel; every other figure in his story is there to reflect glory upon him. Johnson's sources, even though they too are explicitly out to glorify Drake, lay nothing like the same consistent and detailed emphasis on his surpassing of other people.[55]

Johnson presents Drake to us through solid statement rather than any mist of panegyric; but there are areas he leaves unexamined and vague: Drake's purposes and the long-term results of his activities. Although later he consistently rejected a heroic model of imperialist expansion and preferred a humdrum mercantile one, he here provides a paragraph not in his source about the thrilling attraction, in Drake's day, of the new West Indian trade.[56] He communicates the thrill without irony or qualification, in language very like what he later gives to disproportionate aggrandizers of their own schemes. Military gains are associated with advances in navigation, and those presented as benefaction to humanity (*GM*, X (1740), p.352; *Works*, VI, 338–9). No broader scale is invoked here such as, for the debates, the fictional framework and the clash of principle supply. Drake's voyage round the world is self-evidently this 'great enterprise', this 'new attempt' (VI, 338–9). Drake, progressing from obscure beginnings to world-wide renown, fills to perfect satisfaction a traditional role as national hero, the value of whose achievements is understood to need no defence. Johnson presumably intended a contrast with national pusillanimity as perceived by the Opposition of his own day, but this remains only implicit.

To compare Drake with Frederick is to make him appear almost as innocent and ignorant as the South American Indians. Johnson refuses to separate the king of Prussia's actions, modern hero (and bogey) as he is, from their political results, or from the question of their value, and therefore makes his political motives subject to comparison with those of other politicians and with the unchanging standard of morality. It is impossible, except in the limited field of law-giving, to see him, as Johnson sees Drake, as a human benefactor. Johnson's 'memoirs' of him (whether they amount to a 'life' or to a 'gazette's pompous tale') dismantle the whole idea of power politician as hero. F.V. Bernard sees them as supporting Frederick against the French and emphasizing 'the political significance of his rule', and he cites their reworking of material from the *Gentleman's Magazine*'s 1740s 'Foreign History' sections (which may also be by Johnson).[57] The reworking, however, is done in a manner calculated at every step to throw doubt on the significance of 'political significance'.

Frederick never begins to fulfil the requirements for heroism. His early difficulties are overcome by his father's death, not by his own efforts; in any case, his early obscurity has been, for a prince, an advantage rather than a handicap. The scope and purpose of his military operations does not go unexamined, and turns out to be nothing special. 'To enlarge dominions has been the boast of many princes. . . . I shall willingly suspend or contract the history of battles and sieges, to give a larger account of' Frederick's rarer undertaking to reform his country's laws. But even these reforms turn out to be not difficult or in themselves remarkable; it is only remarkable that the effort should be made at all (VI, 440, 449–50).

Frederick's actions enjoy no Drakean monopoly of limelight in Johnson's account of him. At the outset Johnson establishes his present greatness ('whose actions and designs now keep Europe in attention') by contrast with the pettiness of his father, Frederick William, who is little both in the sphere of action and in mind,

> of narrow views, and vehement passions, earnestly engaged in little pursuits, or in schemes terminating in some speedy consequence, without any plan of lasting advantage to himself or his subjects, or any prospect of distant events. (*Works*, VI, 435–6)

Frederick II acts a mighty part beside that of his father, but later comparisons do not work out so much in his favour. He is early contrasted with Maria Theresa. She, although a female in 'distresses', is also heroic in 'the firmness with which she struggled with her difficulties'; Frederick, acting possibly with some justice but 'certainly with very little generosity', has, comparatively, nothing of the hero about him (VI, 445–6).

Johnson does not, however, maintain the same relative view of Maria Theresa and of Frederick. Where the genre of heroic biography presents consistent characters and a coherent structure of progress and triumph, the present work substitutes chanciness of behaviour and the dislocations of historical narrative. The material presented lacks even the structure by means of contrast which Johnson gives the same events in *The Vanity of Human Wishes*.

The poem contrasts (lines 241–54) Charles Albert of Bavaria's moment of glory (when he bursts unexpectedly on 'the dread summits of Cesarean pow'r' and 'sees' as from those summits 'defenceless realms receive his sway') with his subsequent humiliation, his period as the rapacious observer from on high with his later one as the victim of rapacity *from* the hills. At the same time Maria Theresa ('fair Austria') changes from 'defenceless' suppliant for chivalrous aid, to being associated and incorporated with her half-civilized subjects, 'the sons of ravage'. Readers disposed to take the side of the underdog have their response as rudely re-aligned as do those disposed to admire success.

The life of Frederick the Great has as backdrop a similar series of re-alignments, with Charles Albert moving from empire to flight and Maria Theresa from victimization to 'an uninterrupted torrent of success' (VI, 454–5, 459, 460). Frederick takes an objective but then abandons it. Gallantries are performed on both sides: a notable exploit of four Prussian grenadiers against dozens of Austrians is succeeded by Austrian defiance and cowardly flight by Frederick ('This attention to his personal safety has not yet been forgotten': VI, 448–9). Neither side has any monopoly on heroism; Johnson's judgments vary as their actions do, not in a single reversal but in an apparently unlimited sequence. The French, for instance, are first praised for succeeding in a near-impossible exploit, then rebuked for wantonness of destruction, then derided for impossible 'dreams of projected greatness', and finally left after having 'so long kept the world in alarm, [to] be taught, at last, the value of peace' (VI, 460–3).

This technique ensures that neither Frederick nor anyone else shall become the hero of this account. Moreover, the closing stages of the story subject him to a whole series of belittlings which, for this reader at least, finally cancel out any lingering effect of dignity left over from the opening contrast with his father and from his early successes. Having long kept Frederick offstage and concentrated on his rivals, Johnson allows him re-entry to perform a dishonourable and mercenary manoeuvre 'hitherto applied chiefly in petty cheats and slight transactions'. This reverses every aspect of the situation once more and obliges Maria Theresa, as Johnson puts it, 'to fight through the war a second time' (VI, 465–6). This last adds a fine touch of futility. Despite the multiplicity of Drake's recurring attempts, repulses, re-attempts, it is inconceivable that Johnson should have devalued his exploits by suggesting that the *same* thing had to be gone through twice.

The inconsequentiality of Frederick's actions is well exemplified by his relations with the city of Prague. In September 1744 he strikes a medal to commemorate having taken the city three times in three years. 'On the other side were two verses, in which he prayed, "that his conquests might produce peace".' He then leaves Prague with a garrison and savagely enforced curfew, and

> went forward to take the other towns and fortresses. . . . At the approach to the Austrian army the courage of the king of Prussia seemed to have failed him. He retired. . . . It might have been expected, that he should have made some effort to secure[58] Prague; but, after a faint attempt. . .

he retreated. The various trophies he leaves behind, with the medal, form a characteristically unsatisfactory 'dear-bought' recompense to Prague for its three sieges.[59] Johnson denies the likelihood of peace by reminding us, in the midst of this narrative, of the timeless truth that 'every sovereign is growing less' and therefore growing dissatisfied 'as his next neighbour is growing greater' – in which case conquests will produce the reverse of peace. Drake's life is an upward progress, Frederick's a kind of perpetual inconclusive ebb and flow, in which his triumphs are too brief (too little) to command respect.

To close his penultimate instalment, Johnson even expresses positive impatience at having to concern himself at all with Frederick's activities, in language which recalls and reverses the comment on Frederick William. The father concerned himself with little things near at hand, ignoring 'any prospect of distant events'; the son's distant prospects, it seems, only make larger events grow little in their turn.

> Nothing is more tedious than publick records, when they relate to affairs which, by distance of time or place, lose their power to interest the reader. Every thing grows little, as it grows remote; and of things thus diminished, it is sufficient to survey the aggregate without a minute examination of the parts.

After such a pronouncement it is hard to feel elated for Frederick when the final section leaves him 'giving laws to his enemies, and courted by all the powers of Europe' (VI, 467, 474), or to believe that such splendour is anything but delusive. Frederick has become only one figure in a 'tumultuous confusion' (*Adv.* 128: Y, II, 476), associated with littleness and with the demeaning ideas of rapacity, malignity and repetition. Despite his station 'at the height of human greatness,' still 'the event of the present war . . . is yet too early to predict'. Even a prediction of being toppled from his height might confer precarious dignity, but Johnson refuses to make such a prediction: anything, he says, could happen.[60] In gaining the height of human greatness, Frederick seems to have shown it to be far less great than it once appeared beside his father's trivial hobby.

It is unfortunate for the narrow purposes of the literary critic that Frederick lacked the personal bravery and attractive personality which Drake so conspicuously possessed, since this may seem to some to be the whole basis of Johnson's different attitudes towards them. But the root cause lies neither here nor in such differences of circumstance as nationality, or Johnson's sources, or Frederick's irritating status as the idol of the Will Marvels of the day, but in the completion of a shift which took place in Johnson's perspectives at some time during his thirties. He sees war not entirely differently in 1756 from the way he did in 1740. (Events during 1756-7, while his life of Frederick was serially appearing, probably did not radically reshape his increasingly disillusioned view, though they may have played some part.) But he sees human capacity differently. The modern politico-military hero cannot now appear as successor to the heroes of old but only as pretender to a lapsed or questionable title.

Frederick's instant in the whirligig of power invites such questions as 'What for?' and 'Is that all?' Johnson's account, ending *in medias res*, implicitly invokes the advice to judge no man happy before regarding the end, which he had ignored in Drake's case but quoted in *The Vanity of Human Wishes*, lines 313-14. As the *Journey* examines an ancient race of heroes and finds them to be men, as the biographies shift their attention from heroic to imperfect individuals, so the poem examines strivers in every field of human endeavour, and applies a vocabulary and imagery of heroism to their actual achievements and eventual deaths. 'Heroic worth', lines 87-8 suggest, is something which we, the general public, unhesitatingly ascribe to the fortunate and cannot attribute to the unfortunate (cf. above, p.186); since the poem offers no single example of a fortunate end, one of its effects is to deny the possibility of continued heroic status in a mortal.

Johnson gives war twice as much space as politics or scholarship, one third as much again as old age and nearly four times as much as beauty. This dominance is of course largely dictated by Juvenal's original, but also very well fits the heroic theme. But elements of the heroic inform even the least likely of Johnson's exemplars. The scholar (associated with Hercules through the shirt-of-Nessus image) proceeds like a chivalric knight, with many foes to encounter in his quest to invade and vanquish Science and to pay homage at 'the throne of Truth'; the old man flashes out in 'heady rage' and sustains against disease the bodily fortress which is bound to capitulate; the beauty falls a prize to the same siege-warfare tactics (lines 137–8, 141–54, 281, 283–4, 331–4). The advice which Johnson addresses in his own voice to the scholar, 'Nor think the doom of man revers'd for thee' (line 156), is urgently required by every character in the poem. The vainest of human wishes is that to escape the doom, to rise above the human condition, and it is implicit in every wish that Johnson describes. Despite all exploits of conquest over countrymen, other nations, lovers (or, in the case of the scholar and the benevolent old person, over oneself), the last struggle is coming in which defeat is certain.

Wolsey and the military leaders are each presented as wielding more than human power, until some reverse of fortune reveals it to be, like Frederick's, illusory or temporary. Johnson invests Wolsey's physical voice, hand and smile with the power of dispensing the large abstractions: law, fortune, honour, security. It is a vivid picture of hubris. The reader who, having encountered *The Vanity of Human Wishes*, is told in Johnson's Oriental *Ramblers* how the 'voice of Morad was heard from the cliffs of Taurus to the Indian ocean', or how Seged addresses himself at some length on the subject of his own power ('Thy nod is as the earthquake that shakes the mountains. . . . In thy hand is the strength of thousands, and thy health is the health of millions'), feels no surprise when Morad and Seged are rudely reduced to merely human stature (*Ram.* 190, 204: Y, V, 229, 296). In the case of Wolsey, the lines

> Till conquest unresisted ceas'd to please,
> And rights submitted, left him none to seize (107–8)

relate him clearly to Alexander's heroic displeasure at running out of worlds to conquer. Once Wolsey's magic powers are revoked, it is his loss of more trivial, material satisfactions that Johnson dwells on (the 'golden canopy, the glitt'ring plate'), along with his retention of those things which he shares with his most undistinguished fellow-humans: age, cares, maladies, folly (lines 113–20). The hero has become mortal.

The introduction to the military section (lines 175–90) presents contrasting definitions of the 'bribes' which activate the hero (honour and dignity call them 'fame', the poet calls them rusting medals, decaying stones, 'the gazette's pompous tale') and the paradox that the conquerers are conquered by these bribes. (Johnson must surely have remembered his own lines when later in prose he described Frederick wasting nations in the attempt to raise his single name.) After this general belittling of heroism, the individuals Charles XII, Xerxes, and the 'bold Bavarian' each become a 'vanquish'd hero', tracing the same course as Wolsey: from superhumanity, impervious to danger, labour, pleasure, pain or peace, to depending miserably on dependants (lines 193–222); from dominion over 'half mankind', attempted dominion over waves and wind, and even the status of a god, to 'humbler thoughts', flight and dread (lines 225–40).

Yet this denial of ultimate hero status coexists with a poetic celebration of heroic effort which one strand of Johnson's imagery asserts. Our response to the whole poem would be entirely different if he had continued throughout it to see humanity as wavering and anxious in 'dreary paths' (lines 7–8). Much of its energy comes from the drive to compete ('Athirst for wealth, and burning to be great': line 74), much more from the achievements which precede the inevitable downfalls. Johnson associates every one of his exemplars with some combination of the qualities of height, shining, fire, rapid movement and the affronting of difficulty and resistance. Often such difficulty takes the form of personified abstracts (the triumvirate Novelty, Sloth and Beauty which may allure the scholar; Famine, Winter, Want and Cold, which oppose their forces to those of Charles XII, apparently in vain; Resistance which steps forth like a warrior from Spenser or Bunyan to cut back at Xerxes' power) all apparently malevolent forces of larger than life size, which make the combat unequal and the vanquished human combatant pathetic even while his energy and strength excel those of his peers.[61] Human heroes are those who capitulate only to more-than-human foes.

Allowing always for the different requirements of purpose and genre, Johnson during the 1740s abandoned the aim of representing the hero in his glory for that of exploding his claim to heroism (Frederick) or else that of depicting him (as in *The Vanity of Human Wishes* and the potential paintings described in *Idler* 45) confronting the fact that he is after all mortal. Johnson's treatment of Shakespeare in his preface of 1765 is a revised statement of the possibilities of a certain version of the heroic. Johnson calls Shakespeare 'so great a poet', 'this mighty genius', in his dedication for Charlotte Lennox (Y, VII, 48, 49). Yet, paradoxically, Shakespeare founds his greatness on acknowledging the ordinary boundaries of humanity and curbing the drama's tendency to stray beyond them. Shakespeare, says Johnson, turned his fellow writers away from the representation of 'such characters as were never seen' (Y, VII, 63). His peculiar excellence is 'the representation of life':

> his *heroes are men* . . . the love and hatred, the hopes and fears of his chief personages are such as are common to other human beings, and not like those which later times have exhibited, peculiar to phantoms that strut upon the stage.

(By echoing *Macbeth* at the end of that sentence, Johnson implies further that a too-heroic play is 'a tale/Told by an idiot, full of sound and fury,/ Signifying nothing.'[62])

One whose 'heroes are men' must be both a nice discriminator of the quality of heroism as it is actually to be found in life, and a vigilant delineator of false heroisms. Celia in *As You Like It* is a heroine in friendship (Y, VII, 264). Hamlet has a just and 'philosophical' idea of true greatness, yet entertains 'romantick' notions about honour which make him – crushingly – the 'idea of a modern hero' (Y, VIII, 995). Hotspur, whose rhetoric Warburton had regarded as 'the natural movement of an heroic mind', seems to Johnson to possess *only* 'the soldier's virtues, generosity and courage' (Y, VII, 461–2, 523; cf. above, pp.189ff.). Finally and perhaps most significantly of all, Johnson reserves one of his highest panegyrics for the line and a half from *Macbeth*, 'I dare do all that may become a man,/Who dares do more, is none'. This fine discrimination of the human from the would-be superhuman ought almost 'to bestow immortality on the author, though all his other productions had been lost' (Y, VIII, 767).

The paradox in Johnson's criticism of Shakespeare is not that he presumed to find imperfections in the 'mighty genius' (though Sir John Hawkins and some later critics have held this against him).[63] Rather it is that his praise of Shakespeare for attention to 'the genuine progeny of common humanity', not to heroes, is itself couched in terms which strongly suggest the heroic rather than the human. As he believes Shakespeare's power to be 'the power of nature', Johnson employs for him metaphors drawn from the large and splendid aspects of nature. Through centuries of evaluation Shakespeare's plays have vanquished their competitors; Johnson describes the process as not like the aggressive victories of Crichton or Charles XII, but like the tranquil self-revelation of the highest mountain and the deepest river (Y, VII, 62, 73, 60). Like Drake, Shakespeare excels others apparently without trying. Johnson's other images for him take the same tone as this. In his life he shook off poverty and obscurity 'as dewdrops from a lion's mane'. We contemplate his genius through the years between us 'as the eye surveys the sun through artificial opacity'; his commentators are his satellites. The 'whole system of life' whose springs he reveals to us is selected as by a greater Creator's hand from the vast 'chaos' of human activity. His work is the eternal rock, the 'adamant' which resists the 'stream of time'; it is regular yet varied, like a stretch of countryside or like the whole surface of our planet; it is a mine of gold, diamonds and meaner minerals; 'a forest, in which oaks extend their branches, and pines tower in the air . . . filling the eye with awful pomp, and gratifying the mind with endless diversity'.[64] Murray Krieger suggests that the forest image 'rejects the sense of universal order' in recognizing 'the equal role and equal necessity' of brambles with roses. That equal necessity is, however, the order of the living chain in Pope's *Essay on Man*. In Jungian terms Johnson attributes to Shakespeare completeness, not perfection.[65] These images carry a very different force from those of the lion and mountain to which in

Rambler 72 he compares a man who is great without good humour (see above, p.127), because of the accompanying insistence here on humanity. Shakespeare never 'panted for a height of eminence denied to humanity' (*Ram.* 17: Y, III, 96). His superior mind saw the limits of its own works (Y, VII, 112); but those works, with their mixture of gold and meaner minerals, happily modify Johnson's earlier opinion that anyone who 'has abilities to conceive perfection, will not easily be content without it; and since perfection cannot be reached, will lose the opportunity of doing well in the vain hope of unattainable excellence' (*Ram.* 134: Y, IV, 349).

To ascribe to Shakespeare's imperfect, living works the power of inspiring growth, like the sun, or exemplifying it, like trees, is the highest praise that Johnson can give. He had used the same two images to open his *Rambler* criticism of *Paradise Lost*, ostensibly of Addison's criticism but surely with reference to Milton as well (Y, IV, 87). In distorted form he had applied them to Charles XII and Xerxes. He uses a third image to convey the continuing life and growth of Shakespeare's works after their author's death. These plays, 'as they devolved from one generation to another, have received new honours at every transmission', thereby declaring themselves akin to the ancients as Pope described them,

> Whose Honours with Increase of Ages *grow*,
> As Streams roll down, *enlarging* as they flow![66]

Shakespeare is Johnson's most complete single depiction of man as hero, encountering difficulties unassisted (Y, VII, 88–9), benefiting humanity, towering above his fellows and courting comparison with the splendours of nature, yet never seeking to evade the human scale. Johnson cannot forget to assess his hero as man, whom it would be idolatry to rate too highly. In this he follows Dryden, whom he quotes saying that if Shakespeare were uniformly great, he would be *above* 'the greatest of mankind. . . . But he is always great, when some great occasion is presented to him.' Johnson's preface holds in balance judgments of apparently contradictory tendency: Shakespeare's glory is that of having deglorified the theatre, turning from impossible heroes to men; to point out his faults, almost every one of which Johnson mentions in explicit reaction against excessive glorification, is to be a better Shakespearean than those who would make him no man but such a writer as was never seen.[67]

Johnson's Shakespeare 'has long outlived his century' (Y, VII, 61); the preface several times appears about to credit him with immortality. This, however, he has not attained, even in the limited literary sense: 'it is vain to carry wishes beyond the condition of human things; that which must happen to all, has happened to Shakespeare, by accident and time'. Like Achilles, he cannot escape the condition of human things: the one must die, the other must depend on editors and explanatory notes. Indeed, like Laud and other figures in *The Vanity of Human Wishes*, Shakespeare falls victim to his own greatness, to 'that superiority of mind, which despised its own performances, when it compared them with its powers' (Y, VII, 112), and which therefore made no arrangement for preserving them. Johnson's Shakespeare is his most complete delineation of a hero defined according to the *Dictionary*'s second sense, a 'man of the highest class in any respect'. (He shows no trace of the first definition's 'bravery' in the military sense, but only in energy and magnanimity.) Nor is there any trace of the demi-god. Not for Shakespeare is the doom of man or of writer reversed.

11

GREATNESS AND OURSELVES

Nor think the doom of man revers'd for thee.

(*The Vanity of Human Wishes*, line 156)

SUCH GREATNESS as Shakespeare's never lost its hold on Johnson's imagination. His writings continually return to it, and it was regularly canvassed in his talk, both generally and as regards the aspirations of himself and his acquaintance. His natural impulse is regularly to relate the achievements of his subject to the efforts of himself and his audience. Self-identification has been repeatedly detected or debated in this or that Johnsonian biography. To suppose that Johnson actually drew his own portrait under the guise of another is clearly mistaken. It is helpful, on the contrary, to see him as generally associating himself and also ourselves with his pictures of the upward struggle of greatness. Except when he separates his great achievers from us as heroes, he invites us to contemplate them from a lower point on the same scale, and to relate ourselves to them by direct comparison.

As biographer, traveller, history writer, Johnson assesses those examples of greatness which present themselves to his view; in writing more analytically about the workings of the mind he associates himself and us in an enquiry into the means and the obstacles to achieving superiority, into its moral problems, its rewards when achieved, and its circumscription by 'the condition of human things'. He was fond of the text 'Of him, to whom much is given, much shall be required'.[1] As he wrote his essays, his interest in 'hopes of excellence' (*Letters*, no. 686), indubitably his own hopes as well as those of others, was still acute. The essays focus early and steadily on the particular problems of pursuing excellence: withdrawal from others, unrealistic demands of oneself, underconfidence, overconfidence, arrogance, the temptation to take impossible perfection as the goal or to think oneself in any way exempt from the human condition. The kind of false standards of measurement which are merely comic in obviously petty people become a matter of deep, unmocking concern when they afflict those who must be taken seriously.

Most of Johnson's precepts fall into one of two categories: how to cope with obscurity and how to cope with eminence. We are warned, frequently and hilariously, of the figure we shall cut if we persist in overvaluing our own importance; but also we are warned, just as frequently, about the wrong exercise of great talents and about the problems which even the right exercise of them poses. The very number of essays on good humour, 'petty qualities' and 'subaltern endowments' is witness to Johnson's concern with the realization of greatness, for he sees good humour as the necessary counterweight to superiority.

> Heroic generosity, or philosophical discoveries, may compel venera- tion and respect, but love always implies some kind of natural or voluntary equality, and is only to be excited by that levity and chearfulness which disencumbers all minds from awe and solicitude, invites the modest to freedom, and exalts the timorous to confidence. . . .
>
> Every man finds himself differently affected by the sight of fortresses of war, and palaces of pleasure; we look on the height and strength of the bulwarks with a kind of gloomy satisfaction, for we cannot think of defence without admitting images of danger; but we range delighted and jocund through the gay apartments of the palace, because nothing is impressed by them on the mind but joy and festivity. Such is the difference between great and amiable characters; with protectors we are safe, with companions we are happy. (*Ram.* 89: Y, IV, 108–9)

There is, we note, no mention in Johnson's metaphor of a cottage along with its fortress and palace. His argument is addressed to encourage voluntary equality, not natural, to solve the predicament of a genuinely great mind. The second paragraph quoted is likely to leave with the reader an image of a fortress transforming itself into a palace. Johnson does not say that the bulwarks and the gay apartments belong (as historically and archi- tecturally they easily might) to the same building, or advise conversion and defortification. But he does describe, in the other half of his implied simile, 'levity and .chearfulness' not simply meeting an equal response but disencumbering, inviting, exalting; and he does introduce the passage with 'A wise and good man is never so amiable as in his unbended and familiar intervals'. He is, as so often, addressing those who may choose equality, not those who have it thrust upon them, and is recommending cultivation of 'petty qualities' not instead of, but in addition to, great ones.

These essays address themselves to the moral and intellectual problems involved in the pursuit of greatness with a persistence which must make them every bit as barren for readers entirely devoid of ambition as accounts of impossible heroes can be for the unheroic. Though Johnson conceives of them, even more markedly than of his biographies, as taking their subject-matter from unexceptional experience, 'levelled with the general surface of life' (*Idler* 84: Y, II, 262), such as will fit his unexceptional audience, he nevertheless consistently assumes that the drive to achieve excellence is a major preoccupation of that audience. 'The desire of excellence is laudable' in itself (*Ram*. 66: Y, III, 351) no matter how urgently it requires regulation. When he admits that it 'cannot indeed be expected of all to be poets and philosophers' (cf. *Lives*, III, 126) we find ourselves shocked, like Rasselas when the maid breaks the cup, at recognition of the obvious, because in reading the *Rambler* we have had our ambition and our sense of potential stirred, as well as our brains exercised.

When Johnson calls people 'equal in themselves' (see above, p.185), he has in mind no egalitarian mean, but the 'high and low', a prince annoyed by invasion and a farmer by the theft of a cow: distant points, but on the same scale. It is the man 'most elevated above the croud by the importance of his employments or the reputation of his genius' whose essential equality, against all appearances, Johnson most wishes to demonstrate (Y, II, 262–3). Persons of such transcendent abilities absorb much of the essays' attention. A reader of the fifth and sixth paragraphs of *Rambler* 43 would naturally suppose that it intends to balance the particular advantages and disadvantages of on the one hand 'souls suited to great . . . employments . . . formed to soar aloft' and on the other hand those formed for little employments and to 'confine their regard to a narrow sphere'. Not only does Johnson never consider the problems of the second group: in his last paragraph he roundly identifies the first as 'those for whom this essay is designed', having apparently forgotten all about the others (Y, III, 233, 236).

The problems of soaring aloft, to which Johnson thus directs attention, are, according to his system of thought, without solution. To escape the human sphere is impossible; to enlarge it is an attempt fraught with hazard; to perceive oneself as having excelled others is, almost necessarily, in some way to fall below them. The range of advice which Johnson offers to the great and would-be great centres always on the single precept, 'remember you are little'. Examples of the various failures to follow this advice are inexhaustible. The pursuit of intellectual distinction has been variously responsible for the inhuman hard-heartedness of Gelidus, the social ineptness of Verecundulus, and the vanity of the naturalist in *Idler* 55. But Johnson does not propose that we should play safe by refraining from attempts at distinction, only that we should modify the attempt with certain precautions – precautions which have to do with choice of an accurate scale of measurement.

In the quest for superiority, the first obstacle to be encountered is a premature confidence that superiority has already been attained. This error of judgment is a favourite theme of the essays, a favourite starting-point for Johnson's meditations, stated and restated in opening paragraphs.

> Every man is prompted by the love of himself to imagine, that he possesses some qualities, superior, either in kind or in degree, to those which he sees allotted to the rest of the world; and, whatever apparent disadvantages he may suffer in the comparison with others, he has some invisible distinctions, some latent reserve of excellence, which he throws into the balance, and by which he generally fancies that it is turned in his favour. (*Ram.* 21: Y, III, 115–16)

From here he moves into a discussion of how authors consider themselves superior to other people, and how each author considers himself superior to the rest. *Rambler* 146 provides a detailed case-history of such a conviction. A recently published author 'walks out like a monarch in disguise, to learn the various opinions of his readers', with 'an imagination full of his own importance' and with careful resolutions against falling into the vices of eminence. This man is typical: everyone 'endeavour[s] to conceal his own unimportance from himself' through the 'arts of voluntary delusion' (Y, V, 13, 15); it is indeed 'easy . . . to find reasons for esteeming' oneself, to discover in one's own self-interrogation 'many latent excellencies' which no other observer would suspect (*Ram.* 76: Y, IV, 33–4). These essays investigate the processes of applying a distorted scale, either intellectual or moral.

Johnson deliciously, parodically indulges in the thumb in the scale at the end of *Rambler* 193. Here he shares with his readers his own modest exultation at receiving a letter lauding his 'universal learning – unbounded genius – soul of Homer, Pythagoras, and Plato': a letter which comes from himself. The mask which periodical journalists assume for the purpose of writing themselves flattering letters, it appears, is that of full-blown hero-worshipper. This self-as-worshipper, besides linking in the Carlylean manner such disparate names as Homer, Plato and the Rambler,

> always addresses us with the deference due to a superior intelligence . . . offers an objection with trembling diffidence; and at last has no other pretensions to our notice than his profundity of respect, and sincerity of admiration. (Y, V, 247)

The incense which Carlyle describes as beneficially offered to others, Johnson depicts as a furtive, poisonous indulgence which we reserve for ourselves.

It is therefore no surprise that so many of Johnson's references to greatness or to genius are correctively satiric or even sarcastic. The self-acclaimed genius ranks in his works with the hero of the street or the boudoir. As sole *Dictionary* example under *genius* ('2. A man endowed with superiour faculties') he quotes from memory Addison's *Spectator* 160 as, preparatory to considering 'what is properly a great genius', it gives its first paragraph to sweeping up and clearing away debased uses of the word. Johnson as essayist maintains the fiction of genius and keeps it carefully separated from himself. In his first *Rambler*, conscious of making a serious bid for literary greatness in a genre not accorded high status, he acknowledges with a smile the gulf traditionally recognized between 'the lower orders of literature' and those like writers of epic who claim alliance with genius (Y, III, 4). In his penultimate number he smiles again at the same gulf: a common-or-garden author might confess some falling-off towards the end of his work when he got tired or bored, but 'a genius is not to be degraded by the imputation of human failings' (Y, V, 313).

'As all error is meanness', the error of miscalculating one's own stature is the most dangerous of all to that stature itself (*Ram.* 31: Y, III, 173). A conviction of their own greatness is the most common mental handicap of Johnson's imaginary correspondents, and one of the paradigms of *Rambler* experience is premature acclaim which actively destroys the achievement it professes to recognize. The antidote against gratuitous littleness, or the meanness of self-aggrandizement, is to be mindful of inescapable littleness.

> In proportion as perfection is more distinctly conceived, the pleasure of contemplating our own performances will be lessened; it may therefore be observed, that they who most deserve praise, are often afraid to decide in favour of their own performances. (*Ram.* 169: Y, V, 131–2)

The only greatness even potentially available to human beings is that which, as *Ramblers* 31 and 137 and the preface to Shakespeare suggest, can both conceive perfection and recognize that perfection is impossible. The active and enquiring mind needs to be constantly fed with the prospect of greatness beyond itself. An individual who 'easily comprehends all that is before him, and soon exhausts any single subject' will find that 'in proportion as the intellectual eye takes in a wider prospect, it must be gratified with variety by more rapid flights, and bolder excursions' (*Ram.* 150: Y, V, 34). *Ramblers* 150 and 169 both insist that we should see the powers of the mind 'in proportion as' we see not some charismatic hero or genius but the world beyond. Johnson desires not that we should be cowed into submission by contemplating a supra-human scale, but that we should be challenged by the ability of human powers to relate to it.

Souls 'formed to soar aloft' have an equally acute need to relate to a pettier scale of things as well as persons. They are 'apt to place too much confidence in [themselves], and to expect from a vigorous exertion of [their] powers more than spirit or diligence can attain' (*Adv.* 69: Y, II, 394). They

> form schemes of too great extent, and flatter themselves too hastily with success; they feel their own force to be great, and, by the complacency with which every man surveys himself, imagine it still greater: they therefore look out for undertakings worthy of their abilities, and engage in them with very little precaution, for they imagine that without premeditated measures, they shall be able to find expedients in all difficulties. (*Ram.* 43: Y, III, 233)

Against this error too the best preventive is acceptance of littleness and mutuality: of 'common gradations' and 'petty operations, incessantly continued'. By such steps as 'a single stroke of the pick-ax, or . . . one impression of the spade', great designs are realized, and to despise the steps is necessarily to fail of the goal (Y, III, 233, 235). Laughable pottering in search of plants has developed into the science of botanical medicine; hollowing tree-trunks has led to circumnavigating the world. 'If what appears little be universally despised, nothing greater can be attained, for all that is great was at first little, and rose to its present bulk by gradual accessions, and accumulated labours' (*Ram.* 83: Y, IV, 72). Intellectual or moral greatness is built out of littleness as surely as is physical bulk. Johnson makes the same point in criticism when he dwells on the metrics or the first sketches of *Paradise Lost*, the drafts of Pope's *Iliad*, the common humanity of Shakespeare's heroes, the relation of sublime harmony to single sounds, and great works to 'imperfect rudiments' and 'accidental hints' (*Ram.* 88: Y, IV, 99; *Lives*, I, 121–4, III, 119–26). As *Rambler* 137 has it, 'The widest excursions of the mind are made by short flights frequently repeated; the most lofty fabricks of science are formed by the continued accumulation of single propositions' (Y, IV, 361).

Theories of poetry as a matter of inspiration are suspect to Johnson because they attempt to negotiate an escape from human pettiness, a leap beyond the gradual. To pursue a great design successfully, the first requisite is not to expect or to depend upon exemption from the human scale, from single steps taken in single moments of time. *Rambler* 108 describes how, 'from a false estimate of the human powers', we unrealistically defer beginning 'any great project' until a hypothetical 'time of leisure, and a state of settled uniformity' (which of course will never arrive). It glances at the unproved assertion that 'gigantick' (larger than human) intelligences exist which can dispense with 'regular steps through intermediate propositions', but insists on the known fact that many of 'those who have contributed to the advancement of learning' have done so, gradually, 'amidst the tumult of business, the distresses of poverty, or the dissipations of a wandering and unsettled state' (Y, IV, 212–14). Accurate judgment, both of oneself and of the scale of things, will prevent at once the mistakes of overconfidence and of lack of confidence.

> To expect that the intricacies of science will be pierced by a careless glance, or the eminences of fame ascended without labour, is to expect a peculiar privilege, a power denied to the rest of mankind; but to suppose that the maze is inscrutable to diligence, or the heights inaccessible to perseverance, is to submit tamely to the tyranny of fancy, and enchain the mind in voluntary shackles. . . .
>
> It were to be wished that they who devote their lives to study would at once believe nothing too great for their attainment, and consider nothing as too little for their regard. (*Ram.* 137: Y, IV, 362)

All Johnson's demands for wisdom and clear-sightedness, for liberating ourselves from prejudice, are comprehended in the demand for awareness of relativity of scale. Every advance towards greatness makes relativity both harder and more necessary to remember. Therefore the scholar in *The Vanity of Human Wishes*, whose quest for greatness the poet so warmly endorses ('Are these thy views? proceed, illustrious youth,/And virtue guard thee to the throne of Truth!'), nevertheless needs the solemn caution not to think himself exempt (lines 141–2, 156). Therefore the astronomer in *Rasselas*, 'one of the most learned . . . in the world', nevertheless urgently needs the advice to 'keep this thought always prevalent, that you are only one atom of the mass of humanity' (XL, XLVI). This thought leads on, no matter how great the thinker, to awareness of ties to other people, of reliance on petty methods and gradual steps, and finally of the uncertainty and fragility of the rewards of greatness.

Johnson's treatment of fame is a classic example of his insistence on relativity, or the simultaneous entertaining of alternative scales. On the one hand it may be nobly and compellingly described, as in *Ramblers* 49 and 136, as something beyond the individual whose aspiration it crowns. It remains high and weighty amongst terrestrial goals even when the overall significance of such goals is diminished (*Rambler* 118, see above, pp.25–6). Johnson himself distributed the meed of praise to those who had earned it with a clear sense of conferring something valuable.[2] On the other hand he is always reminding us, not only that fame is of briefer duration than contenders for it expect (e.g. *Rambler* 106 and the *Journey*: Y, IV, 200; IX, 151), but also that those contenders perform for an audience whose members they would have despised. Blockheads snooze over what Art and Genius lament; 'names which hoped to range over kingdoms and continents shrink at last into cloisters or colleges'. By this scale, fame is a further instance of the dependence of great people on little, to be classed ultimately with 'bribes' whose reality falls far below the expectation.[3]

Johnson's diminishing of fame often verges on diminishing the very greatness which it rewards. In *Rambler* 20 he compares unearned fame to an ice palace, ready to melt, and even deserved fame to a pinnacle slippery to stand on (Y, III, 115, 114). This repeats a forceful image from no. 17, published ten days earlier, which pictures mankind 'wearing out our lives in endeavours to add new turrets to the fabrick of ambition, when the foundation itself is shaking, and the ground on which it stands is mouldering away'. Johnson hints at Christ's parable of the house built on sand as he repeatedly stresses the inadequate foundations of human achievement: Wolsey's, Swedish Charles's, and in the sermons those of us all. 'There is not time for the most forcible genius, and most active industry, to extend its effects beyond a certain sphere.'[4]

Yet, no matter how radically Johnson reduces the scale of greatness, he still retains his sense of its relative worth. Drawing the *Rambler* series to a close, he expatiates eloquently first on the delight of planning great projects, then on the toil and disappointment of carrying them through in the face of 'the necessity of resting below that perfection which we imagined within our reach' (Y, V, 310–11). The individual – oneself – sinks back into pettiness; the ideal of greatness, unattained, lives on. Johnson's writings frequently couple the adjective *great* with the noun *attempt*. What he seeks is the search itself: any viable alternative to accepted narrowness, or unexamined fantasies of greatness, or rolling 'darkling down the torrent of [our] fate',[5] or to solacing ourselves with delusive fantasies of greatness. As a hack journalist he wrote the lives of the celebrated and the debating speeches of the eminent. As a poet he wrote a vivid indictment of his own environment, London, for its failure to nourish and reward 'those qualities which have a claim to the veneration of mankind' (*Idler* 51: Y, II, 160), and a survey of the way that even the most wished-for achievements fail to satisfy the spirit. As an old man, in *The Lives of the Poets*, he returned to the genre of his apprenticeship to celebrate that which 'can claim praise or admiration' (*Idler* 57: Y, II, 178) in a field of endeavour whose possibilities and whose boundaries he knew from experience, and had already charted in his essays and elsewhere.

The Lives of the English Poets, booksellers' project as it was, must also have been conceived by Johnson simultaneously as a pious rendering of bays, a reminder that the recipients were only mortal, and an investigation of the causes why great plans sometimes ripen into great achievements and sometimes do not. The second and third of these aims reflect changes in Johnson's underlying assumptions since the years of his earlier biographies. During those years the essays had dwelt on success and failure. That 'generous temerity which . . . often succeeds', Johnson concludes, is the same which 'often fails' (*Idler* 57: Y, II, 178); 'unexpected accidents' are liable to snatch deserved success from a 'great or laudable undertaking'

(*Adv.* 111: Y, II, 455). Chance, indeed, has a wider power than merely that of hindering: 'unless some accidental advantage co-operates with merit' that merit will not attract 'honour or remembrance' (*Ram.* 193: Y, V, 244). The *Gentleman's Magazine* pieces show their heroes winning their way, as the young Johnson had once hoped to do, through sheer force of native ability; *The Lives of the Poets* show greatness as much more hazardous.

The *Lives* combine the celebration of realized greatness both with recognition of its chanciness and with that tragic sense of its insufficiency which had animated *The Vanity of Human Wishes*. Scattered remarks in Johnson's essays indicate the preparedness of his mind for such a task. Veneration even for material relics of men 'great and illustrious, is intended as an incitement to labour, and an encouragement to expect the same renown, if it be sought by the same virtues' (*Ram.* 83: Y, IV, 74). But veneration ought to be carefully and parsimoniously dispensed. On the subject of dedications Johnson wrote

> Praise, like gold and diamonds, owes its value only to its scarcity. It becomes cheap as it becomes vulgar, and will not longer raise expectation, or animate enterprize. It is therefore . . . necessary, that . . . goodness be commended only in proportion to its degree; and that the garlands, due to the great benefactors of mankind, be not suffered to fade upon the brow of him who can boast only petty services and easy virtues. (*Ram.* 136: Y, IV, 355–6)

So the distributors of praise must also be measurers and comparers, remembering their duty both to mankind and to 'the great benefactors of mankind' – a phrase Johnson had used, with some variation, in several early biographies. In view of the importance, both social and religious, that Johnson attributes to the life of the mind, it is not surprising that he should believe that common humanity is more truly benefited by the addition of new intellectual or imaginative than by that of new imperial and commercial territory. He also believes in the writer as teacher: a mere human who, although sharing the same wants, pains, pleasures, petty cares and duties as others, is in his books 'the instructor of mankind'. *Idler* 51 professes readiness to venerate the instructor, even while as ordinary mortal in his 'domestick privacies' he can deserve 'very little reverence'.

The several directions of Johnson's endeavour in the *Lives* are mapped in this essay on the behaviour of great men in ordinary circumstances (Y, II, 158–61). Great powers, it says, cannot be exerted except in rare great exigencies. For those who aim at distinction the message is clear: not to strive against nature, but to save their wisdom or valour for special circumstances, and to yield with full understanding to their petty human condition in 'common occurrences'. The *Lives* systematically record the way in which candidates for renown did this, or (like so many subjects of Johnson's essays) did not.

The message of *Idler* 51 to potential adjudicators of renown, and what it says of them, is much more ambiguous. The often-quoted fifth paragraph tells us that having 'neither opportunity nor motive to examine the minuter parts of their lives', we see 'of a hero only his battles, or of a writer only his books'. We see, that is, their superiority but not their littleness; 'we have nothing to allay our ideas of their greatness' – and we depend on the biographer to examine for us their minuter behaviour. But two paragraphs later Johnson's argument reverses itself. He now assumes that we know the lives of the great by direct observation and their achievements only in theory; it is therefore their pettiness that we perforce see, and their greatness that waits for the biographer to reveal it.

Whatever any man may have written or done, his precepts or his valour will scarcely over-ballance the unimportant uniformity which runs thro' his time. We do not easily consider him as great, whom our own eyes shew us to be little; nor labour to keep present to our thoughts the latent excellencies of him who shares with us all our weaknesses and many of our follies.

There can be few such striking instances as *Idler* 51 of the inconsistency of which some critics of Johnson's essays have complained. He finds first the works of the eminent, and then their lives, to be the easier to observe. He calls on the biographer first to counteract too pronounced an impression of greatness, then the reverse. This inconsistent essay goes some way towards explaining why the *Lives* themselves display inconsistencies which 'imputed to man . . . may both be true' (*Rass*. VIII. The stature attainable in an individual's work is in either case higher than that attainable in life; but the discrepancy needing to be redressed seems first to be the dominance of one scale, then of the other.

Johnson's 'very little reverence' for the minuter parts of his subjects' lives is due neither to inadequacy in the subject nor a grudge in the biographer. He relates all their behaviour to their goal of greatness: of Swift's boasting his familiarity with those in power, for instance, he asks not whether it was right or wrong, but whether it was magnanimous or servile (*Lives*, III, 21–2, 61). Most of Johnson's great poets are unexceptional as persons, some even notably petty; Isaac Watts, on the other hand, has a personal greatness which his writings do not capture, and the mediocre poet Blackmore is capable of 'magnanimity' in a way that Dryden and Pope are not (II, 253). It is the moralist's business to urge that neither transcendent achievement nor what *Idler* 51 calls 'domestic degradation' (not humiliation but simply stepping down) should be entirely lost sight of. *The Lives of the Poets* alternates two different lengths of focus.

Johnson opens the *Lives*, as already mentioned (see above, p.29), with a disclaimer of the magnifying and bemisting powers of panegyric. The life of Cowley doubly proclaims his concern with problems of scale: its criticism of the Metaphysicals identifies greatness as an essential quality of poetry, not to be sacrificed for the heaping-up of detail or ornament; its probing behind the false magnifications of flattery recognizes the difficulty of measuring poetic achievement. The first of the *Lives* establishes, for Johnson to refer to later, fundamental propositions about greatness. The lack of ceremony with which he identifies Cowley's father as a grocer sets his tone towards the petty particulars of all the lives, irrespective of the literary stature of the individual concerned.[6] This fact might seem too obvious to mention, did not some critical responses to the *Lives* show that the expectation of reverence for a great man's relics, to which Johnson refers in *Rambler* 83, may be transferred from objects to facts. Boswell, with his delight in investigating such 'particularities' as Johnson's disposal of orange-peel (II, 330–1), was willing as a biographer to arouse and to gratify such feelings; Johnson was much more doubtfully and infrequently so.

Indeed, he came to this work already expecting to find much pettiness in great writers, whether, as he speculates in the life of Pope, because

> men conscious of great reputation think themselves above the reach of censure . . . or that mankind expect from elevated genius an uniformity of greatness, and watch its degradation with malicious wonder; like him who having followed with his eye an eagle into the clouds, should lament that she ever descended to a perch. (*Lives*, III, 135)

Whatever the cause, 'the veneration which learning would procure' is often obstructed 'by follies greater or less to which only learning could betray' (*Adv.* 131: Y, II, 482). Johnson more than once involves us, his readers, in his expectations about greatness: we are to be disillusioned by the small scope of Roscommon's *oeuvre* (*Lives*, I, 234–5), ashamed to discover Dryden's faults (I, 464), disappointed at Swift's failure in his B.A. exam (III, 2); but also, indirectly by association with 'the world', we are to be diverted by the spectacle of greatness stooping to folly (III, 186). I do not believe that Johnson felt or showed malice towards his subjects, nor that he felt degraded in his own eyes by standing comparison with those 'really and naturally great' (see above, p.64). What he did demonstrate is purposeful and steady opposition to the offering of incense to the great as beyond the human scale. Johnson, unlike many, refuses to ask of a distinguished individual that he demonstrate 'superiority in those parts of life, in which all are unavoidably equal'; he sets himself against the school of thought which considers 'those who are placed in ranks of remote [here financial] superiority, as almost another and higher species of beings', against, as it were, those remote peasants who expect kings to be taller than themselves (*Rams.* 180, 58; Y, V, 182, III, 312). This school includes Milton's biographer Richardson, who wishes to find the poet 'discriminated from other men', and William Cowper, who wrote sarcastically in the margin of this life, 'Let us by all means make an ordinary man of him if we can', and Robert Potter, who criticized the *Lives* as drawing attention away from those qualities which differentiate a great man from others, towards those 'paltry circumstances' which level him with them,[7] and ultimately Carlyle.

Johnson always desires to see a great writer levelled with other human beings as far as accuracy demands; and it demands a good deal. Eagles not only perch but stoop. Intellectual excellence may not only co-exist with but actually produce a kind of pettiness. The same essay which insists that all are unavoidably equal in some parts of life also opens the possibility that learning may tend to 'contract the understanding' and leave its possessors 'mean and selfish, ignorant and servile', having 'observed every thing but what passes before their eyes' (Y, V, 182, 184), deaf to *Rambler* 137's advice to relate to both great and little scales (Y, IV, 362). Johnson finds common among his poets both a foolish forgetfulness of human limitation and an equally foolish anxiety for those trappings of status which Longinus thought it greatness to despise (see above, p.50).

Yet Johnson is always attentive to the superiority which appears only in a small, specialized, literary or intellectual part of life, though neither the ignorant venerators of *Rambler* 180 nor the malicious detractors of the life of Pope are so attentive. A short king is still royal. Johnson's great poets *are* discriminated from other men, though not automatically or in every respect. Literary greatness and actual human pettiness do not, however, lie side by side like oil and water, but combine into a whole variety of different relations and consequences. In discussing the resultant patterns, I shall not be concerned with the question of Johnson's accuracy, but intend to consider the portraits he draws almost as if they were fictional characters.

Individual *Lives*, especially their openings, demonstrate the same concern as the opening of 'Cowley' with the establishment of scale, and often with the interrelation of different scales. Johnson played with such interrelations in his comments which Hester Thrale recorded about Pope: 'Pope Madam was a narrow Man. Of Pope as a Writer he had however, the highest Opinion.' He added, of Pope's writings on Shakespeare, 'the little Fellow has done Wonders'.[8] To write poetry at all is to attempt a certain stature, as Johnson makes clear when discussing the poetic trifles of Waller (see above, pp.81–2). Of Ambrose Philips he says, 'little things are not valued but when they are done by those who can do greater' (*Lives*, III, 324). The lives of Butler and of Dryden both open with sweeping claims ('Of the great author of *Hudibras*. . . .' and 'Of the great poet whose life I am about to delineate. . . .'), both later considerably modified. Cowley is repeatedly said to have just failed of greatness through some instance or other of disproportionate judgment (e.g. I, 45, 48, 49, 53). Johnson conveys doubt whether Shenstone's landscape-gardening pursuits are worth the serious attention of a rational being, let alone a poet. He makes Lyttelton appear ridiculous, without any explicit comment, for letting his attention wander from his writings themselves to the minutiae of punctuation and errata (*Lives*, III, 350–1, 453–4). In both these cases it is the dignity of the calling, but not of the man, which he wishes to protect.

The importance even of poetry itself cannot be simply assumed, but the subjects of the earlier *Lives*, being most of them public men as well as writers, give Johnson various opportunities to turn aside and consider the place of poetry in the whole human scheme. It is the care which a poet lavishes on his works, the time and thought they demand from the reader, and their power to affect our lives, which imply a certain weight and importance in the world. The poet claims attention from minds whose limited time is occupied with the serious business of thinking and acting, and he must make good his claim.

In this context writers who do not attempt superiority (like Fenton, who 'may be justly styled an excellent versifier and a good poet', a style which carefully excludes greatness: II, 264) are somewhat anomalous. Johnson can raise only lukewarm interest in Pomfret, whose '*Choice* exhibits a system of life adapted to common notions and equal to common expectations', or in John Philips, who was 'one of those who please by not offending', 'not born to greatness and elevation' (I, 302, 316, 320). For them, unlike the great men of *Idler* 51, the common scale is entirely adequate. Whatever fails to enlarge our comprehension or elevate our fancy, whatever is merely pretty or 'not below mediocrity' (I, 292, II, 24), fails to make its mark on the scale of greatness to which poetry properly belongs.

Johnson does scant justice to Prior. He condescends to Gay as a 'general favourite', 'a play-fellow rather than a partner', having 'not in any great degree the *mens divinior*, the dignity of genius', writing 'little poems' which are 'neither much esteemed, nor totally despised' (II, 268, 282, 284). When at the accession of George II 'Gay was to be great and happy' (II, 274), this is a moment of disproportionate ambition which brings him close to the *Rambler*'s deluded claimants to greatness. Johnson has cast him as one of those hangers-on whom great writers like Addison and Pope attract (III, 129), and gives him in this role an endearing vitality. The episode, in particular, of his tripping on a stool and bringing down a heavy screen when invited to read his work to the royal family (II, 274), is a comic gem which deprives its subject of all dignity, while confirming him as favourite and playfellow to the reader. Behind this 'domestic degradation' no 'latent excellencies' are searched for. To class Gay's works as 'lucky trifles' (II, 271) obviates any need to ask how their effects are achieved or whether their trifling has any serious purpose: whether, in fact, Gay's 'To a Lady on her Passion for Old China' is really the same kind of work as Waller's 'To a

Lady who can do any thing, but sleep when she pleases'. If not actually blamed for it, Gay is certainly dismissed for being little.

Conversely, Johnson treats Edmund Smith (whose 'high opinion of his own merit' and contempt for those who disagreed with him – II, 20 – are traits he shares with more considerable writers) as a false pretender to greatness. Smith is lucky to have attained reputation (like the aristocrats Roscommon and Halifax) without labour, by talent without correspondent performance; it is a piece of luck which Johnson does not forgive. He quotes the whole of Oldisworth's fulsome panegyric, which, identifying Smith as 'the only son of an eminent merchant, one Mr. Neale, by a daughter of the famous Baron Lechmere' (II, 1), recalls nothing so much as the newspaper advertisements aimed at getting a name which Johnson ridiculed in *Idler* 12. Having given Smith's grandfather (a knight) the title of another relation, Oldisworth goes on to credit Smith with natural 'perfections', an 'eager but generous and noble emulation . . . to excel in every art and science' (II, 2–4), and 'a long and perfect intimacy with all the Greek and Latin Classicks' (II, 5): the last a claim more extreme than that which Johnson queried when it was made of Milton (I, 91). Oldisworth presents Smith as philosopher, poet, critic, and finally as a great genius, on the strength largely of fragments and unfinished undertakings (II, 4–11). Even Johnson's judicious praise of poems by Smith as 'best' in their category (II, 12, 16–17) sounds faint after this; his gently deflating statements – that a scheme to make Smith useful failed (II, 14), that his tragedy is remote from life (II, 16), that his best poem can be criticized since 'every human performance has its faults' (II, 17) – read like drastic correctives to Oldisworth's magnification. When Smith's arrogance causes his death, the reader is likely to feel intimations of poetic justice; when Johnson at the end of the life turns away from his subject to indulge himself in reminiscence of Gilbert Walmesley (who, youthfully licentious like Smith, differs from him in acquired piety and in generosity towards the then ignorant young Johnson), and then yet further away to the more solidly based fame of Garrick (II, 20–1), the reader is likely to feel relief.

Gray makes for himself a claim to greatness which Johnson explodes. (Johnson's already formed opinion was perhaps exacerbated by Temple's view that Gray had 'a visible fastidiousness, or contempt and disdain of his inferiors in science': III, 430.) He describes Gray's odes almost entirely in terms of excessive size: they have 'a kind of cumbrous splendour which we wish away', 'pomp of machinery'; stanzas are too long; one of them 'sounds big'; 'The Bard' takes 'a singular event, and swell[s] it to a giant's bulk' (III, 437–8). This size is then shown to be inaccurately perceived. Gray 'has a kind of strutting dignity, and is tall by walking on tiptoe' (III, 440): a little writer feigning size or height. Johnson emphasizes, throughout his account, what Gray imitated from others: Dryden and Horace (III, 435, 438), besides the whole classical and nordic traditions (III, 436, 439). 'Theft is always dangerous', he says of Gray's borrowing from Norse mythology: it is perhaps not fanciful to hear in this accumulation of Johnson's images an echo of one from *Macbeth* (a play Johnson quotes in this life: III, 440), about the usurper feeling his title 'Hang loose about him, like a giant's robe/Upon a dwarfish thief' (V, ii, 21–2). Johnson dismantles the impressive panoply of Gray's magnified images, 'glittering accumulations of ungraceful ornaments' (III, 440), through minute examination, stanza by stanza, almost image by image, exposing with the microscope of criticism.

Johnson never raises Gay above mediocrity (his aspiration to be 'great and happy' is only a momentary aberration). He actively diminishes Smith and Gray, who both pretend to some stature. Writing of Butler, he inherits the conventional paradox of the poverty and obscurity of the brilliant 'great author of *Hudibras*'. He adds another paradox, harder to resolve: that the great author, whose name can perish only with the language, has yet robbed his work of the chance of lasting as well as immediate renown by forming it of materials merely temporary. Cervantes addressed *Don Quixote* to the continuing causes of human folly; Butler addressed *Hudibras* to its particular and local effects (I, 209–10, 213–16). Butler's work not only satirizes the petty fashions of its day, but is too closely associated with their pettiness for its own good. We are left wondering whether we should after all have read this life's opening statement ironically, whether Butler should after all be seen as an example of great potential not properly realized.

Discrepancy between the relative stature of man and writer is a commonplace of the *Lives*. In the life of Milton such discrepancy provides Johnson with matter for multiple comparison, irony, and insistence on the fact that great literary works achieve their being against all expectation, as if we should gather grapes from thorns, or figs from thistles. He maintains throughout this life a steady,[9] unwavering sense of the greatness of the work, especially *Paradise Lost*, before which 'all other greatness shrinks away' (I, 172). Early in his biography he recognizes magnanimity in his subject's temper: 'the usual concomitant of great abilities, a lofty and steady confidence in himself' (I, 94). This recognition, however, comes qualified with a rider: 'perhaps not without some contempt of others', since Milton was parsimonious of praise. His attitude to the university shows 'captious perverseness' and peevishness (I, 90); he thinks too highly of his own juvenilia (I, 87, 161). Already the reader recognizes something petty in the attention of Milton, as portrayed by Johnson, to his own reputation, something unworthy the author of such a great poem and more appropriate to self-important denizens of *Rambler* letters or of the parliament of Magna Lilliputia.

Milton's vanity (pettiness) springs from his abilities (greatness). The two are repeatedly connected. His high standards for marriage precipitate him into the writing of self-justifying pamphlets on divorce (I, 105–6); one work is contemptuous and puritanically savage while the next is calm and nobly self-confident (I, 102). Johnson's moments of joining respectfully in veneration for this great man are closely associated with pinpricks or letdowns: one with a glimpse of him as a politician failing to adjust to loss of influence, another with a jibe at his biographer Richardson ('the fondest of his admirers'), a third with comment on his querulousness, a fourth with his failure to judge his own works impartially (I, 126–7, 134, 140, 147). Milton's courageous defiance of adversaries and of blindness is balanced both by mean, flattering submission to Cromwell (I, 115–16, 118) and by repressive concern to prevent his daughters or other women from 'break[ing] the ranks' (I, 157). All his discreditable behaviour springs from over-concern with his own stature: as a male he believes in the inferiority of women; as an intellectual he believes in the mental decline of mankind since earlier ages because it flatters his desire to feel himself now 'the giant of the pygmies' (I, 157, 138). He is even open to the charge of malignity to both superiors and inferiors, an envious hater and insulter of 'all that is venerable or great', a compeller of mindless labour from women kept ignorant by himself (I, 111, 145). Milton's writing raises him in poetry to his greatest glory, but sinks him in pamphlets to mean expedients: punning on an adversary's name and defending indefensible mistakes (which, says *Rambler* 31, those most superior are generally the readiest to own).[10]

Milton makes great claims both as man and poet; only as poet does he make them good. As poet, on the one hand, he makes promises of future achievement from which, Johnson says, 'might be expected the *Paradise Lost*' (I, 102–3). The poem is based on 'a design so comprehensive that it could be justified only by success' (I, 121) – and it has succeeded. On the other hand, Johnson writes, 'Let not our veneration for Milton forbid us to look with some degree of merriment on great promises and small performance': promises and performance here not in poetry but in action (I, 98).[11] Johnson clearly distinguishes between his attitude to the works, which deserve veneration, and that to the man, who does not; between the works, which outsoar (though not without some concomitant disadvantages) the human scale, and the author, who cannot.

It is an important part of Johnson's intention, in opposition to Richardson, Cowper, Potter and Carlyle, to make his Milton ordinary as well as great. His chief strategy for doing this is to show Milton (and sometimes his biographers) as dwelling on his extraordinariness in ways that can be proved mistaken. On the king's return Milton, to his surprise, finds himself not singled out either for special punishment or special clemency, but put 'in the same condition with his fellow-subjects' (I, 128–30). His politics and more especially his pamphleteering form one area in which Johnson tells us he overestimates his own importance, so that to our compensating eyes he appears petty. His personal relationships are another area in which this happens, and another is a whole sequence of involvements with the less dignified aspects of language and learning. Johnson does not hesitate to use Milton's pedagogic connection to inconsistent and opposing purposes. He mocks the pedantry of his pamphlets as out of scale: 'No man forgets his original trade: the rights of nations and of kings sink into questions of grammar, if grammarians discuss them' (I, 113). Yet he seriously praises him for being ready, after 'defending the supreme powers of his country' and working at *Paradise Lost*, to 'descend from his elevation to rescue children' with a better grammar book, or tyros in philosophy with a textbook in logic (I, 132, 147–8). Though Johnson praises Milton's condescensions, he is amused when he 'hastens home because his countrymen are contending for their liberty, and, when he reaches the scene of action, vapours away his patriotism in a private boarding-school'. In this sequence, as Johnson makes clear, it is not the teaching post which is ridiculous, but its following upon the self-important journey (I, 98).

As a husband Milton is wounded not in his tenderness but in his amour-propre when his wife leaves him after a month of marriage: he 'was too busy to much miss' her but not to resent her absence, for in 'a man whose opinion of his own merit was like Milton's, less provocation than this might have raised violent resentment' (I, 105). To Milton's lofty attribute of accurate belief in his literary abilities, Johnson has added a belief in his national importance which the event did not justify, and a belief in his personal merit which his wife did not share. The greatness which alone could justify his literary arrogance was not forthcoming to justify his political or personal arrogance.

Johnson here presents a man whose assessment of his own stature relative to others is seriously distorted. Though Milton may be praised for voluntary descent, he must also be blamed for intentional withdrawal to superior regions, sometimes aided and abetted by his admirers.[12] This explains Johnson's apparently ambiguous attitude towards the schoolmastering episode. On the one hand he puts forward an unequivocal estimate of merit surely no lower than Milton's own: he 'was not a man who could become mean by a mean employment'. On the other hand he applies to Milton the kind of language which, when Blackmore applies it to poetry, he scornfully calls 'such as Cheapside easily furnished' (*Lives*, II, 238). 'He did not sell literature to all comers at an open shop; he was a chamber-milliner, and measured his commodities only to his friends.' To write of teaching in terms of the drapery trade[13] ridicules not only Milton's shifting, palliating, shrinking biographers, but also Milton himself (I, 109). To say that the biographers shrink (I, 98) is apparently an example of the kind of pun which according to Johnson's principles he should have disapproved, but which he uses fairly frequently and to vivid effect. Milton's biographer

Philips *reduces* Milton's stature through mistaken efforts to enhance it; Johnson having his fun with Philips seems to reduce Milton still further. Philips, he says, viewing the schoolmastering as 'this state of degradation', 'to raise [Milton's] character again, has a mind to invest him with military splendour' and therefore mentions an abortive scheme to give him a commission. In Johnson's sarcastic summary, 'Milton shall be a pedagogue no longer; for, if Philips be not much mistaken, somebody at some time designed him for a soldier'. This is shrinking Milton, the man who had hurried home to save his country, with a vengeance. Philips's misapprehensions (that Milton needs defence as educator of only a select and intimate few instead of 'all the young fry of a parish', and that the character diminished by pedagogy will be enhanced by 'military splendour') result from adhering to a petty or vulgar scale of measurement (I, 109–10). By such a scale, according to which Cowley and Denham the diplomats would be superior to Milton the teacher, not very different from that by which Johnson himself makes political theorists *sink* into grammarians, the lowest teacher would presumably be superior to a milliner, a more select teacher superior again, and a soldier more superior still.[14] Such gradations have no bearing on the stature of epic poetry.

Johnson moves in with gusto for further reductions of Milton, not *to* a pedagogue, but *from* a pedagogue to a milliner, and then to a puppet passively raised and lowered, the sport of stray designs of somebody at some time. The allegedly mean employment gains *some* comparative dignity from this process (Johnson denies, in any case, that it was matter for shame: I, 98). More importantly, he reminds us how wrong we are to yearn after a human employment or a human life exempt from meanness. Johnson is content to leave the creator of a uniquely great literary work in a contemptible social position, whimsically to associate him with millinery as he had accurately associated Cowley with grocery. He similarly combines sardonic comment on Milton's physical appearance with sardonic comment on his admirers' reaction to it: 'not of the heroick stature, but rather below the middle size, according to Mr. Richardson, who mentions him as having narrowly escaped from being "short and thick"' (I, 151). Intellectual dignity is for Johnson independent of socio-economic or sliding-rule considerations, and it is dignity which predominates in the ideal Milton of Johnson's imagination, when *Paradise Lost* is published but not yet admired:

I cannot but conceive him calm and confident, little disappointed, not at all dejected [as Johnson believed Drake could not have been], relying on his own merit with steady consciousness, and waiting without impatience the vicissitudes of opinion and the impartiality of a future generation. (I, 144)

At the end of his life, when blindness is his adversary and acclaim withheld, Milton approaches the status of hero. Not for nothing did the *Dictionary* quote him four times under *magnanimous* and its cognates.

Human, non-literary dignity is threatened by overweening misjudgment of human stature, as Johnson had emphasized in his parliamentary debates. Johnson's Milton, without question a benefactor of humankind, is also a man who tries to break free of the human scale, to evade 'the unimportant uniformity which runs thro' his time' (*Idler* 51: Y, II, 160). Milton's on the whole dislikable personality is intimately linked with his achievement; it is one which ('born for whatever is arduous' and well understanding its own talents: *Lives*, I, 194, 177) would naturally be drawn towards a staggeringly difficult attempt, with the resultant literary faults and virtues which Johnson finds in it.[15] Milton's imagination is 'in the highest degree fervid and active':

> The characteristick quality of his poem is sublimity. He sometimes descends to the elegant, but his element is the great. He can occasionally invest himself with grace; but his natural port is gigantick loftiness. . . .
> The appearances of nature and the occurrences of life did not satiate his appetite of greatness. To paint things as they are requires a minute attention, and employs the memory rather than the fancy. Milton's delight was to sport in the wide regions of possibility; reality was a scene too narrow for his mind. He sent his faculties out upon discovery, into worlds where only imagination can travel, and delighted to form new modes of existence, and furnish sentiment and action to superior beings, to trace the counsels of hell, or accompany the choirs of heaven. (I, 177–8)

Nowhere else in all Johnson's writings does he throw such stress on to the assertion of greatness: this 'poet whatever be done is always great'; his subject and characters are inexpressibly great; no other 'ever soared so high or sustained his flight so long' (I, 180, 172–3, 187).

Emphasizing the comprehensive abilities necessary to produce an epic, Johnson suggests that its author must combine in himself a whole range of superhumanities, like Crichton or the ideal poet portrayed by Imlac. His phrases here (that *Paradise Lost* claims first or second place among human creations, that Milton 'must be confessed to have equalled every other poet': I. 170–1) adopt the terms of the competitive struggle, as does that with which he closes the life: 'his work is not the greatest of heroick poems, only because it is not the first'. This last paragraph once more emphasizes difficulties overcome; it also adds the idea of community to that of competition by pointing out that Milton shares with all later generations in a debt of reverence owed to 'that vigour and amplitude of mind' which invented the epic form (I, 194).

Milton has achieved the literary superiority he sought, which necessarily involves what Damrosch calls overreaching 'the bounds of human nature',[16] distorting the human scale. Johnson's favourite term for him, out of a whole rhetoric of power and authority, is 'master'.[17] He 'never learned the art of doing little things with grace' or that of minute attention (I, 163, 177–8). The lack of human interest in *Paradise Lost* (inevitable from his subject but also from his ignorance of the lesser shades of human character: I, 189) means that his display of his forces wearies the reader, whose mind sinks 'in passive helplessness', 'harassed and overburdened', who 'feels himself in captivity to a higher and a nobler mind' – and may even wish for revenge, by mockery, on what has held him in Carlylean subjection (I, 181–4, 190, 317). Assuming no community with his reader, Milton behaves to us as he did in life: like a tyrant who will make people wish to pull him down. The fault of his greatness is greatness.

The faults of Johnson's Dryden are quite the reverse. Although a great writer, 'whom every English generation must mention with reverence as a critick and a poet', he was also a natural flatterer, one of those 'minds which easily sink into submission, that look on grandeur with undistinguishing reverence' (I, 410, 400). Milton's eyes were not thus prone to look upwards. In some sense Dryden shares Milton's self-confidence: he early begins 'to exercise the domination of conscious genius'; 'he appears to have known in its whole extent the dignity of his character, and to have set a very high value on his own powers and performances', but his 'reverence of his own greatness' is such 'as made him unwilling to expose it to neglect or violation' (I, 338, 395). Where Milton imposes his own scale of measurement on the world, arrogantly expecting it to recognize his greatness, Dryden submits to the world's scale, and anxiously fears it will fail to accord him his due. Johnson represents him as querulous and plaintive in his dealings with his contemporaries and posterity, in a manner which a reader is bound to find disappointing. 'It was throughout his life very much his custom to recommend his works by representation of the difficulties that he had encountered, without appearing to have sufficiently considered that where there is no difficulty there is no praise' (I, 338–9). Johnson conveys distaste for his 'meanness and servility of hyperbolical adulation' (I, 399). Dryden's rivals and adversaries, though none were worthy of him, 'gained from his own temper' a power which Blackmore's worthier rivals never enjoyed, 'the power of vexing him' (I, 370, II, 253). When Settle chalked up a theatrical success, Dryden 'seems to have had his quiet much disturbed' and was unable either to repress or honestly to acknowledge jealousy, 'malignant impatience', and even 'brutal fury' (I, 342, 343): 'and since Settle is sunk into oblivion his libel remains injurious only to himself' (I, 401). Of this play's attention-getting illustrations, Johnson says, 'those ornaments seem to have given poor Dryden great disturbance' (I. 345). That 'poor' (the word which Johnson applies to Gay falling among the royal furniture and to Lyttelton's submissiveness towards reviewers: II, 274, III, 452) is the finishing touch to a section of this life which is designed to arouse pitying contempt.

Johnson several times regrets the amount of petty detail involved in telling Dryden's story, although in fact he suffered from a dearth of solid information. He laments that he has to enumerate tedious theatrical minutiae (I, 336, 368). He quotes what most readers consider too many pages of Settle's quibbling tirades against Dryden, giving their flavour of unwearied littleness as no summary could, and concludes 'Enough of Settle' (I, 354), with a dry dismissiveness which is the very contrary of Dryden's own reaction. The reader is led to share, not Dryden's indignation but Johnson's weariness and regret that Dryden should be reduced to this level. As when writing of Milton, Johnson sometimes links outspoken praise with demeaning comment, Dryden's genius with its disgrace (I, 359). On the 'rage and terrour' provoked by Settle, he comments: 'To see the highest minds thus levelled with the meanest may produce some solace to the consciousness of weakness, and some mortification to the pride of wisdom' (I, 346).

This life incorporates, however, much and noble praise.[18] Dryden's 'compositions are the effects of a vigorous genius operating upon large materials' (I, 457). This too easy flatterer has struck gold in his praise of Shakespeare, which 'may stand as a perpetual model of encomiastick criticism; exact without minuteness, and lofty without exaggeration'. Here Dryden has satisfied the demands of high and low, vast and little; here for once he stands above the competitive struggle. His praise has been converted into smaller change by all the later 'editors and admirers of Shakespeare', including Johnson himself, 'in all their emulation of reverence'. Dryden is praised for qualities diametrically opposed to Milton's, for ease and 'penetrating remarks on human nature' (I, 412, 418, 429). His faults are, not always but usually, 'generous and splendid'; where Milton's greatness is inherent, Dryden's language varies between the genuinely great and the pseudo-great, bulky or tumid (I, 462, 461). Dryden resembles Milton in being competitive to the core, but in a different way. He

> seldom struggled after supreme excellence. . . . nor compare[d] his works, such as they were with what they might be made. He knew to whom he should be opposed. He had more musick than Waller, more vigour than Denham, and more nature than Cowley; and from his contemporaries he was in no danger. Standing therefore in the highest place he had no care to rise by contending with himself; but while there was no name above his own was willing to enjoy fame on the easiest terms. (I, 464–5; cf.I, 413, III, 220–1)

Milton describes the cosmic battle of good with evil, and challenges Homer. Dryden describes blue-blooded patrons and megalomaniac tragic heroes, and fights *à l'outrance* with Settle. Dryden is a man full of weaknesses, fierce in petty quarrels, careless of his talents, great almost in spite of himself, and in spite of an unrestricted participation in common humanity which in the last resort commands Johnson's sympathetic respect.

In his lives of Addison and Swift, Johnson has been seen as ungenerous, damning with faint praise and withholding approval out of prejudice. Addison as a man, like Milton and Dryden, 'knew his own dignity', and had 'a very high opinion of his own merit'; like them, he cannot refrain from malignity against contenders, depreciating Dryden and not only suffering 'too much pain from the prevalence of Pope's poetical reputation' but stooping insidiously to injure him (II, 81, 120). Johnson's probing, minute examination reads pettiness behind some of Addison's actions: he can push himself into finishing *Cato* only by disingenuously enlisting a friend's help; his marriage to a rich and socially superior wife seems accomplished by boot-licking (II, 99, 110–11); the rift in his friendship with Steele, which might be puzzled over in Homeric terms as a secret whose causes only the gods know, involves on Addison's part a dissociating 'contempt of "little *Dicky*, whose trade it was to write pamphlets"' (II, 113, 115); his bashfulness in company is identified with 'servile timidity' (II, 123). Johnson inserts his well-known passage about delicacy in near-contemporary biography, about his fear of giving a pang to survivors by disclosing discreditable truth, directly after recounting Addison's break with Steele (II, 116).[19]

Johnson nevertheless has a high opinion of Addison's literary and personal merit, and sees him as in need of defence against the whirligig of literary fashion. His critical estimation too, however, plays off one scale against another in a manner verging on inconsistency. On the one hand he praises him for the very contrary to greatness: the *Spectator* follows in a tradition of teaching 'the minuter decencies and inferior duties' (II, 92–3). Addison 'had read with critical eyes the important volume of human life'. The knowledge he presents is 'not lofty and austere, but accessible and familiar', and all the better for that (II, 121, 124, 146). Johnson calls his criticism of Milton superficial, presented with 'blandishments' to its readers; but it does both them and Milton the more good for its unpretentiousness, its aiming at no glory for itself (II, 146–7). On the other hand Johnson praises Addison also for greatness: the *Spectator* 'towered far above [its] predecessors; and taught, with great justness of argument and dignity of language, the most important duties and sublime truths' (II, 95–6). To have 'employed wit on the side of virtue and religion' and 'if I may use expressions yet more awful . . . "turned many to righteousness"' is 'an elevation of literary character, "above all Greek, above all Roman fame."'[20]

To measure out acclaim to Addison is no more simple than to measure his achievement. On the one hand 'the profound observers of the present race' make a mistake if they 'repose too securely on the consciousness of their superiority to Addison'; on the other, 'time quickly puts an end to artificial and accidental fame; and Addison is to pass through futurity protected only by his genius' (II, 148, 126). Of this genius Johnson is sparing in his allowance: 'He thinks justly; but he thinks faintly'; his mind is not vigorous; his virtues are those of mediocrity and caution; he does not 'trust his powers enough to be negligent'; he avoids faults but does not attain excellence (II, 127, 145). No grace-notes for Addison. Johnson frequently praises by negatives in the manner of the famous lines from *Cooper's Hill*; in the life of Addison he carries this method to an extreme, and when the reader's ear is attracted by what appears to be a positive, straightforward sentence-structure at last, it turns out to carry as strong a negative implication as any: 'What he attempted, he performed' (II, 149). No great attempts for Addison, except the kind which is great by the alien standard of eternity. He is not, like Milton, 'born for whatever is arduous'; where Dryden complains of difficulties encountered (I, 194, 338–9), Addison evades the encounter. I do not discount Johnson's closing sentence, which recommends the study of Addison by day and by night, when I conclude that Johnson's Addison is a valuable writer but not a great one. That closing sentence, itself so familiar and so elegant, means precisely what it says. Addison will form one's *middle* style; he has not the 'deep mouth', the *mens divinior*.[21]

I have already mentioned (see above, pp. 35–6) Johnson's withholding from Swift the close critical consideration which he gave to other subjects. Swift's style, he says, has no elevations or profundities (*Lives*, III, 52). He is in sober fact a benefactor of the people of Ireland, but Johnson never mentions this without mentioning in the same breath the slightly demeaning circumstance that he is therefore an idol of the mob, and delights in this idolatry. In disposition 'as he exhibits himself to [Johnson's] perception', he is a man addicted to trifles, loving 'la bagatelle' and petty intellectual amusements (III, 63, 45–6), punctilious in detail, describing 'minute occurrences' in a range of different kinds of work, two of which at least are also querulous, peevish or petulant (III, 23, 47–8). These three words and their derivatives, lavishly applied, suggest that Swift as complainer affected Johnson even more disagreeably than Dryden in the same role: 'reiterated wailings' (III, 62) is stronger and more offensive than anything said of Dryden. Johnson sees Swift's peevishness as mean, and associates it with other qualities which, though apparently contrary, are mean as well: he 'shuffles' and flatters those above him, delights in flattery in his turn, and 'predominated over his companions with very high ascendency' (III, 39, 60, 59). By boasting that he is not servile to the great, he manages to have it both ways, flattering himself that he is both favoured and also independent, where a truly 'great mind' would disdain to hold favour by sufferance (III, 21–2, 61). He has it both ways also in impersonally benefiting the inferiors he bullies (III, 57–8), and in concealing by irony his will to power:

> On all common occasions he habitually affects a style of arrogance,[22] and dictates rather than persuades. This authoritative and magisterial language he expected to be received as his peculiar mode of jocularity; but he apparently flattered his own arrogance by an assumed imperiousness, in which he was ironical only to the resentful, and to the submissive sufficiently serious. (III, 60)

As Pope's Addison is willing to wound, and yet afraid to strike,[23] Johnson's Swift is willing to rule, and yet afraid openly to seize the throne. He and his closest friends despise the world and recoil from its pettiness (III, 61), as Milton did from the pygmies of modern times. In despising, too, the saying 'men are but men' and refusing, as Johnson implies, to use it as palliation for mean conduct of his own (III, 32), Swift declares his sense of his own superiority to ordinary human failings. Like so many *Rambler* characters, the central figure of this life is a man with delusions of greatness.

With Pope as his subject, Johnson faced in extreme and even symbolical form the contrast: little man, great poet. He lays purposeful emphasis on Pope's physical littleness, though it is first mentioned in the life as thrown in Pope's face by Dennis (III, 95, 97). This man's 'petty peculiarites' are those of feebleness, weakness, low stature, contracted side, slender legs and proportionate 'little sword'.[24] Johnson's sources for his description (III, 196–8) include the second of Pope's own brave and delightful essays on 'The Club of Little Men' (*Guardian*, nos 91, 92). His whole account, though readers have differed about this, seems to me instinct with the most delicate sympathy, with a sense of how it would *feel* for a man middle-aged and eminent to be unable to dress or undress, to go to bed or 'to hold himself erect' without help from 'a female domestick'.

Yet Johnson does not spare him. He tells, immediately before he describes Pope's 'person', how he made a spiteful and belittling legacy to Ralph Allen because he was 'tottering in the decline of life and unable to resist the violence' of Martha Blount's 'female resentment' against Mrs Allen (III, 195), and immediately afterwards how his ill health made him spoiled, like 'a child whose parents will not hear her cry' (III, 198). Pope is made to appear like an infant – female, to boot – under the dominion of women. Johnson calls his death, if indeed it was caused by heating potted lampreys in a silver saucepan, disproportioned to the lustre of his life; but he hardly shows it as disproportioned to his tea-table stratagems, his cabbage and turnip artifices (III, 200). 'He was fretful and easily displeased, and allowed himself to be capriciously resentful' (III, 202). He loves to talk of his own virtues, and loves money, unlike Johnson's early heroes (III, 196, 204; see above, p.194). Like Milton at his least impressive, like a Lilliputian, he overestimates his own importance (III, 154, 181, 211): he is several times charged with malignity. Like Swift, he is petulant, sneaks and shuffles, loves flattery (III, 195, 151, 154), plumes himself, with 'the common vanity of common men', on the favour of the great and his own self-possession in it (III, 150, 90, 204–6, 211), and is narrow-minded enough to find merit only in his own circle (III, 212).

Yet all this 'domestic degradation' is only an extreme version of our common condition, 'all naked till we are dressed, and hungry till we are fed' (*Idler* 51: Y, II, 159–60). It makes the treasures which Pope offers to his readers more amazing and more mysterious, but cannot seriously diminish them. He is a 'man of such exalted superiority', his 'intelligence perpetually on the wing, excursive, vigorous, and diligent, eager to pursue knowledge, and attentive to retain it' (III, 215, 216), his mind

> active, ambitious, and adventurous, always investigating, always aspiring; in its widest searches still longing to go forward, in its highest flights still wishing to be higher; always imagining something greater than it knows, always endeavouring more than it can do. (III, 217)

In these 'very strong desires of intellectual eminence' and in chafing at the bounds of human achievement, he resembles Milton more than Dryden (III, 94, 220); he is like them both in his self-confidence – and unlike those who delude themselves in their solitude, he has 'the felicity . . . to rate himself at his real value' (III, 89). Johnson describes his fulfilment of his strong desires in terms almost as wholly physical as those applied to his littleness. Eminence is a high place which Pope and Addison contest in a passage dominated by the metaphor of physical struggle: 'now at the head . . . a state of elevation . . . could no longer bear . . . a superior. . . . approached . . . having attained that eminence to which he was himself aspiring. . . . his submission lessened . . . advances . . . contend with him for the highest place. . . . too high . . . mean endeavours to obstruct the progress of rising merit. The contest rose so high. . . . his adversary sunk before him without a blow' (III, 128–9, 131, 132). Ironically, Johnson reserves his description of Pope as 'at the summit of poetical reputation' for a time when as a human being he is doubly bereaved (III, 154).

In this life again the contradictory great and little exist not simply side by side but in various intimate linkings. On the one hand, Pope's desire for greatness betrays him in various ways into pettiness. The phrase 'voracity of fame' sets up a disturbing connection with his undignified gluttony (III,

136). His vanity and resentment are by implication associated with those of his enemies the dunces as 'common' (III, 150). His disciple Warburton, with his fervid mind, 'haughty confidence', 'contemptuous superiority', and taste for being feared even if also hated, is presented almost as a demeaning parody of his master, right in the middle of the account of Pope's period of most active hostilities (III, 165–6). Later, however, Pope's subservience to Martha Blount, enforced by anguished circumstances, and his remark that his delirium gives 'sufficient humiliation of the vanity of man' – the very things that show us 'the contraction of human scope' – serve also, paradoxically, to confer on him the stubborn dignity of pettiness accepted, a dignity which his campaigns to establish superiority lacked.[25] Johnson presents Pope's frugality on the one hand (by aggregation of effects to make it great) as self-reliance, a wise and even magnanimous rejection of temptation, and on the other (by detail of minute circumstances to make it little) as 'petty artifices of parsimony . . . by which perhaps in five years five shillings were saved' (III, 202–3; *Adv.* 128: Y, II, 479). (Even the taskmaster mother of *Idler* 13 was saving five *pounds* in *one* year by her children's enforced labour; Pope is almost more like the man who stole string: see above, pp.96, 79–80.) Such behaviour is a moral puzzle: honest recognition of scanty resources is a sign of stature; wilful co-operation with the narrowing effects of poverty is a sign of pettiness; and the first tips over easily into the second. There is a discreditable link between Pope's high estimate of himself and his friends, and his scorning of mankind in general as 'emmets . . . below his serious attention'. For this the cure would have been for Pope, like Johnson, to recognize his kinship with 'common life' and 'the natural emotions of common men' (III, 212–13, 210).

On the other hand, Pope's literary greatness has nourishing roots in pettiness. When in *An Essay on Man* he 'exalt[s] himself into the chair of wisdom' he can tell us nothing about our restricted place in the scale that we did not know already; but he is at his best when his Homer adds lightness and elegance to dignity, or when *The Rape of the Lock* excels through familiar treatment of 'an event below the common incidents of common life' (III, 243, 239, 234). When he miscarried as editor of Shakespeare, Pope 'hoped to persuade the world' that he had 'a mind too great for such minute employment' (III, 138–9); yet of such minute employments were his greatest achievements formed. He scorns no diligence, no humble source of information, he is careful in detail, and works in 'little fragments', in 'minute and punctilious' retouchings of his greatest works (III, 217, 218, 221). Dryden's mind has 'a larger range', more 'comprehensive speculation', Pope's more 'minute attention'. 'If the flights of Dryden therefore are higher, Pope continues longer on the wing.' When we read this sentence we can hardly have forgotten how recently we have been told that Pope was 'perpetually on the wing', and always in his 'highest flights still wishing to be higher'; the aspiration in which he was Dryden's superior is implicitly present in Johnson's critical parallel. Even though Johnson awards the literary palm, with some suspicion of 'partial fondness', to Dryden (III, 222, 223, 216, 217), the reader of both lives will almost certainly feel that Pope, embattled against his own physical weakness, frequently deluded by his petty failings, striving always to attain the highest place and to surpass those limitations which he could not ignore, is the greater man. Johnson's *Lives of the Poets* conclude with the tumid pseudo-greatness of Gray's verse, and the conventional socially-measured greatness of Lyttelton; but it is the 'little Fellow [who] has done Wonders' who towers over this last volume.

CONCLUSION

TO LOOK INTO any part of Johnson's writings is to see at once how central and consistent was his concern with measuring and comparing. He regularly employs more than one scale of measurement, but he enters into each with full and eager participation. The idea of desired individual superiority, of 'burning to be great',[1] of excelling one's fellows in any field of endeavour, excites and compels him. At the same time it is always natural to him to shift the scale, to see not only vainglorious boasters of their own or their own tribe's prowess, but also serious contenders for renown, in the light of Gulliver presiding in his little chair 'before one of the Salt-sellers'.[2] The idea of humanity's inescapable littleness, the helplessness of death, the looming grandeur of the divine, is an idea just as potent as the other. The jostling of these two ideas is responsible for a sometimes choppy, up-and-down movement in *The Lives of the Poets*. A particular writer is great – but then he is petty – is great – but then he is petty. Neither scale can be dispensed with or escaped from.

Johnson's search for just judgments presses him constantly towards the survey, the detached contemplation of people in the mass, at a distance, individually little; yet his fear of the consequences of superior detachment, his reliance on the ordinarily quotidian and domestic, presses him as constantly to recoil from any position of onlooker or overseer. Such positions are also those which aim, like Observation in *The Vanity of Human Wishes*, Imlac in *Rasselas* X, and Johnson in his preface to his *Dictionary*, at an impossible comprehensiveness. Further movement in his works is produced by his alternation of standing back from the picture he presents, and of dragging his reader and himself forward into the frame.

His works recognize and embody various logical connections between greatness and pettiness. Striving for greatness is itself a cause of meanness, of competition, envy, malice and the attempted devaluation of others; to refuse to strive is, however, pettier still; to strive and accept the inevitability of defeat confers a paradoxical superiority. In purely practical, non-moral terms the following movement dominates human competition: effort begets success, success begets confidence, confidence begets relaxation of effort, relaxation of effort begets failure (*Ram*. 21: Y, III, 120); logically, therefore, we may expect better performance from those of less repute, producing an endless sequence of mounting, shining and being dragged down. In moral terms the effects of superiority are more severe, for achieved superiority does not destroy the desire to diminish others or to measure oneself falsely; it does not cancel our shared, inescapable littleness. Stillingfleet's distinction between excellence and superiority (see above p. 103) was not likely to recommend itself to one so sensitive as Johnson to the derivations of words, for excellence, like superiority, demands someone to be excelled, and there is something inescapably mean in the struggle to render others inferior.

Literary pride (and other kinds of pride work analogously) 'is chiefly to be found amongst those, who have secluded themselves from the world, in pursuit of petty enquiries, and trivial studies' (Sermon 8: Y, XIV, 95) – who have, that is, receded from a true perspective in order to aggrandize their own small concerns. To achieve eminence in any intellectual field requires specialization, and specialization encourages attention to minute details of 'remote and unnecessary subject', to the detriment of that general moral enquiry into 'the various modes of virtue and relations of life' recommended by Socrates (*Ram.* 24: Y, III, 131–2). Lady Bustle's intense pedantic concern with reserving, conserving, preserving, and the proper distinctions between them (with lack of concern for her fellow-mortals), resembles the concerns of the scholar Gelidus (*Ram.* 51, 24) or of others ambitious in areas conventionally considered of broader scope than housewifery: for each the field of contemplation is limited to that of her or his own achievement. The happiness of superiority over all others, which must ultimately be confined to one person, is the narrowest goal of all. Johnson repeatedly depicts people who can place personal happiness in such elevation as ignorant of the higher or broader human purposes and pleasures. The generous desire for excellence leads directly to many varieties of moral pettiness; to rise in moral terms is almost necessarily to fall.

Conversely, as Johnson argued in two separate dedications to the king written for the works of others (the second the last writing, probably, that he prepared for the press before he died), 'It is the privilege of real greatness not to be afraid of diminution by condescending to the notice of little things'; 'Greatness of mind is never more willingly acknowledged, nor more sincerely reverenced, than when it descends into the regions of general life'.[3] These two aphorisms will bear a far fuller freight of general meaning than is allowed them in their original contexts; they point to an ideal of greatness realizing itself through a conscious, voluntary recognition of littleness. Christian forgiveness, similarly, is not condescension but 'greatness of . . . mind'. 'Nothing can be great which is not right' (*Ram.* 185: Y, V, 210, 209) – and the right, for humanity, includes as a high-priority item the recognition, reluctant as it may be, that distinction is not 'the doom of man',[4] that *great* and *human* are more or less mutually exclusive terms. To consider, therefore, the desirability of greatness as a goal entails a continuing, inescapable movement of the mind, back and forth, towards away from.

Johnson's separation from the heroic ideal must not be overstated. Total rejection of the heroic tradition works not only through mock-heroic (that familiar and reassuring genre which tells us that the scale of measuring traditional greatness is still entirely appropriate for our purposes, since its inaccurate application is so risible), but also through non-heroic: that is, a demotion of the grand by the ordinary, a rejection of criteria originally associated with size, strength or courage, an attitude opposed to all our cultural traditions of honouring patriarchy or leadership. Such a rejection Johnson does not make. He can never renounce the ideal of excelling, the imagery of height, size and brightness, even in the most domestic context – even if his idea of voluntary equality, with its concomitant of voluntary descent, may sometimes verge of paradox, on stooping to conquer, or on the ludicrous notion of competing in non-competitiveness.[5] The most one may suggest is that over the years his thought moved more and more towards the acceptance and celebration of *common* humanity: from heroic biographies on the one hand and Lilliputianizing debates on the other to the the honoured yet clay-footed figures of the *Lives*; from the *Rambler's* concern with ambition and intellect, through the *Idler's* frequent impatience with human pettiness, towards the acceptance of that pettiness in the *Journey*; from tragic drama towards little books, little lives and letters upon nothing.

Johnson's thought revolves round two poles: the ideal of excellence, and the ideal of community. 'The known shortness of life, as it ought to moderate our passions, may likewise, with equal propriety, contract our designs' (*Ram*. 17: Y, III, 96) – but it is the contraction of *great* designs which moves us. Although he dutifully recommends the golden mean (in *Rambler* 38, for instance), Johnson is far less interested in and respectful of mediocrity than of failure, which (especially the failure or disappointments of the writer) was one of his favourite topics.[6] Therefore his two great prefaces, to the *Dictionary* and to his edition of Shakespeare, display the same alternating pattern as the *Lives*, balancing great aspirations with menial position (drudge to a great language or to a great writer), vaunted achievement with a sense of the ultimate littleness of achievement.[7]

All greatness, all eminence, is subject to diminishment by a larger scale. This is why Johnson sees honesty or goodness as a first step to greatness (*Works*, VI, 311). 'The utmost excellence at which humanity can arrive, is a constant and determinate pursuit of virtue, without regard to present dangers or advantage' (*Ram*. 185: Y, V, 209). Such a pursuit can be seen in satisfactorily heroic terms; but more importantly, such excellence is the only human quality not susceptible to the indignity of diminution, the only one whose force continues to register on the higher scale. Among the paradoxes of Christianity, it was the greatness of humility and the humility of greatness that took the strongest hold on Johnson's imagination.[8]

Yet even humble goodness may benefit from association with more splendid qualities. The domestic virtue of an Elizabeth Corbett, 'which the dull overlook and the gay despise', needs the genius of a Pope to make its value known and its 'dignity established' (*Lives*, III, 262). The sterling qualities of a Robert Levet will never be remarked by myopic human vision without a realignment such as Johnson supplies in his last considerable poem. 'On the Death of Dr. Robert Levet' (Y, VI, 313–15) is a defiant assertion of the value of unglorified, unmagnified humanity. Howard Erskine-Hill writes that between *The Vanity of Human Wishes* and this poem, between a 'petty fortress, and a dubious hand' and the 'narrow round' and 'single talent',

> 'petty' has changed its position. In the earlier poem . . . it was that which checked and limited the impetuous spirit. . . . [Now] Johnson not only recognizes the littleness of man but, without contraction of his 'extensive view', has come to see it with the eyes of love.[9]

Levet was, on the face of it, no hero. That is, he is not in any respect a 'man of the highest class', though recent criticism has sometimes discerned Christian heroism in his life of service.[10] Since he was a doctor without formal qualification, it seems not unfair to call him a quack. He worked among the very poor, who paid him very little, and he lodged in Johnson's house from mere necessity. When his patients did pay him at all, it was frequently by hospitality that made him drunk in the way of business,[11] an undignified circumstance which Johnson renders as 'No petty gain disdain'd by pride'.

Johnson calls Levet 'Of ev'ry friendless name the friend', a phrase that distinguishes him both from those who build or seek a name for themselves, and from those possessing friends in the sense of powerful backers. The poem recognizes, even stresses, Levet's lack of distinction, genius or greatness. It is his mere humanity whose memory survives the grave:

> Yet still he fills affection's eye,
> Obscurely wise, and coarsely kind;
> Nor, letter'd arrogance, deny
> Thy praise to merit unrefin'd.

In his command to 'letter'd arrogance', Johnson doubtless recalled Gray's 'Let not Ambition mock their useful toil'. Gray, however, by associating Ambition with Grandeur and 'the pomp of pow'r', kept these things as remote from himself as from his humble rustics.[12] Johnson's 'letter'd arrogance', even if not positively self-reproachful,[13] does convey to the reader that the praise which Levet deserves is owed to him precisely from those qualities (learning and the aspiration to greatness) which characterize a poet. Johnson portrays Levet in terms which draw an implicit contrast with extensive flights or great abilities:

> His virtues walk'd their narrow round,
>   Nor made a pause, nor left a void;
> And sure th'Eternal Master found
>   The single talent well employ'd.

Johnson admires Levet's humility, but does not associate himself with it. He had ironically assumed humility in the *Plan* for his *Dictionary* ('beating the tract . . . with sluggish resolution'); Milton had seriously assumed it in the sonnet on his blindness, describing himself as a man of one talent, and Wordsworth was to do something similar within about twenty years in opening *The Prelude*.[14] Johnson, who values the steady self-confidence of genius, will not do this. These stanzas, which compare the two, make the poet the greater but Levet the better.

Yet for Levet as for himself Johnson claims, indirectly, allusively, no matter how incongruously, some elements of greatness in the 'toil of ev'ry day'. 'Obscurely wise, and coarsely kind' associates Levet with Pope's description of the whole human race as 'darkly wise, and rudely great'.[15] Levet therefore becomes a representative of his kind. Johnson also recounts his exploits:

> When fainting Nature call'd for aid,
>   And hov'ring Death prepar'd the blow,
> His vigorous remedy display'd
>   The power of art without the show.
>
> In Misery's darkest caverns known,
>   His ready help was ever nigh.[16]

These lines show him rescuing victims from monsters as surely as ever Theseus or Hercules did. He therefore becomes, despite all appearance to the contrary, a hero. In 'His virtues walk'd their narrow round, / Nor made a pause, nor left a void' the *round* is primarily that of a doctor among his patients; but the word also, especially with the associations of the following line, strongly suggests the rounds of the planets which ceaselessly fulfil the eternal master's command. Levet in his courses – 'from Houndsditch to Marybone': Boswell, I, 243 – reflects the movements of the cosmos, though *narrow* makes the comparison also a contrast. This representative man is a microcosm, reproducing heroic virtues on a miniature scale.

In *The Vanity of Human Wishes*, in *Adventurer* 81, in *Idler* 45, in many of *The Lives of the Poets*, Johnson presents death as the final challenge which explodes a hero's claim to superhuman status. In his poem he revises this situation. Levet has effected rescue out of Misery's darkest caverns and from hovering Death. Yet in his very first stanza Johnson has compared all of us, not only the poor, to imprisoned toilers in 'Hope's delusive mine'. And so in the last stanza Levet becomes not the rescuer but the rescued:

> Then with no throbbing fiery pain,
>   No cold gradations of decay,
> Death broke at once the vital chain,
>   And free'd his soul the nearest way.

The stroke of death, which in stanza four had been a threat, becomes a decisive benefit; Levet, from being an active hero, becomes a passive victim, now delivered.[17] Portrayed as no more than human from the beginning of the poem, he participates briefly, against all apparent likelihood, in heroic effort and heroic achievement – gains some advantages, only temporary, against massively superior adversaries – and subsides again into that mortal helplessness which claims and receives divine aid.

Johnson's appeal to community, unlike that of the sentimentalists, often demands from his reader self-identification not with the helper but with the helped – the smaller, the weaker. Most readers of this poem remember Levet as a puny figure measured both by the ordinary social scale and by the greater-than-human scale at the end. Clearly the poem's power rests on its subject's moving littleness, and it is a fitting work on which to end, since I suspect that while Johnson was strongly attracted from the outset to the subject of greatness 'going off', the power and conviction of his writings about our mutual inescapable littleness increased with time.

Levet is little, but he can hardly be called petty when the poem lays such stress on his dignity: a dignity which lies in accepting the limitations of his lot and yet achieving a kind of greatness through courageous, defiant action against vastly superior antagonists. Precedents for this combination can be drawn from the whole span of Johnson's earlier works: the benevolent old person in *The Vanity of Human Wishes*, Zosima in *Rambler* 12, Mrs Bruce in the *Journey*, among others. In each of these portraits Johnson has reached for grand or heroic associations, no matter how tenuous – for martial or romance imagery or merely for a name – to give a puny individual a foothold on the scale of greatness. In each case he has made their littleness neither an innate deprivation like that of the pettier poets nor a narrowing accomplished during life like that of Nugaculus, but a reflection of the littleness of humanity as such. It is something they have in common with his portraits of greatness, for even Wolsey, Shakespeare, Pope are judged by scales which make them little as well as great. (Indeed, while Pope as poet resembles Milton, Pope as man is more like Mrs Bruce.) In no kind of writing did Johnson make a practice of setting a demarcation line between great individuals and the rest: this would be impossible when for him greatness is evanescent, inhering in particular actions, and is relative, adjudged by comparison with a potentially almost inexhaustible range of objects.

Levet is measured by many scales. He is little in comparison with his fellows (those toilers in the salt mines who are signified by affection and arrogance, whether Johnson means by these abstractions a whole community or merely himself), heroic in comparison with his pathetic clients, pathetically tiny himself in comparison with the powers which kill the body and save the soul.

Nobody else could have written the Levet poem. Many writers perhaps might have celebrated or mourned him as a colourful character, but the poem's early chosen and steadily maintained focus on the question of his stature, its emphasis on and vindication of his littleness as that of unaccommodated humanity, its ingenuity in finding means to make him participate in heroic grandeur and then to relinquish it so totally, in a word its attention to and multiplicity of scales, make it a perfect summary of these arguments about Johnson's dealings with the scale of greatness. In this poem an effort at greatness is relinquished, a scale which diminishes is accepted: all through an imagery which is purely heroic.

NOTES

Short forms have been used for all book titles: for full reference see the List of Works Cited and the List of Abbreviations on p. vii. Commonly recognized abbreviations such as *J.* for *Journal*, *Rev.* for *Review* have been used; other abbreviations are listed below.

Biog. Brit.	Biographia Brittanica, or the Lives of the Most Eminent Persons who have Flourished in Great Britain or Ireland (1747–66)	JHI	Journal of the History of Ideas
		MLN	Modern Language Notes
		MLQ	Modern Language Quarterly
		MLR	Modern Language Review
BIHR	Bulletin of the Institute of Historical Research	MP	Modern Philology
		NLH	New Literary History
BJRL	Bulletin of the John Rylands Library	N & Q	Notes and Queries
		PMLA	Publications of the Modern Language Association of America
BNYPL	Bulletin of the New York Public Library		
		PQ	Philological Quarterly
ECS	Eighteenth-Century Studies	RES	Review of English Studies
EIC	Essays in Criticism	SBHT	Studies in Burke and his Time
ELH	English Literary History	SEL	Studies in English Literature
GM	The Gentleman's Magazine	SP	Studies in Philology
JEGP	Journal of English and Germanic Philology	UTQ	University of Toronto Quarterly
		YES	Yearbook of English Studies.

INTRODUCTION

1. Milton, *Paradise Lost*, I, 14; Shakespeare, *Othello*, III, iii, 360.
2. Thomas Nash, 'Adieu, Farewell Earths Blisse'; James Shirley, *The Contention of Ajax and Ulysses* (1658), I, iii; Boswell, II, 129; *Iliad*, VI, 208 (Loeb transl. by A.T. Murray, 1924–5).
3. Matthew, iv, 8; Luke, iv, 5; Dryden, *The Hind and the Panther* (1687), III, 290; Luke, ix, 48.
4. Lyttelton, *Advice to a Lady* (written 1731, published 1733), 6; Gray, *The Progress of Poesy* (finished 1754, published 1757); Fielding, *The History of Jonathan Wild the Great* (1733), I, i.
5. *Ram.* 5 (Y, III, 25). Johnson deleted *a superior* in his second revision.

6. The same quality is incisively treated by Germaine Greer as 'dimension' (*The Obstacle Race*, 104ff.).

7. Bate, *The Achievement of Samuel Johnson*, vii, x.

8. Robert Voitle, *Samuel Johnson the Moralist*, 144; T. F. Wharton, *Samuel Johnson and the Theme of Hope*, 57; Paul Fussell, *Samuel Johnson and the Life of Writing*, 247 (of the *Lives*); Howard D. Weinbrot, 'Samuel Johnson's *Plan* and Preface to the *Dictionary*', in *New Aspects of Lexicography*, ed. Weinbrot, 94; Donald A. Stauffer, *Biography in Eighteenth Century England*, 393; Eric Rothstein, *Systems of Order*, 50. See also Donald Wesling, 'An ideal of greatness', *UTQ, 34* (1964–5), 133–45.

9. *Trans. Johnson Soc. of Lichfield* (1976), 40.

10. Frequent use will be made of the *Dictionary*, in agreement with W.B.C. Watkins that it 'embodies a personality. . . . Not the Preface alone, but the choice of illustrative quotations, the very definitions of words reflect his character and personal tastes' (*Johnson and English Poetry before 1660*, 1), and with W.K. Wimsatt that it still remains 'an open challenge' to 'students of Johnson's mind' (*Philosophic Words*, xi).

11. Johnson's MS note in a copy of the fourth edition; the change appeared in print in the sixth abridged edition (1778) and the sixth complete edition (1785). See G. J. Kolb and J. H. Sledd, 'The Rylands copy of Johnson's Dictionary', *BJRL, 37* (1954–5), 462.

12. Fussell, *Rhetorical World*, 6.

13. See Marjorie Hope Nicolson, *Science and Imagination*.

14. Y, VI, 21–7. Macaulay suspected influence of Addison's poem on the first book of *Gulliver's Travels*: quoted by Dorothy Moody, 'Johnson's translation of "Addison's "Battle",' *MLR, 31* (1936), 62–6.

15. Pope, *Dunciad* (1743), II, 40, III, 31ff., IV, 73ff.; *Epistle to Burlington*, lines 202, 106–8. See Martin Price, 'The problem of scale: the game of art', in *To the Palace of Wisdom*, 144–55.

16. Stevick, *UTQ, 38* (1968–9), 168.

17. Cf. Margaret J. Osler, 'Certainty, scepticism, and scientific optimism', in *Probability, Time, and Space*, ed. Paula R. Backscheider, 3–28.

18. Keast, 'Johnson and intellectual history', in *New Light on Dr. Johnson*, ed. F.W. Hilles, 254. Fussell writes that the exercise of this discriminatory faculty is required of the humanist by 'man's obligations to the life of value' (*Rhetorical World*, 119).

19. Hawkins, *Life of Samuel Johnson*, ed. Bertram H. Davis, 196, 202, 174–7.

20. *Letters*, nos 130, 298, 515, 561, 605, 613, end of no. 329; Y, IX, 164. Johnson knew of four translations of *Rasselas* in 1773; a Russian one of 1764 had escaped him: see Gwin J. Kolb, 'The early reception of *Rasselas*', in *Greene Centennial Essays*, ed. Paul. J. Korshin and Robert R. Allen, 226–9.

21. In 'The Author's Advertisement to the Third Edition' Johnson pointed out how the *Lives* had grown in the course of completion from 'an undertaking, as it was then presented to my mind, not very extensive or difficult', into something much more ambitious (I, xxv–xxvi and n.).

22. 'Letter to his Cousin Sympson': Swift, *Prose Works*, ed. H. Davis, XI (1941, rev. edn. 1959), xxxiv–xxxv. For Johnson's descriptions of humanity as 'little', see Fussell, *Rhetorical World*, 131–2.

23. Boswell, I, 433, 471, V, 249; Piozzi, *Anecdotes of Samuel Johnson*, ed. A. Sherbo, 126–7.

24. Hobbes, *Leviathan*, I, viii.

25. *Biog. Brit.*, III (1750), 2707; Sermons 14, 25 (1752), 17 (1745): Y, XIV, 154, 269, 294.

26. McIntosh, *The Choice of Life*, 42.

27. *Vanity of Human Wishes*, line 76.

28. Cf. Wimsatt, *Philosophic Words*, 110.

29. *Vanity of Human Wishes*, line 9.

1. COMPARISON

1. *Works*, V, 34. Benjamin Martin uses contraries sparingly and Nathan Bailey hardly at all to define the words discussed here; Johnson added explanations by negatives to many of their basic definitions of simple words: see Martin, *Lingua Britannica Reformata* (1749); Bailey, *Universal Etymological English Dictionary* (1721), its various revisions and its descendant *Dictionarium Britannicum* (1730). Cf. also De Witt T. Starnes and Gertrude E. Noyes, *The English Dictionary from Cawdrey to Johnson*, 158–9.
2. Johnson in 1773 added a couple of negative comparisons. Interestingly, he then used 'opposed to' instead of 'not', here and under *light* (noun), which he radically revised.
3. Locke, *Essay Concerning Human Understanding*, II, viii, 9.
4. Johnson four times quotes Bacon on darkness and silence as privatives (under *privative*, adj. and noun, *contristate*, and *harmonical*).
5. Wimsatt traces the same relationship between Johnson's senses of more recondite words. He considers there are, over the history of language, 'cycles or returns of meaning from physical to psychological and back' (*Philosphic Words*, 46, 14).
6. *Essay Concerning Human Understanding*, II, xxvi, 4.
7. The words come refracted through the double lens of Algarotti's Italian popularization and the re-englishing of that by Johnson's friend Elizabeth Carter. They are flanked on one side by an exposition of how microscopes and telescopes work, and on the other by reference to *Gulliver's Travels* (Algarotti, *Sir Isaac Newton's Philosophy Explain'd* (1739), I, 181).
8. Dryden and Chesterfield each related this idea to the drama, which being less near than life must therefore be larger: see *Essay of Dramatic Poesy*; letter of 23 Jan. 1752, quoted in R.D. Stock, *Samuel Johnson and Neoclassical Dramatic Theory*, 31, 32.
9. Hawkins, *Life of Johnson*, 240.
10. E.g. *Journey* (Y, IX, 146). The same work shows his awareness of the instability of money as quantitative measurement (p. 156 and *passim*).
11. Cf. Longinus: 'In Art the most accurate work is admired, in the works of Nature greatness' (*On the Sublime*, XXXVI, transl. A.O. Prickard).
12. *Lives*, III, 222–3; Daiches, *Critical Approaches to Literature*, 251, 253.
13. Hume, 'Of the Standard of Taste ' (1757), in *Essays and Treatises on Several Subjects* (1768), I, 260–9.
14. The letter of condolence containing this phrase compares death in battle with death from disease and from old age (no. 116).
15. *Lives*, II, 129–30, III, 229, I, 45. Cf. Fussell, *Rhetorical World*, 120.
16. *Idler* 6 (Y, II, 19). Emphasis added.

2. SCALE

1. Y, IX, 121; Madame D'Arblay, *Diary and Letters*, ed. Charlotte Frances Barrett, I, 119–20.
2. Introduction to *The World Displayed* (1759) (*Works*, V, 217).
3. Ruskin, *Works*, ed. E.T. Cook and A. Wedderburn, XXXV (1908), 226. Emphasis added.
4. Virgil, first Eclogue, line 23.
5. Gray, 'Ode on the Spring', lines 19–20; *Lives*, III, 434.
6. Quoted by Hill Boothby in Johnson, *Letters*, ed. G.B. Hill (1892), I, 53 n.1.
7. Condensed from *Paradise Lost*, VIII, 589–92. Raphael is talking to Adam about the non-sensual elements in marital love; his *scale* is glossed by John Carey and Alastair Fowler as 'the Neoplatonic ladder of love' (Milton, *Poems*, 846n.).
8. Macbean was dropped in 1773.

9. This time an exact quotation of *Paradise Lost*, V, 509–12, from Adam's speech to Raphael early in their interview. Milton's modern editors find a Platonic and even a hinted alchemical meaning in the word (*Poems*, 707n.).

10. *Works*, VI, 53. Cf. Arthur O. Lovejoy, *The Great Chain of Being*, 253–4; Robert Eberwein, 'Samuel Johnson, George Cheyne, and the "Cone of Being"', *JHI*, *36* (1975), 153ff.

11. *A Free Inquiry into the Nature and Origin of Evil* (1757), quoted in Johnson, *Works*, VI, 50–1.

12. See Alexandre Koyré, *From the Closed World to the Infinite Universe*.

13. Pascal, *Pensées* in *Oeuvres Complètes*, ed. J. Chevalier, 1105. For Johnson's admiration of Pascal, and for similarities in their thinking, see Chester F. Chapin, 'Johnson and Pascal', in *English Writers of the Eighteenth Century*, ed. John H. Middendorf, 3–16.

14. Locke, *Essay*, II, ii, 3. Johnson quotes one or other part of this sentence under *drawer* and *top* as well as under *immensity*.

15. Shaftesbury, *The Moralists* (1709) in *Characteristics*, II, 114.

16. Nicolson, *Science and Imagination*, 98–9.

17. Pascal, *Pensées*, 1105.

18. Shaftesbury, *Characteristics*, II, 111.

19. Pascal, *Pensées*, 1105–6.

20. Locke, II, i, 24; quoted by Johnson under both *footing* and *tower*. Addison in *Spectator* 420 claimed that even our severely limited fancy may 'enlarge itself' by contemplating the cosmos.

21. Locke, II, vii, 10; quoted by Johnson under both *excursion* and *expansion*.

22. Pope, *Temple of Fame*, lines 11–13; *Essay on Man*, II, 19–30: the latter quoted by Johnson under *empyreal*.

23. Cicero, *De Republica*, VI, 19–20: Y, IV, 265ff. A quotation from 'Somnium Scipionis' or 'Cicero's Dream' appeared at the head of the very last *Spectator* (no.635, 20 Dec. 1714), an essay by Grove anticipating more comprehensive views in a future life.

24. Perhaps a reminiscence of the Biblical parable of the invited guests who made excuses, Luke, xiv, 15–24.

25. *Vanity of Human Wishes*, line 137.

26. W.J. Bate, 'Johnson and satire manqué', in *Eighteenth-Century Studies*, ed. W.H. Bond, 147–8. Frederic V. Bogel writes that 'Johnson's corrosive and reductive vision was countered by a powerful sense of the self-defeating absurdity of reductiveness' ('Structure and substantiality', *Studies in Burke and His Time*, *15* (1973–4), 151). Paradoxical praise-and-dispraise of reductionism becomes unnecessary if its successful use is seen as a matter of accuracy, of degree or scale.

27. *Vanity of Human Wishes*, lines 71–2. Patrick O'Flaherty would have it that Johnson endorses, not questions, the scorn of Democritus: see his 'Johnson as satirist', *ELH*, *34* (1967), esp. 84; also 'The Rambler's rebuff to Juvenal', *English Studies*, *51* (1970), 518, 522. Cf. Wharton, *Samuel Johnson and the Theme of Hope*, 52–3. I agree with Howard D. Weinbrot ('"No mock debate"', *MLQ*, *41* (1980), 252–4, 259) that the reader is invited to assess Democritus with great caution. See below, pp. 159–60.

28. *Letters*, end of no. 318.

29. Noted by W.K. Wimsatt, *Philosophic Words*, 61–2. Johnson was not alone. 'In the allegorical paintings sight is represented by optical instruments': Robert H. Hopkins, who quotes Rosalie Colie's term *scalar disruption* for the effect of the new instruments on seventeenth-century perceptions, 'Swift and the senses', in *Greene Centennial Studies*, ed. Korshin and Allen, 63, 68 n.

30. A.D. Atkinson, 'Dr. Johnson and Newton's *Opticks*', *RES*, n.s. *2* (1951), 229.

31. Pope, *Dunciad* (1728), I, 77–8; Thomson, *Autumn* (1730, 1746), lines 724–7.

32. Hester Piozzi announced her discipleship by opening her *Anecdotes* with the image of magnification and obscurity (p.61).

33. Johnson was not, however, the first biographer of Cowley to disclose the grocer: see Pat Rogers, 'Johnson's *Lives of the Poets* and the biographical dictionaries', *RES*, *31* (1980), 163.

34. Erich Auerbach calls it 'the searchlight device', which falsifies truth by 'overilluminating one small part' at the expense of the whole and its organization (*Mimesis*, transl. W.R. Trask, 404).

35. Johnson responded to Pope's unfairness to Bentley by giving one of these couplets in the *Dictionary* as his second illustration of *microscope*, and taking his first illustration from Bentley himself, arguing that a microscopic eye 'would be a curse, and not a blessing, to us', showing polished crystal as rough and 'the smoothest skin . . . beset all over with ragged scales and bristly hairs'.

36. *Monthly Rev.*, 66, 126, quoted in *Johnson, The Critical Heritage*, ed. J.T. Boulton, 269; e.g. Leopold Damrosch, Jr, *The Uses of Johnson's Criticism*, 145ff.

37. Blake, *The Four Zoas*, V, 121–6, in *Complete Writings*, ed. G. Keynes, 308.

38. Damrosch, *Uses of Johnson's Criticism*, 222.

3. SWIFT AND THE DEBATES IN THE SENATE OF MAGNA LILLIPUTIA

1. Grundy, 'Swift and Johnson', forthcoming, argues that the Swiftian material considered in this chapter is part of a broader pattern of significant references to Swift by Johnson. See also Hopkins, 'Swift and the senses', 68.

2. First published in 1728 as *Intelligencer* no.9: *Prose Works*, XII, 50. Johnson quoted from the same passage in the *Dictionary* under *afford*.

3. *Prose Works*, IV, 253.

4. *Ibid.*, II, xxxv 253.

5. *Gulliver's Travels*, II, i (*Prose Works*, XI, rev. 1959, 71).

6. Grundy, 'Swift and Johnson', 00–0.

7. Gwin J. and Ruth A. Kolb, 'The illustrative quotations in Dr. Johnson's *Dictionary*', in *New Aspects of Lexicography*, ed. Weinbrot, 66. But cf. A.D. Atkinson, 'Dr. Johnson and Newton's *Opticks*', *RES*, n.s 2 (1959), 234n.

8. The only exceptions I have found are *nursery* (4. 'Place where young children are nursed and brought up') and *junto*.

9. *Gulliver's Travels*, III, x, ii (*Prose Works*, XI (1959), 191ff., 148–9); *Adv.* 39; *Idler* 3.

10. Oakleaf, '*Trompe l'oeil*', *UTQ*, 53 (1983–4), 166–80.

11. *Prose Works*, XIII (quoted 123 times in the *Dictionary*: Fussell, *Life of Writing*, 213); *Lives*, III, 56.

12. Quotations, e.g. *adapt*, *chicken*, *innuendo*, *lace* and *spectacles*; Piozzi, *Anecdotes*, ed. A. Sherbo, 115.

13. Adapted from *Prose Works*, II, 58.

14. *Prose Works*, XII, 38–45; quoted at least 21 times in vol. I: see Lewis Freed, *The Sources of Johnson's Dictionary*, 80.

15. Swift, *Poems*, ed. Harold Williams, II, 551–72; see p. 142 above and n. 23.

16. Swift, 'On Censure', lines 11–12 (*Poems*, II, 414).

17. *Prose Works*, IX, 141–9.

18. *Rass.* XLIX; *Gulliver's Travels*, III, x (*Prose Works*, XI, 209–10).

19. Swift, *Intelligencer* no. 19 (*Prose Works*, XII, 55).

20. *Prose Works*, I, 221, 229.

21. Noted by Pat Rogers, who takes it as an index of Gulliver's 'intrusive intellect' and 'over-intent scrutiny of what is better left unexamined' ('Gulliver's glasses', in *The Art of Jonathan Swift*, ed. C.T. Probyn, 183–7).

22. *Prose Works*, X, 89–90, 108; *Gulliver*, III.

23. *Prose Works*, XII, 10–11; Freed, *Sources*, 79.

24. Swift, *Correspondence*, ed. H. Williams, II, 312; *Rambler* 117 (see below, p. 167).

25. *Prose Works*, VI, 55–6; *Vanity of Human Wishes*, lines 187–8.

26. *Prose Works*, III, 21–3.

27. 'A Digression on the nature, usefulness and necessity of Wars and Quarels' (*Prose Works*, I, 289).

28. E.g. Donald Greene's editorial introduction to the Oxford Authors series', *Samuel Johnson* (1984), xv–xvi.

29. That is, between *GM*, XI, 339, and the end of *GM*, XIV: see Boswell, I, 150; dates revised by Benjamin Beard Hoover, *Samuel Johnson's Parliamentary Reporting*, 23–7; Donald Greene, 'Some notes on Johnson and the *Gentleman's Magazine*', *PMLA*, *79* (1959), 77–8; and F.V. Bernard, 'Johnson and the authorship of four debates', *PMLA*, *82* (1967), 408–19.

30. Boswell, I, 502ff (Appendix); J.L. Clifford, *Young Samuel Johnson*, 189; Hoover, *Parliamentary Reporting*, 18–19.

31. Bloom, *Samuel Johnson in Grub Street*, 55.

32. *Gulliver*, IV, xii (*Prose Works*, XI, 296; Y, X, 31, 62, 69, 73). Cf. above, pp. 209–10.

33. Boswell, I, 115; Bloom, *Grub Street*, 8.

34. Hoover, *Parlimentary Reporting*, 15–16.

35. *GM*, VIII, 283–[287] (the square bracket, present in the original, reflects the fact that some page numbers are repeated a few pages later); as 'The State . . . ' in *Samuel Johnson*, ed. Donald Greene (1984), 44ff., and in Johnson, *Shorter Prose*, ed. Greene and O M Brack, Jr, forthcoming; as 'Appendix . . .' in Hoover, *Parliamentary Reporting*, 142–81; Cf. Greene, *The Politics of Samuel Johnson*, 92ff.

36. *GM*, VIII, 284, [286–7]; Hoover, *Parliamentary Reporting*, 173, 179; *Gulliver*, I, iii (*Prose Works*, XI, 38, 42).

37. A later imitator, perhaps influenced by the *GM*, did nicely with *Nodnol* for London and *Namredal* for Alderman: Francis Gentleman, *A Trip to the Moon* (1764), in *Gulliveriana*, ed. J.K. Welcher and G.E. Bush (1970–4), I, xiii. Greene and Brack print as Johnson's 'Proposals for Printing *Anagrammata Rediviva*' (*GM*, VIII (1738), 700), a further milking of the names joke.

38. *London Mag.*, VIII, (1738), 240ff.

39. *GM*, 547–8. Norman Knox mentions this essay as an example of blame by direct praise (*The Word* Irony, 110–11).

40. P.ix.

41. *Gulliver*, I, iii, ii (*Prose Works*, XI, 43, 30).

42. *Prose Works*, XI, xxii–xxiv, 38–9, 69–72.

43. *Gulliver*, I, iv (*Prose Works*, XI, 48). Irvin Ehrenpreis maintains that behind the apparently equal absurdity of both sides, Swift's preference for the High Heels is discernible (*Literary Meaning and Augustan Values*, 98–9).

44. Carl Lennart Carlson, *The First Magazine*, 58.

45. Bloom, 'Johnson on a free press: a study in liberty and subordination', *ELH*, *16*, (1949), 264; Boswell, I, 502.

46. Greene, 'Some notes on Johnson and the *Gentleman's*', 76–7; *Shorter Prose*, ed. Greene and Brack, Appendix; Clifford, *Young Samuel Johnson*, 212, 224.

47. Hoover, *Parliamentary Reporting*, 36, 43–6, 48, 19, 140.

48. *Parlimentary Reporting*, 19.

49. Wimsatt, *Philosophic Words*, 50; Carlson, *The First Magazine*, 96.

50. Y, IV, 301–2. Ehrenpreis points out that Swift delighted in violating the decorum which required 'high personages' to use 'elevated language and imagery', and that in Lilliput the style is 'sober and humorless, although the events are absurd' (*Literary Meaning*, 103, 100) – which, as we shall see, also describes some political events of the 1740s.

51. According to Sheridan's story quoted in Swift, *Prose Works*, I, xxxiii–xxxiv, and to Pope and Gay writing to Caryll: Gay, *Letters*, ed. C.F. Burgess (1966), 19.

52. E.g. *Rass.* X–XI, XLIX; *Ram.* 118. This is W.J. Bate's 'reductionism' (see above p. 26).

53. F.V. Bernard says this reported debate is Guthrie's, not Johnson's; he does not say the same of the editorial comment: 'Johnson and the authorship of four debates', 409–10.

54. *London Mag.*, VII (1738), 434.

55. Hoover, *Parliamentary Reporting*, 139.

56. *London Mag.*, II (1742), 318ff. Secker, whose MS of Lords Debates is printed in *Cobbett's Parliamentary History of England*, IX–XII (1811–12), and who in Johnson's debates is Boship of Odfrox, was later Archbishop of Canterbury. Most of my information on Commons members comes from *The History of Parliament: The House of Commons 1715–1754*, ed. Romney Sedgwick (1970), and on the Lords from G. E. C[okayne], *Complete Peerage*, ed. Gibbs and White (1910–59).

57. Longinus, *On the Sublime*, VII (transl. Prickard).

58. *GM*, XI (Aug. 1741), 418, probably the first wholly reported by Johnson; quoted by Hoover, *Parliamentary Reporting*, 76.

59. *Parliamentary History*, XI, 1063–4.

60. Robert Giddings discusses Johnson's presentation of the anti-Walpole campaign ('The fall of Orgilio', in *Samuel Johnson: New Critical Essays*, ed. Grundy, 86–106).

61. Cf. the comments which Johnson many years later recorded in a letter about reform in representation, a measure 'equitable in itself, but . . . now proposed only to distress the government' (*Letters*, no. 827).

62. *GM*, XII (1742), 344 ff.; *Journals of the House of Commons* quoted in *Parliamentary History*, XII, 215ff.

63. *Rass.* X; *GM*, XI, 676; preface to Shakespeare (Y, VII, 95).

64. It may be relevant that a complaint by Onslow had in 1738 been instrumental in having parliamentary reporting prohibited (see Hoover, *Parliamentary Reporting*, 124–5, 13). In a translated epitaph, Johnson recorded praise of Sir Thomas Hanmer, Speaker 1714–15, for commanding love and veneration (Y, VI, 81), but the poem's tone is nothing like that of the *GM* report.

65. Cf. Hoover, *Parliamentary Reporting*, 137.

66. *Vanity of Human Wishes*, lines 100, 180, 206.

67. Debate on an address to answer the speech from the throne: *GM*, XII (1742), 347; *London Mag.*, XI (1742), 474; *Vanity of Human Wishes*, line 206.

68. *Parliamentary History*, XII, 223.

69. *The London Magazine*'s L. Piso and Secker's Halifax make accusations of triviality or frivolity which, however, lack the context that Johnson gives them: see *London Mag.*, XI (1742), 472; *Parliamentary History*, XII, 226.

70. Hoover, *Parliamentary Reporting*, 86.

71. *Parliamentary History*, XI, 897, 900.

72. *London Mag.*, XI (1742), 114; Hoover, *Parliamentary Reporting*, 78ff., 94ff.; William Coxe, *Memoirs of Sir Robert Walpole*, new edn (1800), III, 157ff.; notes by Dudley Ryder in *The House of Commons*, ed. Sedgwick, I. 90–5, and Thomas Towers in I.G. Doolittle, 'The Commons debates on the removal of Sir Robert Walpole', *BIHR, 53* (1980), 128–31.

73. *A Review of a Late Motion for an Address to his Majesty against a Certain Great Minister*, 1741; Hoover, *Parliamentary Reporting*, 103; *London Mag.*, XI (1742), 178–83; Coxe, *Memoirs*, III, 192–9 (drawing on Walpole's own notes but also on the *GM*); Sedgwick, *Commons*, 94–5; Doolittle, 'Commons debates', 137–9.

74. Hoover, *Parliamentary Reporting*, 117ff.; *GM*, XIII, 563ff.

75. *Parliamentary History*, XII, 1371; cf. *London Mag. XII* (1743) 488–9, 653–4.

76. *London Mag.*, XII (1743), 469–75.

77. Knox, *Irony*, 123, 129–30 (no mention of Johnson).

78. *GM* (1753); L.F. Powell, 'An addition to the canon of Johnson's writings', *Essays and Studies*, 28 (1942), 38–41; *Shorter Prose*, II. Cf. Hoover, *Parliamentary Reporting*, 131; W. Jackson Bate, *Samuel Johnson*, 203; Robert Giddings, 'The fall of Orgilio', 88, 101.

4. VINDICATION OF LITTLENESS

1. *Ram.* 60: Y, III, 320, 321. Robert Folkenflik contrasts Johnson's approach to daily life and vulgar greatness with that of contemporary life-writers such as Robert Potter and Voltaire (*Samuel Johnson, Biographer* (1978), 29, 43).
2. 1744, *Lives*, II, 321–434; 1754, *Works*, VI, 428–35; 1755, in *An Account of an Attempt to Ascertain the Longitude*, *Works*, V, 295–303; 1756, in a review of Elizabeth Harrison's *Miscellanies on Moral and Religious Subjects*, *Works*, VI, 79; 1782, Y, VI, 313–15; see below, pp. 236–9.
3. Contemporary opinions mentioned the 'spirit of detraction diffused so universally through these volumes', the 'overwhelming tide of injustice and malignity', and 'the malevolence that predominates in every part': Robert Potter, Anna Seward and Bishop Newton, quoted in J. Churton Collins, 'Dr. Johnson's "Lives of the Poets"', *Quarterly Rev.*, 208 (1908), 81–3. Modern opinion too often concurs. John Wiltshire finds from what Johnson says of Pope's self-importance in little things that he 'often has a strong antagonism towards his figures' ('Dr. Johnson's seriousness', *Critical Rev.* 10 (1967), 70). K.J.H. Berland reads the life of Dryden as an attacking polemic, 'Johnson's life-writing and the Life of Dryden', *Eighteenth Century*, 23 (1982–3), 197–212. Damrosch finds 'hostility' in more of Johnson's adverse judgments than is warrantable, though he also gives forceful expression to the point made here: see his *Uses of Johnson's Criticism*, 104, 135, 169, 172, 197.
4. *Works*, V, 266; Y, VI, 320; Bloom, 'Symbolic names in Johnson's periodical essays', *MLQ*, 13 (1952), 346. Dustin Griffin calls Johnson's poem on Dr Levet 'perhaps . . . a contemporary version' of this Greek epitaph and the one on Epictetus, in 'Johnson's funeral writings', *ELH*, 41 (1974), 207. Johnson's first sermon, on marriage, also emphasizes the severity of suffering from petty causes: Y, XIV, 6.
5. Michael Rewa, 'Aspects of rhetoric in Johnson's "professedly serious" *Rambler* essays', *Quarterly J. of Speech*, 56 (1970), 81, n.22.
6. *Spectator*, 58, 34, 523. Steele in closing the paper admitted that the authority of his persona 'would look like arrogance in a writer who sets his name to his work' (No. 555: 6 Dec. 1712), a sentiment copied by Johnson (Y, V, 317). Paul Alkon observes Johnson's infrequent use of the imperative mood (*Samuel Johnson and Moral Discipline*, ix).
7. A rhyme used by Henry Carey in ridicule of Ambrose Philips (1729), reprinted 1777, the year before Johnson's letter (*Lives*, III, 326).
8. *Aeneid*, II, 9: *somnum* should read *somnos*.
9. This probably alludes to Martial's epigrams, III, 60.
10. Cf. Grundy, 'Samuel Johnson: man of maxims?', in *Samuel Johnson*, ed. Grundy, 13–30.
11. Horace, *Ars Poetica*, line 142.
12. *Letters*, no. 559, Johnson's chief letter about letter-writing, burlesques the popular epistolary ideal of total sincerity. Nearly six months later he returned to the idea of 'a letter about nothing', and burlesqued 'graceful negligence' (no. 657).
13. Cf. Johnson's renderings: 'adorned with every accomplishment', *Idler* 12 (Y, II, 40).
14. Y, IX, 42, 164. Jeffrey Hart, though he finds the *Journey* heroically tragic, concedes that it 'makes room within itself for the normal, the minimal': 'Johnson's *A Journey to the Western Islands*', *EIC*, 10 (1960), 55.
15. He was indeed criticized for having 'descended to such remarks' as this passage: see Edward Topham, *Letters from Edinburgh* (1776), 141, quoted in G.B. Hill, *Footsteps of Dr. Johnson*, 47.

16. Y, IV, 88, 109; *Georgics*, IV, 6.
17. Wordsworth, *Tintern Abbey*, lines 34–5.
18. 'Magnificat', 8; Herbert, 'The Elixer', *The Temple* (1633), 179.
19. Introductory paragraphs to Gwynn's *Thoughts on the Coronation* (*Works*, V, 451).

5. CRITICISM OF PETTINESS

1. Cf. Fussell, *Rhetorical World*, chapter 10: '"The vermin of nature": hierarchy and moral contempt', 233–61.
2. C.B. Bradford, 'Johnson's revision of the *Rambler*', *RES*, *15* (1939), 311–12. He did the same thing in *Adventure* 50: see Arthur Sherbo, 'Two notes on Johnson's revisions', *MLR*, *50* (1955), 311.
3. *Letters*, nos 237, 254, 258, 264, 281, 282, 557.
4. Piozzi, *Anecdotes*, 135–6.
5. Siebert, 'The scholar as satirist', *SEL*, *15* (1975), 489, 496. For a contrary view see Shirley White Johnston, 'From preface to practice', *Greene Centennial Studies*, 250–70.
6. Y, VIII, 695; Boswell, II, 87. The same evening he made similar remarks on excessive detail in 'the description of night in Macbeth' and in criticism concerning ghosts (II, 90).
7. Y, X, 368, 369. Cf. the description of Sandiland, quoted above, p. 73.
8. In his life of Cave he remarks that 'unequal associations', 'invidious familiarity' with those of higher rank (even though brought about by intellectual superiority) must necessarily end badly, see *Works*, VI, 429, cf. *Ram*. 64: Y, III, 344; *Lives*, III, 422. Dependence on other people is one of the *Rambler*'s central themes, e.g. in a single month early in the series, nos 21, 26, 27, 28: see A.T. Elder, 'Thematic patterning and development in Johnson's essays', *SP*, *62* (1965), 616–17, 628. Cf. Bloom, 'Symbolic names', 349, 350.
9. Bloom, 'Symbolic names', 342. He does not discuss the general significance of diminutives.
10. Y, IV, 187–9, 215–20, V, 155–9; Bloom, 'Symbolic names', 340–1.
11. Bloom, 'Symbolic names', 347, n. 40. The *GM* had reprinted a letter from 'Verecundus' expressing a desire to learn impudence (1738, 358–9).
12. *Ram*, 82: Y, IV, 65–70: the name means 'sweepings' (cf. Bloom, 'Symbolic names', 342).
13. Johnson's house in Gough Square already boasts a stone from the Wall of China, by the generosity of Lord Northcliffe. Admirers of Johnson's 'risibility' might well crawl a snail on that stone and then present its shell, suitably inscribed, to the collection.
14. Noted by Wimsatt, *Philosophic Words*, 139.
15. Hawkins, *Life of Johnson*, 163, 152, 160. This is just a little like thinking *Much Ado about Nothing* or *The Idiot* disparaged by their titles. Fanny Burney wrote of 'the vague and inadequate titles of the Rambler and the Idler', *Memoirs of Doctor Burney*, (1832), I, 117.
16. Boswell was more perceptive, finding in the series 'admirable instances of grave humour' and of the 'power of sophistry' (I, 332). McIntosh thinks nos. 1–3 'Johnson's best prose satire' (*The Choice of Life*, 81), James F. Woodruff that 'in psychological terms' the *Idler* is almost 'the central Johnsonian work' ('Johnson's *Idler* and the "anatomy of idleness"', *English Studies in Canada*, 6 (1980), 34). See also Patrick O'Flaherty, 'Johnson's *Idler*: the equipment of a satirist', *ELH*, *37*, (1970), 211–25.
17. See *Ram*. 106, 98 (above pp. 31, 67).
18. 'Observations' in *Payne's Universal Chronicle*, the same paper where the *Idler* appeared (Y, X, 269, 272); *Idler* 20 (Y, II, 62ff.).
19. This bleakness in the *Idler* has been insufficiently recognized by critics (cf. however, Woodruff, 'Johnson's *Idler*', 22–38 *passim*), who have tended to agree with the Yale editors that

Very few of the character portraits in the *Rambler* or *Adventurer* are favourable, despite the . . . union of charity and sadness that modifies the impatience and exasperation we feel stirring in them. But in the *Idler* the portraits are almost uniformly either favourable or, at least, gentle. (II, xx)

It is hard to know exactly what 'favourable' means here, or to see that it can mean anything without denying the kind of complexity the portraits have; I for one feel much more 'impatience and exasperation' in the *Idler* portraits than in earlier ones. Here we feel the first stirrings of the mood of the 1770s pamphlets.

20. Cf. James F. Woodruff, 'The allusions in Johnson's *Idler* No. 40', *MP*, 76 (1978–9), 384–6; Grundy, 'Man of maxims?' *Samuel Johnson*, 20. The Emperor was, incidentally, far less famous than his wife, Maria Theresa.

21. *Ram*. 41, 8, 85: Y, III, 221, 41, IV, 86. Arieh Sachs devotes the first chapter of *Passionate Intelligence* to 'The vacuity of life'. See also Bate, *Achievement*, 160ff.; Max Byrd, 'Johnson's spiritual anxiety', *MP*, 78 (1981), 373–8.

22. *Ram*, 42: Y, III, 230; 'Epistle To Miss Blount, on her leaving the Town, after the Coronation' (1715), line 18: Pope, *Poems*, VI.

23. E.g. Y, X, 258, 263, II, 19.

24. Swift, *A Tale of a Tub*, II (*Prose Works*, I, 45); Rochester, *Poems* (1680), 59–60. This verse is given to Sackville Earl of Dorset in Rochester's *Complete Poems*, ed. David M. Vieth. Keith Walker prints it as 'possibly' by Rochester (p.130). Cf. also Fielding's Mr. Wilson's 'journal of one day', *Joseph Andrews*, III, iii.

25. *Lives*, I, 224–8; Hawkins, *Life of Johnson*, 10.

26. *Idler* 31 (Y, II, 97–8). Hawkins wrote that Johnson's own 'chemical operations . . . dwindled down to mere distillation' (*Life of Johnson*, 178).

27. 'And some there be, which have no memorial; who are perished, as though they had never been' (*Ecclesiasticus*, xliv.9; cf. above pp. 68–9).

6. COMPETITION

1. Bate, *Samuel Johnson*, 281.

2. Piozzi, *Anecdotes*, 62.

3. By about the 1760s, Hawkins thought, Johnson ceased contending for conversational supremacy (see *Life of Johnson*, 7, 27, 106, 196, 185).

4. Roy Flannagan, 'Bate's Samuel Johnson and Johnson's Life of Milton: puckish or perverse', *Milton Q*., 12 (1978), 147.

5. D'Arblay, *Diary and Letters*, I, 120, 117, II, 215; Duncan Isles, 'The Lennox Collection', *Harvard University Library Bull*., 19 (1971) 38–9. Thirty-six years later 'Burney', quoting Johnson's advice to her, inserted a characteristic humble disclaimer: 'Always aim at the eagle! – even though you expect but to reach a sparrow!' (dedication to *The Wanderer* (1814), I, xix.

6. E.g. *Ram*. 2, 3 (cf. above, p. 112).

7. Pope, *Essay on Man*, II, 191–2.

8. 'Verses on the Death of Dr. Swift', lines 35–6 (see above, pp.37–8).

9. Sermons 17, 11, 23, *Ram*. 183: Y, XIV, 187, 120, 240, V, 200; Bate, *Achievement*, 103 (cf. Wharton, *The Theme of Hope*, 64ff., 74); Hawkins, *Life of Johnson*, 186. See further above, pp. 136–7, 142.

10. Hobbes, *Leviathan*, I, xi. Several modern critics have noted relationship between Johnson and Hobbes, e.g. Bate, *Achievement*, 69; Greene, *Politics of Johnson*, 246; Arieh Sachs, *Passionate Intelligence*, 34.

11. Richardson, *Clarissa*, Everyman edn, II, 134, I, 190, IV, 199.

12. *Anecdotes of William Hogarth, Written by Himself* (1833), 20. Cf. *Ram* 64 (Y, III, 343).

13. 'The Scale of Blessedness' and 'Death and Heaven, Discourse II' (*Works* (1810), I, 134–5, II, 39–40, 76).

14. Chesterfield, 24 Nov. O.S. 1749: *Letters*, ed. B. Dobrée (1932), IV, 1442.
15. Y, II, 400–5. The fact that Johnson dictated this essay to Hawkesworth instead of writing it down himself – see Hawkins, *Life of Johnson*, 2nd edn (1787), 294ff. – seems to have no bearing on the difficulty. It will be apparent how widely this reading differs from Folkenflik's view of Crichton as 'clearly a figure of wish-fulfilment' (*Johnson, Biographer*, 59).
16. Mackenzie, *Lives*, Edinburgh, III, 198–207; Urquhart, *The Jewel*, eds. R.D.S. Jack and R.J. Lyall (1984), 100–37. Cf. Y, II, 402 n. 6. *The Jewel's* amazing flavour emerges clearly in the review by Denton Fox, *London Rev. of Books*, 6 (1984), no. 17, 13–14. Hawkins was puzzled by Johnson's essay, and devoted pp. 294–309 (2nd edn, 1787) to lengthy quotation from it and Urquhart.
17. *Lives*, I, 190, 194; Caroline Goad, *Horace in the Eighteenth Century*, 237. Paul Alkon has discussed Johnson's use of 'admiration' as a term of criticism, *PQ*, 48 (1969), 59–81.
18. Johnson's uncle Andrew of course comes to mind, but is not really relevant. Wrestling and boxing at Smithfield entirely lack the romance connotations of this story.
19. E.g. *Vanity of Human Wishes*, lines 313–14 (the Yale footnote, VI, 106, fails to bring out the significance of this allusion); *Ram.* 17, also 21 (Y, III, 92, 118–19).
20. *Vanity of Human Wishes*, line 221; *Anatomy of Criticism*, 186, 187. Cf. Grundy, 'Samuel Johnson: a writer of lives looks at death', *MLR*, 79 (1984), 257–65.
21. Fussell, *Johnson and the Life of Writing*, 161–2.
22. *Vanity of Human Wishes*, lines 76, 156.

7. COMMUNITY

1. Robert Voitle, *Samuel Johnson the Moralist*, 107; Pope, *An Essay on Man*, IV, 396; Rothstein, *Restoration and Eighteenth-Century Poetry*, xiii.
2. Byrd, *London Transformed*, 4 (cf. 115–16); Y, II, 386; *Ram.* 56: Y, III, 299.
3. Elder, 'Thematic patterning and development', 621–31.
4. Ephesians, iv, 25.
5. Voitle, *Johnson the Moralist*, 13; Wimsatt, *Philosophic Words*, 128, 140.
6. Thomson, *Autumn*, lines 1020–2; *Spring*, lines 301–2.
7. Preface to *The Preceptor: Works*, V, 243; *Ram.* 81, Y, IV, 62.
8. *Lives*, I, 424; *Idler* 51, *Ram.* 60: Y, II, 159–60, III, 320; cf. *Adv.* 95: Y, II, 425–7.
9. Cf. Grundy, 'A writer of lives looks at death', *MLR*, 79.
10. E.g. *Ram.* 23, 25, 52, 83: Y, III, 128, 136, 280, IV, 74; *Lives*, II, 132, III, 441–2.
11. Collins, 'Dr. Johnson's "Lives of the Poets"', 97. Hazlitt in *Lectures on the English Comic Writers* (1819) blamed the *Rambler* for drawing on 'gradual accumulation, the produce of the general intellect' instead of on a single mind (196).
12. A man of 'a temper naturally cool', probably modelled on an individual named *Coulson*, whose name Johnson whimsically adapts (Y, III, 132, n. 3).
13. I John, iv, 18.
14. Italics added where emphasis seems helpful.
15. Bate, *Achievement*, 122. He pursues the point further in 'Johnson and satire manqué', 145–60. See also above, pp. 174–5.
16. IX: *Prose Works*, I, 114.
17. *Lives*, II, 433–4; *Ram*, 83; *Rass*, XLIII; *Idler* 27 (Y, II, 84).
18. B.H. Bronson says this phrase 'has perhaps never been satisfactorily explained by any commentator'. Howard Weinbrot, quoting this, suggests that God's love *may* be meant. (*The Formal Strain*, 213 and n.32) – although, of course, this would destroy the parallel with faith and patience. Ian White, reading it as human love, calls it 'akin to the urge for conquest of millions criticised in the earlier part of the poem' ('*The Vanity of Human Wishes*', *Cambridge Q.*, 6 (1974), 117) – although, of course, the kinship must be that of contraries.

8. MALIGNITY

1. Hobbes, in fact, disbelieved in motiveless malignity (*Leviathan*, I, vi).
2. Boswell, *Life*, V, 211; Hester Chapone, *Posthumous Works* (1807), I, 72–4; Mudford, *Nubilia in Search of a Husband*, 448, 451–2. Robert G. Walker remarks that *Rasselas*, unlike the essays, almost entirely lacks moral – though not physical or metaphysical – evil (*Eighteenth-Century Arguments for Immortality and Johnson's* Rasselas (1977), 47).
3. Noted by Wimsatt, *Philosophic Words*, 104–5.
4. Quinlan, *Samual Johnson, A Layman's Religion*, 106; Voitle, *Johnson the Moralist*, 59.
5. Bailey includes a few more words, and defines in terms of 'spight' and ill-will, but not otherwise of intention (*Dict. Brit.* (1730)).
6. E.g. *Ram.* 111: Y, IV, 228. Blake similarly brackets them when in a letter to Trusler, 23 Aug. 1799, he calls 'Merit in one a Cause of Envy in another, & Serenity & Happiness & Beauty a Cause of Malevolence' (*Complete Writings*, 793).
7. That Johnson was in some ways close to Fielding in thought, though critically grudging about him, is noted by R.E. Moore in 'Dr. Johnson on Fielding and Richardson', *PMLA*, *66* (1951), 162–81, and Mark Kinkead-Weekes in 'Johnson on "The Rise of the Novel"' in *Samuel Johnson*, ed. Grundy, 74–7.
8. *GM*, XII (1742), 666ff.
9. Noted by Bate, *Achievement*, 106.
10. *Lives*, II, 353; 'Observations on the Present State of Affairs': Y, X, 190. Cf. fielding, who draws the lesson from history that 'mankind in general desire power only to do harm' (*Tom Jones*, XII, xii).
11. Y,X,213, 240, 412, 443, 444.
12. It would have been normal for her to retain the title, though at the time under discussion she had become Mrs Brett. Johnson never uses that name for her; indeed, as far as possible he refrains from giving her any name at all.
13. McIntosh, *Choice of Life*, 45.
14. See Benjamin Boyce, 'Johnson's *Life of Savage* and its literary background', *SP*, *53* (1956), 576–98; Damrosch, *Uses of Johnson's Criticism*, 129-30.
15. *Lives*, II, 323; Boyce, *Savage*, 591.
16. Again he resembles Fielding, who writes of slander, 'some black and infernal mind may propose a reward in the thoughts of having procured the ruin and misery of another' (*Tom Jones*, XI, i).
17. Boyce, *Savage*, 594.
18. Tracy, *The Artificial Bastard*, 4, 24.
19. Cf. Boyce, *Savage*, 594–5.
20. 'Biographical sketch', *Johnsonian Miscellanies*, ed. G.B. Hill, II, 378.
21. Y, VII, 512, VIII, 703, 881, 704, 990, 1045. If Johnson intended his 'horrible' to echo the Ghost's 'Oh, horrible! Oh, horrible! most horrible!' he was suggesting that Hamlet's purpose here was as bad as his uncle's action: *Hamlet*, I, v, 80.
22. 'Verses on the Death of Dr. Swift', lines 46, 6 (*Poems*, II, 555, 551). It is in this poem on the indulgence of envious malice that Swift embodies his own most serious claim for merit in his writings. Pope writes of the persistence of envy both at the outset of his career and twenty-six years later (*An Essay on Criticism*, 1711, line 466; *Epistle to Augustus*, 1737, lines 15–18).
23. 'Verses on the Death of Dr. Swift', lines 7–10, 31–2; Johnson, *Letters*, nos 560, 969, 1016; Piozzi, *Anecdotes*, 90, 124; Windham in *Johnsonian Miscellanies*, II, 386; *The Making of the Life of Johnson*, ed. G. Scott, 53. Cf. Boswell, I, 246.
24. 'Verses on the Death of Dr. Swift', lines 33–4.
25. Cf. 'his thinking goes first through everything that will not work, minimizing nothing. . . . only gradually, as one thing after another gives way, do we find left a citadel of unshaken results that have withstood the test' (Bate, *Achievement*, 90).
26. *Rams*, 12, 133, 142, 149 (see above pp. 65–6ff.; Y, IV, 343–4, 393, V, 30).

27. 'Hap' (1866) in Hardy, *Complete Poems*, 9. D.P. Walker traces earlier appearances of the idea of a malignant deity in *The Decline of Hell*, 4–51 and *passim*. Johnson's superhuman torturers probably owe something to Erasmus's gods in *The Praise of Folly* (see above p. 169). On Johnson's fear of a hostile God, see Charles E. Pierce, Jr., *The Religious Life of Samuel Johnson* (1983), 35ff.

28. Walker ascribes to 'a general change in the attitude to other people's suffering, a change which was only just beginning [in the late seventeenth century] and which today is still not completed', the decline of the doctrine that the blessed enjoy watching the torments of the damned (*Decline of Hell*, 29–30). The enjoyment of pain which Johnson imagines in his review of Jenyns closely resembles that long attributed in Christian thinking to the blessed in Heaven.

29. Locke, *Essay Concerning Human Understanding*, II, xxi, 13, xxxiii, 13; Hume, *An Inquiry Concerning Human Understanding*, ed. Charles W. Hendel (1955), 110 (the latter quoted in Richard B. Schwartz, *Samuel Johnson and the Problem of Evil* (1975), 15–16). Johnson in *Irene* made less of Turkish cruelty than might have been expected, and there and in 'Lobo' he deleted references to the rack, XV, 67n.3 (Y, VI, 196). His review also reflects familiarity with recent newspaper reports of the execution in France of Robert-François Damiens.

30. *Lear*, III, vii, 28: Y, VIII, 703; the *Dictionary*'s only example under *corky*.

31. Preface to *The World Displayed: Works*, V, 218; *Idler* 81: Y, II, 253.

32. Johnson quoted this phrase twice in his sermons – nos. 17 and 20: Y, XIV, 189, 224.

33. Milton had picked up the word *sport* from the Biblical account of the Philistines' behaviour, and used it twice in his own version (*Samson Agonistes*, lines 1328, 1679).

34. Note on John Ward: Pope, *Poems*, III, ii, 85.

35. Cf. the torment by incomprehensibility devised by the employer in *Idler* 46.

36. Johnson is an honourable example of the change in attitude noted by D.P. Walker.

37. D'Arblay, *Diary and Letters*, I, 204.

38. McIntosh, *Choice of Life*, 75.

39. Damrosch notes the 'surprising frequency in Johnson's writings during the next couple of years' of 'the imaginative cluster of the Jenyns review' (*Johnson and the Tragic Sense*, 85).

9. SUPERIOR OBSERVERS

1. Y, VIII, 813; Life of Cowley (*Lives*, I, 51), Percy in *Johnsonian Miscellanies*, ed. Hill, II, 215.

2. Patricia Meyer Spacks finds in the poem an 'almost obsessive concern with "seeing", as both fact and metaphor' (*An Argument of Images*, 42).

3. Pope, *Essay on Man*, line 5.

4. McIntosh, *Choice of Life*, pp.199n., 206.

5. Noted by Richard B. Schwartz, 'Johnson's *Journey*', *JEGP*, 69 (1970), 296.

6. Cf. Eric Rothstein, *Systems of Order*, 34–5.

7. Howard Erskine-Hill comments that she, and therefore Johnson himself, resemble Charles XII in seeking comprehensiveness ('Johnson and the petty particular', *Transactions of the Johnson Society of Lichfield* (1976), 40–1).

8. Sachs, *Passionate Intelligence*, 77; Lipking, 'Learning to read Johnson', *ELH*, 43 (1976), 527–8: Hilles, 'Johnson's poetic fire', in *From Sensibility to Romanticism*, ed. Hilles and Bloom, 68–9, 70.

9. Carnochan, *Confinement and Flight*, 162ff; Boyd, 'Vanity and vacuity', *ELH*, 39 (1972), 403.

10. *Job*, xxii, 12–13.

11. Prayer Book version, verses 1–2, 6, 10.

12. *Paradise Lost*, VI, 228, 672–4, III, 555–63; *Paradise Regained*, III, 269ff.

13. *Paradise Lost*, IX, 811–16.
14. *Paradise Lost*, V, 711–12; *Divine Songs* (1715), no. IX. Billy Graham in 1984 repeated exactly the same message in images from modern surveillance technology.
15. Translation in Quinlan, *Samuel Johnson, A Layman's Religion*, 202.
16. *Julius Caesar*, I, ii, 198–200; *Measure for Measure*, I, i, 28–9.
17. Murphy, 'Essay on Johnson's life and genius', *Johnsonian Miscellanies*, I, 439.
18. Y, XIV, 70. Gulliver, in the last chapter of his *Travels*, shares just this incredulity; he only fancies he shares the superiority.
19. This change does not appear in Johnson's marked copy of the 4th edn (now in the John Rylands Library, Manchester), but it reached print in the 7th abridged edn, 1783.
20. Horace, *Odes*, III, 3.
21. *Lives*, I, 20; Damrosch, *Uses of Johnson's Criticism*, 64. Cf. Basney, 'Johnson on Metaphysical poetry', *SBHT*, *16* (1975), 244.
22. Robert Voitle, in 'Stoicism and Samuel Johnson', mentions several of the contexts associated here with Lucretian observation, though, logically enough, he makes no mention of Lucretius (*SP*, extra series no. 4, (1967), 107–27). See also Carey McIntosh, 'Johnson's debate with Stoicism', *ELH*, *33* (1966), 327–36, and Donald Greene, 'Johnson, Stoicism, and the good life', in *The Unknown Samuel Johnson*, ed. Burke and Kay, 17–38.
23. Swift, 'Thoughts on Various Subjects': *Prose Works*, I, 244.
24. Lucretius, *De rerum natura*, II, 1–16: transl. W.A.D. Rouse, rev. M.F. Smith, Loeb Library (1975), 95.
25. Lucretius, II, 323–32: Loeb, 121.
26. A.L. Reade, *Johnsonian Gleanings*, V, 217; Donald Greene, *Samuel Johnson's Library* (1975), 79; J.D. Fleeman, *A Preliminary Handlist of Copies of Books associated with Dr. Samuel Johnson* (1984), 48. Arthur Sherbo believes that Johnson preferred book I of *De rerum natura* to book II, on the grounds of simply counting *Rambler* uses of each (*Samuel Johnson, Editor of Shakespeare*, 169).
27. Brendan O Hehir, *Expans'd Hieroglyphicks*, 79; Carnochan, *Confinement and Flight*, 109–110. Maren-Sofie Røstvig comments on this tradition in English poetry (*The Happy Man*, I, 28, 252–310 *passim*, II, 182–4), and also, as does Marjorie Nicolson, on 'soaring' in non-satirical poetry of Johnson's period: Røstvig, II, 207–89 *passim*; Nicolson, *Mountain Gloom and Mountain Glory*, 330ff., 361ff.
28. R.D. Stock, *Johnson and Neoclassical Dramatic Theory*, 89, 90.
29. Richardson, *Grandison*, III, xix: ed. J. Harris, II, 114; Cowper, *The Task*, IV, 88–102.
30. Watts, *Horae Lyricae*, 2nd edn (1709), 190.
31. Greene, *Johnson's Library*, 78; Woodruff, '*Rasselas* and "Menippean satire"', in *Samuel Johnson*, ed. Grundy, esp. 173ff. D.C. Kay in 'Thomson, Donne, and Wordsworth's "Monstrous Ant-Hill"' does not mention the image's earlier history (*N & Q, 229* (1984), 55–6).
32. Lucian, transl. A.M. Harmon (1915, repr. 1919): Loeb Library, II, 267ff., 287, 297–9.
33. Preface to Shakespeare: Y, VII, 66; *Iliad*, XVIII, 478ff.; *De rerum natura*, II, 576ff.
34. *Vanity of Human Wishes*, lines 308–10; Pope, *The Second Epistle of the Second Book of Horace* (1737), lines 324–5.
35. *Witt against Wisdom, or a Panegyrick upon Folly*, transl. from Erasmus by [White Kennett] (1683), 78–81; Greene, *Johnson's Library*, 56; see above, pp. 152–3.
36. See above, p. 159, and J.S. Cunningham, 'On mirth as it laughs in heaven', in *Augustan Worlds*, ed. Watson, Hilson and Humphreys, 131–51.
37. McIntosh, *Choice of Life*, 199 n.
38. Rothstein, *Systems of Order*, 34.
39. *Rass.* chap. X. For Johnson's undermining of Imlac, see e.g. C.R. Tracy, 'Democritus, arise!', *Yale Review*, *39* (1949–50), 306–7; Alvin Whitley, 'The comedy of *Rasselas*', *ELH*, *23* (1956), 57. Geoffrey Tillotson argues that Johnson thoroughly

endorses the fictional Imlac's conception of poetry: 'Imlac and the business of a poet', in *Studies in Criticism and Aesthetics*, ed. Anderson and Shea (1967), 298.

40. Folkenflik also remarks that this derives from the magniloquence of Renaissance theories of poetry ('The tulip and its streaks: contexts of *Rasselas* X', *Ariel*, *9* (1978), ii, 57–71). The claims of generality and particularity have been much canvassed, notably by Scott Elledge (*PMLA*, *62* (1947), 147–82), W.R. Keast (*PQ*, *27* (1948), 130–2), Arieh Sachs (*SEL*, *5* (1965), 491–511), Howard D. Weinbrot (*ECS*, *5* (1971–2) 80–96), and W. Edinger, (*Samuel Johnson and Poetic Style* (1978), 83–92, 190–1, and *passim*).

41. E.g. by Gwin J. Kolb, 'The use of stoical doctrines in *Rasselas*, Chapter XVIII', *MLN*, *68* (1953), 439–47; Whitley, 'The comedy of *Rasselas*', 59.

42. Fielding, *Joseph Andrews*, III, xi, IV, viii.

43. *Works*, IX, 164; Burke, *Enquiry*, II, vii, quoted in Tillotson, 'Imlac and the business of the poet', 305, n.12.

44. Fussell, *Rhetorical World*, 268, 274; Henry Gifford, '*The Vanity of Human Wishes*', *RES*, n.s. *5* (1955), 161. Notes of Johnson's talk a few months before he died include the tantalizing 'Arguments about that feel [*sic*] which persons on great heights suppose themselves to have of a wish to throw themselves down' (Johnson, *Letters*, ed. G.B. Hill, II, 440).

45. *Vanity of Human Wishes*, line 259; 'On the Death of Dr. Robert Levet', line 14.

46. *GM*, XIV (1744), 65; Y, VII, 4–5, VIII, 753; *Lives*, I, 317–18, II, 129–31; Franklin, letter to Jan Ingenhousz, 16 Jan. 1784, *A Selection from his Personal Letters*, ed. L.W. Labaree and W.J. Bell, Jr., 58.

47. *Paradise Lost*, III, 431–41, 562–3; *Spectator* 159; Swift, see above, p. 39.

48. *GM* debates *passim*, e.g. XIII (1743), 229; XIV (1744), 65; *Falkland's Islands* (Y, X, 384); *Ram.* 38, 115, 153, epigraph to 197; *Adv.* 119 (Y, III, 209, IV, 248, V, 52, 261, II, 464). Carol Becker detects the influence of *Volpone* on the old age passage in *The Vanity of Human Wishes* ('Johnson's "*The Vanity of Human Wishes*" lines 285–90', *N & Q*, *222* (1977), 250–2); for the confiscation passage cf. Howard Erskine-Hill, 'The political character of Samuel Johnson', in *Samuel Johnson*, ed. Grundy, 128.

49. E.L. McAdam, Jr, *Dr Johnson and the English Law*, 84.

50. Boulton, *The Language of Politics*, 39–40; Watt, 'The ironic tradition in Augustan prose', in *Stuart and Georgian Moments*, ed. E. Miner, 184. Wayne C. Booth's *A Rhetoric of Irony* frequently images writer and reader looking down from a shared eminence (e.g. pp. 263, 264). Dustin H. Griffin, *Alexander Pope: The Poet in the Poems*, 149, 154–5, 163–4, finds Pope balancing the first-person plural against 'the judgmental voice of a satirist who presumably exempts himself from the condition he attacks', and, relatedly, the little human scale against the cosmic one. Johnson's ultimate rejection of superior observation is noted by C.L. Manlove, *Literature and Reality 1600–1800*, 163–9, and Robert W. Uphaus, *The Impossible Observer*, 6, 95.

51. *Lives*, III, 350–1; Siebert, 'The scholar as satirist', *SEL*, *15* (1975), 483–4.

10. GREATNESS AND HEROISM

1. McIntosh, *Choice of Life*, 115–16. See also Folkenflik, 'Johnson's heroes', in *Johnson, Biographer*, 56ff., and in *The English Hero, 1660–1800*, ed. Folkenflik, 143ff.

2. T.S. Eliot, 'Burnt Norton', in *Collected Poems 1909–1962* (1963), 189.

3. The 4th edn inserts one from Sidney, remarking the servility of unintelligent people to greatness.

4. Piozzi, *Thraliana*, ed. Balderston, I, 183.

5. Yeats, Prologue to *Responsibilities*, in *Collected Poems* (1965), 113.

6. Edinger, *Samuel Johnson and the Poetic Style* (1978), 82; Boswell, I, 49; Eithne Henson,

'Johnson's romance imagery', *Prose Studies*, 8 (1985), 5–24; review of Joseph Warton's *Essay on Pope: Works*, VI, 40.

7. Y, VII, 81; *Letters*, nos 408, 58; Boswell, IV, 274.

8. 'Dissertation on the Amazons' *GM*, XI (1741), 206; Dussinger, 'Style and intention in Johnson's *Life of Savage*', *ELH*, 37 (1970), 567.

9. Y, VII, 99; Windham's diary; Johnson, *Letters*, ed. G.B. Hill, II, 440. The scenes come from *Metamorphoses*, IX, 166–238, and *Iliad*, XXI, 34–135. Johnson probably had in mind Kirkall's plate for Tonson's 1717 translation of the *Metamorphoses*, IX, which depicts the life and death of Hercules serially though scarcely heroically. Cf. Grundy, 'A writer of lives looks at death', *MLR*, 79 (1984), 261–2.

10. As A.T. Elder has pointed out, this essay functioned as 'an advertisement of a painting contest sponsored by the Society for the Encouragement of Arts and Commerce', to which Johnson had been elected in 1756 ('Thematic patterning and development in Johnson's essays', *SP*, 62 (1965), 611, n.6). The society issued, two months after *Idler* 45, an elaborate list of premiums offered in many fields, of which the largest allotted for the arts was 100 guineas for the best historical painting 'from the English history only, containing not less than three human figures, as large as the life', to have been painted in England since 1 Jan. 1759 and submitted by the last Tuesday in March 1760: see *The Annual Register . . . For the Year 1759*, 152, 155, 158–9. But the prize would not have been Johnson's 'chief' or only motive in writing, especially since his one English subject, introduced with some hesitation, occupies only his last two paragraphs. Benjamin West took up Johnson's other suggestions, but apparently ignored those about Hercules and Achilles: see John Dillenberger, *Benjamin West*, 234–5. For the popularity of serene and instructive death-bed scenes in mid-eighteenth-century painting, see Robert Rosenblum, *Transformations in Late Eighteenth Century Art*, 28ff.

11. Martin, *Lingua Britannica Reformata* (1749).

12. Auden, 'The Shield of Achilles', *Collected Shorter Poems 1927–1957* (1966), 295.

13. Mary Lascelles, 'Johnson and Juvenal', in *New Light on Johnson*, ed. Hilles, 53. Damrosch thinks that Johnson has 'nothing to say' of the tragedies of great heroes, though much to say finely on those of obscure lives (*Samuel Johnson and the Tragic Sense*, 90ff.)

14. Lady Mary Wortley Montagu, *Complete Letters*, ed. R. Halsband, II, 485; Y, V, 9; Boswell, II, 125, n. 4. John Gower and Francis Bacon had also identified the ancient gods with inventors (information from Jonathan Harrington).

15. Y, II, 430; Temple, *Five Miscellaneous Essays*, ed. S.H. Monk, 98; W.K. Wimsatt mentions Johnson's familiarity with Temple's works (*The Prose Style of Samuel Johnson*, repr. 1963, 124–5).

16. Irvin Ehrenpreis, *Swift: The Man, his Works and the Age*, I, 190; cf. F.P. Lock, *The Politics of* Gulliver's Travels, 30. To John Locke, too, conquerors were just robbers writ large: *Second Treatise of Government* (1698), XVI, 176.

17. Dryden, dedication to *Examen Poeticum* (1693): *Poems*, ed. James Kinsley, II, 798–9; Swift, *Prose Works*, I, 57. For the views of the heroic age which were *de rigueur* for each side in the battle of ancients and moderns, see Pope's preface to the *Iliad*: ed. Mack, *Poems*, VII, 13–15. Cf. also Percy G. Adams, 'The anti-hero in eighteenth-century fiction', *Studies in the Literary Imagination*, 9 (1976), 29–51; Peter Hughes, 'Restructuring literary history: implications for the eighteenth century, *NLH*, 8, (1977), 257–77. Augustan attitudes are sometimes seen as reactions against the Restoration tragic heroes, but Martin Price considers Dryden's heroes themselves to be 'statements of the problematic nature of heroism' (*To the Palace of Wisdom*, 35). Richard B. Schwartz links Johnson with Swift and 'nearly every writer in the century' as concerned 'to challenge the twisted notion of public "greatness"' (*Samuel Johnson and the Problem of Evil*, 64).

18. Fielding, *Tom Jones*, XIII, i.

19. Fielding, *Joseph Andrews*, I, i. Bruce W. Wardropper, who quotes Erasmus revealing military heroes to be parasites and scoundrels, says also that the remains of the old idea of heroes fed into the new one of 'great men' ('The epic hero superseded', in *Concepts of the Hero*, ed. Burns and Reagan, 203).
20. Pope, *Essay on Man*, IV, 219ff.; Richardson, *Clarissa*, I, 243, II, 329–30, VI, 514; Richardson, *Selected Letters*, 134; D'Arblay, *Diary and Letters*, V, 66–7.
21. Price, *To the Palace of Wisdom*, 262.
22. Y, X, 370; *London*, lines 230–1; *Ram*. 170 (Y, V, 139); *Letters*, nos 679, 681.
23. Second Vinerian lecture: McAdam, *Johnson and the Law*, 87.
24. Carlyle, *Heroes and Hero-Worship*, *Works* (1897), V; see above, pp.216–17.
25. E.g. *Ram*. 108, *Idler* 37 (Y, IV, 213; II, 116).
26. Carlyle, *Works* (1897), V, 2, 15, 196.
27. Longinus, *On the Sublime*, VII (transl. Prickard).
28. *Adv*. 99 (Y, II, 430–1); also *Letters*, no. 647 (1779).
29. *Idlers*, 32, 44, 51, *Adv*. 39 (Y, II, 99–100, 139, 159–60, 349); *Lives*, I, 98, 109.
30. Carlyle, *Works* (1897), V, 211.
31. 'A Debate Between The Committee . . . and Oliver Cromwell' (Y, X, 92); *Idler* 45 (Y, II, 142).
32. Carlyle, *Works* (1897), V, 43.
33. *Lives*, I, 194, 348–9, II, 132, 135, III, 394; Percy Hazen Houston, *Dr. Johnson, A Study in Eighteenth Century Humanism*, 172.
34. E.g. William Vesterman, *The Stylistic Life of Samuel Johnson*, 106–7; Fredric V. Bogel, 'The rhetoric of substantiality', *ECS*, *12* (1978–9), 468.
35. Cf. P.A. O'Flaherty, 'The art of Johnson's *London*' in *A Festschrift for Edgar Ronald Seary* (1975), 85; John Hardy, 'Johnson's *London*', in *Studies in the Eighteenth Century*, ed. R.F. Brissenden, 257–8.
36. Pope, *Epilogue to the Satires*, 'Dialogue II' (1738), lines 212–16.
37. *Journey* (Y, IX, 57, 110). Critics differ widely about Johnson's attitude to the vanished feudal society (e.g. Jeffrey Hart, 'Johnson's *A Journey*', *EIC*, *10* (1960), 44–59; R.K. Kaul, '*A Journey* reconsidered', *EIC*, *13* (1963) 341–50).
38. Y, IX, 39, 45, 77, 155. The Homeric flavour is noted by George H. Savage, '"Roving among the Hebrides"', *SEL*, *17* (1977), 493–501, and the romance element by Eithne Henson, 'Johnson's quest for "the fictions of romantic chivalry" in Scotland', *Prose Studies*, *7* (1984), 97–128.
39. Fielding, *Tom Jones*, IV, 2.
40. Y, IX, 76, xxvii; G. B. Hill, *Footsteps of Dr. Johnson*, 186–9.
41. Philip C. Yorke, *Life and Letters of Lord Chancellor Hardwicke* (1913), I, 56, quoted in Folkenflik, *Johnson, Biographer*, 62.
42. E.g. *Ram*. 21 (Y, III, 116–17).
43. Cf. Folkenflik, *Johnson, Biographer*, 56–70; Richard R. Reynolds, 'Johnson's heroes before the *Life of Savage*', *New Rambler*, *16* (1975), 10.
44. *Works*, VI, 396 and n. For Drake, Johnson used four earlier pamphlets reprinted for Nicholas Bourne in 1652–3 (*Sir Francis Drake Revived*, *The World Encompassed*, *A Summarie and True Discourse* and *A Full Relation of Another Voyage*), besides, for his opening and closing passages, Nathaniel Crouch's *The English Hero: Or, Sir Francis Drake Reviv'd* (1692), which echoes the remark about emulation from its source's title page. Fontenelle's *éloges* have been discussed by George Armstrong Kelly, 'The history of the new hero', *The Eighteenth Century*, *21* (1980), 18–20. That footnote suggests to O M Brack and Thomas Kaminski that Johnson may have had less than full control over the text proper: 'Johnson, James, and the *Medical Dictionary*', *MP*, *81* (1984) 385, n.22.
45. *Works*, VI, 265, 294–5, J.A.V. Chapple, 'Samuel Johnson's *Proposals for Printing the History of the Council of Trent*, 1738', *BJRL*, *45* (1962–3), 353, n.2; E.L. McAdam, Jr, 'Johnson's lives of Sarpi, Blake, and Drake', *PMLA*, *58* (1943), 471–2, 474–5; J.L.

Abbott, 'Dr. Johnson and the making of "The Life of Father Paul Sarpi"', *BJRL*, *48* (1965–6), 258. Johnson drew on the *General Dictionary* (1734), englished from Pierre Bayle, for Blake: see Johnson, *Shorter Prose*.

46. R. Reynolds, *New Rambler* (1975), 14–15.
47. *Works*, VI, 277–8, 338, 411, 264–6, 270, 310–11, 391, 397; *GM*, XII (1742), 355; Jacob Leed, 'Johnson, DuHalde, and the life of Confucius', *BNYPL*, *70* (1966), 19; Abbott, '"Sarpi"', 260ff.
48. Cf.Frye, *Anatomy of Criticism*, 187.
49. *Works*, VI, 375; Crouch, *The English Hero*, 184.
50. *Works*, VI, 269, 286–7, 384, 403–4, 412, 307; McAdam, 'Sarpi, Blake, and Drake', 469. My comments here are slightly expanded in *MLR* (1984), 263–4.
51. *Works*, VI, 292, 275, 288; Richard Reynolds, 'Johnson's *Life of Boerhaave* in perspective', *YES*, 5 (1975), 127, 129.
52. The *GM* published 'Blake' in June 1740; a year later it printed the first debate entirely written by Johnson: see Hoover, *Parliamentary Reporting*, 24–5.
53. Reynolds, *New Rambler*, 13; McAdam, 'Sarpi, Drake, and Blake', 473.
54. *Works*, VI, 374, 311; McAdam, 'Sarpi, Drake, and Blake', 474.
55. E.g. Bourne pamphlets; Crouch, e.g. pp. 10, 31–2, 41–2.
56. *Works*, VI, 311; McAdam, 'Sarpi, Drake, and Blake', 475.
57. *The Vanity of Human Wishes*, line 177; Bernard, 'A possible source for Johnson's life of the King of Prussia', *PQ*, *47* (1968), 215, 206ff.
58. Thus in *Literary Magazine*.
59. *Vanity of Human Wishes*, line 189; *Works*, VI, 470–1.
60. Johnson's *Literary Magazine* conclusion was dropped when the life was reprinted.
61. Lines 149–51, 207–9, 234; the Yale edition's policy on capitalization obscures some of these personifications.
62. Yale, VII, 49; *Macbeth*, V, v, 26–8. R.D. Stock quotes various contemporary critics who found domestic disasters more moving than those of kings and heroes; he also quotes Warton's *Essay on Pope* on Shakespeare's 'little touches' and '*minute* representations of Nature' (*Johnson and Neoclassical Dramatic Theory*, 38, 43).
63. See above, p.103. Damrosch finds in the preface an 'almost inexplicable severity', though he admits that the final impression is positive (*Uses of Johnson's Criticism*, 104, 119).
64. Y, VII, 89, 59, 99, 62, 66, 70–1, 84. Stock, who cites precedents for some of these images, finds it odd of Johnson to insist on the virtues of Shakespeare's wildness (*Neoclassical Theory*, 154–6); but what he insists on is not so much wildness as nature and vitality.
65. Krieger, 'Fiction, nature, and literary kinds in Johnson's criticism of Shakespeare', *ECS*, *4* (1970–1), 190; C.G. Jung, e.g. *Aeon*, 123: *Collected Works*, ed. H. Read *et al.* (1953–64), IX, ii, 68.
66. Y, VII, 61; Pope, *An Essay on Criticism*, lines 191–2.
67. Y, VII, 112. Elizabeth Montagu compared Shakespeare's fate to that of 'the heroes of the fabulous ages', being first superstitiously hailed as more than human, then later debunked (*An Essay on the Writings and Genius of Shakespear* (1769), 2ff.). Cf. also Pope's praise of Homer as supremely creative but not above humanity: *Iliad* preface, *Odyssey* postscript, *Poems*, VII, 3, X, 394.

11. GREATNESS AND OURSELVES

1. *Ram.* 77 (Y, IV, 44), paraphrased from Luke, xii, 40.
2. Cf. Mary Lascelles, 'Johnson and commemorative writing', in *Samuel Johnson*, ed. Grundy, 186–202.
3. *Vanity of Human Wishes*, lines 173–9, 222; *Ram.* 146: Y, V, 16.

4. Y, III, 93, 96; *Vanity of Human Wishes*, lines 125–8, 191–2.
5. *Vanity of Human Wishes*, line 346.
6. Folkenflik expresses somewhat different opinions on Johnson's view of the relationship between life and works (*Johnson, Biographer*, 118ff. and *passim*).
7. *Lives*, I, 138; J. Copley, 'Cowper on Johnson's Life of Milton', *N & Q, 222* (1977), 314; Potter, *An Inquiry into . . . Dr. Johnson's 'Lives of the Poets'* (1783), 4 (quoted by Folkenflik, *Johnson, Biographer*, 29, who in this chapter, 'Trifles with dignity', deals with this school).
8. Piozzi, *Thraliana*, I, 164.
9. Johnson three times applies *steady* or *steadily* to Milton, with increasing degrees of praise: *Lives*, I, 88, 94, 144.
10. *Lives*, I, 117, 119; Y, III, 171, 173.
11. In an earlier version Johnson directed our merriment 'upon a human head with a fish's tail' – a Horatian image which, however, confuses the issue by associating Milton the man with something non-human. See John H. Middendorf, 'Johnson as editor; some proofs of the "Prefaces"', in *Eighteenth-Century Studies*, ed. W.H. Bond, 103.
12. Stephen Fix notes that Johnson stresses 'Milton's effort to separate himself from the flow of ordinary life', and more generally the 'dangers to an author in living apart' ('Distant genius; Johnson and the art of Milton's Life', *MP, 81* (1984), 244, 256). It is important, however, that Johnson shows Milton trying *unsuccessfully* to set himself apart.
13. *Lives*, I, 109. There is also perhaps an implied comparison with the poet's brother, a lawyer in what Johnson calls 'chamber-practice' (I, 85).
14. For Johnson's own scale cf. Gilbert West, who, though 'some time in the army . . . never sunk into a mere soldier' (*Lives*, III, 328).
15. Cf. Lawrence Lipking, *The Ordering of the Arts in Eighteenth-Century England* (1970), 439; Folkenflik, *Johnson, Biographer*, 165ff.
16. Damrosch, *Uses of Johnson's Criticism*, 99.
17. Stephen Fix, 'Johnson on Shakespeare and Milton', paper at Johnson Bi-Centenary Conference, Pembroke College, Oxford, 10 July 1984.
18. Maximillian E. Novak makes this point ('Johnson, Dryden, and the wild vicissitudes of taste', in *The Unknown Samuel Johnson*, ed. Burke and Kay, 54ff.); K.J.H. Berland is surely on the wrong track (see above, p.247, n.3).
19. Apparently no earlier biographer of Addison had mentioned this rift. *Biographia Britannica* says the friendship 'lasted as long as Mr Addison lived' (I (1747), 31).
20. *Lives*, II, 125–6. The quotations are from Daniel, xii, 3, and Pope's *Epistle to Augustus*, line 26.
21. *Lives*, II, 150, I, 43, II, 282; cf. Piozzi, *Anecdotes*, 101, 127.
22. Altered from 'assumes a style of superiority' (Boswell, IV, 63).
23. Pope, *Epistle to Arbuthnot*, line 203.
24. Howard Erskine-Hill points out the *gallantry* of this ceremonial dress, the account of which is not meant to belittle greatness ('Johnson and the petty particular', 44).
25. *Lives*, III, 195, 190; Folkenflik, *Johnson, Biographer*, 54.

CONCLUSION

1. *Vanity of Human Wishes*, line 74.
2. II, iii: Swift, *Prose Works*, XI, 106.
3. Dedications of George Adams's *Treatise on the Globes* (1766) and Charles Burney's *Commemoration of Handel* (published 1 Feb. 1785): see Allen T. Hazen, *Samuel Johnson's Prefaces and Dedications*, 3, 32. It is noticeable that each work deals modestly with a small area of a large subject.

4. *Vanity of Human Wishes*, line 156.
5. He jestingly challenged Hester Thrale at small talk and at writing about nothing (*Letters*, nos 408, 559; cf. above, p.71).
6. William Vesterman finds that after writing of success in his early works he then concentrated, through two decades which included the *Dictionary*, on the theme of failure: *The Stylistic Life of Samuel Johnson*, 54. Cyril H. Knoblauch finds that 'he is invariably more sensitive to the failure of writing than to its success' ('Samuel Johnson and the composing process', *ECS*, 13 (1979–80), 243).
7. Cf. Howard Weinbrot, 'Samuel Johnson's *Plan* and Preface to the *Dictionary*', in *New Aspects of Lexicography*, ed. Weinbrot (1972), 73–94.
8. Erich Auerbach discusses the impact of this idea on Western thinking: *Mimesis*, transl. Trask, 151 and *passim*.
9. Erskine-Hill, 'Johnson and the petty particular', 46.
10. E.g. Donald C. Mell, 'Johnson's moral elegiacs: theme and structure in "On the Death of Robert Levet"', *Genre*, 5 (1972), 296; Erskine-Hill, 'Petty particular', 46. T.F. Wharton maintains that Levet becomes heroic, one of the 'Johnsonian supermen', by having no imagination (*Theme of Hope*, 162, 163).
11. According to George Steevens in the *GM* (Boswell, I, 243, n.3).
12. Gray, *Elegy written in a Country Church-Yard*, lines 29ff.
13. Vesterman calls it 'the speaker's rebuke to himself' (*Stylistic Life*, 131).
14. Johnson, *Works*, V, 1; *The Prelude*, 1850, I, 268–9; 1805–6, I, 270–1.
15. A fine example of the 'vigorous contraction of some thoughts' which Johnson found in *An Essay on Man* (II, 4; *Lives*, III, 244).
16. Boswell, IV, 139: capitals not in Yale edn.
17. Johnson may have had in mind Isaac Watts's five lyric odes on 'Death and Heaven'. The first begins:

> How am I held a Prisoner now,
>   Far from my God! This mortal Chain
> Binds me to Sorrow.. . .

The next includes:

> triumphant Stroke,
> That rends the Prison of my Clay,
> And I can feel by Fetters broke!

Reliquiae Juveniles (1734), 246–7.

LIST OF
WORKS CITED

Place of publication is given only when it is outside the United Kingdom.
Loeb Library editions of classical authors have been used except where otherwise stated.
Shakespeare has been quoted from the Arden edition. For ease of reference available cheap editions of eighteenth-century novels and poems have sometimes been used.

Abbott, John L., 'Dr. Johnson and the making of "The Life of Father Paul Sarpi"', *BJRL*, *48* (1965–6)

Adams, Percy G., 'The anti-hero in eighteenth-century fiction', *Studies in the Literary Imagination*, *9* (1976)

Algarotti, Francesco (trans. Elizabeth Carter), *Sir Issac Newton's Philosophy Explain'd For the Use of the Ladies* (1739)

Alkon, Paul, K., *Samuel Johnson and Moral Discipline* (Evanston, Ill., 1967)

—, 'Johnson's conception of admiration', *PQ*, *48* (1969)

Annual Register . . . For the year 1759 (1759)

Arblay, Frances D', *Diaries and Letters*, ed [Charlotte Frances Barrett] (1842–6)

—, *Memoirs of Doctor Burney, Arranged from his own Manuscripts, from Family Papers, and from Personal Recollections* (1832)

—, *The Wanderer, or Female Difficulties* (1814)

Atkinson, A.D., 'Dr. Johnson and Newton's *Opticks*', *RES*, n.s. *2* (1951)

Auden, W.H., *Collected Shorter Poems 1927–1957* (1966)

Auerbach, Erich, *Mimesis, The Respresentation of Reality in Western Literature*, Berne, 1946, trans. W.R. Trask (Princeton, 1968, repr. 1974)

Bailey, Nathan, *Dictionarium Britannicum* (1730)

—, *Universal Etymological English Dictionary* (1721 and later editions), eventually incorporated in the *Dict. Brit.*

Basney, Lionel, 'Johnson on Metaphysical poetry and semantic change', *SBHT*, *16* (1975).

Bate, Walter Jackson, *The Achievement of Samuel Johnson* (New York, 1955)

—, *Samuel Johnson* (1975)

—, 'Johnson and satire manqué', in *Eighteenth-Century Studies*, ed W.H. Bond (1970)

Bayle, Pierre, *A General Dictionary, Historical and Critical*, translated and revised (1734–41)

Becker, Carol, 'Johnson's "The Vanity of Human Wishes" lines 285–90', *N & Q*, *222* (1977)

Berland, K.J.H., 'Johnson's life-writing and the Life of Dryden', *Eighteenth Century*, *23* (1982–3)

Bernard, F.V., 'Johnson and the authorship of four Debates', *PMLA*, *82* (1967)

—, 'A possible source for Johnson's Life of the King of Prussia', *PQ*, *47* (1968)

—, *Biographia Britannica, or the Lives of the Most Eminent Persons who have flourished in Great Britain and Ireland* (1747–66)

Blake, William, *Complete Writings*, ed. Geoffrey Keynes (1957, repr. 1966)

Bloom, Edward, A., *Samuel Johnson in Grub Street* (Providence, R.I., 1957)

—, 'Johnson on a free press: a study in liberty and subordination', *ELH*, *16* (1949)

—, 'Symbolic names in Johnson's periodical essays', *MLQ*, *13* (1952)

Bogel, Fredric V., 'The rhetoric of substantiality: Johnson and the later eighteenth century', *ECS*, *12* (1979)

—, 'Structure and substantiality in later eighteenth-century literature', *SBHT*, *15* (1974)

Bond, W.H. (ed.), *Eighteenth-Century Studies in Honor of Donald F. Hyde* (New York, 1970)

Booth, Wayne, C., *A Rhetoric of Irony* (1974)

Boulton, James. T., *The Language of Politics in the Age of Wilkes and Burke* (1963)

— (ed.), *Johnson, The Critical Heritage* (1971)

Bourne, Nicholas, publisher, re-issue of four earlier pamphlets on Drake: *Sir Francis Drake Revived; The World Encompassed; A Summarie and True Discoverie . . .; A Full Relation of Another Voyage* (1652–3)

Boyce, Benjamin, 'Johnson's *Life of Savage* and its literary background', *SP*, *53* (1956)

Boyd, D.V., 'Vanity and vacuity: a reading of Johnson's verse satires', *ELH*, *39* (1972)

Brack, O M, and Thomas Kaminski, 'Johnson, James, and the *Medicinal Dictionary*, *MP*, *81* (1984)

Bradford, C.B., 'Johnson's revision of the *Rambler*', *RES*, *15* (1939)

Burke, John, J. Jr, and Donald Kay (eds), *The Unknown Samuel Johnson* (Madison, Wis., 1983)

Burney, Frances, *see* Arblay, D'

Byrd, Max, *London Transformed: Images of the City in the Eighteenth Century* (1978)

—, 'Johnson's spiritual anxiety', *MP*, *78* (1981)

Carlson, Carl Lennart, *The First Magazine: A History of the Gentleman's Magazine, with an account of Dr. Johnson's editorial activity and of the notice given America in the magazine* (Providence, R.I., 1938)

Carlyle, Thomas, *Works* (1896–9), vol. V

Carnochan, W.B., *Confinement and Flight: An Essay on English Literature of the Eighteenth Century* (1977)

Chapin, Chester F., 'Johnson and Pascal', in *English Writers of the Eighteenth Century*, ed. Middendorf (1971)

Chapone, Hester, *Posthumous Works* (1807)

Chapple, J.A.V., 'Samuel Johnson's *Proposals for Printing the History of the Council of Trent*, [1738]', *BJRL*, *45* (1962–3)

Chesterfield, Philip Stanhope, Earl of, *Letters*, ed Bonamy Dobrée (1932)

Clifford, J.L., *Young Samuel Johnson* (1955)

Cobbett's Parliamentary History of England, *IX-XII* (1811–12)

C[okayne], G.E., *Complete Peerage*, ed. Vicary Gibbs *et al.* (1910–59)

Collins, J. Churton, 'Dr. Johnson's "Lives of the Poets"', *Quarterly Review*, *208* (1908)

Copley, J., 'Cowper on Johnson's Life of Milton', *N & Q*, *222* (1977)

Coxe, William, *Memoirs of the Life and Administration of Sir Robert Walpole*, new edn (1800)

Crouch, Nathaniel, *The English Hero, or Sr Francis Drake Reviv'd* (1692)

Cunningham, J.S., 'On mirth as it laughs in heaven: mirth and the "frigorifick wisdom"', in *Augustan Worlds: Essays in Honour of A.R. Humphreys*, ed. J.C. Hilson, M.M.B. Jones and J.R. Watson (1978)

Daiches, David, *Critical Approaches to Literature* (1956)

Damrosch, Leopold, Jr, *Samuel Johnson and the Tragic Sense* (Princeton, 1972)

—, *The Uses of Johnson's Criticism* (Charlottesville, Va., 1976)

Denham, Sir John, *Expans'd Hieroglyphicks: A Critical Edition of Sir John Denham's Cooper's Hill*, ed. Brendan O Hehir (Berkeley and Los Angeles, 1969)

Dillenberger, John, *Benjamin West, The Context of His Life's Work* (1977)

Doolittle, I.G., 'A first-hand account of the Commons Debate on the removal of Sir Robert Walpole, 13 Feb. 1741', *BIHR*, *53* (1980)

Dryden, *Poems*, ed. James Kinsley (1958)

Dussinger, John A., 'Style and intention in Johnson's *Life of Savage*', *ELH*, *37* (1970)

Eberwein, Robert, 'Samuel Johnson, George Cheyne, and the "Cone of Being"', *JHI*, *36* (1975)

Edinger, William, *Samuel Johnson, and Poetic Style* (1978)

Ehrenpreis, Irvin, *Literary Meaning and Augustan Values* (Charlottesville, Va., 1974)

—, *Swift: The Man, his Works and the Age*, I, (1962)

Elder, A. T., 'Thematic patterning and development in Johnson's essays', *SP*, *62* (1965)

Eliot, T. S., *Collected Poems 1909–1962* (1963)

Elledge, Scott, 'The background and development in English criticism of the theories of generality and particularity', *PMLA*, *62* (1947)

Erasmus, Desiderius, *Witt against Wisdom, or a Panegyrick upon Folly*, trans. [White Kennet] (1683)

Erskine-Hill, Howard, 'Johnson and the petty particular', *Transactions of the Johnson Society of Lichfield* (1976)

—, 'The political character of Samuel Johnson', in *Samuel Johnson*, ed. Grundy (1984)

Finch, Jeremiah, S., *Sir Thomas Browne, A Doctor's Life of Science and Faith* (New York, 1950)

Fix, Stephen, 'Distant genius: Johnson and the art of Milton's Life', *MP, 81* (1984)

—, 'Johnson on Shakespeare and Milton', paper at Johnson Bi-Centenary Conference, Pembroke College, Oxford, 10 July 1984

Flannagan, Roy, 'Bate's Samuel Johnson and Johnson's Life of Milton: puckish or perverse', *Milton Quarterly, 12* (1978)

Fleeman, J. D., *A Preliminary Handlist of Copies of Books associated with Dr. Samuel Johnson* (1984)

Folkenflik, Robert, *Samuel Johnson, Biographer* (1978)

—, (ed.), *The English Hero, 1660–1800* (1984)

—, 'The tulip and its streaks: contexts of *Rasselas* X', *Ariel, 9* (1978)

Fox, Denton, review of Thomas Urquhart's *The Jewel*, in *London Review of Books, 6*, no. 17 (1984)

Franklin, Benjamin, *Mr Franklin, A Selection from his Personal Letters*, ed. L. W. Labaree and W. J. Bell, Jr (1956)

Freed, Lewis, *The Sources of Johnson's Dictionary*, Cornell Ph.D. thesis (1939)

Frye, Northrop, *Anatomy of Criticism: Four Essays* (Princeton, 1957)

Fussell, Paul, *The Rhetorical World of Augustan Humanism, Ethics and Imagery from Swift to Burke* (1965)

—, *Samuel Johnson and the Life of Writing* (1972)

Gay, John, *Letters*, ed. C.F. Burgess (1966)

Gentleman's Magazine, The, VIII (1738ff.)

Giddings, Robert, 'The fall of Orgilio: Samuel Johnson as parliamentary reporter', in *Samuel Johnson*, ed. Grundy (1984)

Gifford, Henry, '*The Vanity of Human Wishes*', *RES*, n.s. 5 (1955)

Goad, Caroline, *Horace in the English Literature of the Eighteenth Century* (New Haven, 1918)

Gray, Thomas, and William Collins, *Poetical Works*, ed. Roger Lonsdale (1977)

Greene, Donald J., *The Politics of Samuel Johnson* (New Haven, 1960)

—, *Samuel Johnson's Library, An Annotated Guide* (Victoria, B.C., 1975)

—, 'Johnson, Stoicism, and the good life', in *The Unknown Samuel Johnson*, ed. Burke and Kay (1983)

—, 'Some notes on Johnson and the *Gentleman's Magazine*', *PMLA, 79* (1959)

Greer, Germaine, *The Obstacle Race: The Fortune of Women Painters and their Work* (1979)

Griffin, Dustin A., *Alexander Pope; The Poet in the Poems* (1978)

—, 'Johnson's funeral writings', *ELH, 41* (1974)

Grundy, Isobel (ed.), *Samuel Johnson: New Critical Essays* (1984)

—, 'Samuel Johnson: a writer of lives looks at death', *MLR, 79* (1984)

—, 'Samuel Johnson: man of maxims?', in *Samuel Johnson*, ed. Grundy (1984)

Hardy, John, 'Johnson's *London*: the country versus the city', in *Studies in the Eighteenth Century: Papers Presented at the David Nichol Smith Memorial Seminar, Canberra, 1966*, ed. R. F. Brissenden (1968)

Hardy, Thomas, *Complete Poems*, ed James Gibson (1976)

Hart, Jeffrey, 'Johnson's *A Journey to the Western Islands*: history as art', *EIC, 10* (1960)

Hawkins, Sir John, *The Life of Samuel Johnson, LL.D.*, ed. and abridged by Bertram H. Davis (1962)

Hazen, Allen T., *Samuel Johnson's Prefaces and Dedications* (New Haven, 1937)

Hazlitt, William, *Lectures on the English Comic Writers* (1819)

Henson, Eithne, 'Johnson's romance imagery', *Prose Studies, 8* (1985)

—, 'Johnson's quest for "the fictions of romantic chivalry in Scotland', *Prose Studies, 7* (1984)

Hill, George Birkbeck, *Footsteps of Dr. Johnson* (1980)

—, (ed.) *Johnsonian Miscellanies* (1897, repr. 1966)

Hilles, Frederick W. (ed.), *New Light on Dr. Johnson: Essays on the Occasion of his 250th Birthday* (New Haven, 1959)

—, and Harold Bloom (eds), *From Sensibility to Romanticism, Essays Presented to Frederick A. Pottle* (New York, 1965)

—, 'Johnson's poetic fire', in *From Sensibility to Romanticism*, ed. Hilles and Bloom (1965)

Hobbes, Thomas, *Leviathan* (1651), ed. C.B. Macpherson (1968)

Hogarth, William, *Anecdotes of William Hogarth, Written by Himself* (1833)

Hoover, Benjamin Beard, *Samuel Johnson's Parliamentary Reporting, Debates in the Senate of Lilliput* (Berkeley and Los Angeles, 1953)

Hopkins, Robert H., 'Swift and the senses', in *Greene Centennial Essays*, ed. Korshin and Allen (1984)

Houston, Percy Hazen, *Dr. Johnson, A Study in Eighteenth Century Humanism* (Cambridge, Mass., 1923)

Hughes, Peter, 'Restructuring literary history: implications for the eighteenth century', *NLH*, 8 (1977)

Hume, David, *Essays and Treatises on Several Subjects* (1768)

Isles, Duncan, 'The Lennox Collection', *Harvard Library University Bulletin*, 18, 19 (1970, 1971)

Johnson, Samuel (see also abbreviations listed above p.vii)

—, *A Dictionary of the English Language* (1755; 4th edn, rev., 1773)

—, *Letters*, ed. G.B. Hill (1892)

—, *Samuel Johnson*, ed. Donald Greene (Oxford Authors) (1984)

—, *Shorter Prose*, ed. Donald Greene and O M Brack, Jr (forthcoming)

Johnston, Shirley White, 'From Preface to practice: Samuel Johnson's editorship of Shakespeare', in *Greene Centennial Essays*, ed. Korshin and Allen (1984)

Jung, C.G., *Aeon, Researches into the Phenomenology of the Self: Collected Works*, ed. H. Read *et al.* (1953–64)

Kaul, R.K., '*A Journey to the Western Islands* reconsidered', *EIC*, 13 (1963)

Kay, D.C., 'Thomson, Donne, and Wordsworth's "monstrous ant-hill"', *N & Q*, 229 (1984)

Keast, William R., 'Johnson and intellectual history', in *New Light on Dr. Johnson*, ed. Hilles (1959)

—, 'Johnson and intellectual history', *PQ*, 27 (1948)

Kelly, George Armstrong, 'The history of the new hero: eulogy and its sources in eighteenth-century France', *The Eighteenth Century: Theory and Interpretation*, 21 (1980)

Kinkead-Weekes, Mark, 'Johnson on "the rise of the novel"', in *Samuel Johnson*, ed. Grundy (1984)

Knoblauch, Cyril, 'Samuel Johnson and the composing process', *ECS*, 13 (1979–80)

Knox, Norman, *The Word* Irony *and its Context, 1500–1755* (Durham, N.C., 1961)

Kolb, Gwin J., 'The early reception of *Rasselas*' in *Greene Centennial Essays*, ed. Korshin and Allen (1984)

—, 'The use of Stoical doctrines in *Rasselas*, chapter XVIII', *MLN*, 68 (1953)

— and Ruth A. Kolb, 'The selection and use of the illustrative quotations in Dr. Johnson's *Dictionary*', in *New Aspects of Lexicography*, ed. Weinbrot (1972)

— and J. H. Sledd, 'The Reynolds copy of Johnson's *Dictionary*', *BJRL*, 37 (1954–5)

Korshin, Paul J., and Robert R. Allen (eds) *Greene Centennial Essays: Essays presented to Donald Greene in the Centennial Year of the University of Southern California* (Charlottesville, Va., 1984)

Koyré, Alexandre, *From the Closed World to the Infinite Universe* (Baltimore, 1957, repr. 1970)

Krieger, Murray, 'Fiction, nature, and the literary kinds in Johnson's criticism of Shakespeare', *ECS*, 4 (1971)

Lascelles, Mary, 'Johnson and commemorative writing', in *Samuel Johnson*, ed. Grundy (1984)

—, 'Johnson and Juvenal', in *New Light on Johnson*, ed. Hilles (1959)

Leed, Jacob, 'Johnson, DuHalde, and the Life of Confucius', *BNYPL*, 70 (1966)

Lipking, Lawrence, *The Ordering of the Arts in Eighteenth-Century England* (Princeton, 1970)

—, 'Learning to read Johnson: *The Vision of Theodore* and *The Vanity of Human Wishes*', *ELH*, *43* (1976)

Lock, F.P., *The Politics of* Gulliver's Travels (1980)

Locke, John, *An Essay Concerning Human Understanding* (1690), abridged and ed. A.D. Woozley (1964, repr. 1975)

—, *Second Treatise of Government* (1698)

London Magazine, The, VII, 1738ff.

Longinus, *On the Sublime*, trans. A.O. Prickard (1906, repr. 1949)

Lovejoy, Arthur O., *The Great Chain of Being, A Study of the History of an Idea* (Cambridge, Mass., 1936 repr. 1970)

McAdam, E.L. Jr, *Dr. Johnson and the English Law* (Syracuse, N.Y., 1951)

—, 'Johnson's Lives of Sarpi, Blake, and Drake', *PMLA*, *58* (1943)

Mackenzie, George, *The Lives and Characters of the most Eminent Writers of the Scots Nation* (1708–22)

McIntosh, Carey, *The Choice of Life, Samuel Johnson and the World of Fiction* (1973)

—, 'Johnson's debate with Stoicism', *ELH*, *33* (1966)

Manlove, C.L., *Literature and Reality, 1600–1800* (1978)

Martin, Benjamin, *Lingua Britannica Reformata: Or, A New English Dictionary* (1749)

Mell, Donald C., Jr, 'Johnson's moral elegiacs: theme and structure in "On the Death of Robert Levet"', *Genre*, *5* (1972)

Middendorf, John H. (ed.), *English Writers of the Eighteenth Century* (1971)

—, 'Johnson as editor: some proofs of the "Prefaces"', in *Eighteenth-Century Studies*, ed. Bond (1970)

Milton, John, *Poems*, ed. John Carey and Alistair Fowler (1968)

Montagu, Elizabeth, *An Essay on the Writings and Genius of Shakespear* (1769)

Montagu, Lady Mary Wortley, *Complete Letters*, ed. Robert Halsband (1965–7)

Moody, Dorothy, 'Johnson's translation of Addison's "Battle of the Cranes and Pygmies"', *MLR*, *31* (1936)

Moore, R.E., 'Dr. Johnson on Fielding and Richardson', *PMLA*, *66* (1951)

Mudford, William, *Nubilia in Search of a Husband, including Sketches of Modern Society, and Interspersed with Moral and Literary Disquisitions* (1809)

Nicolson, Marjorie Hope, *Mountain Gloom and Mountain Glory: The Development of the Aesthetics of the Infinite* (Ithaca, N.Y., 1959)

—, *Science and Imagination* (Ithaca, N.Y., 1956)

Novak, Maximillian E., 'Johnson, Dryden, and the wild vicissitudes of taste', in *The Unknown Samuel Johnson*, ed. Burke and Kay (1983)

O'Flaherty, Patrick, 'The art of Johnson's *London*', in *A Festschrift for Edgar Ronald Seary* (St Johns, Newfoundland, 1975)

—, 'Johnson as satirist: a new look at *The Vanity of Human Wishes*', *ELH*, *34* (1967)

—, 'Johnson's *Idler*: the equipment of a satirist', *ELH*, *37* (1970)

—, 'The Rambler's rebuff to Juvenal: Johnson's pessimism reconsidered', *English Studies*, *51* (1970)

O Hehir, Brendan, *see* Denham

Oakleaf, David, '*Trompe L'Oeil*: Gulliver and the distortions of the observing eye', *UTQ*, *53* (1983–4)

Osler, Margaret J., 'Certainty, scepticism, and scientific optimism: the roots of eighteenth-century attitudes toward scientific knowledge', in *Probability, Time, and Space in Eighteenth-Century Literature*, ed. Paula R. Backscheider (1979)

Ovid, *Metamorphoses, Translated by the Most Eminent Hands* (1717)

Pascal, Blaise, *Oeuvres Complètes*, ed. J. Chevalier (Paris, 1957)

Pierce, Charles E., Jr., *The Religious Life of Samuel Johnson* (1983)

Piozzi, Hester Lynch, *Anecdotes of the late Samuel Johnson, LL.D., during the Last Twenty Years of his Life* (1786), ed. Arthur Sherbo (1974)

—, *Thraliana, The Diary of Mrs. Hester Lynch Thrale (Later Mrs. Piozzi) 1776–1809*, ed. K.C. Balderston (1942, 2nd edn 1951)

Pope, Alexander, *Poems*, ed. John Butt *et al.*, (1940–69): *Iliad* and *Odyssey*, ed. Maynard Mack (1967)

Powell, L.F., 'An addition to the canon of Johnson's writings', *Essays and Studies by Members of the English Association, 28* (1942)

Price, Martin, *To the Palace of Wisdom, Studies in Order and Energy from Dryden to Blake* (Garden City, N.Y., 1964)

Quinlan, Maurice J., *Samuel Johnson, A Layman's Religion* (Madison, Wis., 1964)

Reade, Aleyn Lyell, *Johnsonian Gleanings* (1909–52)

Review of a Late Motion for an Address to his Majesty against a Certain Great Minister, A (1741)

Reynolds, Richard R., 'Johnson's heroes before the *Life of Savage*', *New Rambler, 16* (1975)

Rewa, Michael P., 'Aspects of rhetoric in Johnson's "professedly serious" *Rambler* essays', *Quarterly J of Speech, 56* (1970)

Richardson, Samuel, *Clarissa: or The History of a Young Lady* (1748–9, Everyman edn 1932, repr. 1976)

—, *The History of Sir Charles Grandison* (1754), ed. Jocelyn Harris (1972)

—, *Selected Letters*, ed. John Carroll (1964)

Rochester, John Wilmot, Earl of, *Complete Poems*, ed. David M. Vieth (1968)

—, *Poems*, ed. Keith Walker (1984)

Rogers, Pat, 'Gulliver's glasses', in *The Art of Jonathan Swift*, ed. C.T. Probyn (1978)

—, 'Johnson's *Lives of the Poets* and the Biographic Dictionaries', *RES, 31* (1980)

Rosenblum, Robert, *Transformations in Late Eighteenth Century Art* (Princeton, 1967)

Røstvig, Maren-Sofie, *The Happy Man, Studies in the Metamorphoses of a Classical Ideal* (Oslo and New York, 2nd edn 1962, 1971)

Rothstein, Eric, *Restoration and Eighteenth Century Poetry 1660–1780* (1981)

—, *Systems of Order and Inquiry in Later Eighteenth-Century Fiction* (1975)

Ruskin, John, *Works*, ed. E.T. Cook and A. Wedderburn (1903–12)

Sachs, Arieh, *Passionate Intelligence: Imagination and Reason in the Work of Samuel Johnson* (Baltimore, 1967)

—, 'Generality and particularity in Johnson's thought', *SEL, 5* (1965)

Savage, George H., "Roving among the Hebrides": the Odyssey of Samuel Johnson', *SEL, 17* (1977)

Schwartz, Richard B., *Samuel Johnson and the Problem of Evil* (1975)

—, 'Johnson's *Journey*', *JEGP, 69* (1970)

Scott, Geoffrey (ed.), *The Making of the Life of Johnson, as Shown in Boswell's First Notes* (Mount Vernon, N.Y., 1929): vol. VI of *The Private Papers of James Boswell from Malahide Castle.*

Sedgwick, Romney (ed.), *The History of Parliament: The House of Commons 1715–1754* (1970)

Shaftesbury, Anthony Ashley Cooper, Earl of, *Characteristics of Men, Manners, Opinions, Times* (1711), ed. J.M. Robertson (1900, repr. N.Y. 1964)

Sherbo, Arthur, *Samuel Johnson, Editor of Shakespeare, with an Essay on* The Adventurer, Illinois Studies in Language and Literature, no. 42 (Urbana, 1956)

—, 'Two notes on Johnson's revisions'. *MLR, 50* (1955)

Siebert, Donald T., Jr, 'The scholar as satirist: Johnson's edition of Shakespeare', *SEL, 15* (1975)

Spacks, Patricia Meyer, *An Argument of Images: The Poetry of Alexander Pope* (Cambridge, Mass., 1971)

Starnes, De Witt T., and Gertrude E. Noyes, *The English Dictionary from Cawdrey to Johnson 1604–1755* (Chapel Hill, N. C., 1946)

Stauffer, Donald A., *The Art of Biography in Eighteenth Century England* (Princeton, 1941)

Stevick, Philip, 'Miniaturization in eighteenth-century English literature', *UTQ, 38* (1969)

Stock, R. D., *Samuel Johnson and Neoclassical Dramatic Theory: The Intellectual Context of the Preface to Shakespeare* (Lincoln, Neb., 1973)

Swift, Jonathan, *Correspondence*, ed. Harold Williams (1963, repr. 1965)

—, *Poems*, ed. Harold Williams (1937)

—, *Prose Works*, ed. Herbert Davis (1939–68: vol. XI rev. 1959)

Temple, Sir William, *Five Miscellaneous Essays*, ed. S.H. Monk (Ann Arbor, Mich., 1963)

Thomson, James, *The Seasons* and *The Castle of Indolence*, ed. James Sambrook (1972)

Thrale, Hester Lynch, *see* Piozzi

Tillotson, Geoffrey, 'Imlac and the business of a poet', in *Studies in Criticism and Aesthetics, 1660–1800: Essays in Honor of Samuel Holt Monk*, ed. Howard Anderson and John S. Shea (Minneapolis, 1967)

Tracy, Clarence, *The Artificial Bastard, A Biography of Richard Savage* (1953)

—, 'Democritus, arise! A study of Dr. Johnson's humour', *Yale Review, 39* (1949–50)

Uphaus, Robert W., *The Impossible Observer: Reason and the Reader in 18th-Century Prose* (Lexington, Kentucky, 1979)

Urquhart, Sir Thomas, *Ekskubalauron: or, The Discovery of A most exquisite Jewel*, ed. R. D. S. Jack and R. J. Lyall (1984)

Vesterman, William, *The Stylistic Life of Samuel Johnson* (New Brunswick, N.J., 1977)

Voitle, Robert, *Samuel Johnson the Moralist* (Cambridge, Mass., 1961)

—, 'Stoicism and Samuel Johnson', *SP*, extra series no 4 (1967)

Walker, Daniel Pickering, *The Decline of Hell, Seventeeth-Century Discussion of Eternal Torment* (1964)

Walker, Robert G., *Eighteenth-Century Arguments for Immortality and Johnson's* Rasselas (Victoria, B.C., 1977)

Wardropper, Bruce W., 'The epic hero superseded', in *Concepts of the Hero in the Middle Ages and the Renaissance*, ed. Norman T. Burns and Christopher Reagan (1976)

Watkins, W.B.C., *Johnson and English Poetry before 1660* (Princeton, 1936)

Watt, Ian, 'The ironic tradition in Augustan prose from Swift to Johnson', in *Stuart and Georgian Moments*, Clark Library Seminar Papers on Seventeenth- and Eighteenth-Century English Literature, ed. Earl Miner (Berkeley and Los Angeles, 1972)

Watts, Isaac, *Divine Songs Attempted in Easy Language for the Use of Children* (1715)

—, *Horae Lyricae, Poems Chiefly of the Lyric Kind* (1706, 2nd edn 1709)

—, *Reliquiae Juveniles: Miscellaneous Thoughts in Prose and Verse* (1734)

—, *Works* (1753, repr. 1810)

Weinbrot, Howard D., *The Formal Strain, Studies in Augustan Imitation and Satire* (Chicago, 1969)

—, (ed.), *New Aspects of Lexicography: Literary Criticism, Intellectual History, and Social Change* (1972)

—, 'The reader, the general, and the particular: Johnson and Imlac in chapter ten of *Rasselas*', *ECS, 5* (1971)

—, 'No "mock debate": questions and answers in *The Vanity of Human Wishes*', *MLQ, 41* (1980)

—, 'Samuel Johnson's *Plan* and Preface to the *Dictionary*: the growth of a lexicographer's mind', in *New Aspects of Lexicography*, ed. Weinbrot (1972)

Welcher, J.K., and G.E. Bush (eds), *Gulliveriana* (Gainesville, Fla, 1970–4)

Wesling, Donald, 'An ideal of greatness: ethical implications in Johnson's critical vocabulary', *UTQ, 34* (1964–5)

Wharton, T.F., *Samuel Johnson and the Theme of Hope* (1984)

White, Ian, 'The Vanity of Human Wishes', *Cambridge Quarterly, 6* (1974)

Wiltshire, John, 'Dr. Johnson's seriousness', *Critical Rev.* (Melbourne, Sydney), *10* (1967)

Wimsatt, William Kurtz, *The Prose Style of Samuel Johnson* (New Haven, 1941, repr. 1963)

—, *Philosophic Words: A Study of Style and Meaning in the* Rambler *and* Dictionary *of Samuel Johnson* (New Haven, 1948)

Woodruff, James F., 'The allusions in Johnson's *Idler* no. 40', *MP, 76* (1979)

—, 'Johnson's *Idler* and the anatomy of idleness', *English Studies in Canada, 6* (1980)

— '*Rasselas* and the traditions of "Menippean satire"', in *Samuel Johnson*, ed. Grundy (1984)

Wordsworth, William, *Poetical Works*, ed. T. Hutchinson, rev. E. de Selincourt (1904, repr. 1961)

Yeats, W. B., *Collected Poems* (1965)

INDEX

Abbott, J. L., 256–7
Achilles, 144, 178, 187, 191; in *Iliad*, 179–80, 190, 204
Adams, George, 234 and n.3
Adams, Percy G., 255
Addison, Joseph: Johnson on, 36, 76, 124–5, 127, 145, 204, 218, 227–8, 229, 230; and malignity, 145; and Lucretius, 167, in *Dictionary*, 210; and Pope, 229, 230; and cosmos, 243; Battle of the Pygmies and 'Cranes', 5–6, 20; *Cato*, 187, 227; essays, 69, 76, 134, 167, 173 and n.47, 204, 210, 243
Aeneas, 71, 179
Africa, 20
Ajax, 180
Alexander the Great, 74, 178–186 *passim*, 201; in *Vanity of Human Wishes*, 166; Pope on, 181
Algarotti, Francesco, 242
Alkon, Paul, 247, 250
Allèn, Ralph, 229
Allen, Mrs Elizabeth, 229
America, 7, 83–4, 86, 126, 138, 190–1
Arblay, D', Frances, see Burney
Archimedes, 68, 69
Argyll, Archibald Campbell, Duke of (formerly Lord Islay), 56, 59
Argyll, John Campbell, Duke of, 55, 56
Aristotle, 1, 104, 105, 116
Ashbourne, 70, 79
Aston, Elizabeth, 71
Atkinson, A. D., 243, 244
Auden, Wystan Hugh, 180
Auerbach, Erich, 244, 259
Augustus, Emperor, 183
Auknasheals, Ross, 75
Austria, 59, 198–9

Bacon, Sir Francis, 155; in *Dictionary*, 69, 242
Bailey, Nathan, 13 n.1, 251
Baker, Henry, 24, 25
Baretti, Giuseppe, 70
Barnard, Sir John, 60
Barretier, Philip, 192, 193
Barthius (Kaspar von Barth), 187
Basney, Lionel, 253
Bate, Walter Jackson, 3, 26, 102, 131 and n.15, 155, 246, 247, 249, 251

Bavaria, see Charles Albert
Bayle, Pierre, 257
Becker, Carol, 254
Beckford, William, 141
Bellarmino, Roberto Francesco, 103
Bentley, Richard, 32
Berland, K. J. H., 247, 258
Bernard, F. V., 197, 245, 246
Bible: in *Dictionary*, 4, 150; Sir Thomas Browne and, 64; Old Testament, 160; Daniel, 227–8 and n.20; Ecclesiasticus, 100; Ephesians, 121 and n.4; Genesis, 4, 160; Isaiah, 5; Job, 160, 161; Judges, 150; Luke, 1 and n.3, 206 and n.1, 243; Matthew 1 and n.3, 213 and n.4; Proverbs, 150 and n.32, 163, 164, 169; Psalms, 160; St John 1, 129
Biographia Britannica, 9, 258
Blackmore, Sir Richard, 215, 222, 225
Blake, Robert, 43, 192, 193
Blake, William, 32, 251
Blenheim, battle of, 152
Bloom, Edward A., 41, 45, 66, 87, 248
Blount, Martha, 229, 231
Blount, Teresa, 98
Boerhaave, Herman, 3, 193, 194, 195
Bogel, Fredric V., 187 and n.34, 243
Booth, Wayne C., 254
Boothby, Hill, 242
Boswell, James: and Mrs Bruce, 74; on *False Alarm*, 85; Johnson advises, 98; and Johnson's talk, 102, 107; and 'particularities', 216; on *Idler*, 248
  Life of Johnson, 1 and n.2, 8, 10, 18, 32, 36, 80 and n.6, 108, 124, 134 and n.2, 136, 161–2, 179 and n. 7, 182–3, 186, 237, 245, 248, 258
Boulton, James T., 174
Bourne, Nicholas, 256, 257
Boyce, Benjamin, 251
Boyd, D. V., 159
Brack, OM, 245, 256
Bradford, C. B., 79 and n.2
Britain, see England
Bronson, Bertrand H., 250
Browne, Sir Thomas, 63–5, 77, 111
Bruce, Mrs, 74, 75, 238
Buchan, Buller of, 172

Shakespeare, 204, 226; and other writers, 226; and Pope, 230, 231–2; and scale, 242
  Examen Poeticum, 181 and n.17; *The Hind and the Panther*, 1; Juvenal trans., 25; Lucretius trans., 154, 166; plays, 141, 187, 255; Virgil trans., 71
Dussinger, John A., 179

Eberwein, Robert, 243
Edinger, William C., 179, 254
Ehrenpreis, Irvin, 180–1, 245
Elder, A. T., 121, 248, 255
Eliot, George, 69
Eliot, Thomas Stearns, 177 and n.2
Elledge, Scott, 254
England (see also Parliament): and Ireland, 38, 39; and Spain, 44, 46, 86; trade of, 49–50; and France, 55–6, 95, 195; foreign relations of, 84, 99, 195–7
Epictetus, 74, 247
Epicureans, 165–7, 168, 171
Erasmus, Desiderius, 154, 169, 181, 184, 252
Erskine-Hill, Howard, 3, 236, 252, 254, 258
Europe, 44ff., 195–200; Europeans, 150

Fenton, Elijah, 218
Fielding, Henry: and greatness, 1, 3, 5, 181, 184; Johnson and, 5, 135, 171, 181–4; and malignity, 135, 150, 251; and Stoicism, 171; and heroes, 181, 182, 183;
  Covent Garden Journal, 181; *Jonathan Wild*, 1, 3, 181, 184; *Joseph Andrews*, 135, 171, 181, 249; *Tom Jones*, 135, 181 and n.18, 191, 251; *Tom Thumb*, 5, 181
Fix, Stephen, 258
Flannagan, Roy, 103 and n.4
Fleeman, J. D., 253
Folkenflik, Robert, 170, 247, 250, 254, 256, 258
Fontenelle, Bernard le Bovier de, 192
Ford, Cornelius, 102
Fowler, Alistair, 242
Fox, Denton, 250
Fox, Henry, 48, 55
France: as Blefuscu, 48, 55, 56; and England, 55–6, 95, 195–6; and Canada, 99; mobs in, 181; French in London, 187; in Seven Years War, 198
Franklin, Benjamin, 172
Frederick the Great: in Johnson's life, 29, 85, 195–200, 201; in *Idler*, 96, 98
Frederick William of Prussia, 20, 197, 198, 199
Freed, Lewis, 37 and n.14, 245

Frye, Northrop, 118, 257
Fussell, Paul, 3 and n.8, 5, 118, 241, 242, 244, 248, 254

Galileo, Galilei, 30
Ganges, River, 25, 110
Garrick, David, 219
Gay, John: and parody, 47–8; Johnson on, 218, 220, 226
Gentleman, Francis, 245
Gentleman's Magazine, The (see Johnson: Works: Debates, 40ff.; Early Lives, 192ff.; State of Affairs in Lilliput, 41ff.): Swift in, 41; and ban on parliamentary reporting, 41ff.; readers of, 43, 44, 47; 'Eubulus' letter, 43; 'T. B.' in, 43; advertisement, 1738, 45; prefaces, 45; index to, 61; 'Foreign History', 197; Verecundus letter, 248; Steevens in, 259
George II, 46, 218
Germany, Francis of Lorraine, Emperor of, 96, 97 and n.20
Giddings, Robert, 246, 247
Gifford, Henry, 254
Goad, Caroline, 250
Goldsmith, Oliver, 32
Gower, John, 255
Graham, Billy, 253
Gray, Thomas: and greatness, 1, 2–3, 21, 219–20, 232, 236; and community, 124; Johnson on, 219–20, 232, 236
  Elegy, 124, 236; 'Ode on the Spring', 21; odes, 219–20, 232; 'Progress of Poesy', 1, 2–3
Great Chain of Being, The, 21–2, 121, 156, 203
Greek Anthology, The, 66, 74, 180
Greeks, 188
Greene, Donald J., 40 and n.28, 245, 249, 253
Greer, Germaine, 241
Griffin, Dustin H., 247, 254
Grove, Henry, 243
Grundy, Isobel, 244, 247, 249, 250, 255
Guardian, The, 229
Guthrie, William, 246
Gwynn, John, 248

Hadrian, Emperor, 86
Halifax, George Montagu, Earl of, 219
Halifax, George Montagu Dunk, Earl of, 246
Hanmer, Sir Thomas, 246
Hardwicke, Philip Yorke, Earl of, 60, 191–2
Hardy, John, 256

Hardy, Thomas, 148
Harleian Library, The, 75
Harrington, Jonathan, 255
Harrison, William, 34
Hart, Jeffrey, 247, 256
Hawkesworth, John, 250
Hawkins, Sir John: on Johnson, 6–7, 16, 93, 100, 102–3, 104, 107, 184, 185, 203, 249, 250; on *Adventurer*, 250; on *Idler*, 93; on Shakespeare preface, 6, 16, 103, 115, 203
Hazen, Allen T., 258
Hazlitt, William, 250
Hebrides: Johnson on (see also Highlands), 6, 19, 73, 124, 159, 167, 179, 185, 188–91
Hector, 144, 179, 180
Henson, Eithne, 179 and n.6, 256
Herbert, George, 77
Hercules, 116, 152, 185, 237; death of, 72, 179–80, 187; Swift on, 181; and *Vanity of Human Wishes*, 200
Hervey, John, Lord, 46, 56–9
Highlands: Johnson on, 73ff., 125, 157, 163, 172, 188, 190–1
Hill, Aaron, 137
Hill, George Birkbeck, 247, 256
Hilles, Frederick W., 159
Hobbes, Thomas, 8, 105, 106, 133
Hogarth, William, 85, 105
Holder, William, 21
Homer: 64; Johnson and, 1, 73, 103, 124, 155, 169, 179–80, 188, 209, 224; heroes of, 1, 179–80, 181, 188; Milton and, 224, 227 *Iliad*, 1, 73, 103, 160, 179–80 and n.9, 190; *Odyssey*, 155
Hoover, Benjamin Beard, 40 and n.29, 42 and nn.35 and 36, 47, 50, 53, 54–5, 56, 247, 257
Hopkins, Robert H., 243
Horace (Quintus Horatius Flaccus): Johnson and, 72, 114, 115, 155, 165
Houghton Hall, Norfolk, 56
Houston, Percy Hazen, 187 and n.33
Howe, John, 48
Hughes, John: Johnson on, 9, 11, 123, 193
Hughes, Peter, 255
Hume, David, 17, 149, 167

Imperialis, Joannes, 114
Iona, Island of, 73, 179
Ireland, 38, 39, 228
Islay, Lord, see Argyll, Duke of (Archibald Campbell)
Isles, Duncan, 249

Jenyns, Soame (for review of, see Johnson: Works: Jenyns review): Johnson and, 22, 25, 148, 149, 152–3; and Great Chain, 22, 156
Johnson, Andrew, 102, 250
Johnson, Esther (Stella), 7, 37
Johnson, Samuel:
I. LIFE:
At Ashbourne, 70, 79; his books, 157, 166, 168, 169; and Fanny Burney, 103; career, 102–3, 213; combativeness, 7, 62, 102–3; competitiveness, 102–3; as editor, 40, 46; health, 71, 72; and Harleian Library, 75; head for heights, 171–2; at Lichfield, 70–1; mathematics, love of, 17, 83, 157; and orange peel, 216; at Oxford, 102, 166; physical activity, 20, 102; and romances, 179; in Scotland, 19, 20, 73–5, 157, 172, 179, 191; self-examination, 83; sensitivity, 70, 141; short sight, 156; and Society for Encouragement of Arts and Commerce, 255; talk, 7, 102, 103, 107, 108, 119, 161–2, 179, 206, 254;
II. LITERARY TECHNIQUES (This and the following two sections are necessarily incomplete, but may nevertheless be useful as pointers.)
aphorisms, 60, 234; belittling, 40ff., 61, 62, 94, 198–200, 212–3, 217ff.; contempt, 79, 81–2, 83–4, 87, 94; detail, 94; diction, 99, 130–1, 157, 177–8, 182, 189, 190, 193, 209–10, 213, 225–6; double perspective, 3, 6, 11, 32, 40, 57–8, 112, 157, 170–1, 188ff., 215ff., 235, 238–9; humour, 19, 20, 40, 41, 46, 48, 52–3, 68, 70, 71, 72, 92ff., 96, 151, 206–7, 209–10; imagery, 11, 25–32, 39–40, 55–6, 67, 72, 85–6, 107, 111, 121, 139, 144–5, 149, 151–2, 164, 170, 172, 173, 179, 183, 185–6, 191–2, 200–4, 207, 236–8, 239; interweaving of themes, 10–11, 36, 37; irony, 48–9, 53, 55, 59, 94–5, 117–8, 131, 182, 222–3; naming, 43, 66, 68–9, 86ff., 93, 155, 236; oblique openings, 42, 49; participation by himself, 7, 66–7, 69, 75, 93, 100, 101, 108, 111–2, 131 and n.15, 132, 142, 143, 155, 174–5, 206, 209, 210, 236–7, 239; periphrasis, 9–10, 118; personae, 41, 42, 43, 84–5, 93, 96–7, 99, 108; puns, 90, 222; reductionism, 26, 62, 95; reversals of argument, 118, 147, 215; satire, 61, 86ff., 94, 165, 209–10; shift in scale, 36, 48, 60,

61; structure, 11, 163, 198; style, 47, 50, 67, 95; tone, 53–4; truisms, 71

III. MIND AND OPINIONS:

development of ideas: 193–5, 200, 202, 235, 236

on admiration, 115; on advice, 103–4, 112; on biography, 62–3, 185, 186; on chance, 186, 213–4; on children, 108, 146–7; and Christianity, 1–2, 65, 77, 83, 100, 120–1, 129, 132, 133, 148, 160–3, 167, 174, 176, 227–8, 235–9; on colonialism, 20, 150, 196–7; concrete and abstract, 4–5, 11, 14, 18, 20–1; contraries, 13–14, 19, 56ff.; and cosmos, 21–7, 183, 237; critical judgments, 16–19, 32–3; on critical theory, 211; on death, 9–10, 68, 69, 97, 117–9, 122–3, 128, 162, 193, 201, 204–5, 237–8, 239; on detail, 144, 170–1; on diaries, 80, 98; on diction, 82; on didacticism, 67, 69; English poetry, 142–5; and etymology, 234; on fame, 25–6, 212–3, 214; on fiction, 187; humility, 2; on general and particular, 58; on genius (literary), 2; on good humour, 67, 207; and Great Chain of Being, 22, 121; and great men, 184ff.; on history, 199, 206; on imagery, 18–19, 144, 155; on incongruity, 20; on intimacy, 128; and jokes, 8, 70; on journalism, 47, 52, 146; on letters, 70, 73, 76; on microscope and telescope, 29ff.; on native peoples, 20, 196; and *nothing*, 98–101; on parenthood, 146–7; on patronage, 87, 129; and politics, 43, 45, 47, 60, 83–5, 125–6, 147, 197, 200; and poverty, 17–18, 149; on progress of science, 123–4, 211; on relics, 91; and retirement, 98, 122, 167; and romances, 20, 179, 183, 187, 188; on rulers, 163–4; and slavery, 66; on sport, 139, 150–3; on Stoics and Epicureans, 165–7; on storms, 167; and Swift, 3–4, 5, 8, 11, 20, 28, 31, 34–62 *passim*, 80, 84, 85, 95, 99, 131–2, 134, 141, 142, 162 and n.18, 170, 173, 174, 182, 228–9, 233; and travel-writers, 18, 27; on truisms, 21, 71–2, 77; and veneration, 51, 52, 53, 184, 195, 214, 215, 216, 221; on versification, 76, 125; and war, 86, 140, 172–3, 182–3, 189–91, 195–200; on writers, 110–1, 112, 142–3, 154–60 *passim*, 170, 214, 218

IV. THEMES:

achievement, 1, 3, 4–5, 8–9, 102, 114; common life, 37, 49–50, 57–8, 67–9, 70,

77, 79–80, 86, 89, 97, 119, 128, 178, 185, 187, 191, 202–5, 207, 208, 214–5, 216–7, 221–32 *passim*, 236–9; community, 10, 38, 113, 120–32; comparison, 5, 11, 13–20, 54, 107, 184, 196, 233; competition, 8–10, 11, 102–20, 126, 130–1, 133, 141, 233; detail, 80; envy, 104, 108, 133, 135, 136–7, 145, 185, 192, 195; goodness and greatness, relation of, 2, 4–5, 10, 12, 13, 176–7, 234–6; greatness, 206–39; heroism, 116, 176–206, 237–8; human littleness, 7–8, 40–61 *passim*, 62–101, 208, 215–34 *passim*; isolation, 120, 126–7; malignity, 11, 38–9, 108, 133–53, 194; measuring, 6, 25, 26, 40, 80, 83, 177, 191; mutuality, 121, 129–32; perception, 6, 29–33, 80–1, 154–76 *passim*, 199; superior observers, 24–6, 59, 61, 66, 85, 100–1, 154–75, 233; superiority, 11, 12, 38, 52, 103–19 *passim*, 122, 127, 128, 141–7, 153, 195, 204ff., 233–4; ultimate scale, 6, 9, 28, 65, 77, 96, 97, 201, 239

V. WORKS:

dedications: 234; for Charlotte Lennox, 202

34, 47; no. 126, 73; no. 127, 169; no. 129, 108, 124; no. 130, 110–1; no. 131, 125; no. 133, 147–8 and n.26; no. 134, 93, 204; no. 135, 122; no. 136, 212, 214; no. 137, 67, 120, 127, 128–9, 183, 210, 211–2, 217; no. 141, 99; no. 142, 147–8, and n.26; no. 143, 142–3; no. 144, 136, 143–4, no. 145, 76, 180; no. 146, 122, 143, 209, 212 and n.3; no. 147, 66; no. 148, 129, 136, 146–7, 149, 151; no. 149, 87, 147–8 and n.26; no. 150, 210; no. 151, 122; no. 152, 70; no. 154, 112; no. 157, 89, 90, 208; no. 158, 155; no. 159, 89, 90, no. 161, 67–70; no. 162, 87; no. 163, 135; no. 164, 109; no. 165, 104, 108; no. 167, 143; no. 168, 82; no. 169, 90, 210; no. 170, 182 and n.22; no. 171, 156; no. 172, 108, 143; no. 174, 87–8; no. 175, 136, 143, 151–2; no. 176, 31, 141, 150, 152; no. 177, 90–1, 96; no. 180, 216, 217; no. 182, 87; no. 183, 102, 104, 133, 136–7, 142; no. 185, 2, 135, 234, 235; no. 186, 19; no. 188, 99, 130–1; no. 189, 87, 108; no. 190, 201; no. 192, 6; no. 193, 106, 209, 213–4; no. 195, 99; no. 196, 99; no. 198, 108; no. 200, 122–3, 126; no. 202, 17–18, 75, 82; no. 203, 100–1, 113; no. 204, 201; no. 205, 107; no. 206, 87, 89; no. 207, 210, 213; no. 208, 69

Rasselas, 9, 13, 48 and n.52, 50, 52–3, 132, 215, 224; double perception in, 3, 32; translations of, 7 and n.21; scale, 28–9; superiority in, 38, 154, 172; benefaction in, 122, 131, 147; malignity in, 136, 148, 150, 172; observation in, 154, 157, 158, 160, 161, 163–4, 169–71, 233

reviews (see also Jenyns): of Elizabeth Harrison, 63 and n.2; of Warton, 179 and n.6

Scriblerian works, 40, 41, 65

sermons, 213, 252; competition in, 8–9; periphrasis in, 9–10, 118; envy in, 104 no. 1, 247; no. 2, 148, 162; no. 3, 2, 110; no. 6, 162; no. 8, 157, 234; no. 10, 162; no. 11, 10, 38, 126, 163, 249; no. 12, 107, 113; no. 14, 105, 107–8; no. 16, 15; no. 17, 249, 252; no. 20, 252; no. 23, 126, 249; no. 26, 163, 164; no. 27, 126, 135

Shakespeare edn: 6, 93, 115; Johnson's criticism in, 103 notes, 31, 32–3, 80–1, 98, 141, 149, 155, 162–3, 172

preface, 20, 32, 52 and n.63, 111; comparison in 16–17; critical distance recommended, 31; tragi-comedy, 169 and n.34; dramatic illusion, 171, 179; imagery, 183, 203ff.; no heroes, 187, 202ff., 211; and perfection, 210; double perspective, 235, 238

'Short Song of Congratulation', 152

'State of Affairs in Lilliput' or 'Appendix to Capt. Lemuel Gulliver's Account', 41–5, 61, 196

Taxation no Tyranny, 83, 85, 86, 125–6

translations: Addison, 5–6, 20; from Greek, 66, 74, 180; Lobo, 252

Vanity of Human Wishes, 12 and n.29, 25, 26 and n.25, 27, 40 and n.25, 53–4, 57, 84, 102, 110, 116 and n.19, 117, 118, 119, 132, 137, 144, 146, 151, 157, 158–60, 161, 164, 166, 169, 172, 173, 176, 195, 197, 198, 199, 200–2, 204–5, 206, 212, 213, 214, 233, 236, 237, 238; and scale, 11; MS of, 174

verse, 41; to Hester Thrale, 37; early, 110

Vinerian lectures, 173, 182

'Vision of Theodore', 156, 172

World Displayed introduction, 20 and n.2, 150 and n.31

Yale ed., 39, 67, 92, 93, 142, 248–9, 250, 257

Johnson, Sarah, 97

Johnston, Shirley White, 248

Jonson, Ben, 173

Journals of the House of Commons, 53, 246

Jung, C. G., 203

Juvenal, 25, 200

Kaminski, Thomas, 256

Kaul, R. K., 256

Keast, William R., 6, 254

Kelly, George Armstrong, 256

Kennett, White, 154

Kinkead-Weekes, Mark, 251

Kirkall, Elisha, 255

Knoblauch, Cyril H., 259

Knox, Norman, 59 and n.77, 245

Kolb, Gwin J., 241, 244, 254

Kolb, Ruth A., 244

Koyré, Alexandre, 243

Krieger, Murray, 203

La Bruyère, Jean de, 27

La Rochefoucault, François, duc de, 142, 167

Lascelles, Mary, 180, 191, 257

Laud, William, 159, 204–5

Lechmere family, 219

193–4; names in, 42–3, 46–7; satire on, 43–61 *passim*; advertisement to debates, 45; sketches of members, 45–6; veneration for, 50ff

Commons debate on speech from throne, 43; Commons on securing trade to America, 44, 46, 50; Commons on raising new regiments, 48, 55; Commons on public enquiry, 48; Commons on mutiny and desertion, 48, 54; Lords on the army, 48; Commons on buttons and button-holes, 49–50; Lords on indemnifying evidence, 50, 60; Lords on removing Walpole, 51; Commons on Speaker, 52–3; Commons on removing Walpole, 54, 55–6; Lords on speech from throne, 54; Lords on spirituous liquors, 56–60; Commons on seamen's bill, 60–1

Parnell, Thomas, 4–5
Pascal, Blaise, 22, 23, 24, 25, 28
Passerat, Jean, 100
Payne's Universal Chronicle, 248
Pelham, Henry, 52, 53
Penthesilea, 179
Percy, Thomas, 72
Persepolis, 91
Peter the Great, 183, 191
Philips, Ambrose, 217, 247
Philips, John, 218
Phillips, Edward, 222–3
Pierce, Charles E., Jr, 252
Pindar, 81
Piozzi, Hester, see Thrale
Pitt, William, 42
Plato, 25, 209
Pomfret, John, 123, 156, 218
Pond, Miss, 94–5, 118
Pope, Alexander, 9; in *Dictionary*, 4, 151, 155, 178; and scale, 5, 6, 8; Johnson and, 8, 17, 18, 32, 63, 124, 125, 127, 168, 179, 215–8, 229–32; and Dryden, 17, 231–2; imagery, 18; and cosmos, 24–5; death of, 123, 193, 229–30; and Homer, 124, 125, 155, 257; and Shakespeare, 125, 217, 231; and perception, 155–6, 157; and satire, 174, 188; on heroes, 181, 183, 255; stature of, 215–8, 229–32, 238; and Gay, 218; and Addison, 227, 230
   Dunciad, 6, 29, 32, 64, 91, 94, 156; *Epilogue to the Satires*, 55–6, 187–8; *Epistle to Arbuthnot*, 229 and n.23; 'Epistle to Atticus', 145; *Epistle to Augustus*, 228 and n.20, 251; *Epistle to Burlington*, 6, 178; 'Epistle to

Miss Blount...after the Coronation', 98 and n.22; epitaph on Elizabeth Corbett, 236; *Essay on Criticism*, 18, 204, 251; *Essay on Man*, 24–5, 104, 120, 155–6, 157, 160, 181, 231, 237; Homer trans., 125, 257; *Iliad*, 211, 255; 'Ode on St Cecilia's Day', 179, 195; *Odyssey*, 155; *Rape of the Lock*, 5, 64, 231; *Second Epistle of the Second Book of Horace*, 169 and n.34; Shakespeare edn, 125; *Temple of Fame*, 24, 156
Porter, Lucy, 71, 72, 73
Portuguese, 20
Potter, Robert, 217, 221, 247
Powell, L. F., 247
Prague, 152, 199
Prayer Book: Magnificat, 77
Priam, 74, 179, 180
Price, Martin, 182 and n.21, 241, 255
Prior, Matthew, 218
Prussia, see Frederick the Great
Pulteney, William, 42, 55
Pythagoras, 209

Quinlan, Maurice J., 134

Raasay, 191
Reade, Aleyn Lyell, 253
Restoration, writers of, 99, 105
Review of a Late Motion, 56 and n.73
Rewa, Michael, 69 and n.5
Reynolds, Sir Joshua, 124
Reynolds, Richard, 156, 257, 292
Richardson, Jonathan, 124, 216–7, 221, 223
Richardson, Samuel, 105, 167–8, 181
Rivers, Richard Savage, Earl, 137–8, 146
Rochester, John Wilmot, Earl of, 99–100
Rogers, Pat, 244
Romans, 54, 97, 146, 148, 166
Rome, 40, 115
Roscommon, Wentworth Dillon, Earl of, 69, 216, 219
Rosenblum, Robert, 255
Røstvig, Maren-Sofie, 253
Rothstein, Eric, 3 and n.8, 120, 170, 252
Rowe, Elizabeth, 63
Rowe, Nicholas, 4
Ruskin, John, 21
Ryder, Dudley, 246

Sachs, Arieh, 158, 249, 254
St Andrews, 74
Sandiland, 73–4
Sandys, Samuel, 54–5
Sarpi, Paul, 192, 193

Thrale, Hester (later Piozzi), 18, 37, 251; appearance of, 20; Johnson's letters to, 70–3, 79, 101, 259; electioneering, 71–2, 85; bears daughter, 73
 Anecdotes of Johnson, 8, 79–80, 100, 102, 243, 258; *Thraliana*, 178 and n.4, 217, 232
Thrale, Hester Maria (Queeney), 72–3, 183
Thrale, Susannah, 103
Thucydides, 188
Tillotson, Geoffrey, 172, 253–4
Tonson, Jacob, 255
Topham, Edward, 247
Towers, Thomas, 246
Tracy, Clarence, 138, 253
Tunbridge Wells, 30
Turkey, 49
Tyers, Thomas, 141

Uphaus, Robert W., 254
Urquhart, Sir Thomas, 114–8 *passim*

Vanbrugh, Sir John, 34
Vesterman, William, 187 and n.34, 259
Virgil (Publius Vergilius Maro), 21, 64, 71, 76, 181
Voltaire (Jean François Marie Arouet de), 247
Voitle, Robert, 3 and n.8, 121, 134, 250

Walker, D. P., 252
Walker, Robert G., 251
Waller, Edmund, 81–2, 124–5, 217; and Dryden, 226
Walmesley, Gilbert, 219
Walpole, Sir Robert: as great man, 3, 4; in debates, 41–60 *passim*; on political journalists, 52; removal of, 51–6, 59; and navy, 60
Warburton, William, 231

Wardropper, Bruce W., 256
Warton, Joseph, 255, 257
Watkins, W. B. C., 241
Watt, Ian, 174
Watts, Isaac, 63, 67, 75, 215; and competition, 105–6; verse, 161, 168, 259
Weinbrot, Howard D., 3 and n.8, 243, 250, 254, 259
Wesling, Donald, 241
West, Benjamin, 255
West, Gilbert, 258
West Indies, 196·
Wharton, T. F., 3 and n.8, 243, 249, 259
White, Ian, 250
Whitehead, A. N., 3
Whitley, Alvin, 253, 254
Wight, Isle of, 94
Wilkes, John, 85–6
Williams, Anna, 63
Williams, Zachariah, 63
Wiltshire, John, 247
Wimsatt, William Kurtz, 47, 241, 242, 243, 248, 250, 255
Windham, William, 251
Wolsey, Thomas: in *Vanity of Human Wishes*, 11, 53–4, 132, 159, 201, 213, 238; in Shakespeare, 178
Woodruff, James F., 168, 248, 249
Wordsworth, William, 77 and n.17, 178, 237
Wowerus, Joannes, 64
Wynne, Watkins William, 43

Xerxes, 132, 159, 201–2, 204

Yeats, William Butler, 178
Yorke, Philip C., 256
Young, Edward, 73, 187

Zosima, 65–6, 74